Case Studies in Abnormal Behavior

Robert G. Meyer
University of Louisville

Yvonne Hardaway Osborne
Louisiana State University

ALLYN AND BACON, INC.

Boston   London   Sydney   Toronto

To Monika; truly a case,
but a delightful one,
and
to our parents

Library of Congress Cataloging in Publication Data

Meyer, Robert G.
  Case studies in abnormal behavior.

  Bibliography: p.
  Includes index.
  1. Mental illness—Case studies. I. Osborne, Yvonne
Hardaway, 1950- . II. Title.
RC465.M44   616.89'09   81-19107
ISBN 0-205-07744-7   AACR2

10 9 8 7 6 5 4 3 2   87 86 85 84 83 82
Printed in the United States of America.

Contents

Preface

Research articles in abnormal psychology necessarily focus on specific theories and experiments; texts in this area are concerned with integrating a vast array of literature on historical, descriptive, research, diagnostic, and treatment issues. Some texts do a good job of bringing in "chunks" of case material to demonstrate particular points. However, texts cannot do justice to their other goals if they provide any significant number of cases in depth. *Case Sudies in Abnormal Behavior* fills this niche. This text helps the reader regain a sense of how the whole person experiences and reacts to the diverse factors studied in abnormal psychology. The abstract and conflicting concepts of this field can thus be seen in the context that eventually counts—the totality of an actual person who has the disorder.

The cases presented in *Case Studies in Abnormal Behavior* are based on actual, recent cases, though identifying details have, of course, been changed to protect people from even a small chance that they would be recognized. Most cases originate in the experience of the authors; a few were donated by other clinicians who have substantial experience or special expertise with a particular disorder. For example, Dr. Paul Salmon, a clinical neuropsychologist at the University of Louisville who also works with children, was kind enough to provide most of the cases in Chapter 2 on Organic Mental Disorders, as well as the case of Delano, the child with a developmental language disorder in Chapter 1 on Childhood Disorders. We have also included several cases published in journals. These cases either make an original point or examine a subcategory of disorder that is important theoretically yet rarely studied in any depth by most clinicians. Hajal and Leach's article on the Gilles de la Tourette Syndrome and Pallis and Bamji's article on the Factitious Disorder are examples of such cases.

Readers will note that cases that are provided by the authors and that are not reprints from other journals are assigned names with a logical or mnemonic (i.e., sounds like) relationship to the syndrome being studied; for example, Agnes–Agoraphobia, and Perry–Paranoid Schizophrenia. Granted, this may at times sound a bit corny, we have nevertheless found it to be a helpful technique for most readers. Our students have found this to be a useful device, since it adds clarity to classroom discussion and also enhances the remembrance of the cases if needed during a test.

The reader may note the high number of case studies in this book. Feedback from our own students and from other professors and their students indicated that most felt that case studies in other books were too long and included irrelevant detail. The cases in this book contain the full details of background material that are relevant to etiological, diagnostic, and therapeutic considerations and yet hopefully are not overly long. This allows us to provide a full spectrum of case studies, perhaps more than in any previous case study book. It also allows us to detail cases from all categories of DSM-III and to provide contrast cases within the major categories.

Relevant and detailed family and social history data are presented in almost all of these case studies, since such data give the reader clear ideas about how specific behavior patterns were generated and maintained. A few of the case studies have little background data such as in the case of Harry, in which an abrupt organic trauma is the focus of disorder, or where it seems highly probable that genetic factors dominated the development of the disorder. In cases such as Harry's, we present more detailed information regarding present behavior and the responses in psychological evaluations. We follow all cases through to their natural conclusion, even though it cannot always be termed a success. As in most experiences, much can be learned from failure.

The authors wish to thank the many teachers, colleagues, and students who contributed so much to the knowledge and experience that led to this book. There are far too many to thank individually, though our primary mentors such as Albert Rabin, Bertram Karon, Norman Abeles, Mary Clarke, Will Edgerton, Guy Renzaglia, and Warren Webb deserve a special thank you. Much appreciation is extended to Bill Barke, Allyn and Bacon editor, for his support and advice. We would also like to acknowledge Mike Moll's helpful input, as well as the extensive help in organizing and typing this book provided by Frances Knox, and also by Belinda Pearson, Mary Ellen Brown, Kathleen McDaniel, Pamela Brooks, and Darlene Posey. Finally, Diane Follingstad and Dennis Sacuzzo read the manuscript in draft form and made excellent suggestions for revision, and Terri Whitfield and Mary Millican assisted in preparing the indices.

R.G.M.
Y.H.O.

Introduction

The field of abnormal psychology has evolved through many theoretical orientations. In the first half of this century, the Freudian *psychoanalytic* model, already developing a more broad spectrum *psychodynamic* orientation, was clearly dominating the study of abnormal psychology in North America (Wolpe, 1981). At the same time, the seminal behavioral studies of John Watson and Mary Cover Jones (1924; reprinted in this book) established behaviorism as an important influence in the study of abnormal behavior. While behaviorism was coming into bloom in the 1950s and 60s (Wolpe, 1958; Ayllon & Azrin, 1968), a "third force" also was emerging, marked by diverse theories, many new psychotherapies (Garfield, 1981), and a varying and differing interest in diagnosis and etiology. At the same time, psychodynamic theory was further diversifying (Kohut, 1977) and showing a renewed concern for experimental verification (Silverman, 1976). Behaviorism was meanwhile becoming less wedded to theory (Lazarus, 1971) and also expanding its concern back to at least some aspects of the mind under the influence of the cognitive behavior modifiers (Meichenbaum, 1977), and into a broader perspective on environmental variables under the social learning theorists (Bandura & Walters, 1963; Mischel, 1969).

Teachers and practitioners alike have reflected the increasing sophistication that is inherent in this maturing and diversification process. Very few would now argue that any one technique or theoretical approach answers all or even most of the diagnostic, etiological, and treatment questions that arise. Certain theories and techniques have more relevance to certain disorders. In this vein, it is interesting that the "sphere of relevance" of an approach is most closely centered on the original group that was studied or treated when the approach came into being.

1

Freud's specific theories became less relevant as society lost some of the repressions of the Victorian era (possibly only to take on repressions in other dimensions). Jung's treatment techniques, which focus on uncovering "spiritual" yearnings and on creating a sense of meaning, arose primarily in the therapy of middle-aged males who had "made it big" financially and in their careers, but who lived the feelings expressed in the songstress Peggy Lee's classic refrain "Is that all there is to that?". Just as the client-centered therapy techniques of Carl Rogers seem most appropriate to bright and introspective clients (similar to the graduate ministerial and psychology students he first worked with), the behaviorist's "token economy" is most effective when dealing with clients who are institutionalized and who show marked deficits in basic social and interpersonal skills.

Concomitant with this growing awareness that no one theory holds all the answers is the concept that a number of diverse techniques may be necessary to handle any one case most efficiently. This "multimodal" approach is an underlying assumption in this book; it is dramatically emphasized in the case of Roger, which is based around an earlier journal article by the senior author and Dr. Mitchell Hendrix.

The eclecticism inherent in the ideas stated above is another assumption in this book. The authors also confess to leaning toward a social learning formulation in most instances, and for several reasons. First, social learning theory's broad-based acceptance of many cause-paths to disorder allows a more comfortable melding with most specific theories. For example, biological causes of behavior are neither contrary to nor contradictory of a social learning approach. Also, the absence of an "in-group" language and theory structure in social learning theory allows easier communication with specific theorists and facilitates an emphasis on empirical verification.

The terminology used to designate the disorder patterns in this book is that of the *Diagnostic and Statistical Manual*, third edition (DSM-III), published by the American Psychiatric Association (1980). The use of this terminology should not be viewed as indicating a belief that this is a perfect, or even excellent system. There have been telling criticisms from various quarters (Schacht & Nathan, 1977; Garmezy, 1978; Zubin, 1978). However, it is clear that (1) no other system is even close to the level of acceptance accorded to DSM-III, (2) there are increasing demands from third-party payers (the insurance companies and the government) for specific DSM-III diagnoses in even routine or minor client contacts, and (3) the DSM-III system has attempted to operationalize the criteria for diagnoses (unfortunately, more so in the initial drafts of DSM-III), and thus is open to change in future editions based on accumulated data. The authors thus feel it would be a major disservice to all readers substantially to ignore the DSM-III system, and de-emphasizing it at all would particularly hurt those people (such as psychology, pre-med, nursing, social work, and education majors) who are likely to have to deal with this system later in their careers.

This book begins with cases from the beginning years of life. The cases on Early Infantile Autism, Developmental Language Disorder, and Hyperactivity point to three of the most critical disorders that emerge in early childhood. The Oppositional Disorder and the Separation Disorder document two common maladaptive channels for the strivings for identity and selfhood that are a common concern in middle childhood and adolescence. A classic disorder of adolescence, Anorexia Nervosa, is often caused by these same conflicts, yet it usually first appears later in adolescence. The last case study in this section, on Child Abuse, allows a transition to disorders seen predominantly in adulthood, as the case portrays the effects in adult life of a childhood marked by abusive parenting.

Chapter 2, the Organic Mental Disorders, studies several syndromes in which a clear organic factor has caused psychological symptomatology. The first case in this chapter documents a person's virtually complete recovery of psychological functioning subsequent to having an entire half of the brain surgically removed. This is all the more impressive since the half removed was the "dominant side," which controls most language functions.

The next case shows how depression can result from organic trauma; the third case here indicates probable organic causation for an unusual disorder, the Gilles de la Tourette's Syndrome, in which grunting and the barking of obscenities are consistent symptoms. The last case here is about legal "incompetence" as a result of brain dysfunction from aging and alcohol and, as such, is a good transition to the next section on the Substance Use Disorders. The cases in that latter chapter focus on two of the most common disorder patterns in our society, Alcohol Dependence and Prescription Drug Abuse.

The third chapter considers two severe disorders whose labels have become part of the standard language patterns of society, the schizophrenic and paranoid disorders. Schizophrenia is a subgroup within the overall conceptual category of "psychosis," which essentially designates a loss of reality contact. The two schizophrenia cases allow a contrast between Paranoid Schizophrenia, the most well-integrated form, and Disorganized Schizophrenia, in which the behavior is especially fragmented. These two forms are then compared with the nonpsychotic Paranoid Personality Disorder pattern also discussed here.

The important patterns of Major Depressive Disorder and Bipolar Disorder (Manic-Depressive Disorder) are discussed next, in the Affective Disorders in chapter 5. The other case here examines a common problem in modern society—depression in older adults. The cases in chapter 6, on the Anxiety Disorders, contrast the Simple Phobia (the classic study by Mary Cover Jones) with the severe anxiety-ridden and disabling Agoraphobia syndrome, and then with the severe but more ordered Obsessive-Compulsive Disorder.

Chapter 7 includes a study of Mr. McIlroy, the probable all-time champion of the Factitious Disorder, or Munchausen Syndrome, who managed by faking illness to obtain thousands of blood tests, 48 spinal taps, and at least 207 separate hospital admissions. In this pattern, the person is aware that the symptoms are not real, whereas in the case of Psychogenic Pain Disorder, the deception remains at an unconscious level. The Dissociative Disorders chapter documents the loss of identity and sense of self in the Psychogenic Fugue and Depersonalization Disorders.

The spectrum of the Psychosexual Disorders are then presented, in chapter 8. The Gender Disorders and Paraphilias (Sexual Deviations) are discussed in cases of Transvestism, Autocastration, and Exhibitionism. The Psychosexual Dysfunctions are represented by cases of Impotence and Vaginismus.

The Disorders of Impulse Control, chapter 9, are denoted by cases of Pathological Gambling and Kleptomania. Personality Disorders, chapter 10, (seldom detailed in most case books even though they are very common) are represented here by three different patterns, as well as in the case of Lloyd, which appears in an earlier chapter in order to contrast it with a *psychotic* paranoid pattern, the case of Perry. After presenting the Supplementary Cases on Family and Marital Problems, in chapter 11, the book closes with an especially interesting "normal" case—the case of Pyotr Grigorenko, a major general of the Soviet Red Army, found to be paranoid by psychiatrists in his homeland, but seen as normal by the clinicians examining him in the United States.

This full spectrum of cases should provide an awareness of the diversity inherent in the modern study of abnormal psychology. We hope that readers find the cases as interesting as we did when we studied and organized them.

REFERENCES

Ayllon, T., and Azrin, N. *The token economy: A motivational system for therapy and rehabilitation.* New York: Appleton-Century-Crofts, 1968.

Bandura, A., and Walters, R. *Social learning and personality development.* New York: Holt, Rinehart, 1963.

Garfield, S. Psychotherapy: A 40-year appraisal. *American Psychologist,* 1981, *36,* 174–183.

Garmezy, N. Never mind the psychologists: It is good for the children. *The Clinical Psychologist,* 1978, *31,* 1, 4–6.

Kohut, H. *The restoration of the self.* New York: International Universities Press, 1977.

Lazarus, A. *Behavior therapy and beyond.* New York: McGraw-Hill, 1971.

Meichenbaum, D. *Cognitive behavior modification.* New York: Plenum, 1977.

Mischel, W. Continuity and change in personality. *American Psychologist,* 1969, *24,* 1012–1018.

Schacht, T. and Nathan, P. But is it good for psychologists? Appraisal and status of DSM-III. *American Psychologist,* 1977, *32,* 1017–1025.

Silverman, L. Psychoanalytic theory: The reports of my death are greatly exaggerated. *American Psychologist*, 1976, *31*, 621–637.

Wolpe, J. Behavior therapy versus psychoanalysis: Therapeutic and social implications. *American Psychologist*, 1981, *36*, 159–164.

Wolpe, J. *Psychotherapy by reciprocal inhibition*. Stanford: Stanford University Press, 1958.

Zubin, J. But is it good for science? *The Clinical Psychologist*, 1978, *31*, 1, 5–7.

1

Disorders First Manifest in Infancy, Childhood, and Adolescence

This first section documents cases that are characteristic of the beginning years of life. As in all of the following sections, representative cases have been chosen to sample the range of disorders relevant to that section. We also present here a sampling of cases from different age ranges. Symptoms of the first three cases, Developmental Language Disorder, Hyperactivity, and Early Infantile Autism, are usually evident in early childhood. As with many of the childhood disorders, however, they may not cause a major disruption in the child and/or family's world until the child moves into the structured social demands of day care and formal schooling. The first case, Delano, a child with the Development Language Disorder, is a particularly good example of this phenomenon. Although the disorder did not emerge until he went to school, there was hard evidence of disorder as early as eighteen months of age. Even though all three of these disorders may take a severe toll on the child's later adjustment, Delano's symptomatology is subtle when compared to that seen in the Early Infantile Autism case.

The next two disorders discussed, The Oppositional Disorder and The Separation Disorder, are more characteristic of middle childhood, particularly the early school years, though again the initial symptoms may appear much earlier. These disorders present contrasting styles of coping with a major developmental task—the establishment of a new and separate sense of identity. In the Separation Disorder, a too-fearful coping style makes adequate separation very difficult, whereas in The Oppositional Disorder, uncontrolled assertiveness blocks an adequate adjustment.

The next disorder discussed, Anorexia Nervosa, listed in the DSM-III as an Eating Disorder, is most often found in adolescence, particularly in middle- to upper-class females. This disorder, which first focuses on attention to dieting and marked weight loss, may not initially cause parents much concern. However, once the trend progresses to a substantial disorder pattern, the possibility that it will result in death is variously estimated at from 5 percent to 20 percent. This possibility is especially of concern since there is evidence that this condition is on the rise (Jones et al., 1980).

The last disorder in this section focuses on child abuse, a problem of much concern in modern society. It is well known that children who have been abused are likely to replicate this behavior when they become parents. Yet, little attention has been given to other pathological outcomes in the later lives of children who have been abused. The cases from the article by Barrett and Fine (1980) document some of these effects. Since these cases examine the effects of abuse experienced as a child on later adjustment as an adult, they provide a fitting transition to the following sections of this book on disorders that are primarily (though not exclusively) manifested in adulthood.

A number of other childhood disorder patterns also have an analogous pattern in adult syndromes. For example, an unsocialized Conduct Disorder (either aggressive or nonaggressive) in childhood is likely to reappear in subsequent maladjustment as a Personality Disorder, particularly the Antisocial Personality Disorder, which is discussed in chapter 10. Anxiety-based childhood disorders, such as phobias and avoidance patterns, are similar in many respects to the patterns discussed in the section on The Anxiety Disorders. The same analogy holds for many of the other adult cases discussed in this book.

REFERENCE

Jones, D., Fox, M., Babigian, H., and Hutton, H. Epidemiology of anorexia nervosa —Monroe County, New York: 1960–1976. *Psychosomatic Medicine*, 1980, 42, 551–557.

Developmental Language Disorder

The Case of Delano   Children with school-related problems comprise a significant source of referrals for psychological assessment. In such cases, the psychologist's role often focuses on evaluating the child's level of cognitive and intellectual skills and on making recommendations for intervention within the school system. Such intervention often requires the integration of a great deal of history from a variety of sources, with the consequent problem of organizing a small mountain of information into a diagnostic impression of the child.

The term *learning disabled* is often used to describe children who encounter more than the usual degree of difficulty in mastering basic school subjects. Any implication that such children have central nervous system impairment is not accurate. A 1980 Federal law *Education for all handicapped children* (P.L. 94–142) incorporates a definition of the learning disabled child that is useful here, since it is broad enough to encompass many of the types of school-related problems that clinical psychologists are called on to deal with.

"Specific learning disability" means a disorder in one or more of the basic psychological processes involved in understanding or in using language, spoken or written, which may manifest itself in an imperfect ability to listen, think, speak, read, write, spell, or to do mathematical calculations. The term includes such conditions as perceptual handicaps, brain injury, minimal brain disfunction, dyslexia, and developmental aphasia. The term does not include children who have learning problems which are primarily the result of visual, hearing, or motor handicaps, or mental retardation, or of environmental, cultural, or economic disadvantage. (P.L. 94–142, sect. 121a. 5(9))

Implicit in such a definition is that a child with a learning disability possesses skills in other areas and is not simply deficient in performance abilities across the board. P.L. 94–142 is one of a series of efforts to characterize adequately a wide range of disorders, all of which appear to have some significance with respect to behavior in educational settings. The long history of efforts to systematize the discussion of these disorders testifies to the perennial interest of specialists from a wide range of disciplines in factors that affect a child's performance (Rie & Rie, 1980).

In a general way, DSM-III aids in the identification of school-related disorders owing to its expanded treatment of childhood disorders. In particular, a group of disorders termed *Specific Developmental Disorders* encompasses many of the school-related difficulties encountered by young children. The most commonly identified of these include developmental disorders of reading and language. The former condition is diagnosed when there is a significant discrepancy between a child's IQ score and a standardized assessment of reading proficiency. Developmental reading disorders are generally first identified *after* a child has been in school for some time—long enough for a discrepancy between reading and intellectual skills to develop. In many instances, however, developmental reading disorders may be preceded by the second major category of Specific Developmental Disorders, which involve language.

DSM-III classifies language disorders according to whether: a) language is acquired at all; b) the language deficit is acquired subsequent to normal development; or c) the onset of language is delayed. The last of these, termed a Developmental Language Disorder, is the most prevalent and is generally thought to reflect the relatively slow maturation of brain structures that mediate linguistic skills. Depending on whether the language deficit predominantly involves problems in understanding or using spoken language, it is termed a receptive or expressive developmental language disorder.

Other specific developmental disorders include a Developmental Articulation Disorder (in which speech has a "babyish" quality), and a relatively rare disorder involving calculation skills, termed a Developmental Arithmetic Disorder. It is not uncommon for children with expressive or receptive developmental language disorders to manifest specific academic disabilities when they enter school; hence, all of these specific developmental disorders bear some relation to each other and frequently occur in combination. The following case, Delano, illustrates a situation in which both a receptive Developmental Language Disorder and a Developmental Reading Disorder were concurrently diagnosed.

Specific developmental disorders are recorded on Axis II of the DSM-III multi-axial system, since they are frequently found in conjunction with certain of the mental disorders identified on Axis I (such as Anxiety reactions or Avoidance reactions). Moreover, in keeping with the other major group of disorders recorded on Axis II (Personality Disorders), Developmental Disorders convey a sense of being long-standing chronic conditions, in contrast to the often dramatic and florid symptom patterns of Axis I disorders.

In Delano's case, a comprehensive psychological evaluation revealed evidence of specific developmental disorders affecting both receptive language and reading ability. Although the child's problems became most obvious once he had started school, their origin could be traced to evidence of central nervous system impairment evident at a very early age, at which time epileptic seizures first occurred.

Delano

Del was referred to a local psychology clinic for a series of tests to determine his overall ability level. Although seven-and-one-half years old, he was still in first grade, having failed his first time through. Del's parents could not understand his poor school performance and had been of the impression that he possessed at least average intelligence. They described him as a quiet, well-mannered child who was well liked by both classmates and teacher.

According to the developmental history supplied by the parents, Del, one of three children, was the product of a planned pregnancy and normal delivery. He was described as a "good baby" but manifested a series of medical problems, including allergies, ear infections, pneumonia, and psychomotor seizures—the latter first diagnosed when Del was about eighteen months old. At this time, both parents had noticed that Del would occasionally become pre-occupied with the movement of his hands and also seemed to withdraw from social contact and take on a glassy-eyed stare. These episodes were reported as occurring before sleep or on first waking, then later began to occur during the day as well. According to the parents, these trance-like states could usually be interrupted by calling Del's name.

Shortly after these episodes began, Del was taken to the family pediatrician, who recommended a neurological examination. As part of the exam, an electroencephalogram (EEG) recording was made. In this technique, small electrodes placed on various parts of the head are used to monitor electrical activity in brain tissue immediately underneath. Because certain characteristic brain-wave patterns emanate from various locations, any abnormalities are readily evident.

In Del's case, the EEG report indicated "mild dysrhythmia," with evidence of a "focal discharge" in the posterior region of the temporal lobe of the left hemisphere. That is, electrical activity in Del's brain was mildly irregular and also was comparatively uncontrolled in one specific location. Numerous studies have demonstrated that this region of the brain plays a significant role in understanding speech and language. The presence of irregular electrical activity in this portion of Del's brain suggested that there may have been some disruption of brain structures involved in the ability to understand language. The seizure activity and the underlying irregular brain wave activity were subsequently controlled with a medication called Phenobarbitol, and at the time of the assessment, Del had not had a seizure in years. Nevertheless, it was apparent that the early brain trauma associated with the seizures somewhat curtailed his development of certain skills during the critical early formative years.

Thus, it was not surprising to discover that his speech and language skills were slow to develop. He did not speak clearly until nearly age three, and his parents reported that it was often necessary to repeat instructions endlessly, after which time there was still no guarantee that he would do what he had been told. At the age of three, he was enrolled in a nursery school, where he displayed a behavior pattern characterized by a short attention span, low frustration tolerance, and social immaturity. This pattern continued into first grade. Despite attending a summer tutoring program before entering school, he did not do well in first grade, which he was repeating when the psychological assessment was made.

One of the most obvious things about Del was that he was a likable child. At the time the psychological testing was carried out, he proved easy to get along with and worked industriously if given clear structure. He was very attentive to task instructions but occasionally misunderstood the examiner, especially when asked to define words. For example, he confused the word donkey with doggie and repeated the word diamond several times, as if trying to form the memory of a word that he had never heard—yet he knew what a diamond was. It seemed that tasks such as word definitions gave Del the most problem; he did best on test items that provided a lot of contextual cues that aided comprehension. It was characteristic of Del to adopt a rather passive stance toward testing—almost timid at times. He was reluctant to ask for repetitions of test questions, even when it was evident that he did not clearly understand them.

In addition, he created the general impression of a somewhat shy child, less talkative than many children of similar age. As it turned out, Del had developed this style as a result of feeling sensitive about having to ask people to repeat things that he did not understand the first time; he felt that others thought him stupid. Indeed, several of the kids at school, with their unerring ability to focus on other children's weaknesses, had taken to calling him "Spaceman," because he seemed to be "out of it" a great deal of the time. Nonetheless, despite the reserve apparent in Del's behavior, he was an appealing and likable child.

The results of the psychological assessment revealed that Del did possess average intellectual skills, indicating that he possessed the overall mental ability necessary to handle normal academic demands. Even this level was felt to be an underestimate of his actual potential, due to the language disturbance, which inhibited the expression of intelligent behavior. Not surprisingly, a standardized test of intellectual abilities, known as the Wechsler Intelligence Scale for Children (WISC)—Revised, revealed that Del's verbal skills were less highly developed than abilities that made use of nonverbal activity, such as visual-motor coordination. The examiner had access to Del's scores on the same test when it had been administered about one year earlier; it was significant to note that Del's language skills were not keeping pace with his development in other areas. One of the most significant results of the assessment revealed that Del's performance improved markedly whenever he was able to process test information visually. For example, he performed rather poorly on a vocabulary test in which the examiner read words for Del to define. His performance improved dramatically when vocabulary was assessed by having the examiner show Del pictures of objects or events and ask him to select those that corresponded to words read.

Performance on a number of the tests revealed that Del was quite adept at using contextual cues to obtain meaning from what was going on around him. In this regard, it was fascinating to find that, despite markedly subaverage performance on measures that evaluate basic reading skills—for example, word and letter identifi-

cation, and word comprehension—Del was able to read and comprehend passages in grade-school readers at nearly a second-grade level. It appeared that Del had developed a reading strategy in which he used contextual cues to understand much of what he read. For example, he appeared to search for familiar words in a passage and then to try to fit them together with words whose meaning he was unable to decipher. In the absence of such contextual cues, as when word comprehension was tested, he was at a considerable disadvantage because he was not able to sound words out effectively. (Word sounding is an invaluable skill that helps many readers in triggering acoustic memories that are associated with the visual images of words). Del, in contrast, relied almost solely on visual cues to make sense out of what he read and was thereby clearly handicapped in his efforts to read all except materials that were intimately familiar to him.

The overall results of the psychological assessment indicated that, despite possessing visual comprehension skills and reasoning abilities well in excess of his current grade level, Del manifested a significant deficit in auditory processing—specifically, in comprehension. It was found that Del required frequent repetitions of task instructions and items and that his ability to remember auditorially presented information for immediate recall was markedly below average.

The results of the assessment helped tie together a number of observations that had been made about Del. It became evident that his difficulty in comprehending spoken language went back a long way—to the early stages of language development—and as a result may have reduced the amount of information about his surroundings that Del was able to assimilate. His difficulty in understanding others led him to become somewhat shy and withdrawn in social situations. He preferred to appear as if he understood what was going on rather than to risk peer censure (comments such as "Earth to Del, Earth to Del . . ."), which inevitably followed his attempts to have people repeat things. The language impairment became a real handicap when he entered school, where he was forced to repeat first grade despite possessing average intelligence. He appeared to have developed moderately effective compensatory strategies in school-related areas, including the use of visual and other contextual cues. However, the numerous indications that receptive language development had not kept up with relatively normal development in other cognitive skills made this a prime target for remediation recommendations.

By way of summarizing these observations, the following DSM-III diagnosis was made:

Axis I: *313.21. Avoidant Disorder of Childhood*
Axis II: *315.31 Developmental Language Disorder,*
      Receptive type
Axis III: *Mild residual cerebral trauma, dominant*
      temporal lobe seizures
Axis IV: *Severity of Psychosocial stressors: Moderate*
Axis V: *Highest level of adaptive functioning, past*
      year: Fair

Treatment A number of specific recommendations were made to help Del overcome the effects of his language disability. First, it was recommended that he receive intensive training in basic auditory encoding skills necessary for reading. For children who need work in this area, a format such as that provided by the television program *Sesame Street* is often quite effective—sounds are accompanied by visual representations in animated form. This format permitted Del to apply his visualization skills to aid him in such auditory encoding skills as word attack and comprehension. As he became more familiar with the basic sound combinations, the use of visual prompts was gradually phased out.

Second, it was felt that Del should participate in *second*-grade reading classes, since his overall comprehension level was considerably in advance of his first-grade placement. It was felt that since much of the second-grade reading material used extensive pictorial cues, Del would be able to use these in understanding what he read. Moreover, as the additional training in auditory encoding began to have an effect, it was thought that his reading skills would increase even more. Efforts were also made to develop rewards for reading, including giving Del access to appropriate comic books and other texts that employed a lot of visual cues. Del's parents were encouraged to spend time with him going through magazines and other such materials, giving Del additional reading experience, as well as access to the modeling of adult reading behavior. (See Bandura [1971] for a good discussion on the powerful effects of modeling.)

An issue related to developmental language delays concerns Del's difficulty in organizing his approach to various tasks. It is well known that much of our purposeful behavior is shaped and guided by language, and one of the outgrowths of early development is that language comes to play an increasingly significant role in regulating behavior. Del's subaverage language skills had the results of not only cutting down on effective communication with others, but also of making it difficult for him to regulate his own behavior.

Children with this sort of problem profit from several strategies. First, they learn from exposure to role models who provide visual cues regarding task performance and also talk their way through tasks, explaining each step in turn, with frequent repetitions. Second, it is often helpful to sit down with such children before beginning a new task and have them verbally rehearse the steps to be followed, while perhaps jotting them down either in written or pictorial form (Meichenbaum, 1977). Many situations existed both at school and at home where it was possible to build such routines into Del's daily activities. For example, his father began to work with Del on building plastic models and adopted an approach in which he would explain, rehearse, and demonstrate the sequences of necessary steps for Del as a means of helping him develop a more organized, less impulsive approach. Model building soon became a favored activity and provided the basis for more emotional closeness between father and son.

If the list of recommendations seems extensive, it is because deficits in language skills have so many far-reaching implications that must be addressed in planning intervention. In Del's case, every effort was made to keep him in a regular classroom, in order to avoid further stigmatizing him. Both school officials and parents responded positively to the recommendations and were able to implement most of them without significantly altering Del's daily activities. Within six months, Del had shown marked improvement in basic reading skills and continued to do well in his second-grade reading class. His parents reported that he was becoming socially more responsive around other children and less defensive about his difficulties in understanding. At last report, he was doing well in school, and the administrators were considering a phased promotion plan that would permit Del to move gradually into more advanced classes as his abilities permitted.

Comment Del's development history was notable for the extensive array of medical symptoms, the most significant of which were the reported seizures. As described by his parents, they fit the description of temporal lobe seizures (also known as psychomotor seizures), which are characterized by: 1) bizarre, episodic stereotyped movement patterns, 2) "phasing out" or clouding of consciousness during the seizure, and 3) partial or total inability to remember an event (Bakwin & Bakwin, 1972). EEG records of temporal lobe seizure activity commonly show irregularities in the anterior region of the temporal lobes on one or both sides of the cerebral cortex. The significance of this in Del's case lay in the site of the seizure activity and in the reported delays in language acquisition. The area of the brain in which seizures were triggered mediates much of the language acquisition process. The good prognosis for control and eventual elimination of seizure activity in young children would suggest that Del's language development may continue relatively unhindered from this point on and will eventually permit him to overcome the effects of the mild cerebral impairment, which apparently delayed his development of language skills. Lacking skills in this area, Del may have been at a disadvantage in nursery school, both in terms of verbal regulation of his own behavior and of engaging in interpersonal communication.

Children who manifest early indications of biological vulnerability and developmental delays are often slow to develop socially and interpersonally. They frequently feel themselves to be somehow different from other children, though are often unable to articulate their concerns effectively. Prompt recognition and treatment of conditions that compromise a child's development and contribute to the child's sense of psychological vulnerability assure the greatest potential for subsequent adequate adjustment. Del appears to have weathered more than his share of developmental problems, and consistent efforts by his parents to seek treatment appear to have helped him greatly in achieving a satisfactory level of adjustment.

REFERENCES

Bakwin, H., and Bakwin, R. M. *Behavior disorders in children* (4th ed.). Philadelphia: W. B. Saunders, 1972.

Bandura, A. Analysis of modeling processes. In A. Bandura (Ed.), *Psychological modeling*. Chicago: Atherton-Aldine, 1971.

Meichenbaum, D. *Cognitive behavior modification*. New York: Plenum, 1977.

Rie, H. E., and Rie, E. D. *Handbook of minimal brain dysfunctions: A critical view*. New York: John Wiley, 1980.

Hyperactivity

The following case on hyperactivity, written by T. Cornwall and D. Freeman (1980), is a good example of how psychotherapy can be effective with issues in hyperactivity. In one sense, however, the case is unusual, as the focus in many hyperactives is on control by chemotherapy rather than by psychotherapy. Hyperactivity, sometimes referred to as the Hyperkinetic Syndrome, is a common problem in children, particularly males; it is estimated that about 5 percent of United States elementary school children can be considered hyperactive. Hyperactivity has become a problematic diagnosis, because it apparently incorporates a wide diversity of different patterns under the same category. For that reason, many of these individuals are now better labeled in the DSM-III framework as Attentional Deficit Disorder. The major symptom is simply exaggerated motoric behavior. These individuals are often unable to sit through a lesson at school, and even when forced to stay in one place, they fidget and are constantly distracted by any stimuli around them. They are draining on both teachers and parents and are often shunned by peers.

As is evident in this article, Minimal Brain Damage (MBD) is often thought to be a major factor in this disorder. Yet, the label is problematic; what it really means is that "we think there may be some organic dysfunction, but we have no clear evidence for it." The particular problem with this type of labeling is that brain damage signifies a permanent condition (though the psychological effects may not be—see the case of Harry), and the labeling tends to stay with these individuals for many years. There is some evidence that at least in some children with hyperactivity, genetic and/or birth trauma factors are important (Safer, 1976), although other researchers cite environmental toxins and allergic responses as critical. As is evident in the following case, psychological factors can also be crucial in generating this pattern.

Many children with hyperactivity are treated with stimulant drugs, since this may result in a "paradoxical effect" wherein the stimulant drug seems to push the behavior to a peak and then it tends to extinguish. No one is actually clear as to why this paradoxical effect occurs. Yet, this class of drugs is the most efficient here. The drugs do have substantial side effects, in some cases retarding both height and weight growth patterns, as compared to normal growth patterns (Safer, 1976). In some minor cases of hyperactivity, tranquilizers can be useful as an adjunct therapy; in most cases, however, the dosage required to slow such children down also makes them so lethargic that they can not interact meaningfully with their school or home environment.

Let us now turn to the case of Sammy, as described by Cornwall and Freeman. Even though birth trauma factors undoubtedly played a role in Sammy's disorder, the authors note how psychological factors were also generic. Also, instead of the usual treatment for behavioral control problems through behavior modification, they work successfully with Sammy from a psychodynamic perspective.

REFERENCE

Safer, D. *Hyperactive children: Diagnosis and management.* Baltimore: University Park Press. 1976.

The Hyperactive Child With Primary Emotional Problems

Thomas P. Cornwall and David F. Freeman

Many authors have written about the hyperactive child. Safer, in his 1976 book, *Hyperactive Children,*[1] lists well over 300 references from the last

From: Cornwall, T., and D. Freeman. "The Hyperactive Child with Primary Emotional Problems," *Psychiatric Opinion*, Volume 17, Number 1, January, 1980, pp. 35–38. Reprinted by permission of Opinion Publications, Inc. (Shelburne Falls, Mass.).

two decades. The great preponderance of this literature has dealt with research into organic and genetic causes of hyperactivity, with various psychometric studies, and with treatment by means of drugs, behavior management and brief psychotherapy. Cantwell summarizes this literature in *The Hyperactive Child: Diagnosis, Management and Current Treatment.*[2]

Unfortunately, this emphasis in the literature has led to emotional factors in hyperactivity—either as causes or effects—being overlooked or underestimated. This is not a new problem, but rather seems to be a recurrent cycle that was first mentioned in 1935 by Childers,[3] who wrote, "The literature on this subject . . . has mostly to do with post-encephalitic conditions, choreas, and other organic neurological syndromes of a chronic nature. . . . In our experience, only a minor proportion of cases seemed directly related to definite neurological disease.

Hyperactivity is usually due to a number of factors, physical and environmental." He included emotional factors among the environmental causes.

Stella Chess,[4] in a statistical analysis of hyperactive children presented at the American Psychiatric Association in 1959, found that 22 percent of her clinic's sample of hyperactive children were diagnosed as neurotic or reactive behavior disorders. She separated neurotic conflicts secondary to the hyperactivity from primary neurotic problems and recommended treatment of the neurotic problem with psychotherapy.

The case report which follows illustrates the need for professionals to be more aware of emotional factors as a cause of hyperactivity.

Case Report

Sammy R., an eight-year-old boy, was referred to a university clinic by his mother because she was "worried he's hyperactive" and that he "may be brain damaged." Sammy's teacher had referred Mr. R. to an educational consultant who, after administering several psychological tests, recommended a "trial of medication to see if it eases any of his emotions and activity level." Based on this Mrs. R. took Sammy to his pediatrician, who prescribed methylphenidate HCl because "even though I am not impressed that hyperactivity, as a symptom, is as prevalent a sign for minimal brain damage (MBD) as it is for emotional disorder, I feel that a trial of methylphenidate (HCl) is often indicated to see if MBD may be a component of the child's symptom complex." He reported a normal neurological exam.

Neither parent had severe emotional problems, nor was there a family history of emotional problems. Sammy's early history was compatible with that of a potentially MBD child. He was the third pregnancy for Mrs. R., who was a childhood-onset diabetic controlled on insulin and diet. Her previous pregnancies had ended in miscarriage and stillbirth. Sammy was seven weeks premature due to an induced labor. At birth he was fed through his umbilical cord to prevent insulin shock. Sammy suffered from hyaline membrane dis-

ease and was jaundiced for a time but did not require transfusions. He was discharged one week after birth. During the first month Sammy slept almost constantly. He was breast fed until he was 10 months old.

Developmentally, Sammy walked well by 12 months and talked well by 18 months. He was toilet trained between two and three years of age with bedwetting until he was six. His mother stayed at home during his preschool years while his father served in the Navy.

When Sammy was nine months old his mother became pregnant and his father left on a one-year cruise in the Pacific. Sammy and his mother went to live with her parents. Mrs. R. noted that Sammy seemed to miss his father, and she was ineffective in controlling him during the year when he was 9 to 21 months of age. Sammy, at 18 months of age, had little overt reaction to his younger brother's birth. The younger brother, Jeff, became the maternal grandparents' favorite. Sammy reportedly was always very protective of Jeff.

After the one-year cruise, Mr. R. came back and Sammy reportedly ran to him with open arms. Mr. and Mrs. R. then had three years together during which they fought more and more over petty things. Mr. R. spent much time away from home and less and less time with his children. When Sammy was five and a half years old, Mr. and Mrs. R. separated and Mrs. R. then went to work. About this time both children became upset. When Sammy started first grade six months later, his teacher described him as disruptive and hyperactive. At home he was intensely frustrated over anything he could not do perfectly. He regularly became very angry with his younger brother. His mother commented that Sammy "expects too much of himself; his mind has grown faster than his body." Sammy began and persisted in showing his affection to her in rather adult ways. He repeatedly attempted to kiss her passionately on the lips and to squeeze her breasts. Mrs. R. could not effectively curb his actions. She would sometimes feel guilty about Sammy's not getting enough attention and would walk by and squeeze his foot while he watched TV, after which he became very active. After the separation Sammy had nightmares several times a week. He would wake up screaming in fear and would sleep in his mother's bed for the rest of the night.

When Sammy was seven years old, Mrs. R. began dating Mr. Q. When Mr. Q. would come over, Sammy would be very disruptive, not let them talk, refuse to go to bed, or even shout "shut up" at his mother. Mrs. R. married Mr. Q. when Sammy was seven and a half years old. Mr. Q. was a very dedicated professional student who appreciated his stability.

When Sammy started on methylphenidate HCl at age eight, his teacher thought he became less active for a short time but he continued to have nightmares, overactivity at home, and poor school reports. Methylphenidate HCl was discontinued after this unsuccessful trial and he was referred for psychotherapy.

On psychological testing, Sammy's full-scale IQ was 136. All scores were two to five years above his chronological age. On the Draw-A-Person and Bender Gestalt he tested a year above his chronological age in visual motor abilities. On projective testing he showed many fears related to an unresolved oedipal struggle and also showed much freely expressed rage, low self-esteem, and poor impulse controls.

Sammy came twice weekly for two years of insight-oriented psychotherapy, with concurrent collaborative therapy with mother and stepfather. The parent therapy focused on appropriate limit setting and support for Sammy.

Sammy walked rapidly with me to the therapy room for our first session. He seemed eager to please and made overly mature statements about the waiting room area. He was active in his chair, playing with his hands or turning various ways. He had pressured speech and was obviously anxious. I told him I was a talking doctor, not one who gave shots. He said, "Good. You know I'm afraid of blood." He said this started when he was three years old and fell off his mother's lap while she was sewing. "My thumb had to be cut by a doctor when I was two because I'd been sucking it too much." Next he remembered he had cut his toe recently; "I almost fainted when I saw all that blood." The dream started after his dad left when his mother moved Sammy and Jeff into the kingsize bed while she took a single bed. In the dream Sammy was with a friend walking along a jungle path. Suddenly they came upon a green plantlike monster that had teeth in a hole half way up his trunk. It grabbed them with its branches but they ran away, back down the path through other green things. After they had run some distance, they came upon a man cut in pieces and bleeding on the path. With this Sammy woke up screaming for his mother. In his associations to this dream he remembered another dream of the headless horseman. He told a story of a girl's finger being cut off, wrapped in newspaper, and thrown away. Then the finger came back and bled all over people.

Comments.   Sammy was a very active child. This activity was caused by severe anxiety related to his concerns about castration and aggression that came pouring out in this session. As he talked about these concerns, he was able to sit still and stick to the task at hand.

In our second session, Sammy began to draw a "big racing car." He commented that the driver was lying down in the car. Then he drew a smaller racing car with a "wind-up engine" in front of the bigger car. He drew a race track and talked of a race between the big and little cars. The driver of the smaller car fell out and injured his back before he could win. He was then picked up by a helicopter ambulance, shrunk by his mother in a washing machine, and finally taken to the hospital where he asked, "Where's my wife?" before he had surgery on his hand.

Comments. In this session the element of racing possibly was related to his overactivity and competitive conflict with a father figure. The result of near oedipal victory was to be not only hurt in a wreck, but to be shrunk by mother and symbolically castrated at the hospital.

These themes were repeated in various forms and with a great deal of anxiety for the first 12 sessions. He was unable to listen to supportive statements or inquiries from me without more anxiety and further stories. Finally in the 13th session he told his version of the movie, Chitty Chitty Bang Bang—the flying car. He played this out with a car he had built with Legos (small interlocking plastic blocks). His car had some friends who were stolen by pirates and placed in a castle. The car flew in the air after the pirates and circled faster and faster around the castle. The car could not figure out how to save his friends so it started backfiring. I asked if the car felt upset. "Yes, he was nervous and angry," Sammy said. I said maybe we could help him learn how to deal with those feelings without having to fly around faster and faster. We might help him understand what had happened to his friends or even get to know and not feel so upset by the pirates. Sammy sighed, relaxed, had his car land and said, "His engine's too big. It's too much for that small frame." He then built a smaller engine for his car which now stayed on the ground and became a police car.

Comments. Here Sammy enacted his overactivity in play. His anxiety and anger over losing his mother to the pirate fathers and brother was relieved by a clarifying statement about how talking therapy could work. He was then able to play out being the right size and to begin to incorporate, temporarily, some superego controls in the form of the police car.

Over the next four months of therapy we began to identify and work through what we called his "Chitty Chitty Bang Bang" feelings. He began to develop very competitive feelings towards me that he played out over and over again by losing at a game with me and smashing the pieces of the game. He talked more and more directly of his "greed" for his mother's attention and his fury at his brother, stepfather and me for taking her away from him. He became less anxious and much less active in sessions. In school he began learning up to his abilities and was able to attend to his work. At home, with some proper parental limit setting, he became less excited about his mother and was able to sleep undisturbed. About a year after therapy began, he talked of his newfound friends at school, of feeling proud that he could sit and do things that he had not been able to do before. He spontaneously said,

"This works better than that medicine." I asked him what he meant. He said, "I just acted better when they gave me that medicine so I could keep secret the special feelings about mom."

Comments. The working through of his competitive feelings and his wish to be number one with his mother led to a cessation of the hyperactivity at school and also the major behavior problems at home. Also, he was able to verbalize directly what his conflicts had centered on and to provide insight into the partial control of his hyperactivity on methylphenidate HCl. In his mind, if he took the medicine and behaved better for a time, he would not have to give in and lose being number one with his mother in his unresolved oedipal fantasies.

Discussion This case report demonstrates that there are primary emotional causes for hyperactivity which respond to long-term, insight-oriented psychotherapy. Fowler[5] has also reported the successful analysis of the neurotic factors in a boy with hyperactivity. Our emphasis on the neurotic factors is not an attempt to minimize the common organic or even the more serious emotional causes for hyperactivity. Rather it is an attempt to emphasize that when a child's hyperactivity is caused by neurotic conflicts, the option of psychotherapy must be kept open. Realistically speaking, this option can be available only if people seeing children are as aware of the emotional factors that can cause hyperactivity as they are of the organic factors.

REFERENCES

1. Safer, D. *Hyperactive Children: Diagnosis and Management,* University Park Press, Baltimore, MD., 1976.
2. Cantwell, D. *The Hyperactive Child: Diagnosis Management and Current Treatment.* Spectrum Publications. New York. 1975.
3. Childers, A. "Hyperactivity in Children Having Behavior Disorders," *American Journal of Orthopsychiatry.* Vol. 5. 1935, pp. 227–243.
4. Chess, S. "Diagnosis and Treatment of the Hyperactive Child," *New York State Journal of Medicine ,* Vol. 60, August, 1950. pp. 2379–2385.
5. Fowler, John A. "The Hyperactive Child: A Psychoanalytic Case Study of Motility," unpublished manuscript.

Comment The success of psychotherapy with Sammy supports the theories that propose that hyperactivity is at least partially a reaction to faulty child-rearing practices or other psychogenic factors, such as destructive or impulsive models and conflicting environmental expectations. Though the acceptance of the influence of psychogenic factors is increasing among professionals, the prevalent view is biological; that is, that hyperactivity is attributed to abnormal cortical arousal or other brain dysfunction.

As noted regarding treatment, the favored approach has been chemotherapy—either stimulants (Ritalin or Dexedrine) or tranquilizers (Thorazine or other phenothiazines). However, Simmons (1975) points out three reasons for considering treatment approaches other than chemotherapy, regardless of the ultimate resolution of the controversy about the etiology of the hyperkinetic syndrome. The first reason is the usual risk of undesirable side effects with chronic drug intake by developing children (Safer, 1976). Second, pharmacologic treatments do not add adaptive responses to the child's repertoire; such responses are important and are necessary to successful adjustment. Finally, Simmons cites the uneven effectiveness with Ritalin and similar drugs as evidence of a heterogeneous etiological picture, which implies the need for more varied treatment decisions. Rie et al. (1976) have added a fourth consideration—that Ritalin can suppress behavior to the extent that other behavioral and attentional problems are actually masked by less disruptive (but equally problematic) inactivity and lethargy. Most children are currently treated with some combination of medication and psychotherapy. In addition to the psychodynamic conflict-resolution approach that was successful with Sammy, contingency management and modification of the child's environment have been effective psychological treatments for hyperactivity. Based on the assumption that overactivity is attributable to an inability to inhibit and delay incoming and background stimuli, some success has been achieved with purposeful restriction of the environmental stimulation (Strauss & Lehitinen, 1947; Cruickshank et al., 1961; Gorton, 1972). Although the preliminary results of these efforts were promising, there have been no conclusive replications of these data to date. Contingency management within token economy programs has yielded the most promising results (Rimm & Masters, 1974; Lovaas & Willis, 1974; Knopf, 1979). Ayllon et al. (1975) reported increased performance in mathematics, reading, and the control of the hyperactivity with token economy programs for children who had heretofore been treated with Ritalin.

It should be noted here that hyperactivity in childhood has been associated with several adult emotional disturbances, including schizophrenia, occupational maladjustment, antisocial personality disorders, and juvenile aggression. However, advances in treatment approaches have resulted in adequate adjustment for many youngsters, particularly if controlled before the onset of puberty. Consequently, prognostic statements for hyperactive children are becoming increasingly favorable.

REFERENCES

Ayllon, R., Layman, D., and Kandel, H. A behavioral educational alternative to drug control of hyperactive children. *Journal of Applied Behavioral Analysis,* 1975, *8,* 137–146.

Cruickshank, W., Bentzen, F., Ratzeburg, F., and Tannjausser, M. *A teaching method for brain injured and hyperactive children.* Syracuse, N.Y.: Syracuse University Press, 1961.

Gorton, C. The effects of various classroom environments on performance of a mental task by mentally retarded and normal children. *Education and Training of the Mentally Retarded*, 1972, 7, 28–38.

Knopf, I. *Childhood psychopathology: A developmental approach.* Englewood Cliffs, N.J.: Prentice-Hall, Inc., 1979.

Lovaas, O., and Willis, T. Behavioral control of a hyperactive child. Unpublished manuscript, 1974.

Rie, H., Rie, E., Stewart, S., and Ambuel, J. Effects of methylphenidate on under-achieving children. *Journal of Consulting and Clinical Psychology*, 1976, 44, 250–260.

Rimm, D., and Masters, J. *Behavior therapy: Techniques and empirical findings.* New York: Academic Press, 1974.

Safer, D. *Hyperactive children: Diagnosis and management.* Baltimore: University Park Press, 1976.

Simmons, J. Behavioral management of the hyperactive child. In D. Cantwell (Ed.), *The Hyperactive Child.* New York: Spectrum Publications, 1975.

Strauss, A., and Lehitinen, L. *Psychopathology and education of the brain injured child.* New York: Grune and Stratton, 1947.

Early Infantile Autism

The Case of Earl

Early Infantile Autism (EIA) is a behavioral syndrome first identified by Leo Kanner (1943) to describe a group of young children who failed to develop normal communicative skills. The primary symptom of EIA was termed "extreme autistic aloneness" by Kanner, referring to these children's apparent inability to tolerate social contact and their marked preference for being alone. Associated symptoms noted by Kanner and others have included resistance to change in the environment, irritability, self-stimulation, ritualistic behavior, and unusual speech patterns. According to the DSM-III diagnostic criteria, EIA (which is referred to in DSM-III simply as Infantile Autism) is classified as a Pervasive Developmental Disorder, indicating the extent to which widespread social and cognitive deficits are manifested in this disorder. Specific DSM-III diagnostic criteria include: onset before thirty months of age, social unresponsiveness, language deficits, and bizarre responses to the environment.

Important and distinctive features of autistic children's behavior are that they often possess well-developed motor skills, and, in addition, often possess highly developed "splinter skills," despite evidence of otherwise poorly developed cognitive abilities. This pattern of irregular cognitive development is one feature that discriminates autistic from mentally retarded children (Rutter, 1978).

A distinction that has historically been less clear cut involves EIA and a psychotic disorder termed *Childhood Schizophrenia*. The latter disorder, characterized by extreme withdrawal and apathy, was first described by Potter (1933) and has since been extensively studied by researchers, including Bender (1953), Mahler (Mahler & Furer, 1972), and others. An important distinction has emerged between EIA and Childhood Schizophrenia concerning age of onset: EIA is believed to be present at birth (or within the first thirty months), whereas Childhood Schizophrenia is generally viewed as an acquired disorder, following a period of apparently normal development. According to Kolvin (1971), other factors that differentiate these two disorders include familial social class (higher levels in families of children with EIA), family history of psychotherapy (lower among families of EIA children), and likelihood of associated central nervous system impairments (higher in children with EIA).

Kanner originally attributed autism to social factors, specifically to unsatisfactory interactions with parents characterized as cold and unfeeling. In light of more recent research, this position has given way to the belief that autistic behavior patterns are typically present at birth and not the product of early child-parent interactions (Ornitz & Ritvo, 1976). In fact, it is reasonable to suggest that parents of EIA children who appear distant or aloof may very well have felt rejected by an unresponsive infant. In contrast to the etiology of Childhood Schizophrenia, social factors do not appear to play a significant role in EIA. In fact, Ornitz and Ritvo (1976) have gone so far as to state that there is no known environmental cause—social or otherwise—of EIA.

The essence of effective psychological intervention in dealing with autistic children involves training in language and social skills. Generally, behavioral approaches have been most widely employed, following the lead of Ferster (1961) and more recently of Lovaas (Lovaas, Schreibman, & Koegel, 1976). The goals of therapy typically focus on increasing the child's responsive behaviors, such as making and maintaining eye contact, responding to one's name, and following simple instructions. When rudimentary response patterns have been reliably established, it is often possible to attempt to train more sophisticated language and social skills, depending on the degree of impairment present. In the early stages of treatment, efforts are simply focused on getting the child's attention, which is a necessary prerequisite to any type of training. Once a child has learned to attend to another person consistently, treatment goals may include response generalization to other persons and the development of communicative speech and of more complex social skills. The liberal use of positive reinforcement (including such tangibles as cookies and M & M's or praise and encouragement) aids in the acquisition and generalization of these behaviors.

Techniques derived from learning theory are also used to treat behaviors associated with EIA that may be harmful to the child, such as pica (repetitive eating of nonnutritive substances) or self-mutilation, which interfere with attention and learning. Here, the treatment of choice is typically aversive conditioning, employing such stimuli as noxious odors, loud noises, or even mild electric shock in response to undesirable or potentially harmful behaviors. Though the use of aversive conditioning has been criticized, it has been shown to eliminate maladaptive behaviors rapidly and effectively, a factor clearly in the child's best interest.

The case of Earl involved a less dramatic form of aversive conditioning—known as overcorrection—to treat social isolation and withdrawal successfully. Overcorrection is a procedure in which the child's limbs (usually arms) are repeatedly moved by the therapist in a fatiguing fashion in response to inappropriate behavior. The fatigue and constriction resulting from these manipulations are often sufficiently noxious to alter the preceding behavior and yet are presumably less anxiety-provoking than are more drastic aversive stimuli. In addition, such procedures are less unpleasant for parents to administer, and so can be incorporated relatively easily into home training programs.

Earl

Earl was three years old when his parents were referred to the School for Autistic Children following a neurological evaluation. His pediatrician had become concerned by the mother's descriptions of Earl's peculiar behaviors and unusual developmental history. He had preferred to be left alone since birth, and efforts to hold and cuddle him were met with squirming, fretting, and apparent irritation. Earl was content to stare at his crib mobiles and later to manipulate colored blocks repetitively, the only toys with which he would play. He sat up, stood, and walked within the average developmental range, but never crawled. Language development was retarded. Though Earl occasionally said "mama" and "dada" by the time he was two, he was otherwise mute and did not respond reliably to his name. However, he could hum several radio and church songs from memory, and he was impressively adept at manipulating building blocks.

Both the pediatrician and the neurologist considered Earl's physical health and development to be age appropriate. The pediatrician suspected generalized central nervous system (CNS) dysfunction, but the neurologist obtained normal EEGs and reflex measures. The neurologist diagnosed EIA and referred the parents to the school's early intervention program.

The school's psychoeducational evaluation of Earl's development was consistent with the neurologist's diagnosis of EIA. Earl's com-

municative language was so impaired that a valid assessment of his intellectual ability could not be obtained. Though Earl manipulated some of the test materials correctly, cooperation was erratic and then limited only to manipulation tasks. The examiner suspected that these correct scores were more the results of spontaneous attractions for certain tasks than of purposeful responses to instructions. When Earl was not attending to test materials, he turned away from the examiner and hummed to himself. Occasionally, he rocked back and forth, but most of the time sat very still.

In motor development, Earl evidenced accelerated progress. His skill with building blocks was observed on one of the subscales of an IQ test, though interestingly enough, the designs that Earl produced were complex variations rather than copies of the originals suggested by the examiner. His performance on two of the tests was in the superior range. In addition, Earl walked and ran effortlessly and accurately imitated the examiner in alternate arm and knee lifts, hopping, skipping, and sit-ups—skills usually observed reliably only in older children.

Treatment   This information, combined with Earl's social unresponsiveness throughout his visit at the school and his parents' descriptions of his behavior at home, were incorporated into a treatment plan. The initial step was to train Earl to establish eye contact with the examiner in response to his name. The shaping procedure required four fifteen-minute sessions per day for three days. Earl's mother sat across a small table from Earl and allowed him to play with building blocks as he gradually learned to maintain eye contact for three seconds when she called his name. When Earl did not respond within fifteen seconds, the trainer stood behind him and exercised his arms for ten seconds. Ten seconds after the overcorrection exercise, Earl's mother repeated his name and another trial was initiated. The first day, Earl turned in his mother's direction several times, yet did not establish eye contact with her. The arm exercises were apparently ignored the first two sessions, but Earl resisted in subsequent sessions and was obviously annoyed by the manipulation. By the fourth day, however, Earl was responding highly reliably, and he was placed on a variable ratio (randomly spaced) reinforcement schedule. After ten days, Earl was responding to his name at home without immediate reinforcement.

Similar procedures were implemented for more complex social skills and verbal imitation. The shaping procedures were lengthy for the introduction of increasingly complex response requirements, though Earl maintained reliable response rates once skills were acquired. Undoubtedly, the persistence and patience of Earl's mother were significant contributing factors in the effectiveness of maintenance procedures. She and her husband were consistent with Earl at home, and after a few weeks they implemented strategies of their own to help Earl learn to dress and feed himself and to play with toys other than building blocks.

After several months, Earl had acquired some basic social skills. He would greet people who entered the room, say "please," "thank you" and "excuse me," call several people by name, and follow simple verbal instructions without modeling assistance. However, Earl evidenced little spontaneous generalization of these responses, and his rocking and humming continued. At this point, avoidance conditioning procedures were implemented at school and at home to eliminate these autistic behaviors during designated social interaction periods. The arm exercises were administered if Earl exhibited these or similar behaviors during three fifteen-minute sessions per day. This strategy reduced the frequency of autistic behaviors within prescribed periods and generalized to other time periods as well. Also, Earl's focused attention improved significantly, as evidenced by dramatic reductions in the length of shaping procedures.

Shortly thereafter, Earl began to evidence increasing generalization of social and communicative language skills. Tolerance of physical affection gradually increased, and after a year of treatment, Earl spontaneously hugged his mother and most frequent trainer. The subjective impressions of the staff were that Earl's behavior was less stilted and mechanical and probably was associated with genuinely experienced emotions.

Given these indications that generalized social contact had acquired reinforcement properties for Earl, he was placed in a classroom with four other autistic children (ages three to five years) and four teacher-trainers. Earl's initial reactions were extreme withdrawal and a refusal to exhibit any behaviors acquired in the preceding year. Earl's mother was asked to sit with Earl and model correct responses in the classroom. Again, the affectionate perseverance of Earl's mother was impressive throughout the lengthy shaping procedure that had accompanied his previous exposures to novel environmental demands.

Attempts to fade out his mother's modeling were successful, though Earl would not tolerate her absence from the classroom. So each day for a year, Earl's mother accompanied him to class and sat with him during the two hours of instruction. Fortunately, Earl had learned to play games and activities during the afternoon without his mother's presence. Earl eventually functioned in the classroom without his mother's attention and prompting, so she could attend to the newspaper or sewing as long as she did not leave the room. Earl's mother would periodically attempt to sneak out of the room when Earl seemed involved in class activities. But he would notice immediately, cease participating in class, and exhibit the otherwise infrequent autistic behaviors described earlier. Nevertheless, the intensity of these behaviors appeared to decrease, and as Earl's mother continued to leave and reappear, he became more tolerant of her exits.

Over the next two years, Earl's treatment program focused on language skills and reading readiness activities. He made steady though gradual progress. There were several temporary behavior reversals that were associated with significant events in Earl's life, including the birth of his sister, having substitute teachers, and moving to a new house. These behavior reversals were characterized by extreme withdrawal, autistic rocking, and refusal of affection. In actuality, these reactions were encouraging prognostic signs. Heretofore, Earl had been unresponsive to similar external events, including the birth of his brother eighteen months earlier and the death of an elderly relative who lived with his family.

When Earl was six, he was promoted to a "regular" classroom at the autistic school. The overcorrection procedure was discontinued since Earl would now respond socially and educationally to the social praise, time-out, and special privileges used in the classroom token economy program. At home, Earl relates more harmoniously with his family, yet continues to evidence a preference for aloneness. Earl's language skills are delayed by about two years, but prereading skills (shape discrimination, letter recognition, interpreting picture stories) are slowly improving.

Comment   Early Infantile Autism is a pervasive disorder with long-lasting effects. Few people are ever completely "cured." For example, Havelkova (1968) reported that nearly 80 percent of children with EIA continued to manifest significant intellectual deficits throughout their lives. The development of initial language skills before the age of five appears crucial to a positive prognosis (Lovaas et al., 1976). Generally speaking, prognosis appears to vary as a function of the degree of language, social, and neurological impairment present before age five. To this extent, children with EIA do vary in their responsiveness to treatment.

In Earl's case, the prognosis for social and educational adaptation is guarded but favorable, and it appears likely that his academic achievement may actually reach age-appropriate levels within two or three years. His progress to date has been facilitated by effective training strategies within the school, as well as by his parents' consistent and cooperative implementation of behavioral intervention techniques at home.

Earl's response to out-patient treatment was fortunate since a poorer prognosis has been associated with in-patient treatment for EIA (Lovaas, 1977; Kennedy, 1965; Eisenberg, 1956). A common outcome for autistic children in the past has been institutionalization and final diagnosis in adulthood of mental retardation and/or schizophrenia. However, current treatment practices emphasize brief hospitalization and active involvement of parents in training the child. Fortunately, the empirically unsupported and punitive notion of parental rejection as generic is subsiding among practitioners. Consequently, significant advances have occurred in the development and refinement of behavioral strategies for correcting the child's social, cognitive, and linguistic deficits. These strategies have been impressively successful and have significantly increased the probability of eventual adaptive functioning for children with EIA.

REFERENCES

Bender, L. Childhood schizophrenia. *Psychiatric Quarterly*, 1953, 27, 663–681.

Eisenberg, L. The autistic child in adolescence. *American Journal of Psychiatry*, 1956, *112*, 607–612.

Ferster, C. Positive reinforcement and behavioral deficits of autistic children. *Child Development*, 1961, *32*, 437–456.

Havelkova, M. Follow-up study of 71 children diagnosed as psychotic in pre-school age. *American Journal of Orthopsychiatry*, 1968, *38*, 846–857.

Kanner, L. Autistic disturbances of affective contact. *Nervous Child*, 1943. *2*, 217–250.

Kennedy, W. School phobia: Rapid treatment of fifty cases. *Journal of Abnormal Psychology*, 1965, *70*, 285–289.

Kolvin, I. Psychoses in childhood—a comparative study. In M. Rutter (Ed.), *Infantile autism: Concepts, characteristics and treatment.* Edinburgh: Churchill Livingstone, 1971.

Lovaas, O. *The autistic child: Language development through behavior modification.* New York: Irvington, 1977.

Lovaas, O., Schreibman, L., and Koegel, R. A behavior modification approach to the treatment of autistic children. In E. Schopler and R. Reichler (Eds.), *Psychopathology and child development: Research and treatment.* New York: Plenum Press, 1976.

Mahler, M., and Furer, M. Child psychosis: A theoretical statement and its implications. *Journal of Autism and Childhood Schizophrenia*, 1972, *2*, 213–218.

Ornitz, E., and Ritvo, E. The syndrome of autism: A critical review. *American Journal of Psychiatry*, 1976, *133*, 609–621.

Potter, H. Schizophrenia in children. *American Journal of Psychiatry*, 1933, *12*, 1253–1268.

Rutter, R. (Ed.). *Autism: A reappraisal of concepts and treatment.* New York: Plenum, 1978.

The Oppositional Disorder

The Case of Phyllis The Oppositional Disorder is characterized by intensely negative responses to attempts by parents or other authority figures to control the behavior of the child or adolescent. Stubborn and/or hostile resistance is manifested in a variety of behavior patterns, including consistent violation of minor rules and pouting with an occasional temper flare-up. Oppositional Disorder can be diagnosed as early as three years of age (it receives a lay diagnosis even before then in the phrase "terrible twos"). When it emerges most strongly in adolescence, as it often does, (and as it does in the case of Phyllis) similar behaviors usually had been evident in the child's earlier behavioral history.

Adolescence is commonly a stressful period for teenagers, their families, and school officials. Pubertal changes, the task of identity formation, the renegotiation of relationships with parents, and rapid changes in

29

the social environment can precipitate a variety of problematic behaviors for teenagers. Certain adolescents are unable to effect a logical or objective break from their earlier emotional bonds with parents, and thus teenagers' struggle for an autonomous relationship with parents may be a significant source of problems. As a result, teenagers may become rebellious, emotional, or hypercritical in order to convince parents that they are no longer "children," and so must be accorded greater independence.

Though a degree of rebellion in adolescence is considered normal, some teenagers believe that true autonomy can be attained only by making a complete break with their parents. These youngsters are openly and consistently defiant of parental authority and may solve their problems by moving out of the home. Other teenagers remain in the home, yet resist parental and school authority as being excessive and unreasonable. In extreme cases, these teenagers may take such exception to rules and regulations that their behavior is intensely hostile and antisocial. The usual diagnosis in these cases is one of the conduct disorders.

Another group of adolescents, who perceive the expectations of parents, teachers, and peers as overwhelming, respond with the growth-inhibiting symptoms of adolescent anxiety disorders. A third group of teenagers evidence continued disruption of emotional development that is a result of pervasive developmental disorders, mental retardation, or other disorders with childhood onset. A final group of rebellious adolescents respond to age-appropriate developmental tasks with a confused self-definition that manifests itself in temper tantrums, disobedience, negativism, and provocative violations of minor rules, resulting in a diagnosis of Oppositional Disorder. These strategies, however, remain within the boundaries of age-appropriate social norms and do not violate others' rights to the extent evidenced in adolescent conduct disorders.

Oppositional teenagers, though emotionally unpredictable and argumentative, may elicit a generally positive response from others and may evidence stubbornness and emotionality rather than an antisocial value system or deliberate disregard for the feelings of others. Also, oppositional behavior has a compulsive component, which maintains the problematic behavior despite detrimental (and undesired) consequences (Rachman, 1980). Oppositional behavior is consistent with the traditional concept of the neurotic paradox; that is, the behavior is goal-directed (aimed toward emotional autonomy and independent thinking), but not goal-attaining (usually resulting in descriptors such as immature or irresponsible). As in the case of Phyllis, compulsive violations and seemingly reflexive negative responses toward authority figures merely elicit mistrust and anxiety from them, resulting in criticism and further restrictions of freedom, to which the oppositional person responds with intensified negativism. Consequently, relationships with authority figures deteriorate and become increasingly conflict-ridden and frustrating for everyone involved.

Phyllis

Throughout Phyllis's childhood, her parents were United States embassy officials in several South American countries. When Phyllis entered high school, her parents moved back to the States and joined the political science department of a small private college. Phyllis attended public high school for two years and was suspended four times. Her parents enrolled her in a private girls' academy, hoping the structured atmosphere would "settle her down." However, Phyllis was suspended from the academy twice in the first semester, and the principal had threatened permanent expulsion if her school behavior did not improve. The school had a weekly "detention hall" for students who had broken rules. Phyllis's suspensions resulted primarily from noncompliance with detention hall and the sheer number of outstanding detentions. The infractions for which she received detention were generally minor, such as talking during class, violations of dress code, and tardiness for detention hall.

Phyllis, the youngest of five girls, was the only daughter who still lived with her parents at the time she was referred by her school's guidance counselor to a clinical psychologist. Phyllis's married sisters lived in other states and were employed as nurse, kindergarten teacher, medical technologist, and engineer respectively. There were four years separating Phyllis and the next youngest sister (the medical technologist). Phyllis's parents described the family as close and loving. They said that the older girls had gone through brief periods of rebellion during adolescence but that they all grew out of it. The family was very achievement-oriented, and everyone except Phyllis had distinguished academic records.

Phyllis had been normal behaviorally through childhood, though she had been very stubborn and difficult when three years old and had often been prone to temper tantrums, causing her father to semi-affectionately dub her as "the little witch." Phyllis had always produced an inconsistent academic performance. Throughout grammar school, she often earned above-average grades, yet her teachers consistently concluded that Phyllis's potential was higher than her grades indicated. Junior high school was characterized by a particularly erratic performance. Phyllis received her first failing grade in seventh grade, and from then on would fail one or two subjects each grading period. Her parents would restrict her privileges and closely supervise Phyllis's homework in the failed subject(s). In subsequent grading periods, Phyllis would earn high marks in the previously failed subject(s), only to fail a different subject. After transferring to the academy, Phyllis's overall performance level improved, though it remained inconsistent.

Similar inconsistencies were observed in Phyllis's social rela-

tionships. She had several "personality conflicts" with teachers, on whom she blamed her low grades, and her parents described her as "moody and difficult to get along with" as she neared adolescence. At home, frequent arguments erupted over Phyllis's grades and her failure to complete household chores. When the tension in the home became intolerable, Phyllis would visit one of her sisters. However, these visits were often prematurely terminated by some disagreement with her sister or brother-in-law concerning Phyllis's curfew.

In grade school, Phyllis apparently got along fairly well with her classmates. The family moved every two or three years, however, and Phyllis had not continued any of her childhood friendships. In high school, she moved from one close girlfriend to another, often within a few weeks. These friendships seemed to die from lack of interest on the other girls' parts and seldom resulted in an actual argument. Phyllis dated frequently but did not have a steady boyfriend. This was an additional source of conflict in the family, since her mother suspected, without any hard evidence, that Phyllis was sexually active.

Etiology   Adolescence has been described by Erikson (1959) as a period in which one must resolve the crisis of self-definition by committing oneself to a role and adopting an ideology (attitudes, beliefs, moral values). The apparent ideology and role adopted by Phyllis is one of counterdependence. That is, although her behavior is directed toward demonstrating autonomy, she remains defined by the external environment because her coping strategy is generally limited to acting in the opposite direction of perceived external forces. These dynamics are generally frustrating for everyone involved— including Phyllis. In addition to the predictable negative reactions of parents, peers, and teachers, the oppositional adolescent's behavior does not result in feelings of autonomy or independence. Rather, they are likely to feel that emotionally charged situations escalate too quickly and that they are unable to control their behavior. Phyllis said, "Sometimes I just get mad because someone's ordering me around. So I just don't do it, and then I get in trouble I'm sorry for later."

How adolescents arrive at maladaptive ideologies and roles is a phenomenon about which there is considerable speculation and scant empirical data. Generally, behavior problems in adolescents are attributed to: 1) predisposing family dynamics, and/or 2) deficient coping skills on the part of the teenager (Schwartz & Johnson, 1981). In Phyllis's case, both groups of variables contributed to her poor adjustment. She was the youngest in her family and was no doubt accustomed to relatively unconditional affection, despite implicit expectations of high achievement. In addition to the typical problems experienced by adolescents with successful older siblings, Phyllis's process of self-definition was hampered by her family's indulgence and overprotection, which resulted in her lack of experience with problem solving. Phyllis was able to meet the social and educational demands of grammar school with minimal effort. However, the level of Phyllis's effort and coping ability remained rather constant despite the increased demands of adolescence.

Moreover, because of the family's many moves, and differences in age from her sisters, Phyllis's only stable relationships were with her parents (who had become part of the problem). Harry Stack Sullivan (1953) found that an important predictor of problematic interpersonal relationships is the absence of an intimate same-sex relationship in preadolescence. Sullivan thought these friendships could correct egocentrism, childishness, yearning for everyone's approval, and other maladaptive behavior patterns acquired in childhood. These friendships provide experiences with intimacy, essential reality testing, and a broader perspective from the combined experiences. Phyllis had missed this significant experience in childhood, and the constantly changing environments and associated behavioral norms (complicated by cultural differences among her numerous schools) had interfered with her development of a consistent set of attitudes and behaviors. It is not surprising that she adopted a rigid approach to the environment, which was defined by being *against* the expectations of her parents and teachers.

Treatment The many approaches to treatment with adolescents often correspond with theoretical orientations of therapists, such as behavior therapy, psychoanalysis, client-centered therapy, Gestalt therapy, adolescent group therapy, and community mental health. Bowman and Spanier (1978) have identified six principles that are useful here, regardless of the therapeutic approach: rapport, ventilation, interpretation, insight, support, and motivation.

In addition, some professionals are skeptical about the effectiveness of any treatment program for adolescents that does not include parents and other family members (Framo, 1979). These professionals conceive of adolescent behavior problems as overt manifestations of a larger problem with the interpersonal dynamics of the family. At the same time, it is important to remember that the oppositional disorder is functionally similar in many respects to the passive-aggressive personality disorder (Barrett, 1980). Thus, the treatment principles useful for that syndrome are relevant here (see the case of Patsy, in chapter 10).

Since persons with an oppositional disorder often avoid accepting responsibility for the difficulties they encounter in their world, the Reality Therapy techniques that William Glasser (Glasser, 1980) developed while working with delinquent adolescent girls, who are especially inclined to avoid responsibility, can be appropriate here. Adlerian therapy (Garfinkle et al., 1980), which melds some analogous approaches into a traditional psychodynamic therapy, is also successfully applied here.

Once some of the oppositional tendencies can be muted, either client-centered or nondirective therapies (variations of the original explorations by Carl Rogers, 1951) can be used to explore the conflicts over defining one's identity while adjusting to parental constraints. Similarly, Gestalt Therapy techniques (Perls et al., 1958; Nichols & Fine, 1980) can help the oppositional disorder confront the underlying feelings toward parental figures, often in the "empty chair technique." Here, the adolescent pretends the parent is in a chair and holds a dialogue by taking both parts, which helps the teenager get in touch with the parent's perspective.

Phyllis's Treatment

Phyllis's treatment took place over ten individual therapy sessions, which included Adlerian and Gestalt techniques, followed by weekly adolescent group therapy for three months. Her parents were given advice on reactions to Phyllis's behavior and a list of books and magazine articles written especially for parents of teenagers. Phyllis was slow to disclose spontaneously with the therapist, though she was willing to answer questions and negotiate contracts for more appropriate behaviors. She was motivated both by the threat of expulsion from school and by her desire to effect more harmonious relationships with her parents, teachers, and peers. As is often the case with adolescents, a major portion of Phyllis's problems stemmed from inadequate social skills and an inability to communicate feelings in socially appropriate ways. Consequently, individual sessions concentrated on more appropriate assertive behaviors for Phyllis, including contracts for in vivo trials with parents and peers. These strategies dramatically reduced the intense tension between Phyllis and her parents.

The therapy group in which Phyllis participated consisted of eight to ten teenagers who had similar problems in relationships with authority figures, school achievement, and maintaining stable peer relationships. This group functioned in a manner similar to the intimate preadolescent friendships described by Sullivan (1953). Group members assisted one another in problem-solving and reality-testing within an accepting atmosphere. The group was open-ended—members could enter and then "graduate" as their individual needs were met. Some of the group members became close friends and continued their relationships even after they left the group. Phyllis was more disclosing in the group setting and was relieved to discover the similarities with the experiences of other group members. Behavioral contracting and behavior rehearsal were used extensively in these group meetings (Lutzker & Martin, 1981). These techniques were particularly successful for Phyllis, and she gradually abandoned her oppositional position.

After three months, Phyllis's improvement was evidenced by more pleasant interactions with her parents, significant decreases in school detentions, and better grades. She has maintained the friendships formed in the group, enjoys more stable relationships with schoolmates, and the school has removed the threat of expulsion. Also, Phyllis now reports that she simply is happier and more confident.

Comment   As the oppositional coping strategy generalizes and behavioral controls increase with maturation, the individual may refine this strategy instead of acquiring more adaptive ones. If so, the self-destructive and compulsive features are replaced with the more subtle manipulations of the passive-aggressive personality (see the case of Patsy). However, Phyllis has acquired an adaptive repertoire of coping behaviors that will probably preclude recurrent episodes of oppositional disorder and the subsequent development of a passive-aggressive personality disorder.

Behavioral contracting and group therapy are treatments of choice with adolescents in general for several reasons. First of all, both therapeutic strategies are consistent with normal developmental tasks. Contracting provides them with opportunities to exhibit responsible and independent behavior without parental "nagging" (which irritates adolescents and often provokes even more oppositional behavior). Also, behavioral contracts structure situations, particularly parent-child relationships, in such a way that the expectations of everyone are clear and thus provide consistency in feedback about the appropriateness of behaviors. This consistency serves to reduce the emotionality of relationships and thus to increase opportunities for positive reinforcement and enhanced self-esteem.

Phyllis's case is an example of how singularly unremarkable life circumstances can in combination predispose adjustment problems in adolescence. The developmental tasks of adolescence are such that teenagers must draw on the experiences of childhood and/or social resources for adequate resolution of the identity crisis (Erikson, 1959). Phyllis's childhood experiences, though superior in many ways, did not include adequate practice in frustration tolerance or in the maintenance of long-term peer relationships. Also, her status as the family's youngest and later as the only child in the home combined with deficits in social skills to restrict her socially. Phyllis did not know how to rely on the support of peers or siblings for credible feedback about her behavior, and she was forced to use the expectations of her parents and teachers as guidelines for judgments. Many teenagers in this position abandon efforts to attain autonomy and consequently conform without protest to the expectations of adults. Such conformity may simply delay rebellion until early adulthood (or even much later), when the social consequences are more serious and the environment considerably less tolerant of oppositional behavior. Phyllis had chosen to rebel early (within limits) and fortunately was eventually directed into more positive patterns.

REFERENCES

Barrett, C. Personality (character) disorders. In R. Woody (Ed.), *The encyclopedia of clinical assessment*. San Francisco: Jossey-Bass, 1980.

Bowman, H., and Spanier, G. *Modern marriage* (8th ed.). New York: McGraw-Hill, 1978.

Erikson, E. Identity and the life cycle. *Psychological Issues*, 1959, *1*, 18–164.

Framo, J. Family theory and therapy. *American Psychologist*, 1979, *34*, 988–992.

Garfinkle, M., Massey, R., and Mendel, E. Two cases in Adlerian child therapy. In G. Belkin (Ed.), *Contemporary psychotherapies*. Chicago: Rand McNally, 1980.

Glasser, W. Two cases in reality therapy. In G. Belkin (Ed.), *Contemporary psychotherapies*. Chicago: Rand McNally, 1980.

Lutzker, J., and Martin, J. *Behavior change*. Monterey, Ca.: Brooks/Cole, 1981.

Nichols, F., and Fine, H. Gestalt therapy: Some aspects of independence and responsibility. *Psychotherapy, Theory, Research and Practice*, 1980, *17*, 124–135.

Perls, F., Hefferline, R., and Goodman, P. *Gestalt therapy*. New York: Julian, 1958.

Rachman, S. *Obsessions and compulsions*. Englewood Cliffs, N.J.: Prentice-Hall, 1980.

Rogers, C. *Client-centered therapy*. Boston: Hougton Mifflin, 1951.

Schwartz, S., and Johnson, J. *Psychopathology of childhood*. New York: Pergamon, 1981.

Sullivan, H. *The interpersonal theory of psychiatry*. New York: Norton, 1953.

Separation Anxiety Disorder

The Case of Seth

A degree of separation anxiety is considered a normal phenomenon in the second year of a child's life (Rheingold, 1969; Gardner, 1978). Upset and protest when children are suddenly separated from their mothers (and/or other caretakers) are typically observed at about 10 to 12 months in American children (Ainsworth, 1970; Fleener & Cairns, 1970). The appearance of separation anxiety and the related phenomenon of "stranger anxiety" have generally been interpreted as signs of developing perceptual and cognitive differentiation, such as the ability to discriminate among human faces and the ability to recognize the discrepant qualities of separation from familiar people. As children experience more frequent separations and become increasingly capable of interpreting caretaker's absences, separation anxiety disappears. By age 20 to 24 months, most children are able to tolerate periodic separation with minimal protest and are able to form close attachments with an increasing number of people (Gardner, 1978; Ross, 1980).

In some children, however, separation anxiety persists beyond early childhood or reappears later in childhood or adolescence. These children develop elaborate (and generally successful) strategies for avoiding separation from the involved attachment figure. The most common fears of separation involve mothers, though siblings, grandparents, babysitters, and unrelated loved ones may also be involved. Essentially, children with separation anxiety disorder believe that some catastrophic event(s) can be avoided if they remain with this special person. Yet, some children include the entire nuclear family as the focus of separation fears and exhibit considerable anxiety whenever the family is physically separated for school, work, or short trips (Gardner, 1978).

When fear of separation from a major attachment figure occurs with school-aged children, impairments in social functioning and academic achievement are almost inevitable. Sleep disturbances, somatic complaints, temper tantrums, and deceitful behaviors related to separation avoidance are frequently associated features. Parents of children with separation anxiety disorders usually first seek professional help for the specific symptoms of school refusal, panic attacks, and/or nightmares. Most of these patterns are evident in the case of Seth.

Seth

Seth's mother took him to a clinical psychologist when efforts to send him to school had been unsuccessful for almost six weeks. Initially, Seth had avoided school with various physical ailments, which prompted his mother to take him to several pediatricians and allergy specialists. The results of these examinations were generally negative, although he was given many prescriptions for analgesics, antacids, and tonics. Finally, Seth's mother simply insisted that he was well enough to attend school and sent him despite his extreme protest. Seth left for school, but sneaked back and spent the day in his backyard tree house (he was discovered by a neighbor, who called his mother). Thereafter, Seth's mother attempted to return him to school through a number of ineffective strategies, including firm lectures, sympathetic encouragement, angry threats, whippings, and taking him to the school door. These measures only served to worsen Seth's problems since he merely implemented more extreme avoidance maneuvers. His mother reported intense tantrums, deliberate vomiting, hiding in closets, and returning home to his treehouse after being taken to school.

Seth is an only child whose father was killed in a car accident when Seth was three months old. Since that time, he and his mother had lived with her widowed father, the only relative who lived nearby. Though Seth would not discuss his reasons for refusing school attendance, his mother thought he was mourning his grandfather, who had died two months earlier. Thus, Seth was deprived of his only known father figure and was unable to reassure himself that other caretakers would be available in the event of his mother's death. Otherwise, Seth's birth, infancy, and childhood had been reasonably normal, though he did seem to be a bit more anxious and fretful (though not hyperactive) than most children.

Seth's mother reported other unusual habits and fears that Seth had developed since his grandfather's death: he refused to fall asleep in his bed and was afraid of darkness. His mother allowed him to fall asleep in her bed while she watched television. After he fell asleep, she returned Seth to his room, though several mornings she found him asleep on the floor beside her bed. Also, Seth had stopped playing outside, or at the homes of neighborhood children. He was popular with these children and at first they visited him often. However, when Seth continually declined their invitations to play outside his home, the children stopped visiting him. Seth spent most of his time with such solitary activities as watching television, reading stories, and building model airplanes.

These patterns, combined with Seth's prolonged absence from school, had resulted in almost total social isolation for Seth. His only outings were shopping or attending church with his mother, and he insisted on accompanying her whenever she left the house. Seth's mother was afraid that Seth's attachment to her was abnormally close, and she had talked with him about his withdrawal from friends. His only response was to insist that he would rather stay home. He would not elaborate further in these conversations with his mother and would try to leave the room.

Seth was surprisingly disclosing in his initial interview with the clinical psychologist. After being assured that his mother would wait for him in another office, Seth accompanied the psychologist to the playroom. Though he was interested in several toys there, Seth was willing to discuss his problems. After ten minutes or so, Seth ignored the toys completely and entered into a lengthy conversation with the clinician. When asked why he did not want to attend school, Seth said that his mother needed him at home. Seth sadly said that his grandfather had died alone at home because no one was there to help him; and now that there were only he and his mother, they had to look out for one another. Seth clearly believed that the only way he and his mother could protect one another from harm was to keep in virtually constant and close proximity to each other. He went on to describe, with morbid detail, a number of tragic accidents which might befall his mother in his absence, including dangerous intruders, explosions, and tornadoes. Seth believed that he could (and should) intercede in these events in ways that no one else could. When asked how long he planned to do this, Seth seemed amazed by the question and said "a long time."

Etiology   The predisposing factors in the development of separation anxiety disorder are not clearly known. The disorder is included among the three Anxiety Disorders of Childhood and Adolescence in DSM-III, in which the specific focus of the anxiety is the prominent clinical feature and distinguishing characteristic of each one. In the Avoidant disorder, the child is fearful (though desirous) of social contact with unfamiliar people. Children with an

Overanxious disorder exhibit generalized fearfulness and excessive worrying, which pervade significant life situations, yet are not obviously related to identifiable psychosocial stress.

Regarding the overall grouping of anxious or "neurotic" children, etiological variables that have been suggested include unusual constitutional sensitivity, overprotective parents, overattachment and mutual dependence in family relationships, secondary gains, and the presence of anxious models in the environment (Knopf, 1979; Schwartz & Johnson, 1981). Data that are most pertinent to the current concept of separation anxiety have come from studies of school phobia. Evidence of separation anxiety, dependence, and depression in a significant proportion of school phobics is a consistently reported finding (Johnson et al., 1941; Kelly, 1973; Waldron et al., 1975). Some writers have suggested that the most frequent cause of school phobia is the specific type of separation anxiety in which mother and child have a mutual fear of separation (Kelly, 1973; Berg & McGuire, 1974; Veltkamp, 1975). Depending on the theoretical perspective of the writer, the origins of these separation fears have been attributed to psychosexual frustrations, unfulfilled dynamic needs and drives, and generalization from acute fear and anxiety-provoking experiences.

In the case of Seth, an episode of separation anxiety in an eight-year-old boy was clearly precipitated by the death of his grandfather. Seth's father's death shortly after his birth was probably a catalyst here. Seth's higher than average level of anxiety and "fretfulness" very likely predisposed him to such a pattern. Other factors that seemed related to Seth's extreme reaction were the absence of close relatives other than his mother and the coincidence of Seth's class trip when his grandfather died alone at home.

Seth's egocentric conceptualization of his problems is characteristic of children who experience significant yet incomprehensible loss. Younger children evidence awareness of major loss with mourning, searching, or frustration reactions. However, they have not begun to question cause-effect relationships and so do not evidence the bewilderment frequently observed in middle childhood. By the onset of adolescence, children have usually formulated a personal philosophy that can explain why things happen as they do. Though these personal philosophies often vary in content, consistency, and adaptiveness, they provide a conceptual framework for interpreting significant events in one's life. Thus, during ages seven through twelve, children are aware of cause-effect questions, yet their answers to these questions are limited by their level of cognitive development and uneven life experiences. Consequently, the process of interpreting life events in this age group is characterized by idiosyncratic associations and immature logic.

Moreover, children in middle childhood experience difficulty considering causal factors beyond their own personal experiences. Hence, they come to the conclusion that changes in the environment are caused by themselves more frequently than do children in other age groups. If they occur regularly, these factors lead to inaccurate predictions and inappropriate judgments that cause significant social impairment. It is perhaps the frequency with which these impairments occur that accounts for the prominence of childhood experience in theories of adult psychopathology and the assertion by some theorists that all children encounter psychological problems in middle childhood (Mussen et al., 1974; Coopersmith, 1967; Rosen et al., 1964). Children usually have some resources within their social environment (such as parents, siblings, special relatives, and friends) who provide adequate feedback on the appropriateness of judgments. Seth, however, would not risk upsetting his mother, had lost his grandfather, and had no other available "parental" figures.

Treatment Options

The psychologist in Seth's case had several treatment options available: family therapy, individual play therapy, in vivo desensitization, and even hypnosis. Children Seth's age are particularly suggestible (Barber, 1978), and post-hypnotic suggestions have been successful with a number of anxiety symptoms that occur in middle childhood (Knapp et al., 1976; Barber, 1978), However, some professionals believe that hypnosis encourages maladaptive magical thinking and consider it an extreme measure to use with children.

Insight-oriented psychotherapy might eventually be successful in alt ring Seth's cognitive and affective distortions, and he apparently felt comfortable discussing his problems with the therapist. However, Seth was at risk for being retained in third grade because of his extended absence from school. The therapist thought it unlikely that psychotherapy alone would effect change quickly enough and was concerned that Seth's current adjustment problems might be exacerbated by school failure.

In vivo desensitization, a procedure to eliminate avoidance behaviors, involves systematically exposing the person to a graded series of situations involving the actual fear-arousing stimulus (separation from mother in this instance). This procedure, sometimes referred to as counter-conditioning has been shown to decrease separation anxiety and/or eliminate school refusal within a few sessions (Kennedy, 1965; Montenegro, 1968).

Seth's Treatment

Seth's treatment program included a combination of insight psychotherapy and in vivo desensitization. Beginning the day after the interview, Seth's mother left him at the psychologist's office before school started. The first day, Seth talked with the therapist for thirty minutes and spent twenty minutes waiting for his mother in the playroom. These required waiting periods were increased to three hours over a four-day period. On the fifth day, Seth's mother returned after the therapy session and drove him to school. The hierarchy agreed on by Seth, his mother, and the psychologist required Seth to participate in school for only half of this day. However, when his mother returned for him before lunch on the third day, Seth said he would stay through the entire day, for which he received much praise and reinforcement. Seth attended a few other sessions with his therapist before school, quickly renewed his friendships with school mates and his former interest in school achievement.

The therapy sessions were primarily cathartic with Seth. He expressed his grief for his grandfather and the intense fear he experienced when his mother was not with him. Seth's most disturbing fears were that his mother would leave him (through death or illness) and that no one would take care of him. After a few sessions, he was persuaded to communicate these feelings to his mother, who in turn reassured him that arrangements had been made with friends to care for him even in the very unlikely event that she would die. Seth was surprised that his mother had considered the problem and was agreeable to his mother's plans, which included the parents of his closest friend. It was this discussion that appeared to have the most pronounced effectiveness on Seth's general anxiety level and the related sleep disturbance. His mother reported that he was calmer, less distracted, and was again visiting with his friends.

Similar changes were observed in Seth's school behavior. His performance in school before the episode of refusal had been adequate though unremarkable. He had apparently been preoccupied with anticipated abandonment even before his grandfather's death, as evidenced by his significant improvements in schoolwork even beyond his previous level of functioning. Currently, Seth's grade reports are above average, with consistently superior performance in math and spelling. Further, Seth and his mother now have regular conversations about his interpretations of significant events in his life. At first, these discussions were initiated by his mother, but Seth eventually began to initiate them himself, an especially positive prognostic sign (Schwartz & Johnson, 1981).

Outcome Seth was able to meet the required school attendance criteria and was promoted to the fourth grade. Follow-up sessions with Seth and his mother were conducted by the psychologist at three-month intervals for one year. Seth continued to evidence above average achievement in school, and no indications of separation anxiety have been observed by his mother or teachers. Prognostically, there is every reason to believe that his episode of separation anxiety was an isolated (albeit severe) event and that his current adjustment level can be maintained without significant remissions. In Seth's case, the factors that contributed to successful treatment and favorable prognosis were early intervention, his mother's cooperation, and his willingness to communicate his interpretations (first with the psychologist and later with his mother). Other children may not respond as positively to "talk therapy" and/or may have more limited personal and interpersonal resources. For these children, the course of separation anxiety disorder may become chronic and result in extensive social, academic, and emotional impairment. A few children maintain such high levels of separation anxiety that truly autonomous functioning is never achieved. Thus, they forego college, independent living, and even marriage in order to remain with parents or other major attachment figures. By the time these extreme (and generally rare) cases come to the attention of professionals, social and achievement deficits are quite pronounced and successful treatment is extremely difficult.

Conclusions and Comments

On balance, separation anxiety disorder is characterized by the inappropriate preference of children to remain in the constant presence of one or more major attachment figures. Fear and anxiety associated with anticipated separation are manifest by disturbed sleep patterns, excessive worry about the welfare of loved ones, morbid fantasies about catastrophic events and/or permanent separations, and elaborate maneuvers to avoid or minimize separation. Forced separations are characterized by intense distress and efforts to reunite with the attachment figure(s). The resulting impairments in social functioning and school achievement are frequently the symptoms that precipitate referrals for professional help. The usual presenting psychological problems are nightmares and school refusal (Kelly, 1973; Veltkamp, 1975).

Seth's episode of separation anxiety disorder was successfully treated with a combination of supportive psychotherapy and in vivo desensitization. Several sessions of insight-oriented therapy were helpful in correcting Seth's inaccurate conclusion that he could prevent permanent separation from his mother with his constant presence. This conclusion and the associated distortions in Seth's interpretations of major life events are typical errors in middle childhood. The extent to which this developmental stage is characterized by evolving (and therefore malleable) interpretations of cause-effect relationships probably accounts for Seth's willingness to relinquish his maladaptive beliefs. The in vivo desensitization was effective in rapidly eliminating Seth's school refusal and was aided by insight psychotherapy to maintain his overall gains.

REFERENCES

Ainsworth, M., and Bell, S. Attachment, exploration and separation: Illustrated by the behavior of one year olds in strange situations. *Child Development*, 1970, *41*, 49–67.

Barber, T. *Hypnosis and psychosomatics: A collection of reference materials.* San Francisco: Proseminar Institute, 1978.

Berg, I., and McGuire, R. Are mothers of school phobia adolescents overprotective? *British Journal of Psychiatry*, 1974, *124*, 10–13.

Coopersmith, S. *Antecedents of self-esteem.* San Francisco: Freeman, 1967.

Fleener, D., and Cairns, R. Attachment behaviors in human infants: Discriminative vocalization on maternal separation. *Developmental Psychology*, 1970, *2*, 215–223.

Gardner, W. *Children with learning and behavior problems*. Boston: Allyn and Bacon, 1978.

Johnson, A., Falstein, E., Szurek, S., and Svendsen, M. School phobia. *American Journal of Orthopsychiatry*, 1941, *11*, 702–711.

Kelly, E. School phobia: A review of theory and treatment. *Psychology in the Schools*, 1973, *10*, 33–42.

Kennedy, W. School phobia: Rapid treatment of fifty cases. *Journal of Abnormal Psychology*, 1965, *70*, 285–289.

Knapp, P., Mathé, S., and Vachon, L. Psychosomatic aspects of bronchial asthma. In E. Weiss and M. Segal (Eds.), *Bronchial asthma: Mechanisms and therapeutics*. Boston: Little, Brown, 1976.

Knopf, I. *Childhood psychopathology: A developmental approach*. Englewood Cliffs, N.J.: Prentice-Hall, 1979.

Montenegro, H. Severe separation anxiety in two preschool children: Successfully treated by reciprocal inhibition. *Journal of Child Psychology and Psychiatry*, 1968, *9*, 93–103.

Mussen, P., Conger, J., and Kagan, J. *Child development and personality* (4th ed). New York: Harper and Row, 1974.

Mussen, P. (Ed.). *Carmichael's manual of child psychology*. New York: Wiley, 1970.

Rheingold, H. The effect of a strange environment on the behavior of infants. In B. Fass (Ed.), *Determinants of infant behavior* (Vol. 4). New York: Barnes and Noble, 1969.

Rosen, B., Barn, A., and Cramer, M. Demographic and diagnostic characteristics of psychiatric clinic outpatients in the USA, 1961. *American Journal of Orthopsychiatry*, 1964, *34*, 455–468.

Ross, A. *Psychological disorders of children: A behavioral approach to theory, research and therapy* (2nd ed). New York: McGraw-Hill, 1980.

Schwartz, S., and Johnson, J. *Psychopathology of childhood*. New York: Pergamon, 1981.

Waldron, S., Shrier, D., Stove, B., and Tobin, F. School phobia and other childhood neuroses: A systematic study of the children and their families. *American Journal of Psychiatry*, 1975, *132*, 802–808.

Veltkamp, L. School phobia. *Journal of Family Counseling*, 1975, *3*, 47–51.

Anorexia Nervosa

The Case of Anna   Anorexia nervosa (which literally translated means not eating because of nervous causes) refers to a strong and persistent concern about becoming too fat, usually accompanied by a feeling that one is fat even when there has been some weight loss. The DSM-III also requires evidence of an eventual loss of approximately 25 percent of original body weight, depending on age and previous weight. Even though Anorexia Nervosa is listed simply as an eating disorder in DSM-III, we include it here as a disorder of childhood and adolescence since it so commonly originates in middle and late adolescence.

This disorder most often occurs in middle- to upper-middle class female adolescents, and approximately 1 in 250 females between ages 12 and 18 develops it. There is usually a manifest disinterest in sex, and as the disorder progresses, there is also a disruption if not a complete cessation of menstrual flow (Amenorrhea). Other indications of associated physiological disorder appear as the disorder continues. Estimates of eventual death from this disorder range from 5 percent to 20 percent (Halmi, 1974; Bruch, 1978).

A number of anorectics also show episodes of bulimia, another DSM-III eating disorder. The term *bulimia*, which derives from the Greek words for ox and hunger, refers to a pattern of binge eating. Overall, those anorectics who also show associated bulimia are more disturbed than anorectics who do not (Casper et al., 1980).

Anorectics are usually shy and inhibited and at the same time are passively controlling and stubborn. The parents of anorectics are characteristically loving and devoted. At the same time, the parents are also controlling, show high expectancies for academic and moral performance; they usually punish a child by expressing disappointment and inculcating guilt. Anorectics use the focus on food to regain a sense of control in their psychological world. Significant others are often enmeshed in frustrating attempts to prepare foods that the anorectic will eat, and the whole issue often becomes the family focus for a long period of time. Most of these characteristics are evident in Anna's case, which we will now consider.

Anna

Anna had a rather quiet though pleasant childhood. She was unusually resistant of attempts to toilet train her, yet otherwise showed no real problems in development. As a shy but bright child, she quickly became "the apple of her father's eye," and he would occasionally use the example of Anna's good behavior to chastise her older brother, who more often violated his parent's rules.

Anna's father owned a large and successful insurance agency. Her mother was an industrious and even compulsive housewife and was deeply involved in a number of church and community activities. Neither parent felt comfortable using physical punishment with Anna, though on rare occasions her father would lose his temper and give her a very hard spanking. Their more usual mode of punishment was to sit Anna down and talk to her about how she had been "bad" and had disappointed them. Her parents would tell friends that they never tried to pressure Anna or her brother to achieve academically beyond their ability. This was true as regards any overt statements. In many subtle ways, however, they made it clear that they had high expectations for both of their children, and they would show "hurt" rather than anger when either child did not "measure up" in ways that were critical of them as parents.

Anna's brother was able to escape the brunt of the guilt that can easily develop as a result of such a parenting style. Anna's father expressed a common double standard of behavior; while Anna was expected to be quiet and conforming, her brother was allowed exuberance and occasional rule infractions under the rubric "that's just the way boys are."

As Anna entered adolescence, several situations were disturbing her apparently calm adjustment to life. Sexual impulses were emerging, and she had little in the way of instruction about this area, except for a single almost formal lecture from her mother that only focused on anatomy. In addition, there were both overt and implied messages from her parents that sex was "bad" and "dirty." Anna had also just received her first C in school, and she was beginning to tire of the piano lessons she had been taking regularly since she was five years old. Yet, when her initial complaints about the piano lessons were ignored by her parents, she did not persist in any direct attempt to stop practicing.

At this time, three months after her fifteenth birthday, Anna announced to her family that she wanted to diet and lose some weight. She then weighed 110 and stood 5'3" tall. Of course, that weight and height mean she was not really significantly overweight. Her brother had occasionally called her "Fatty," as had a boy at school whom Anna had some romantic interest in.

Shortly after beginning her diet, she announced that she was going to be a vegetarian. When her family tried to talk her out of this, she would show them studies in health magazines lauding the vegetarian lifestyle, and she adamantly refused to eat meat. Her parents became concerned about her evident weight loss and began devising special diets for her, especially in order to make up for the protein she was missing in not eating meat or seafood. Anna became more and more finicky with her food. She would only eat at certain specific times and only after she went through several preparatory rituals, which were analogous to the obsessive-compulsive patterns noted in the case of Bess in chapter 6 of this book.

Anna's parents had taken her to their family doctor just after the start of her diet. She told them it was "just a phase" and not to be concerned unless Anna started getting sick. However, it soon became apparent that Anna was losing more than just a little weight. They returned to their physician, who referred them to a clinical psychologist specializing in child and adolescent disorders. He saw Anna and immediately suggested that she start in individual therapy, but just as importantly, that the family as a whole also enter therapy.

This angered Anna's father, as he could not see it as other than a physical problem and/or "Anna's damned stubbornness."

Unfortunately, by this point Anna had by now lost about 30 pounds. Her mother discovered that Anna was often going to the bathroom and purposely vomiting up some of the small amounts of food she was eating. Her school work was getting progressively worse, and she was gradually withdrawing from her friends. Anna, who had always been healthy, now seemed to have a constant cold and was obviously very weak. An internist who was called in to consult advised hospitalization and Anna's parents agreed.

Etiology   Some early theorists pointed to the disturbed menstrual flow (amenorrhea) that is commonly associated with Anorexia Nervosa to support the hypothesis that an underlying physiological disorder is the causal agent. However, there has been little in the way of other data to support this hypothesis. Also, there is good evidence that any condition that leads to significant starvation is also likely to cause a menstrual disorder (Halmi, 1974; Bruch, 1978).

Psychoanalysts have also taken note of the amenorrhea but have related it to conflicts around sexual impulses. Specifically, anorexia has been seen as reflecting symbolic conflict and denial of fantasies of oral impregnation by the father (Waller et al., 1964). There has been little in the way of empirical validation of this theory, and there was no evidence to suggest that it was meaningful in Anna's case.

Behaviorists have not spent much effort in trying to formulate the etiology of Anorexia. Rather, they have focused on devising token economy, aversion therapy, and contracting programs that have been a useful factor in the overall treatment package for Anorexia (Leitenberg et al., 1968; Lutzker & Martin, 1981).

In addition to these behavioral approaches, psychotherapy designed to give clients a better awareness of their denial of *both* dependence and stubborn manipulativeness is also usually critical. Family therapy, which is an acknowledgment that this disorder is at least in part reflective of a disturbed family system, is usually necessary if the anorectic is to make and maintain a full recovery.

Treatment   The hospital treatment for Anna centered around a behavior modification program (Lutzker & Martin, 1981). This treatment was instituted only after a long session with Anna and her parents, during which time the program was fully described and permission to proceed was obtained. Naturally enough, the first goal was weight gain. If Anna avoided eating, she was subjected to intravenous and/or forced feeding, which she found to be very aversive. Eating at least a minimal amount of food gained her a minimum though sparse level of privileges (such as amount of television time, things she was allowed to have in her room, amount of time allowed for visits, participation in desired activities, amount of time for visits to home). As she ate and gained more weight, a correspondingly greater amount of privileges were allowed.

As Anna improved, the focus of treatment shifted to *how* she ate rather than just *how much,* and then to the accompanying patterns of emotional disorder. She was now rewarded for eating a greater variety of foods, in diverse settings, and for doing so without resorting to the rituals that she had needed in the past. One technique that was useful in counteracting the rituals was a form of Paradoxical Intention. She was first asked if she could *increase* the ritual patterns. She clearly saw this request as stupid, but complied. She was then asked to vary the rituals in all sorts of ways. As she did this, the message that she did have some control became apparent. She was then gradually able to reduce them.

At the same time, she was seen in individual psychotherapy three times a week. Through these sessions, Anna finally came to an awareness of how she had been using her anoretic patterns to regain a sense of control in her interactions with her parents. She also came in touch with a great deal of hostility toward them, as well as with how difficult their "hurt and disappointment" parenting patterns had made it for her to express criticism or anger. Whenever she had begun to show anger, they had quickly made her feel guilty for hurting such loving parents. The logical next step for Anna was a regimen of assertiveness training (Lutzker & Martin, 1981). She was enabled to begin to express her anger more openly and to make demands appropriate to her reasonable needs for privacy and in line with the need to make more of her own decisions.

Anna's parents easily agreed in principle to supporting these changes. However, after nine weeks, when Anna returned from the hospital, having made a number of moderate changes, all did not go smoothly. Her parents did not so easily accept her more assertive behaviors and tried to mold her back to the quiet and docile child they had been used to. As a result, family therapy (Framo, 1979) was necessary. The particularly difficult task here was to get the family members to see that they were not doing this "for Anna"; rather, that her disorder was in large part the natural evolutionary result of a specific system of family expectations, values, and controls. It was only when Anna stopped being "the patient" and the family became "the client" that real improvement was noted.

It is also very interesting that as Anna improved, particularly in the ability to make her own decisions, her father began to show a number of psychophysiological complaints (especially headaches) and also occasionally erupted into tantrums of rage. He attempted, without much success, to control the headaches with medication and was quite resistant toward accepting the idea that they were psychologically generated. The focus in the family sessions had now swung from Anna to him. Finally, during one session he lost his temper, and began accusing the family of not loving him. He said he felt that they only loved him because he made the money they needed. He then gradually came to realize how he had needed his sense of sacrifice as a means of self-affirmation and whenever his children and his wife made moves away from needing him *in that mode,* he felt very threatened. The other family members gradually began to realize how they had taken his role for granted. More importantly, he began to move more into activities that he had always expressed a desire for ("I've always wanted to get a houseboat, and really get into that") yet had put off because "we need to save money." This is not a bad goal at all, but the family had already saved well more than they would need for most contingencies. He eventually was able to ask his wife to go back to work and was pleasantly surprised that she seemed happy that he asked.

Anna's improvement continued and was generally complete. She did become less rigid in her behavior patterns, though she later went into accounting, where success does require at least a degree of compulsivity. It is interesting that later in life she became a well-informed gourmet and periodically taught cooking classes. Both of these latter examples suggest how residual behavioral patterns can be channeled in to more adaptive behaviors.

Comment Since Anorexia nervosa is often a life-threatening pattern, it is important to be aware of how a focus on dieting, physical attractiveness, and conflict over self-expression can juxtapose into this disorder, particularly in middle- to upper-class adolescent females. In addition to examining the intrapsychic issues and the specific behavioral reinforcements that may perpetuate the anorexia, intervention into the family system may be required. At least one of the parents is usually highly invested in passively controlling the children and/or spouse. Also, just as in other systems in which disorder emerges at one point, control of that point is likely to result in disorder elsewhere (in this case, Anna's father's headaches and rage reactions), until some change in the overall system occurs.

REFERENCES

Bruch, H. *The golden cage: The enigma of anorexia nervosa.* Cambridge, Ma.: Harvard University Press, 1978.

Casper, R., Eckert, E., Halmi, K., Goldberg, S., and Davis, J. Bulimia. *Archives of General Psychiatry,* 1980, *37,* 1030–1035.

Framo, J. Family theory and therapy. *American Psychologist,* 1979, *34,* 988–992.

Halmi, K. Anorexia nervosa: Demographic and clinical features in 94 cases. *Psychosomatic Medicine,* 1974, *36,* 18–25.

Leitenberg, H., Agras, W., and Thomson, L. A sequential analysis of the effect of selective positive reinforcement in modifying anorexia nervosa. *Behavior Research and Therapy,* 1968, *6,* 211–218.

Lutzker, J., and Martin, J. *Behavior change.* Monterey, Ca.: Brooks/Cole, 1981.

Waller, J., Kaufman, M., and Deutsch, F. Anorexia nervosa: A psychosomatic entity. In M. Kaufman and M. Heiman (Eds.), *Evolution of psychosomatic concepts.* New York: International Universities Press, 1964.

Child Abuse

The problem of child abuse has received increasing attention in Western cultures, not only because of the inherent horror in the abuse of a child, but also because of the increasing realization of the extensive pathology in adulthood that is related to previous child abuse. It is clear that this is a self-perpetuating pattern—children who are abused are highly likely to abuse their own children (Blair & Justice, 1979).

Child abusers show low impulse control and an inability to control aggression. What may be somewhat surprising is that the problems in impulse control are not always the critical issue. In many cases, early modeling for abuse and parenting has been combined with an ignorance of any positive ways of coping with the problems of parenting. This ignorance can be furthered if the parent and/or parents feel as if they are alone and without resources in their tasks as parents. For that reason, treatment approaches for child abusers place a strong emphasis on education in parenting, as well as in group contact with other abusing parents. This group contact gives them a way to share their vulnerability and feelings of inadequacy and at the same time to try out, at first in discussion, new and more effective ways of coping with their children.

Even though increasing efforts have been made toward intervening and changing abusive parenting patterns and dealing with the immediate problems of these children, there has not been much in the way of follow-up as to what happens to these victims as they age, except to note that they often do become child abusers themselves. As In and McDermott (1976) point out, "It is paradoxical that the dramatic national concern for protection for these children has not been accompanied by an appropriate psychotherapeutic program aimed at restoring healthy development for their future lives" (p. 440).

The following two cases from Barrett and Fine (1980) show some of the different patterns of child abuse, as well as some of the different results in later functioning that can be expected.

A Child Was Being Beaten: The Therapy of Battered Children as Adults

Deirdre L. Barrett and Harold J. Fine

These cases reflect variation in adaptation and pathology in adulthood after a history of child beating. Due to the horror of the battered child syndrome, legislatures have expended large amounts of funds creating necesary careers manned by professionals who sometimes are naïve about child development. Most of this is necessary as crisis intervention—but it provides little hope in

From: Barrett, D., and Fine, H. A child was being beaten: The therapy of battered children as adults. *Psychotherapy: Theory, Research and Practice*, 1980, *17*, 285–298. Reprinted by permission of *Psychotherapy: Theory, Research and Practice*.

changing the epidemiological statistics in one important dimension in children's developmental sequela to adulthood. These cases are testimonies to the complex variation, adaptations, and psychopathology that may ensue after a child is beaten. In some cases, the abuse has a sexual component as well as violent, but we do not undertake to examine the type of "child abuse" represented by non-violent seduction here.

Case One

Nancy is a 21-year-old who was seen for one year. She previously has been in therapy with two other therapists for similar lengths of time. Most of the time she displays a classic cheerful, superficial, hysteric style. Under periods of stress, however, she reveals a borderline personality: Her logic breaks down, she acts very regressed, has amnesia for significant events, and occasionally hallucinates. Nancy and all four of her siblings were physically abused by her mother to a medium extent—beating with belts, slapping, kicking, frequent withholding of meals. Her mother also once threw a butcher knife at Nancy, missing her narrowly. Nancy suffered many cuts and bruises but no near fatal injuries. She was never treated at any hospital or clinic because her father was a physician. Nancy never remembered feeling close to her mother or wanting to. Her main focus was upon avoiding abuse, and all of the siblings cooperated in staying out of their mother's way and warning each other when she was in an especially bad mood.

Nancy's father was a very warm, good figure in her earliest memories. He fixed physical injuries, was warm and loving to her himself; she observed that her mother never struck her in front of her father. This led to a belief that if she ever did, her father would save her and probably retaliate against the mother. This fantasy was clearly destroyed one morning when she was about five. Her mother became angry with her at the breakfast table, hit her, knocked her out of her chair to the floor and began kicking her in the ribs and stomach in front of the father. His response was to shriek, "Stop it, you'll kill her." over and over without making any physical moves to intervene. She heard the fear and helplessness in his voice and, for the first time, really began to believe she could be killed by her mother. This incident was traumatically inconsistent with her image of her father, in contrast to the rather consistent violence of her mother. The stresses which precipitate her breakdown in defenses now have more to do with this realization that there is no omnipotent benevolent one to save her than with the presence of hostile forces in her life. Although the significance of the actual abuse cannot be denied, the impact of the betrayal and impotence of her beloved father really seemed the most central agent in the formation of this woman's psychology.

Case Two

Susie is an 18-year-old, plump, little girlish-looking freshman who was seen in her first week of college. Her presenting complaint was that she was afraid to be around or talk to male strangers and she immediately stated that this was probably due to the fact that she had been sexually molested as a child. She had only been slightly afraid of men until recently, but moving from a small town where she had lived for eighteen years to a huge state university where she was surrounded by strangers had greatly aggravated her fears.

The first and most severe incident in which Susie was molested occurred when she was six. A teenage neighbor forcibly dragged her off into some woods, tore her clothes off, attempted to rape her, and settled for ejaculating on her thigh. Her father refused to report the incident to the police, but appeared to have been making plans to murder the boy until the latter was arrested a few days later for molesting another child. Susie was warned never to discuss this with anyone.

Before puberty, Susie was sexually molested by two other men. One was a business associate of her father who one day while waiting at her house for her father to return, unzipped his pants and briefly forced her to touch his erection; she ran from the room and he did not pursue her. Her paternal grandfather moved into the house after he was quite senile and he repeatedly for several years tried to corner her and sexually fondle her. She told only her mother about these later incidents and she was instructed never to mention them to her father or anyone else.

Susie felt very guilty about these incidents without understanding why. The therapist's initial impression was that this must have been totally externally imposed guilt from the patient's mother's reactions; this interpretation was accompanied by some rather feminist outrage on the therapist's part. Another picture slowly emerged which did imply some responsibility to her for the later events. First, no one in the family ever touched each other affectionately. She could not remember being hugged or kissed as a child. The sexual molestations were literally the only times she recalled any adults touching her. She also began to recall in the first incident that in spite of genuinely real fear there was also an element of surprise that anyone was that intensely interested in her in any way or wanted to touch her. She became aware that she had somewhat wanted the advances of the later two men; not in terms of any sexual need, but as a sign of interest and affection.

51

At this point the fear of her talking to men and her initial distaste for their sexual interests disappeared. Issues of fear of rejection by them and fear of handling the sexual attraction she wanted to elicit became more the focus. She left therapy satisfied with achieving what she had initially sought. This therapist would have preferred to continued therapy, next working on some more basic aspects of her strongly hysteric character style.

We feel this was a case where an apparently traumatic incident contained not only the obvious fearful significance but also actually provided a way out of an already existing pathological situation (that she felt no one noticed her much and certainly no one would ever show her any physical affection). Even though her sense of sex as a way of getting affection was a pathological solution at that age, this reaction was better than believing that she was totally undesirable. The abuse certainly contributed aspects of fear and guilt to her life, but also probably some sense of hope—that previously hopeless aspects of her identity could change. [End of Barrett and Fine excerpt]

Comment These cases are examples of the most frequently reported types of child abuse: the battered child syndrome and sexual abuse. The battered child syndrome, a term coined by Henry Kempe in 1961, refers to persistent physical abuse of children that may result in physical injury or death (Lord & Weisfeld, 1974). Assessment of the battered child syndrome is usually made by medical professionals when children are presented to emergency rooms with numerous, poorly explained injuries. However, Nancy's many cuts and bruises were treated by her father, so there was no cumulative medical history, which is critical to the accurate identification of the battered child syndrome. In other cases, battered children are overlooked because the parents use several hospitals or pediatricians and/or because the child has been labeled hyperactive or accident prone. Even when repeated injuries occur and are observed by physicians, it is difficult to distinguish between accidental and intentional injuries. For these reasons, and because of the sociocultural taboos that interfere with reliable reporting practices, the actual incidence of the battered child syndrome cannot be confidently determined. Kaplun and Reich (1976) report the alarming statistic that 140 children were killed by their parents in New York City between 1968 and 1969.

Sexual child abuse refers to a variety of sexually intrusive behaviors on the part of siblings and parents (incest) and unrelated adults (pedophilia) and ranging in severity from petting and fondling (molesting a minor) to intercourse (Statutory rape) (Meiselman, 1978; Blair & Justice, 1979). Sexual abuse within families most commonly occurs between daughters and fathers and/or paramours (of the mother) and is generally associated with disturbed marital (or paramour) relationships—particularly with regard to disturbed sexual dynamics (Henderson, 1975; Gutheil & Avery, 1977). The case of Susie is an example of pedophilia. The prevalance of sexual abuse of children is even more difficult to determine than is the battered child syndrome, due to extreme social taboos, reactivity of police and courts, and collusions among family members. As in Susie's case, family members often react with shame and the refusal to acknowledge the event(s) publicly. Other forms of child abuse include physical neglect, subtle or overt psychological cruelty, and/or withholding of affection.

The issue of treatment with abused children is clouded by the different diagnostic problems and by the heterogeneous response patterns observed with battered, sexually abused, neglected, and psychologically damaged children. Some children react with increased aggression toward peers or aggressive acting-out in other situations. Many children withdraw from social contact in varying degrees, such as excessive shyness. A third group of abused children exhibits anxious and somatic symptoms and/or fails to achieve in school. Some children can escape from home or learn to avoid punishment and do not evidence long-term reactions to abuse. Other children are unable to escape and are thus conditioned to accept abusive relationships. These children often experience difficulty establishing stable close relationships in adulthood because of their disturbed affective associations and distorted interpretations of other's motives. The particular emotional response of a child to abuse is related to the following factors: 1) the nature, extent, and duration of abusive incidents; 2) the relationships (and implications thereof) between abusers and victims; 3) reactions of adults from whom the children seek support; 4) the developmental phase of the child; and 5) the subjective interpretations of these events made by children themselves. Treatment decisions are made in consideration of the particular behavior patterns but must include modification of the abuse environment. Family therapy is often successful in eliminating abusive events; in extreme cases, however, the child may be legally (temporarily or permanently) removed from parental custody.

Timely intervention appears to be crucial with abused children (Meiselman, 1980; Blair & Justice, 1979). As can be seen with Nancy and Susie, abused children can develop such distorted self-perceptions and maladaptive beliefs about sexuality that subsequent emotional adjustment is severely impaired. Treatment for adults who were abused (without intervention) as children is likely to be for such generalized and inflexible deficits in interpersonal skills that the diagnosis of a personality disorder is appropriate. This treatment is likely to be long-term and essentially involves personality restructuring. The likelihood is for only partially successful outcomes from intervention, such as Nancy's previous treatment experience. It is probable that Susie will eventually resume treatment, as her therapist identified a continued hysterical pattern which may become problematic in romantic involvements and relationships with employers and coworkers (See the later case of Hilde in The Personality Disorders, chapter 10).

A community-based counseling and support group is available to abusing parents in Parents Anonymous. This organization works in the same manner as Alcoholics Anonymous (see the case of Allen, chapter 3) or Gamblers Anonymous (see the case of Gary, chapter 9). Contact with other abusers and the opportunities to share problems with sympathetic and understanding others are helpful for parents for whom abusive behaviors are triggered by psychosocial stressors. Other parents, for whom abusive behavior is associated with some identifiable psychopathology, may respond to some form of voluntary and/or legally imposed intervention.

REFERENCES

Barrett, D., and Fine, H. A child was being beaten: The therapy of battered children as adults. *Psychotherapy: Theory, Research & Practice*, 1980, *17*, 285–298.

Blair, J., and Justice, R. *The broken taboo*. New York: Human Sciences Press, 1979.

Guthiel, T., and Avery, N. Multiple overt incest as family defense against loss. *Family Process*, 1977, *16*, 105–116.

Henderson, D. Incest. In A. Freedman, H. Kaplan, and B. Sadock (Eds.), *Comprehensive textbook of psychiatry*/II. Baltimore: Williams and Wilkins, 1975.

In, P., and McDermott, J. The treatment of child abuse: Play therapy with a four-year-old child. *Journal of the American Academy of Child Psychiatry*, 1976, *15*, 430–440.

Kaplun, D., and Reich, R. The murdered child and his killer. *American Journal of Psychiatry*, 1976, 7, 809–813.

Lord, E., and Weisfeld, D. The abused child. In A. Roberts (Ed.), *Childhood deprivation*. Springfield, Ill.: Charles C Thomas, 1974.

Meiselman, K. *Incest*. San Francisco: Jossey-Bass, 1980.

2

Organic Mental Disorders

Organic mental disorders are behavioral, affective, and intellectual patterns of disturbance that result when there has been damage to the normal brain. Brain cells can be functionally impaired or destroyed by a wide variety of injuries, diseases, and toxic chemicals. Damage to these brain structures, which are involved in cognition, affect, and/or impulse control, can lead to inadequate psychological functioning. The extent to which a person's psychological functioning is impaired depends on the location and extent of neural damage, the person's prior psychological adjustment, and the quality of the person's lifestyle. The effects of an organic mental disorder can range from mild memory disturbances to severe psychotic reactions.

The DSM-III distinguishes between "Organic Mental Disorders" and "Organic Brain Syndrome"; the former label is applied when there is a known or easily inferred etiology. Thus, Organic Brain Syndrome would apply to disorders in which no real reference is made to etiology, which is usually only the first stage of diagnosis.

The first two cases (Harry and Bjorn) in this section could be formally considered as Organic Mental Disorders; the latter two could not. The third case discusses the rare Gilles de la Tourette's syndrome. The authors suggest that general physiological disorder (probably involving a brain structure) is possibly involved in this pattern, although DSM-III rather arbitrarily assigns this diagnostic group to the subcategory of "Stereotyped Movement Disorders" of the main category of Disorders usually First Evident in Infancy, Childhood, or Adolescence. Thus, while that case technically belongs in the first section of this book, we felt it would be more valuable to present it here, in the context of other organic disorders.

In the fourth case, Ingrid, there ultimately turns out to be little evidence of central nervous system disorder. (Most researchers and practitioners in this area prefer this term to either *Organic Brain Syndrome* or *Organic Mental Disorder.*) But since that was the diagnostic issue at hand, the case is most appropriate here.

We will now turn to the first case, the examination of a rather incredible situation in which a person had an entire hemisphere (one-half of the brain) surgically removed in his youth. Not only did he survive to live a somewhat normal life, but he actually achieved an overall adjustment at well above the average level.

Recovery of Functions Following Removal of Dominant Brain Hemisphere

The Case of Harry
The human brain is a remarkably adaptable organ. People have been known to sustain massive amounts of brain damage due to motor vehicle accidents, tumors, and other lesions, yet show remarkable degrees of recovery (Kertesz, 1979). Of course, the eventual level of recovery depends on a number of factors, including age at the time of injury, severity of damage, and the particular region (or regions) of the brain that sustained damage (Smith, 1962). The psychological assessment of people who have sustained brain injuries should therefore consider changes in performance that are likely to occur for some time after the original insult. For this reason, many clinical neuropsychologists make it a habit to follow up on their clients and to retest them periodically in order to document changes that occur over time.

The processes by which the brain recovers from injury are currently being studied by a number of investigators, most of whom emphasize the capacity of nondamaged brain areas to help compensate for injury to other areas by assuming new functional roles. This line of reasoning implies that there is not a strict one-to-one correspondence between brain structures and behavioral or mental activity, even though under ordinary circumstances certain regions of the brain appear to exert dominant influence over specific functions.

Many years ago, it was believed that there existed a strict correspondence between brain regions and behavior. According to this model, popularly called *Phrenology*, discrete regions of the brain controlled very specific behaviors or mental processes. Thus, specific brain regions allegedly were responsible for such states as euphoria, anger, and intellectual superiority. An implication of this view of brain functions is that damage to a given region would be expected to affect only certain psychological functions, leaving others relatively intact. Indeed, early anatomical studies tended to lend some support to this theory. For example, in the late nineteenth century, French neurologist Paul Broca discovered that impairment of expressive speech followed damage to a relatively circumscribed region of the left (or dominant) cerebral hemisphere (Wooldridge, 1963).

Subsequent attempts to localize brain centers that control particular functions have met with varying degrees of success. At present, it is evident that even though there is certainly a general relationship between brain structures and psychological functions, the correlation is by no means exact (Walsh, 1978). It is well known, for example, that the two cerebral hemispheres each control some relatively distinct functions. In healthy and mature right-handed persons, the left cerebral hemisphere plays the dominant role in mediating language skills and the right cerebral hemisphere exerts correspondingly more control over what are known as visuospatial abilities. Visuospatial abilities are manifested in activities such as drawing, finding directions, and being able to visualize spatial arrangements such as one might encounter in geometry problems. At a more general level, a distinction regarding the two hemispheres emphasizes the capacity of the left hemisphere for rational, logical, and analytic thought processes, in contrast to the right hemisphere's role in more holistic, intuitive processes (Bogen, 1969).

The axis of the brain extending from front to back is referred to as the anterior-posterior dimension. Luria (1973) has suggested that the front-most regions play a significant role in planning and executing behavior patterns. Structures in the posterior regions appear to be more involved in processing information taken in by the various sensory systems.

A third part of the brain extends inward from the surface of the brain. Surface regions—collectively called the cortical mantle—appear to mediate most of what are called higher mental processes, such as language, abstract thought, and reasoning abilities. Areas of the brain beneath the cortical mantle, by contrast, control a wide range of activities, including vegetative (life support), reflexive, appetitive, and emotive functions. From an evolutionary standpoint, these regions comprise the oldest, most primitive regions of the brain, collectively referred to as the allocortex, in contrast to the outermost cortical regions, known as the neocortex.

Regarding the functional localization and implications for recovery processes, it is evident that regions, or zones, of the brain are usually responsible for mediating certain psychological functions. We have grouped these functions according to three dimensions—left/right, anterior/posterior, and brain surface/inner regions. Although these dimensions do imply a degree of functional specificity, there is by no means a precise 1-to-1 correspondence between circumscribed regions of brain tissue and specific behavior patterns or thought processes (Walsh, 1978).

It is interesting to note that this absence of a strict 1-to-1 correspondence holds true to a greater degree for the so-called higher than for the lower functions. For example, lesions in regions of the visual system concerned with basic perceptual processes may have very pronounced and permanent effects, such as blind spots, or reductions in the visual fields (the area of sight extending from one visual periphery to the other). By contrast, brain lesions in areas controlling cognitive activities such as language may disrupt certain linguistic processes, without such clear-cut effects, however. There are several possible explanations for this. One is that language, because it is such a complex process, is mediated by a greater proportion of brain tissue than are relatively less complex functions. As a result, focal damage is less likely to affect adversely all of the regions involved in this skill. A second possibility is that higher level functions such as language may be re-duplicated in adjacent or even in more distant brain regions. Thus, damage to a zone that ordinarily controls or mediates may be compensated for by other structures, which provide a sort of back-up coverage.

Along these lines, it has been suggested by several researchers (for example, Kinbourne, 1971) that both the right and the left cerebral hemi-spheres manifest language capabilities, though to different degrees; ordinarily, the left hemisphere is considered dominant. Until recently, the role of the right hemisphere in language activity was not well understood. However, the results of studies of patients who have undergone certain surgical procedures have made it clear that the right (or nondominant) hemisphere has a capacity for language-related activity. In one such pro-cedure (termed a *hemispherectomy*), an entire cerebral hemisphere is removed, leaving the individual with essentially only half a brain. Understandably, relatively few of these operations are performed. Those that are have been carried out either to arrest malignant tumors that have infiltrated one hemisphere, or as a means of controlling severe seizure activ-ity that has not responded to less dramatic therapy.

The case of Harry is one of the most dramatic instances reported in the literature. Early in childhood, the left hemisphere of Harry's brain was removed. The removal was followed by a remarkable recovery of speech and language functions, as assessed by follow-up evaluations years later. Originally described in an article by Smith and Sugar (1975), Harry (not his real name) was briefly seen by the author some three years later, at which time a follow-up evaluation was being performed.

Harry

The product of a full-term, cesarean birth, Harry soon afterwards began to manifest signs of significant brain impairment in the form of seizures. These seizures increased to nearly a dozen per day by the time he was five years old. A left hemispherectomy was performed shortly thereafter, and within a few months, the seizure activity had abated. Testing prior to surgery had revealed distorted speech, doubt-less due to the disruptive effects of damage in the left hemisphere.

Remarkably, Harry's performance on tests of language and other abilities improved significantly in the months and years follow-ing surgery, despite nearly complete removal of the cerebral hemi-

sphere that normally mediates language skills. Follow-up testing of Harry 15½ and 21 years after surgery in fact revealed that he was performing in the high average range of intelligence, with a verbal IQ score in the superior range.

Subsequent contact with Harry suggested that these high performance levels had been sustained, and that he was adjusting extremely well. He successfully graduated from college and at last report was working in an executive-level position for an industrial company and contemplating attending graduate school. He had compensated remarkably well for the aftereffects of surgery, which included loss of sight in the right visual field and motor-control problems on the right side (it is characteristic of damage to either hemisphere that control of the contralateral *side of the body is affected). Harry was a talkative, quick-witted person who undoubtedly was functioning very effectively with half of an intact brain.*

Comment   The case of Harry contains several important implications concerning the long-term effects of brain injury on behavior. First, the development of above average language capabilities following removal of the cerebral hemisphere that normally mediates these functions suggests that the non-dominant hemisphere may possess greater linguistic capabilities than previously realized. More generally, it is at least evident that brain-behavior relationships do not correspond to a strict 1-to-1 functional relationships. Instead, compensation for, or reduplication of control mechanisms appear to exist for certain cognitive processes.

In Harry's case, it may be concluded that right hemisphere structures were responsible for subsequent development of language skills, despite the fact that the right hemisphere's role in language skills is normally thought to be comparatively minor. Finally, the radical changes and improvements in Harry's mental functions underscore the importance of assessing the effects of brain injury over time and emphasizes the recuperative powers of the central nervous system in certain situations. As noted in the introduction, the brain and related nervous system structures comprise an incredibly complex yet flexible and adaptive system.

As far as Harry is concerned, it is likely that the early age at which surgery occurred enhanced his recovery potential, since brain structures do become more rigid as one ages. Furthermore, the degree of recovery may indicate that Harry possessed exceptional potential to begin with, and for this reason does not provide a truly representative picture of recovery potential. Nonetheless, a discussion of this case is important as a means of counteracting tendencies either to view various functions as being strictly localized in the brain, or to assume that any brain damage results in a corresponding permanent loss in psychological abilities.

REFERENCES

Bogen, J. The other side of the brain II. An appositional mind. *Bulletin of the Los Angeles Neurological Society*, 1969, *34*, 135–162.

Luria, A. *A working brain.* New York: Basic Books. 1973.

Kertesz, A. Recovery and treatment. In K. Heilman and E. Valenstein (Eds.), *Clinical neuropsychology.* New York: Oxford University Press, 1979.

Kinbourne, M. The minor cerebral hemisphere as a source of aphasic speech. *Archives of Neurology*, 1971, *25*, 302–306.

Smith, A. Ambiguities in concepts and studies of "brain damage" and "organicity." *Journal of Nervous and Mental Diseases*, 1962, *135*, 311–326.

Smith, A., and Sugar, O. Development of above normal language and intelligence 21 years after left hemispherectomy. *Neurology*, 1975, *25*, 813–818.

Walsh, K. *Neuropsychology.* New York: Churchill Livingstone, 1978.

Wooldridge, D. *The machinery of the brain.* New York: McGraw-Hill, 1963.

Organic Affective Syndrome

The Case of Bjorn   An advantage of the DSM-III classification system over its predecessor lies in its expanded treatment of mental disorders based on central nervous system (CNS) impairments. The multi-axial system permits the diagnostician to address a number of issues crucial to an assessment of the psychological impact of CNS damage. These issues include: 1) specific mental disorders associated with CNS trauma (Axis I); 2) specification of the underlying structural damage (Axis III); 3) associated psychosocial stressors that frequently accompany brain damage in an individual (Axis IV); and 4) an estimate of the client's previous level of functioning (Axis V). Axis II—Personality Disorders and Pervasive Developmental disorders—is somewhat less frequently used; although in certain instances, characteristics of a long-standing personality disorder either are exacerbated by the effects of CNS trauma or else result in maladaptive recovery patterns.

The following case illustrates some of the psychological correlates of CNS trauma that resulted in a diagnosis of Organic Affective Syndrome. In this condition, the most prominent psychological sequel to CNS impairment is a distinct change in mood or emotion. The case involves Bjorn, a twenty-one-year-old student who, prior to a motor vehicle accident, was reportedly well adjusted and an active participant in school activities.

Changes in mood or emotion are quite common in cases of CNS trauma (Walsh, 1978). Perhaps the most commonly reported reaction is one of depression, which probably reflects both an overall slowing of responsiveness due to the impact of trauma on the brain, and a personal reaction as the individual becomes aware of loss of abilities and of newly imposed limitations on behavior. Generally, depression is succeeded by a more optimistic outlook as recovery proceeds and by the gradual return of cognitive and behavioral capabilities. Of course, not everyone recovers from the effects of CNS trauma. Factors such as severity, region or regions of the brain affected, and the age of the individual all play a role in determining the likelihood of subsequent recovery. To the extent that depression continues unabated despite evidence of recovery of other functions, it is likely that it reflects a functional disorder rather than a direct result of CNS trauma. Pervasive depression and passivity can be a real impediment to recovery (Kertesz, 1979), as the following case illustrates.

Bjorn

Bjorn and Tom were working on a construction crew during the summer to help earn some money for school tuition. They had been good friends ever since childhood and were constant companions throughout high school and in college. They had scanned the work ads earlier that summer in search of jobs and were sufficiently enterprising to convince the foreman of a local construction crew to hire them despite a lack of experience.

One afternoon, while enroute at a high speed to deliver some supplies from the warehouse, their pick-up truck lurched off the unpaved access road to the construction site and overturned. Tom, the passenger, luckily escaped uninjured. Bjorn, who was driving, was thrown forward against the windshield pillar with considerable force. He apparently turned his head at the last instant as if to avert direct impact and as a result was struck on the left side of his head. The blow fractured his skull and caused contusions in the underlying brain tissue. Bjorn lost consciousness, to awaken some time later in the local hospital's emergency room.

Subsequent physical and neurological examinations revealed him to be groggy and lethargic. Within the first week of recovery, two grand mal seizures were recorded. An electroencephalogram (EEG) made at this time revealed a focal electrical discharge in the left posterior region of the brain, corresponding to an area known as the angular gyrus. Bjorn was subsequently placed on a low dosage of Dilantin, a medication effective in controlling seizure activity. His condition improved markedly from this point on, and no further seizure activity was noted. Bjorn was subsequently discharged from the hospital and appeared to be on the way to a good recovery. The skull fracture healed, and subsequent EEGs revealed a decrease in abnormal brain wave activity. A subsequent neurological examination revealed that the degree of residual cerebral trauma was comparatively mild. By this time, the fall semester was about to begin, and Bjorn made plans to return to college and resume his studies.

During this period, both Tom and members of Bjorn's family noted that his behavior had undergone a definite change despite medical evidence of only minimal residual cerebral impairment. Before the accident, he had been a studious, hard-working chemistry major who also was highly sociable and quite active in campus activities. He now spent all his time either studying or sleeping. He had become increasingly irritable and complained about many physical maladies, for which he blamed the accident. Although his school grades did not decline significantly, Bjorn spent a great deal more time than before on class and laboratory preparation. He complained that he found it difficult to concentrate, and that his attention frequently wandered. In addition, despite no real difficulties in understanding either lectures or demonstrations, it was now more difficult to take notes and integrate the material into a form that he could readily understand. Somewhat surprisingly, his memory appeared to be relatively intact, which he attributed to the use of memorization strategies that he had learned and practiced early in college.

The complaints of persisting, recurrent physical pains became more frequent as time went on, and Bjorn appeared to be quite depressed and lethargic. He stopped dating at one point and became involved in a conservative religious sect that advocated the cultivation of spirituality through personal meditation while discouraging physical expressiveness. Somewhat alarmed at these developments, Bjorn's parents decided to have him hospitalized for observation some eighteen months following the accident. At the time of admission, he was quiet and somewhat withdrawn, complaining only of pain in his lower back. He proved to be a willng patient, cooperating fully with the hospital staff, and actually appeared to enjoy all of the attention that he received.

Etiology A full battery of medical and psychological tests were carried out during the five days that Bjorn was hospitalized. A thorough neuropsychological evaluation revealed a pattern of cognitive deficits compatible with mild residual cerebral trauma, though not of sufficient magnitude to interfere markedly with his day-to-day functioning. Indeed, his intelligence quotient fell in the high average range (an IQ of 108) of intellectual achievement, which compared favorably with estimates of prior levels of functioning.

It did appear that the locus of the cerebral injury that Bjorn had incurred had some specific effects on his behavior. The region of the brain in which damage had occurred—the angular gyrus of the dominant hemisphere—appears to integrate information processed by the various systems. Many brain specialists believe that this region is one of the cornerstones of distinctly human thought processes (Walsh, 1978). The impact of damage in this region was rather subtle in Bjorn's case, being manifested primarily in his very slow responses to questions, plus evident difficulty in making new associations between stimulus materials, even despite evidence that his sensory abilities were basically intact. This finding was compatible with Bjorn's reported difficulty in integrating his class material, which he had partially compensated for by making extensive use of tape recordings that he played again and again. Additional evidence of residual cerebral impairment rested chiefly on indications of impaired attention and concentration, mild slowing of the right (dominant) hand on tests of manual dexterity, and a mild form of speech dysfluency known as dysarthria, in which the pronunciation of long words is slurred.

The predominant impression conveyed by Bjorn was one of depression, motoric slowness, and emotional flatness. As part of the evaluation, he completed the Minnesota Multiphasic Personality Inventory (MMPI) so that these observations also could be validated. Not surprisingly, clinical scales on the MMPI that are sensitive to depression, withdrawal, and alienation were significantly elevated. These results were consistent with both the observations of Bjorn's behavior and background information obtained during an interview and history taking. Since the indications of depression appeared to comprise the chief manifestation of the residual effects of cerebral trauma, a diagnosis of Organic Affective Syndrome was made. According to DSM-III criteria, this disorder is diagnosed when a mood disturbance without significant loss of intellectual abilities accompanies diagnosed CNS impairment.

As the assessment of Bjorn continued, it became evident that there was no apparent physical basis for his numerous physical complaints. What became strikingly clear instead was a pattern of behaviors that had evolved within Bjorn's family that tended to reinforce his passivity and unresponsiveness. These behaviors included overly solicitous responses to Bjorn's reports of pain, such as suggestions that he immediately lie down and not exert himself. Moreover, family members frequently made unsolicited comments such as, "Gee, you sure don't look well—is something wrong?," or "We hope you'll get back to being the same person you used to be pretty soon!" Bjorn's response to comments like the last one was to withdraw in confusion and ruminate on just what it was that made him so different.

Another factor that evidently played a role in the dynamics of Bjorn's behavior was the frequency with which medical advice was sought. By becoming increasingly reclusive, Bjorn had a great deal more time to focus on and monitor his internal state, with the result that he became highly sensitive to even minor fluctuations of his various bodily systems (Meister, 1980). It turned out that in the intervening months since the accident, Bjorn had had more than three dozen appointments with the family physician beyond those required for routine checkups! Despite this, the results of the comprehensive assessment carried out eighteen months after the accident were negative with respect to evidence of significant physical or central nervous system trauma. Based on these findings, a diagnosis based on DSM-III criteria was made as follows:

Axis I: (293.83) Organic Affective Syndrome
Axis II: Deferred
Axis III: Mild residual cerebral trauma, left posterior cerebral hemisphere
Axis IV: Severity of psychosocial stressors: Moderate
Axis V: Highest level of adaptive functioning, past year: Fair

Treatment One recommendation stemming from this assessment was for family therapy (Framo, 1979). The intent of this recommendation was to help both Bjorn and his family deemphasize reactions to complaints of pain, as well as to discourage excessive medical consultation beyond normal checkups. In a series of therapy sessions, family members were coached in ways to encourage Bjorn's skills and competencies, without comparing present and past behavior. It became evident that family members experienced considerable frustration in dealing with the prominent shift in Bjorn's moods following the accident, yet were afraid to confront him for fear of disrupting his "delicate" condition. At the same time, Bjorn was encouraged to become more responsive to others as a means of counteracting his introspective tendencies. Privileges that had been denied him out of well-intentioned but misplaced concern were reinstated, including driving and staying out at night. As a result, Bjorn began to feel like less of a prisoner at home and began acting more spontaneously toward family members and friends. A follow-up interview with Bjorn six months later revealed that he was making a satisfactory adjustment both at home and in school and that he had not sought medical consultation in the interim, aside from a routine checkup.

Conclusions Bjorn's case is interesting for several reasons. First, it illustrates the broad scope of issues relating to behavior that psychologists may be called on to evaluate. In Bjorn's case, these issues ranged from assessing the behavioral effects of localized brain injury to evaluating the social context of his behavior.

Second, it demonstrates that the presence of documented cerebral impairment does not rule out the possibility of effective psychological intervention (Smith et al., 1972; Walsh, 1978). In this case, the psychologist working with Bjorn and his family focused on aspects of the social environment that acted to exaggerate and maintain physical symptomatology beyond a time when there was any obvious biological basis for these complaints. Psychologists have long recognized that change in the status of a family member can disrupt accustomed relationship patterns, the outcome of which can be either a gradual return to health and familial equilibrium, or, in some cases, a reorganization of communication patterns in a way that promotes dependence and passivity in the affected member (Haley, 1971).

In Bjorn's case, there is no question that the accident had resulted in actual brain damage: this was documented by neurological examinations, EEGs, and other measures at the time of the accident. Moreover, subtle signs of residual cerebral impairment were evident nearly two years following the accident, as documented by the neuropsychological assessment. However, the fact that at this later time Bjorn was functioning in a high average range of intelligence and was doing reasonably well in school, suggested that the residual effects of brain trauma *per se* were relatively slight and could not by themselves account for the chronic depressed state into which Bjorn had lapsed following the accident. Thus, the family system appeared the logical place on which to focus psychological intervention and ultimately proved effective in altering these problems.

Also, a clear implication of the assessment results is that the diagnosis of a mental disorder in an individual—even when based on verified cerebral impairment—should not exclude consideration of the role of social networks in the maintenance of symptomatology (Framo, 1979). Perhaps in Bjorn's case it would have been equally appropriate to characterize his entire family as in a depressive state, rather than singling out any individual.

Finally, the reports of significant changes in behavior and eventual recovery attest to the marvelous recuperative powers of the central nervous system (Smith & Sugar, 1975; Walsh, 1978). Bjorn's age undoubtedly was a factor in his recovery; had he sustained the injury at a more advanced age, the level of recovery might not have been as complete. Nonetheless, it is evident that recuperation from even serious CNS traumas routinely occurs, although the exact mechanisms through which this takes place are not as yet completely understood.

REFERENCES

Framo, J. Family theory and therapy, *American Psychologist*, 1979, 34, 988–992.

Haley, J. (Ed.). *Changing families. A family therapy reader*. New York: Grune and Stratton, 1971.

Kertesz, A. Recovery and treatment, In K. M. Heilman and E. Valenstein (Eds.), *Clinical neuropsychology*. New York: Oxford University Press, 1979.

Meister, R. *Hypochondria*. New York: Taplinger, 1980.

Smith, A., and Sugar, O. Development of above normal language and intelligence 21 years after left hemispherectomy. *Neurology*, 1975, 25, 813–818.

Smith, A., Chamoux, R., Leri, J., London, R., and Muraski, A. *Diagnosis, intelligence, and rehabilitation of chronic aphasics*. Ann Arbor: University of Michigan Department of Physical Medicine and Rehabilitation, 1972.

Walsh, K. W. *Neuropsychology*. New York: Churchill Livingstone, 1978.

Gilles de la Tourette's Syndrome

The Cases of Ms. A and Mr. B

The following article describes one of the more baffling disorders studied in psychopathology, the Gilles de la Tourette's Syndrome. This disorder has variously been considered as a factitious disorder, malingering, a somatoform disorder, a conversion disorder, or simply an organic disorder. Hajal and Leach (1981) are inclined to view this disorder as reflecting organic dysfunction, (that is, neurophysiological disorder) that is probably of genetic origin. Yet, the fact that it occurs with consistency in families does not prove that hypothesis, since modeling of behavior or consistent though unique diet patterns could just as easily explain this consistency within families. Even though it is clear that an upsurge of anxiety is critical in setting off the actual incident, the authors of this book agree that neurophysiological disorder is at least involved as a precursor of these incidents.

The DSM-III only applies this term when the onset is between two and fifteen years of age; thus, in the cases of both Ms. A and Mr. B., the label would be appropriate. A variety of treatment techniques have been tried with this disorder, but without much evidence that they are critical to successful treatment. Two approaches are helpful here. First is the use of behavioral techniques to control the problematic physical behaviors in this pattern and to make sure that there is no reinforcement for the pattern by allowing individuals to avoid demands in their environment. Secondly, some chemotherapies, particularly haloperidol, have been reported as helpful.

Familial Aspects of Gilles de la Tourette Syndrome

Fady Hajal and Ann M. Leach

The multiple tic syndrome initially described by Itard (1) in 1825 and later by Gilles de la Tourette in his classic paper published in 1885 (2) is a relatively rare condition characterized by sudden, involuntary movements including vulgar gestures, explosive involuntary utterances (both inarticulate noises and articulated words, at times obscenities and coprolalia), and imitative phenomena (echolalia and echopraxia).

In case 1, the boy was admitted at the same institution where his mother had been hospitalized as a child. It was relatively easy to find her chart, which turned out to be well documented. In case 2, the child was hospitalized, and the history of family antecedents of Tourette syndrome emerged in the course of working with his parents.

From: Hajal, F., and Leach, A. Familial aspects of Gilles de la Tourette syndrome. (*The American Journal of Psychiatry*, vol. 138:1, pp. 90–92, 1981.) Copyright 1981, the American Psychiatric Association. Reprinted by permission.

Case Reports

Case 1. Ms. A. was 9 years old when she began showing some unusual motor behavior such as frequently hoisting up her blue jeans, skipping excessively, and intermittent jerking movements of the head and trunk. A few months later the vocalization began and she began to cross herself frequently for no apparent reason.

As the verbal and motor tics worsened, Ms. A, who was then 11, was admitted to the hospital with the chief complaint of "spasmodic vocalizations resembling hiccoughs," which according to her mother sounded more like "four-letter words." In the hospital she was described as being tense and fearful and exhibited hypermotility and restlessness in her various activities. She was suggestible and prone to identify with other patients; for example, she reported having the same dreams, substituting names, etc. During her hospital stay the quality, frequency, and intensity of the tics showed marked fluctuations. The vocalizations become clearer and consisted of obscene words. She admitted to being able to halt the tics on some occasions as well to voluntarily reproduce her vocal and muscular tics. Her vocal tic was generally followed by a body tic. She also showed some prominent sucking habits with drawing of the mouth and a tendency to put objects in her mouth.

She was discharged on a trial basis, although her tic symptoms improved only moderately during her hospitalization; a few months later the tics occurred with increased frequency and she was placed in a home for girls. When returned home at age 14, the tics seemed to have subsided completely. Ms. A, now in her late 20s, has stated that the tics never recurred; however, a recent medical report noted that some verbal tics have been observed at times of stress. This was confirmed by her mother.

Ms. A's son Tim was 9 years old when he was admitted to the same hospital with a diagnosis of Gilles de la Tourette syndrome. Because he had been an extremely active baby and child, his maternal grandfather had expressed concern that Tim might have a Tourette syndrome as his mother had. He crawled at the appropriate age but could only crawl backward. He walked at 12 months but generally did so sideways until he was 14 months old. His speech development was slow. He was still relying on a form of baby talk at age 3½. He continued to talk, but his words were garbled and ran into each other. He also persisted up to the time of his hospitalization in a tendency to "mouth" all kinds of objects; his parents attributed this behavior to his "extreme curiosity."

The motor tics began when Tim was 3 years, 1 month, in the form of excessive eye blinking and shaking of the head and shoulders, with a typical waxing and waning pattern. The tics became more pronounced and diversified following the death of his grandfather, and a number of new tics developed: jerking of the head, skipping, and "dancing." The vocal tics, which started exactly 1 year later, first showed in "sticking out" movements of the tongue, followed within the month by a rapid firing of loud noises sounding like "huh." The vocal tics increased progressively in frequency and volume and soon his symptoms included laughing noises and coprolalia and later copropraxia, at which point he was administered haloperidol. Since the tics were not altogether affected by haloperidol, he was hospitalized 3 years later and thoroughly evaluated. Various examinations, including an EEG, showed normal results.

Case 2

Mr. B. was 10 years old when he began flexing and shrugging his shoulders. These movements were quickly replaced by facial tics, i.e., wiggling his nose and rolling his eyes upward and sideways, and by trunk movements, i.e., stomach contractions. These tics occurred one at a time. Later on vocal tics appeared—a cough that sounded at first as if he was clearing his throat and then like grunting. The tics were spontaneous, appeared in all kinds of situations and occurred frequently (every day, generally several times an hour). He felt uneasy and embarrassed and tried to hide his eye rolling by rubbing his forehead which appeared to be another tic-like movement. His tics were attributed by his family to his being a nervous child, and no professional help was sought since these symptoms did not seem to interfere with his school and social adjustment. The tics disappeared around his 13th year and have not returned except for an occasional wiggling of his nose, noticed by his wife.

When Mr. B's nephew Robert began to walk, he was clumsy and uncoordinated, often dragging his left foot. Robert also had articulation problems, often spoke with a peculiar accent, and generally favored nonverbal communication such as pointing. His infantile speech, together with his low frustration tolerance and his aggressive behavior, made him unmanageable at home and school. He was referred for intensive psychotherapy at age 7. The therapist noted that Robert was showing a great many motor discharges, primarily multiple facial tics. Later, persistent vocal tics with high-pitch screeching appeared following by spitting and coprolalia. He developed a number of ritualistic mannerisms such as mechanically touching his finger to his forehead or his fork to his hair. He began to cling excessively to others by pawing, mouthing, or hanging on to them. At this point Robert started to take haloperidol but he improved only slightly and was later hospitalized. Routine tests, EEG and neurological examinations were within normal limits. During his hospitalization a typical waxing and waning pattern was observed:

his "mannerisms" vacillated from being extreme to being barely noticeable.

Discussion When we first explored the possibility of other people in the family (i.e., the previous generation) having suffered from Tourette syndrome or having shown any type of tic behavior, Robert's relatives (case 2) told us that none was ever observed. Because Robert was in a residential treatment facility and we saw his parents regularly, we were able to return many times to our question about family antecedents. After more than 1 year of persistence we were told that Robert's maternal uncle may have had a similar syndrome. He consented to be interviewed by us and he described the motor and vocal tics that began in late latency. Because of the initial denial we encountered with this family, we wonder about the real incidence of multiple family cases of Tourette syndrome. It is possible that many cases of family occurrence of Tourette syndrome may have been missed because the family felt guilty or ashamed and therefore denied it or because it was buried deep in the past and simply forgotten.

When we studied our patients' clinical pictures more closely, we noted several shared features. One such feature is the persistence of a number of oral and sensory-motor habits. Ms. A showed definite sucking habits, with drawing of the mouth and a tendency to "mouth" things. Her son showed a persistent tendency to "mouth" all kinds of objects within his grasp. Another common feature we found was the high degree of suggestibility exhibited by our patients. Ms. A was described as being prone to identify with other patients to the point of reporting dreams similar to theirs, substituting names, and Tim was described as a very compliant child, adapting his behavior to presumed adult expectations. Robert's marked robot-type movements at one point resembled his mother's dyskinesia so closely that he seemed to be mimicking her. This suggestibility may be another form of the more typically imitative phenomena described in Tourette's as echolalia and echopraxia.

We were struck by the clinical evolution of the syndrome from one generation to the other. The clinical picture seemed to be worse in the second generation in both of these families. In the first generation, the onset of the syndrome was in late latency, whereas the onset was much earlier in the second generation (at 3 and 6–7 years, respectively.) Both boys in the second generation showed a number of premorbid difficulties in their development, whereas none was reported in the early development of their first generation relatives. The symptoms also seemed more severe in the second generation. The frequency, intensity, and persistence of the vocal and motor tics were much greater in the second-generation patients, and the degree of interference with psychological development was more marked, which led to substantial psychological disturbances as well as difficulties in family, peer, and social relationships. The cases suggest a hypothesis of the increasing constitutional predisposition of a tendency to react to stresses (internal as well as external) in an undifferentiated sensory-motor manner, more typical of a preverbal child. It is difficult, at this point, to draw any conclusions from this trend.

REFERENCES

1. Itard JMG: Memoire sur quelques fonctions involontaires des appareils de la locomotion de la prehension et de la voix. *Arch Gen Med* 8:385, 1825.
2. Gilles de la Tourette G: Etude sur une affection nerveuse, caracterisee par de l'incoordination motrice, accompagnee d'echolalie et de coprolalie. *Arch Neurol* 9:19–42, 158–200, 1885.

Comment   Recent evidence suggests that the Tourette's syndrome may be more common than originally thought. However, it is still often misdiagnosed as schizophrenia, or some similar disorder. Recently, the syndrome was the subject of an episode of the *Quincy* program on television. After the program, callers deluged the switchboard to get more information about the disorder. In several cases, people realized that they had been misdiagnosed and eventually improved after seeking more appropriate treatment.

Aversion techniques to control some of the bizarre behavior and EMG (biofeedback of specific muscle movements) have been helpful here. As noted earlier, haloperidol and certain other drugs can also be useful. The irony is that haloperidol is also used to treat schizophrenia. Large doses are appropriate for schizophrenia, smaller doses for the Tourette's syndrome. Thus, even when Tourette patients are misdiagnosed as schizophrenic, the large haloperidol dose knocks out most of the twitching and all the rest of their functioning as well (psychotic patients tolerate these large doses somewhat better).

Central Nervous System Dysfunction and Legal Incompetence from Aging and/or Alcohol

The Case of Ingrid   Psychologists are frequently called on to address the issue of an individual's mental competence. "Competence" in the legal arena can refer to competence to manage one's day-to-day affairs, competence to make a will, or competence to stand trial (defined in Dusky v. United States, 362 U.S. 402 [1960], as the ability to consult rationally with an attorney and to understand the relevant legal proceedings). For the purpose of this case, competence refers to the extent to which individuals are presumed capable of managing their day-to-day affairs. This concept is especially important when applied to older persons. Although the majority of people will remain mentally alert (and presumably competent) throughout most of their lives, aging processes are accompanied by increasing changes that may compromise a person's mental status for any of several reasons, most commonly due to deterioration of the central nervous system (CNS) (Botwinick, 1981).

The term *dementia* is often used to signify the presence of CNS-based mental deterioration sufficient to interfere with a person's functioning and is more commonly though inaccurately termed *senility*. As discussed in DSM-III, dementia is diagnosed when there is evidence of significant intellectual decline, plus evidence of more specific cognitive deficits, one of which involves memory loss. Dementia need not have a specific cause; rather, it can result from a wide range of conditions that adversely affect the brain and other CNS structures.

Dementia is often thought of as an essentially irreversible condition, particularly when evident in older persons; yet this is not always the case. For example, in many older persons, the arteries that supply blood to the brain gradually become occluded due to accumulated deposits of fatty substances (arteriosclerosis). This process curtails blood flow to the brain, reduces metabolic efficiency, and thereby lowers the activation level of the CNS. Accompanying behavioral signs include indications of increasing forgetfulness, absentmindedness, and a general lowering of behavioral efficiency—in short, every indication of dementia, particularly when the condition has progressed to the point at which brain blood supply is markedly reduced. A significant effect of surgery to help restore brain blood supply (called an endarterectomy) is the often abrupt reversal of symptoms of dementia and the restoration of mental alertness.

Signs of evident dementia may diminish or reverse themselves in other instances, also. For example, unremitting alcohol consumption may cause a deterioration of mental functioning; this process can be reversed when the person gains control over the drinking. Whether or not dementia is actually present in such cases depends on whether it can be established that the contributory condition has had a demonstrable effect on CNS functioning.

The assessment of mental competence thus often involves a determination of whether dementia is present to a significant degree. This task may be complicated somewhat by the fact that other mental disorders—particularly depression—can easily be confused with dementia. This distinction is a very important one to make when assessing older persons, who in addition to being more biologically vulnerable to factors underlying true dementia are quite likely to experience events that trigger depressive reactions. For example, the death of a spouse or other loved one typically results in a depressive reaction characterized by brooding, preoccupation, and withdrawal. To outsiders, these reactions may appear as a condition indicative of dementia (or its more popularized cousin, senility).

An evaluation of mental competence in older persons thus requires a careful evaluation of events surrounding the reported onset of symptoms. In addition to carrying out formal psychological testing, the psychologist must obtain a detailed history of the client's problems. It is of crucial importance to be able to distinguish true dementia from a depressive reaction, since the latter condition is by definition transient, with a correspondingly good prognosis. Furthermore, it is important to evaluate symptoms of dementia to see if the underlying process is progressive or in remission.

The following case highlights some of the issues involved in the determination of mental competence. It is a description of Ingrid, a 77-year-old woman who was referred for an extensive psychological assessment to aid the court in a determination of her mental competence.

Ingrid

Ingrid's husband Charlie had died three years earlier, following a long series of illnesses. They had been a devoted couple, and his death sent Ingrid into a deep depression. For the first time in her life, Ingrid began to drink heavily as a means of washing away the emotional pain that accompanied Charlie's death. She appeared to others to become absentminded and forgetful, as if lost in a dream-like reverie. On several occasions, Ingrid's neighbors noticed her doing strange things, such as working in her garden in midwinter, and taking out the trash when only partially dressed. Charlie had left her a sizeable estate—ample to meet her needs plus an inheritance for the children. On one or two occasions, she talked about giving all the money away to a charity, as if any reminder of Charlie's former presence was too much to bear.

Alarmed at these developments—particularly at the prospect of having his inheritance jeopardized—Ingrid's son (aged 53) petitioned to have his mother declared legally incompetent to manage her own affairs. The petition was upheld in a court hearing, and Ingrid's financial holdings were turned over to a court-appointed trustee, who provided her with ample funds to live on in a local nursing home. At the hearing, the attorney retained by Ingrid's son argued that her advanced age made it reasonable to assume that the depression following Charlie's death was only part of a broader picture of mental deterioration indicative of encroaching senility. By way of contrast, expert testimony included the report of a clinical psychologist who, although agreeing that Ingrid showed signs of significant mental impairment, felt that the condition was only temporary and should not be presumed to be accompanied by dementia (senility) merely because of the client's advanced age. He recommended that Ingrid's condition be reevaluated several months hence, should it appear that she showed signs of remission.

Eighteen months later, Ingrid herself wrote a meticulously worded, impeccably reasoned letter to the judge requesting that her case be reopened, and at the same time she hired a new attorney. She was in much better spirits and seemed optimistic that they would succeed in overturning the earlier ruling. As part of the proceedings, a thorough neuropsychological assessment was carried out. In addition to evaluating global intellectual performance, it assessed five groups of cognitive skills that are sensitive to CNS impairment: speech and language skills, visuospatial abilities, attention and concentration, memory, and sensory-motor areas.

The results of this assessment suggested that Ingrid appeared mentally competent, and that whatever condition(s) had been responsible for her earlier mental relapses were no longer apparent. There was no indication of dementia—Ingrid manifested an intelligence quotient in the upper portion of the average range, possessed adequate memory skills, and showed no significant indications of other specific thinking disorders. She appeared to have compensated well for some sensory and motor impairments (poor eyesight, slight hearing loss, plus an obvious motor tremor) and appeared for the assessment as a socially alert, cooperative, well-groomed woman, fully aware of the purpose of the evaluation and related events. As stated in the evaluation (reproduced here in summary form):

> *On the Wechsler Adult Intelligence Scale (WAIS), Mrs. A [Ingrid] achieved a Full Scale IQ score which places her at a level slightly above average for individuals of similar age. Her performance was highly consistent, notable for the absence of diagnostic indicators on the WAIS associated with signs of cerebral impairment. These results were obtained despite evidence of sensory and motor deficits including pronounced motor tremor, bilateral cataracts, and possibly transient hearing difficulty. Mrs. A appears to have developed compensatory strategies which included guiding the right hand with the left to minimize tremor; use of a magnifying glass, plus slow visual scanning patterns; and postural adjustments to maximize auditory volume, along with requests for repetition of test items on occasion. Overall, results of the WAIS were compatible with the client's educational and job history, and reveal normal age-related slowing of response speed and information processing efficiency, without evidence of additional intrusive factors which would interfere with intellectual performance.*

> *Overall, the assessment of this 78-year-old woman reveals intellectual and cognitive capabilities in an above-average range, above-average memory abilities, and a well-focused, organized approach to the tests. Verbal and linguistic fluency appears developed to a higher degree than corresponding skills in visuo-perceptual areas—a discrepancy which may be enhanced by the visual and motor problems apparent to casual observation.*

A court verdict in Ingrid's favor was returned, legally restoring her rights and privileges to manage her own affairs.

The results of formal testing give only a hint of the range of observations needed to provide a clear picture of Ingrid's mental status. These observations contributed to a three-dimensional image of a competent, well-adjusted individual. We will now discuss some of these factors in more detail.

The evaluation was conducted in two different locations—first, in the examiner's office, and then at the nursing home where Ingrid lived. By carrying out the assessment at two different times and in two different locations, it was possible to evaluate the consistency of Ingrid's behavior. On both occasions, she was neatly groomed and dressed and acted in a most cordial fashion. When seen in her own room at the nursing home, it was immediately apparent that Ingrid's living environment reflected active interests. A desk, set up near the bed, contained neatly organized materials—pencils, pens, a work lamp, stationery, plus a vase of freshly cut flowers. She had organized her business papers in a section of the desk; and on one occasion, after stating that she wished to show the examiner some pertinent material, unerringly located them without hesitation or confusion. The material turned out to be a handwritten copy of the letter she had recently sent to the judge requesting a new competency hearing.

Ingrid proved well aware of the purpose of the evaluation and was able to explain clearly the events leading up to the current situation. She was quite frank in discussing the particulars of her history, readily admitting that the grief, fear, and even anger engendered by her husband's death had caused her to do some unfortunate things. Neither her manner and affect, nor the details of her account of these events varied appreciably between the two assessment sessions.

Her response to the testing was characteristic of many older persons faced with taking tests—she was anxious (Schaie & Schaie, 1977). She expressed some trepidation regarding the nature of the tests and was concerned that her lack of recent experience with similar sorts of activities would markedly compromise her performance. In addition, she was dismayed at the prospect of having to analyze problems without the aid of paper and pencil (or her new calculator, which she had recently learned to use as an aid in analyzing her financial investments). It is important to consider a client's reaction to the tests themselves, as extreme anxiety can have a markedly adverse effect on performance. Ingrid was well aware that the results of the assessment would be used in the determination of her legal competency, yet she managed to master whatever anxiety she felt and did perform well on the tests.

During the initial assessment session, Ingrid failed to solve an arithmetic problem involving the computation of a percentage. As a former bookkeeper, she was quite upset at her performance on this particular test item.

She remembered the details of the problem, however, and at the beginning of the following session five days later, produced the correct solution, along with the results of several similar problems that she had made up. This gave evidence of a number of things, including excellent memory skills, persistence in problem solving, a desire to improve on performance, and perhaps a degree of over-compensation and compulsiveness. It was evident that well into her advanced years Ingrid had retained a strong desire to both please and impress people. The only difference was that now she found herself trying to please subordinates both in age and experience and to prove to them (us) that she could perform up to standards that people far younger than she had set.

Additional indications of mental competency accrue from other sources. A sense of humor, for example, is frequently treated as a sign of mental alertness. Ingrid possessed a mildly self-deprecatory sense of humor, and more generally, an overall attitude that appeared uplifting and optimistic. A number of test responses indicated interpersonal sensitivity and awareness of social conventions. Thus, her behavior in this regard was much in keeping with social norms. Finally, a chance question asked during a mental status examination—"Who is President of the United States?"—revealed additional evidence of considerable mental alertness: Ingrid replied that Jimmy Carter had been President up until that very morning but had now been replaced by Ronald Reagan!

These and other indications of behavioral consistency, alertness, and socially apt behavior, apparent during the course of two test sessions, provided evidence of mental competence that amplified on and individualized the rather bland assertion that Ingrid possessed "average intellectual functioning." A comprehensive description of Ingrid based on these observations took on additional significance in light of the impression that people were prone to form of her based on first impressions. For example, at the onset of the evaluation, she stated that the examiner would have to speak somewhat loudly, and she closed in to a distance that violated usual though unspoken standards regarding how close two people normally get. Unless able to use a magnifying glass, she resorted to scanning visual materials with her face very close to the page. When writing, she had to steady her right hand with the left in order to lessen the effects of a pronounced motor tremor. Such behavior, from a distance, could easily create a stereotyped image of an incompetent individual. And yet it was precisely this sort of behaviors that at-

tested to Ingrid's awareness of her limitations and to her successful efforts to adapt to them. It is not uncommon to find individuals of any age who appear superficially competent simply because they are not active and do not behave in ways that might betray their limitations or to find still others whose behavior is maladaptive because they are not aware of their limitations. By comparison, Ingrid really was quite competent and well adjusted.

Treatment   No formal psychological intervention was undertaken in Ingrid's case. When she learned of the favorable decision, she promptly reinvested a portion of her estate in money market funds, sold the family homestead, and purchased a condominium in a progressive retirement community that provided increasing levels of health care as needed by the members. Having quickly dispatched these tasks, she took her first vacation in years—a long cruise. She commented that the outcome of the hearing had given her a new lease on life—at age 78!

Comment   The results of the extensive neuropsychological assessment carried out on this woman corroborated other diagnostic tests. All of the tests concluded that Ingrid's mental status was unimpaired and that there were no indications of any underlying CNS impairment which would seriously compromise her ability to think and reason effectively. The assessment did turn up evidence of normal age-related changes in test performance—chiefly a slowing of reaction time and somewhat lower flexibility when confronted with new information. Nevertheless, it was concluded that these factors would not impede Ingrid from carrying out her day-to-day affairs—a conclusion amply confirmed by her subsequent behavior.

Beyond merely ruling out the presence of dementia, the thorough assessment of cognitive, intellectual, and social skills tended to highlight Ingrid's patterns of strengths and weaknesses and served to individualize her as a person. Thoroughness is important because a comprehensive assessment can help to counteract a tendency to view older persons (or any other nominal group) as homogeneous with respect to almost any characteristic (Neugarten et al., 1964). Although events associated with aging may predispose individuals to undergo deterioration of mental capabilities, it is inappropriate to assume that such decline is inevitable, as demonstrated in Ingrid's case.

The most significant aspect of Ingrid's situation concerns the reversal of a competency ruling in a person of relatively advanced age. The outcome of her case further counteracts the popular tendency to view mental abilities in older persons as suspect (at best) and, if compromised, not readily recovered.

REFERENCES

Botwinick, J. Neuropsychology of aging. In B. Filskov and T. Boll (Eds.), *Handbook of clinical neuropsychology.* New York: Wiley, 1981.

Neugarten, B., Crotty, W., and Tobin, S. *Personality in middle and later life.* New York: Atherton Press, 1964.

Schaie, K., and Schaie, J. Clinical assessment and aging. In J. E. Birren and K. Schaie (Eds.), *Handbook of the psychology of aging.* New York: Van Nostrand Reinhold, 1977.

3

Substance Use Disorders

Our society considers the use of drugs in order to modify mood, behavior, or comfort to be appropriate under certain circumstances. For many people, however, drug abuse and dependence have become serious obstacles to adjustment. Only recently have public and professional conceptualizations of drug problems (including alcohol) changed from the archaic indictment of demonic influence or sinfulness to a consideration of the individual's maladaptive choices and response patterns. Fortunately, the newer approaches have stimulated investigation of both causal factors and effective treatments. These research efforts have also broadened the category of potentially abused drugs. Heretofore, attention was primarily limited to alcohol and heroin. However, DSM-III lists ten types of substances: alcohol, barbiturate, opioid, cocaine, amphetamine, phencyclidine (PCP), hallucinogen, cannabis, caffeine, and tobacco. A common pattern in today's society, Prescription Drug Abuse, is not formally included, though that is the subject of the second case in this chapter.

The diagnostic class of substance use disorders includes undesirable behavioral changes caused by regular use of substances that affect the central nervous system. The distinction is made between mental disorders associated with drug use and nonpathological use for recreational or medical purposes. Substance use disorders are of two types: Substance *Abuse* and Substance *Dependence*. Substance Abuse is defined by a pathological pattern of use (such as the need for consistent use) and by impairment in social or occupational functioning due to use that has lasted for at least one month. Substance Dependence is defined by tolerance (need for significantly increased amounts in order to achieve this desired effect) or by withdrawal (development of physiological and/or psychological symptomatology contingent on cessation of use), in addition to the requirements for substance abuse.

Allen, the first case described in this chapter, received the diagnoses of Alcoholic Hallucinosis (because of his alcohol-generated symptom of hearing voices that were not real) and Alcohol Withdrawal because of the symptoms of vomiting, trembling, and high anxiety generated by the alcohol. Since there was withdrawal, plus consistent use and family disruption over a period of time, he would also eventually receive a diagnosis of Alcohol Dependence (after an adequate history was gathered).

The introduction to this section notes some of the several DSM-III diagnoses that the various problematic patterns of alcohol use can receive. The variety here reflects the fact that alcohol-related psychopathology is a major cause of placement in a mental hospital (not to mention the high cost in related physical illnesses, family and social disruption, auto accidents, and so on).

In the last two decades, society has moved from seeing alcoholism as a product of sinfulness or the power of alcohol itself ("demon rum") to viewing it as an "illness." The fortunate consequence of this trend has been the increased awareness of a need for treatment. The focus on "illness," however, has led many alcoholics to ignore the critical importance of their own motivation to change ("You're the Doc; I hope you can cure me"). In this vein, researchers such as Alan Marlatt (see, for example, Lang, Goechner, Adesso, & Marlatt, 1975) and Terrance Wilson (see also Abrams & Wilson, 1979; Lansky & Wilson, 1981) have found that the uncontrolled expression of sexual and aggressive behavior under the actual or alleged influence of alcohol is related more to a *belief* that one has ingested alcohol, than to *actually* having done so.

REFERENCES

Abrams, D., and Wilson, T. Effects of alcohol on social anxiety in women: Cognitive versus physiological processes. *Journal of Abnormal Psychology*, 1979, *88*, 161–73.

Lang, A., Goechner, D., Adesso, V., and Marlatt, A. Effects of alcohol on aggression in male social drinkers. *Journal of Abnormal Psychology*, 1975, *85*, 508–518.

Lansky, D., and Wilson, T. Alcohol, expectations, and sexual arousal in males: An information processing analysis. *Journal of Abnormal Psychology*, 1981, *90*, 34–45.

Alcohol Dependence

The Case of Allen DePrez   Many people still accept the fallacy that alcohol is a stimulant. In actuality, alcohol acts pharmacologically first to depress higher brain centers, which consequently results in a loss of inhibition in overt behaviors. With continued alcohol intake, the more complex functions of all brain centers are also suppressed, eventually resulting in unconsciousness. Interestingly enough, alcohol is not digested, but is directly absorbed through the intestinal walls and stomach, and then metabolized in the liver by oxidation. In the average person, the liver can only break down about 1 ounce of 100 proof whiskey, or its equivalent, in one hour. Amounts in excess of that remain in the blood stream and begin to affect the brain, as noted above.

Alcohol has been used as long as any drug available today. As far back as 8000 B.C., in the Paleolithic Age, mead, an alcoholic beverage derived from honey, was used. Beer and berry wine were imbibed as early as 6400 B.C. Alcohol has almost certainly been abused for as long as it has been used. The costs to the abuser have always been high, physiologically and psychologically. Alcoholism is especially costly to society at large in our present era, as it exacts an enormous toll through alcohol-caused accidents (especially auto accidents), disruption of family life, and inefficiency and loss in the business realm. (Brandsma, 1979; Begleiter, et al., 1981). Such costs are evident in the case of Allen.

Allen

One Wednesday night, Allen came home from work, greeted his family, and took his normal place in his easy chair and read the paper. Then he ate dinner with his wife and two teenage daughters. After dinner, he worked in his shop for a while on some furniture he was refinishing; but he stopped early and went to his bedroom. Wondering why Allen had quit so early, his wife went in and saw him crawling around the bedroom floor. Allen exclaimed that the "voices" kept telling him to crawl because of his "sins." He was trembling and sweating, had vomited on the floor, and refused to let his wife near him. An ambulance was called and Allen was taken to the hospital emergency room. The attending physician found him highly anxious, suffering from auditory hallucinations (hearing things that are not there), and confused about time and place.

Allen's wife was questioned for any possible causes or explanations for his agitated state. She reported that Allen had been somewhat irritable and restless lately; but she was unaware of any unusual behaviors. She said that Allen had seen a clinical psychologist because of alcoholism. At this point, Allen's episode was diagnosed as Alcohol Withdrawal (because of the trembling, vomiting, and anxiety) and Alcohol Hallucinosis (because of the hallucinations). He was sedated and admitted to the detoxification unit. The clinical psychologist was consulted and Allen's wife was interviewed extensively. The staff of the detoxification team were then able to reconstruct the events that led to Allen's emergency admission.

Allen DePrez is a thirty-eight-year-old air traffic controller who grew up in a small, rural Kansas community. At age eighteen, he left his hometown to attend the state university, returning only for brief visits. After graduating from college, with a degree in aeronautical engineering, Allen remained in the city as an airplane designer. During the next ten years, he worked his way up into managerial positions and then trained for the air traffic controller job. He had held his controller position with the metropolitan airport for five years.

Allen's father was a skilled mechanic and owned a small garage. Allen's mother did not work outside their home and was very devoted to Allen, his two older brothers, and his younger sister. Both parents were high school graduates who strongly encouraged their children to attend college. Presently, Allen's brothers are successful real estate brokers and his sister is a physical therapist. All three returned to their hometown after college and married local residents. Mrs. DePrez was of the opinion that Allen's brothers drank excessively and described his sister as a religious abstainer. Mrs. DePrez also reported that Allen's father was a chronic alcoholic, but that his mother would not drink for religious reasons.

The disagreements between Allen's parents over the morality of drinking were frequent occurrences during family gatherings and apparently began before Allen was born. Allen's father could occasionally be persuaded to admit himself to alcohol abuse units and would stop drinking for a few months. The couple would be reconciled and the family atmosphere would be more pleasant. Interestingly enough, Allen's father's work habits were disrupted only when he was hospitalized. He often presented these facts in his defense and contended that as long as he was able to provide for his family he wasn't a "real" alcoholic.

Allen was very close to his brothers in childhood and made every effort to win their approval. They encouraged Allen to drink as an adolescent and included him in their social functions, which usually included drinking. Allen continued to drink in college and pledged a fraternity known for giving "drunk" parties. Up until this point, Allen's drinking was confined to weekends. During the week he attended classes, worked as a mechanic in the university motor pool, and earned good grades. He met his wife in his sophomore year, when she was a freshman "little sister" with the fraternity. Mrs. DePrez recalls that Allen's drinking habits were similar to those of many students and did not seem out of control at the time.

Allen and his wife generally had few disagreements about his drinking. Mrs. DePrez describes their lifestyle as one that included alcohol at most social functions. Their friends are frequent drinkers, and the DePrez family kept a full bar in their home. She remembered several occasions on which her husband's heavy drinking had led to embarrassing accidents in public, yet considered these episodes as rare and atypical for him. Also, until recently, Mrs. DePrez admired her husband's ability to control his drinking when compared with the obvious excesses of his father and brothers. She said that her husband first began to complain about the pressures he felt in his job about three years ago. Yet, he decided to continue as a controller for five years so that he could apply for the less stressful position of controller supervisor. He took on extra assignments to broaden his experience and worked hard to build an exceptional record as a controller. The previous year, the airport opened several new runways, which doubled air traffic, increased the responsibilities of controllers, and intensified competition for supervisor positions. Allen became noticeably more anxious and began to drink during the week.

Throughout the past year, Allen's drinking became more disruptive to his family life and work performance. He was irritable with his children and only sporadically affectionate with his wife (though at the same time dependent on her). Also, his drinking made it difficult for him to get to work on time and to perform well once he arrived. His job requires him to track several planes simultaneously and to make sure that their flight patterns do not cross. He had temporarily "misplaced" several planes in the past few weeks, but there had been no crashes or major crises. These problems had come to the attention of Allen's superiors, who suggested the clinical psychologist. However, at the time Allen was admitted to the hospital, he had attended only one session with the psychologist. During this session, the psychologist had taken Allen's history and arranged for him to be admitted to the alcohol detoxification unit for withdrawal. Allen had agreed to take two weeks of sick leave from work to participate in the detoxification program and to continue supportive psychotherapy later as an outpatient. He then told his wife that he was sure that he could again control his drinking, and that he was afraid that entering the hospital for detoxification was admitting that he was an alcoholic. He also feared that such an admission would jeopardize his chances for a supervisory position. Thus, he had abruptly discontinued drinking on the day before his admission, which precipitated the withdrawal reaction that resulted in the emergency admission to the detoxification unit.

Etiology The symptoms of severe alcohol withdrawal often include sleep disorders; tremors; agitation and depression; sweating; and, occasionally, auditory, visual, and/or tactile hallucinations. Thus, the reaction may be diagnosed in the emergency room as a psychotic episode. Allen's self-prescribed "cold turkey" program had ironically worsened his pre-existing alcohol problems and ineffective coping style. The symptoms of partial withdrawal and/or supervised detoxification are usually more moderate than abrupt cessation. However, there are some factors in Allen's psychosocial history that probably predisposed him to implement the cold turkey program.

First of all, Allen's father and brothers were models of alcohol abuse. Not only did they set an example for Allen to drink excessively, but they also provided him with an inaccurate decision rule for determining when his drinking was out of control. Allen thought that as long as he could restrict his consumption to nonworking hours, he was not an alcoholic. Such self-deluding decision rules ("I never drink before noon") are common among alcoholics. [These rules often follow from the notion alcoholism is a moral weakness and/or disease of will power. Thus, any restrictions on drinking are incorrectly interpreted by the person as evidence that he or she is not *really* dependent on alcohol.] Allen's drinking had increased during the past year, however, and had generated the social impairments that are part of the DSM-III diagnoses.

There is evidence that Allen was less prepared than most people for the demanding vigilance and responsibility of a position such as air traffic controller. He was the youngest of three boys and identified more strongly with his brothers' lifestyle than with the religious values of his mother. He was protected by his brothers (probably overprotected) and consequently had minimal experience with stressful situations. Until he began to have problems as a controller, Allen had not experienced any significant problems. He went through high school, college, marriage, children, and a career with the aeronautics firm without noticeable frustrations or disappointments. These ostensibly idyllic conditions were, in fact, obstacles to his development of mature and adaptive responses to stress. Negative results from a lack of coping methods generated in response to minor stress are also seen as a factor in the case of the "Postman," discussed in chapter 6.

When the initial pressures of Allen's job were intensified by the airport expansion, he became even more anxious about obtaining the supervisory position (his planned escape route). Thus, a man with a limited experience in coping with stress was exposed to increasingly stressful circumstances from which he could not escape. As Costello (1978) notes, anxiety and ambivalent dependency are common in one type of alcoholic, while more direct aggression and less anxiety mark another type. An attempt to self-medicate depression is also important in many cases. Allen turned to the only mechanism he had learned that could relieve him of his anxiety—alcohol. Then, from Allen's point of view, the "cure" for the alcoholism was more unattractive than the problem. Allen felt that entering the detoxification unit would be more threatening to his future than would be his declining work performance; thus, the ill-advised "cold turkey" technique.

Finally, it is possible that Allen was physiologically vulnerable to alcoholism. Some researchers have suggested that a person can inherit a physiological predisposition to alcoholism, which leads to an unusual craving for alcohol once it has been experienced. Such a predisposition can also be increased by the body's physiological adaptation to chronic drinking, an adaptation that eventually includes a degree of brain dysfunction (Begleiter et al., 1981). The fact that Allen's father and brothers were excessive drinkers is consistent with the concept of genetic vulnerability. However, genetic vulnerability as a significant factor in the development of alcohol problems has not yet been proven, although there is evidence that alcohol dependence tends to run in families (Winokur et al., 1970; Goodwin, 1979). Also, some researchers have found high rates of alcoholism in natural children of alcoholics who were adopted by nonalcoholic parents (Goodwin et al., 1973). However, it is also known that the majority of children with alcoholic parents do not develop a drinking problem. Thus, the role played by genetic factors in alcohol dependence is not felt to be a determining one.

Treatment Options Since alcohol problems are generated and maintained by many causal factors, a treatment approach that employs at least a significant number of the following options is going to be needed in most cases.

1. *Detoxification:* Most alcoholics, such as Allen, need an initial phase in a controlled treatment setting in which to "dry out." This process helps to control the impulse to return to alcohol, especially while their system is physiologically readjusting to the absence of alcohol.
2. *Antabuse:* Antabuse (disulfiram) binds molybdenum, a trace material needed by the liver to detoxify alcohol. Without it, acetaldehyde, a product of that breakdown, is increased, which generates nausea and violent vasomotor spasms. This terribly aversive response only occurs if one drinks alcohol, so Antabuse helps to control that impulse. The only problem is that alcoholics tend to avoid or forget to take it, so it is of limited use (Krasegnor, 1980).
3. *Tranquilizers:* Tranquilizing medication can be used to help lessen the emotional distress of withdrawal. However, there are the dangers of a secondary addiction and untoward side effects (Major et al., 1979), as is discussed in the case of Barbara, the next presentation in this chapter.
4. *Aversion Therapy:* Aversion Therapy helps to suppress specific habits that facilitate alcoholism; it can be combined with the modeling of more appropriate behaviors. Indications are that the use of nausea-inducing drugs is superior to the use of electric shock (Cannon & Baker, 1981).
5. *Biofeedback:* Alcoholics are surprisingly worse (considering their extensive experience) than normals at accurately assessing their blood levels of alcohol. Biofeedback can help them more readily recognize differential bodily reactions with different levels of alcohol intake, a critical step if they are ever to return to a moderate drinking pattern (Lovibond & Caddy, 1970).
6. *Alcoholics Anonymous:* Although not as effective as proponents of AA (who have a vested interest in favorable results) assert, this organization does provide the alcoholic with a system of support, a place for emotional catharsis, and a source of nondrinking friends.

7. *Psychotherapy:* This is helpful, particularly in the early months of treatment, to enable the alcoholic to see the many conflicts and unresolved emotions that facilitate and maintain the alcoholism (Brandsma, 1979).

8. *Family and/or Marital Therapy:* Therapy is critical to long-term adjustment, since it helps to heal the wounds in the systems that are so critical in supporting the more positive behaviors now being initiated by the alcoholic.

Allen's Treatment

Allen spent three days in the detoxification unit. Alcohol withdrawal used to be a long and painful process, but tranquilizers do help, albeit introducing a risk of a second drug dependence. Also, vitamins and supplemental intravenous feedings to maintain nutritional balance are included in most modern detoxification programs. These programs have greatly reduced some of the side effects of alcohol detoxification, such as self-injury, distress, convulsions, and hepatitis.

After detoxification, Allen was retained on the unit for one day of medical observation. When Allen's physical strength was satisfactory, he was transferred to the psychiatry unit for three weeks of inpatient psychotherapy. Allen met with his therapist daily for individual sessions, underwent aversion therapy, and participated in group therapy for two hours each morning. In addition to allowing Allen the opportunity to examine his problems in a comfortable and unpressured milieu, the hospitalization assured his continued abstinence. In the therapy sessions, Allen learned to verbalize the frustrations he experienced with his career and the pressures he felt from his wife in trying to provide for his family. He described his elaborate strategies for appearing sober while continuing to imbibe. As Allen became more open with his therapist and the group members, he was able to devise useful strategies to continue his abstinence after his release from the hospital. He decided to resign his position as air traffic controller and was able to return to the aeronautics firm as a sales manager, with a comparable salary.

After his release from the hospital, Allen continued therapy as an outpatient. In addition to individual psychotherapy, his therapist recommended several sessions with his wife and children. After six months of outpatient therapy, Allen joined Alcoholics Anonymous. In the three years since his release from the hospital, Allen continues to abstain from alcohol. His relationship with his wife and children has greatly improved, and his lifestyle and stress-coping habits have changed. Since he no longer drinks, he and his wife have participated in fewer cocktail parties and have learned interpersonal strategies to avoid pressures to take a drink.

Conclusions

Alcoholism has been a pre-eminent disorder since alcohol was first used at least 10,000 years ago. It causes extensive psychological and physiological damage. It is usually generated by multiple causes, and similarly requires a variety of treatments. Unfortunately, most treatment programs for alcoholism have not shown marked success, particularly in the long run.

However, the prognosis for Allen is good. For one thing, he does not show the schizoid aspects that are a negative prognostic sign (Zivich, 1981). He has stopped drinking and has taken on a less stressful occupation. Further, Allen has rearranged his lifestyle so that: 1) exposure to alcohol is minimized; 2) overall stress is considerably reduced; and 3) more adaptive strategies for stress relief are available to him. Consistent with the philosophy of AA, Allen and his family still consider him an alcoholic. Allen believes that one drink could trigger the self-destructive cycle that precipitated his hospitalization. It should be noted that there have been several published reports of alcoholics who have learned to drink in moderation. However, the total abstinence strategy is efficient, and most therapists recommend total abstinence at least for a substantial period of time for persons who are alcoholic.

REFERENCES

Begleiter, H., Porjesz, B., and Chou, C. Auditory brainstem potentials in chronic alcoholics. *Science*, 1981, *211*, 1064–1066.

Brandsma, J. *Outpatient treatment of alcoholism.* Baltimore: University Park, 1979.

Cannon, D., and Baker, T. Emetic and electric shock alcohol aversion therapy: Assessment of conditioning. *Journal of Consulting and Clinical Psychology*, 1981, *49*, 20–33.

Costello, R. Empirical derivation of a partial personality typology of alcoholics. *Journal of Studies of Alcoholism*, 1978, *39*, 1258–1266.

Goodwin, D. Alcoholism and heredity. *Archives of General Psychiatry*, 1979, *36*, 57–64.

Goodwin, D., Schulsinger, F., Moller, N., Hermansen, L., Winokur, G., and Guze, S. Alcohol problems in adoptees raised apart from alcoholic biological parents. *Archives of General Psychiatry*, 1973, *31*, 238–243.

Krasegnor, N. Analysis and modification of substance abuse. *Behavior Modification*, 1980, *4*, 35–56.

Lovibond, S., and Caddy, G. Discriminated aversive control in the modification of alcoholic's drinking behavior. *Behavior Therapy*, 1970, *1*, 437–444.

Major, L., Murphy, D., Gershon, E., and Brown, G. The role of plasma amine oxidase, platelet monoamine oxidase, and red cell catechol-O-methyl transferase in severe behavioral reactions to disulfiram. *American Journal of Psychiatry*, 1979, *136*, 717–718.

Winokur, G., Reich, T., Rimmer, J., and Pitts, F. Alcoholism III: Diagnosis and familial psychiatric illness in 259 alcoholic probands. *Archives of General Psychiatry*, 1970, *23*, 104–111.

Zivich, J. Alcoholic subtypes and treatment effectiveness. *Journal of Consulting and Clinical Psychology*, 1981, *49*, 72–80.

Prescription Drug Abuse

The Case of Barbara

Even though the DSM-III does refer to the abuse of specific drugs that are occasionally obtained through prescriptions, such as the amphetamines, the specific designation of prescription drug abuse does not exist. This situation is ironic since such a category at least indirectly implicates the people who formulate the DSM-III categories in the first place—those who do the prescribing.

The most commonly abused prescription drug is diazepam (Valium), one of the benzodiazepines (Blackwell, 1979). This drug was abused heavily by Barbara. Blackwell found that during the latter years of the 1970s, more than two billion Valium tablets a year were prescribed in the United States. Even though diazepam has been the most frequently used drug in the United States for many years, it is only one drug in the benzodiazepine family, which in turn is only one group of the minor tranquilizers. The benzodiazepines primarily act to lessen anxiety and cause muscle relaxation. They are easily habituated to and in severe cases may react with alcohol to cause death by drug overdose.

There is also a danger in triggering a psychotic reaction. Major et al. (1979) assessed thirty-two male alcoholics who were being administered Valium. Seven of these individuals experienced a psychotic reaction as a result of the Valium, and all who reacted had certain blood plasma differences from normal; that is, low levels of monoamine oxidase (MAO). Valium is often administered to alcoholics to help them ease the pain of withdrawal. Major's study suggests that an assessment of MAO blood levels before administering Valium to alcoholics could be very useful.

The DSM-III does not focus on the concept of addiction as much as the earlier DSM's did. As noted, the two major DSM-III concepts (Substance Abuse and Substance Dependence) could be applied as diagnostic labels in this case of prescription drug abuse, using the same criteria as was applied in the case of Allen.

Barbara

Barbara is a forty-two-year-old, recently widowed, Caucasian female who now lives alone. Her only child, a son, is on active duty in the Navy. Barbara is the second of four children and was born in a small midwestern town. She still lives there and in general feels comfortable in her community. Her family life as she grew up was from her perspective a positive experience. She related well with her siblings and still maintains moderately active relationships with them.

She remembers her father as a generally good provider who seemed to care about his children, though he had difficulty openly expressing his affection for them. He was an assembly line worker at a local factory and had a high school education.

Barbara reports that the major stresses in her early life occurred when her father developed heavy debts, which made him upset and irritable. At such times, he would often come home and vividly curse the bill collectors.

While he drank himself into a stupor, Barbara's mother stayed home as a housewife, took care of her children, and was apparently a good homemaker. She did suffer occasional "spells," during which time she would "have to go under a doctor's care."

Barbara very much enjoyed her high school years, as she was active in several organizations and had many friends. She obtained good grades and graduated in the top third of her class, but did not continue her education. She married during the summer after her high school graduation.

Barbara worked for two years as a clerk in a local department store and then became a full-time housewife with the birth of their son. Her husband had left high school without graduating but had a good paying job as an ironworker. Her memories of her marriage were quite pleasant. Her husband was killed in a work-related accident when she was thirty-eight years old.

Barbara naturally experienced depression in the period after her husband's death. As she puts it, "There was a huge void in my life for a time, and it actually became worse when I realized my son needed to leave home and get out on his own."

Barbara's pattern of involvement in numerous interest groups in high school had subsided during the marriage, and she had little activity to fill up her world when her husband died and her son began to assert his independence. She was very depressed for the first couple of months, and even though that lessened to a moderate level, she still experienced insomnia and "nervousness." Barbara first used over-the-counter sedatives and aspirin to combat her upset, and she usually downed these with a "good strong drink." As a result of concern about several cysts, she went into the hospital and had a partial hysterectomy. Her attending physician was apparently unaware of her alcohol use and generously prescribed Valium during and after her stay in the hospital. Valium proved to be more efficient and more pleasant for sleep than was the self-prescribed medication. She asked her physician for a continued prescription after her release from the hospital and he acquiesced, although he did try to reduce the prescription gradually.

Shortly after her release, her son left the home, leaving her without any meaningful interpersonal contacts. Her father then died shortly thereafter of a heart attack. Even though they had not been extremely close in the past several years, his death was another stress for her. She began to see another doctor, as well as continuing the contacts with the physician who had performed the hysterectomy. Both doctors were prescribing Valium and in addition she periodically obtained other tranquilizers from neighbors who had prescriptions that they had not used.

Over the four-year period following the death of her husband, Barbara gradually increased her intake and tolerance to the Valium to approximately 80 milligrams a day. In addition, she occasionally took the other similar-acting prescription drugs and also indulged in alcohol to a mild degree. Finally, she was threatened with the loss of her job because of the absenteeism and lethargy that were a direct result of the drug abuse.

Her supervisor at the department store at which she was working had become aware of her abuse pattern through the reports of several of her coworkers. He told her he would fire her if she did not immediately seek professional help. Through an acquaintance at work, Barbara became aware of a research program on prescription drug abuse at the medical school in a nearby city and volunteered to participate in the treatment program.

Etiology Several variables in Barbara's personal history might predict drug abuse of some sort. However, she has few qualities that would push her toward *illegal* drug abuse; thus, it is not surprising that she first resorted to alcohol and over-the-counter drugs. Later, she felt more comfortable when using a prescribed drug, both because it has the surface appearance of legitimacy and also because it did not threaten her self-image by forcing her to label herself as a drug abuser.

Before we proceed to discuss the variables in her personal history, it is important to note some overall cultural factors that contribute to a high level of prescription drug abuse, and, of course, affect an individual such as Barbara.

Prescription drugs serve many purposes beyond effecting the physiological changes, which are the alleged primary role. Such drugs are the charms and fetishes of our modern society. Some physicians too easily resort to the use of a drug when reassurance and understanding would be sufficient. The change from the bedside manner model of medical care to the office visit model has demanded an efficient cue with which the physician can quickly wrap up the patient contact and at the same time leave the patient satisfied. The prescription does both. When the physician begins to write out a prescription, patients know that the session is over. In fact, many patients feel dissatisfied if no prescription is given; it is as if their problem is not serious enough to warrant the attention they had anticipated. Mellinger and his colleagues (1978) found that when patients saw a family physician with rather ill defined symptoms (and about 70 percent of medical patients actually fall into this category) they benefited equally well if they were given reassurance that they were all right and needed no medication. But the important point is that this was only effective when they were given adequate attention and discussion time. Chowka (1979) found that the average consultation time for an office visit with a physician in 1972 was only seventeen minutes, and it may be less than that today.

Another factor contributing to the ease with which mood-altering medication is dispensed is the fact that most such medication is prescribed by nonpsychiatrist physicians, as was the case in the Mellinger study. Unfortunately, these nonpsychiatric physicians are even more likely to use a prescription in lieu of reassurance and explanation of the psychological issues and also are more unaware than are psychiatrists of the potential for abuse and habituation.

Certainly a share of the blame for the high rate of prescription drug abuse in our society belongs with some drug companies. Drug companies are constantly and intensively promoting the use of their drugs by individual physicians. This intensity can lead them to de-emphasize issues such as potential abuse, side effects, and other alternative methods that do not have the inherent problems of drug use.

In Barbara's individual history, several factors made her drug abuse a likely occurrence. The situational factors that led to her depression are important. They left her with a void of social relationships, without a sense of meaning in her world. Her skills at turning this pattern around through new behaviors were minimal; as a result, she needed to dilute the anxiety and apprehension that occurred.

Her history manifests clear models for drug abuse. Her father would drink himself into unconsciousness as the stress from his debts mounted. Her mother would use the umbrella concept of "the doctor's care" to avoid demands at various periods when stress became too much for her.

When she went into the hospital for her hysterectomy, her physician routinely prescribed Valium. It is a common practice for such medication to be prescribed well before any signs of anxiety are present. Naturally enough, the fact that a physician has prescribed it attaches a label of legitimacy to it. Barbara found that the Valium more effectively calmed her and helped her sleep than alcohol did, though she still occasionally continued to include alcohol (Schuckit & Morrissey, 1979).

After Barbara left the hospital, she continued the medication, which dulled the anxiety she first experienced when she realized her son was going to leave home, and then shortly thereafter, when she had to adjust to the death of her father. By this time, she was habituated to using the Valium, not only to counter anxiety and apprehension, but also to go to sleep most nights. She was in the position of fearing to skip the Valium since she did not know if anxiety would occur or not. It became a magic fetish for her, such that taking it warded off the possibility of anxiety. As with many people, the fear of fear itself, or "discomfort anxiety" (Ellis, 1979), is a prime motivator for such behavior. This negative pattern became routine until situational factors intruded on this stability. Fortunately, the threatened loss of her job was enough for Barbara to reflect on her behavior, to the point at which she *decided* (critical step) that she was willing to proceed into treatment (Bugental, 1980).

Barbara is typical of many individuals who develop prescription drug abuse. The drug is first used to counter real problems that a physician labels as legitimate, and the process of habituation is rather slow, with increasing dosages occurring gradually. The drug then begins to take on other functions in the world of the abuser (such as sedative, anxiety preventer, and so forth), just as it did with Barbara. Also, her status as a middle-age, middle-class individual is typical fo the prescription drug abuser. She would feel uncomfortable using any illicit drugs, and, in fact, might verbalize hostility towards persons who do use such drugs, without awareness that her drug abuse is similar to theirs.

Treatment Even though there has been some discussion of the etiology of prescription drug abuse in the literature, its treatment has not been researched to any significant degree. Physicians are naturally oriented to prescribe medication and occasionally downplay the abuse potential. Also, virtually all psychiatric journals are heavily funded by drug company ads. This circumstance does not lead to a pattern of direct control, but it certainly exerts an omnipresent influence.

Barbara was well motivated to change her pattern of behavior. Such motivation is not atypical since prescription drug abusers generally have middle-class values. Once they are directly aware of the fact they are drug abusers, they are more likely to be willing to change than are people who have abused nonprescription drugs.

Her treatment first required a detoxification of her system, which was done with medical support. She was placed on another drug, hydroxyzine pamoate, which researchers have found to reduce the need for the benzodiazepines and other tranquilizers, as helps to subdue any withdrawal symptoms. (This method is not dissimilar to the use of methadone, which, though it is an addicting drug, is used to help reduce the heroin addict's pattern of substance dependence.)

For the first three weeks, Barbara attended the clinic daily in order to have the drug administered and to allow the clinicians to check on her motivation and progress. The hydroxyzine pamoate was administered in gradually decreasing dosages over the three weeks; and at the end of this time, Barbara felt she was able to go without it and also without the Valium.

It was also necessary to deal with the psychological issues that had been primary in promoting her pattern. Her psychotherapist was a clinical psychologist on the staff of the medical center and together they discussed her various conflicts and coping styles. It quickly became clear that Barbara needed to deal with a sense of meaninglessness in her world (Bugental, 1980) that had resulted from the loss of her husband, her father, and the immediate relationship with her son. She had few social contacts, and though she verbalized a desire to increase them, she seemed unaware as to how to do so. She was immediately included in a group therapy situation. This gave her an arena in which to discuss her problems and also allowed her to meet new people with whom she could spin into new social systems. Most importantly, an examination of her vocational situation revealed that she did not feel satisfied with the rewards of her present position. She was tested, found to be bright normal to superior in intelligence, and was encouraged to enroll in further education. This would increase both her alternatives through mobility and affluence and her self-esteem. She chose to pursue a degree program in business administration and stated she hoped to eventually obtain her masters degree.

Since one stated purpose of the therapy group was to help the participants increase the effectiveness of their social behaviors, the group was perfect for Barbara. She learned ways of being more assertive in meeting people and began to have a few dates, which she had not done since the death of her husband. She also made two close female friends, who gave her an outlet for her feelings and facilitated her social contacts.

Barbara was also taught a relaxation technique called Progressive Relaxation. This technique involves learning to tense and then relax individual muscle groups. She used this to counter upsurges of anxiety, which in the past had been a cue for her to start abusing drugs. She was also counseled in better methods of coping with occasional insomnia, which she felt was an initiating cue for her to abuse both alcohol and Valium.

During the treatment, which lasted nine months, Barbara occasionally slipped into the pattern of using drugs and alcohol. However, by this time she had developed trust in a number of the other group members and could disclose this to them. As a result, she had support so that an individual failure did not signify to her a total failure and did not generate any negative self-labeling. As she progressed in her school work and found she could be successful, her self-esteem markedly increased. This positive cycle led to increased social contacts, and then to more effective dating patterns. In that sense, Barbara achieved what could be termed a significant cure that persisted for at least the two years of occasional contact she kept with the center.

Comment As mentioned, minor tranquilizers (such as Miltown, Librium, and Valium) are the most frequently abused prescription drugs (Blackwell, 1979; Chowka, 1979). Unfortunately, some physicians and their patients minimize (or deny) the potential problems associated with the routine prescription and chronic use of these medications. Aside from the physiological side effects (including addiction) of long-term use, the patient is at risk socially, emotionally, and occupationally. Barbara's grief over her husband's death and her distress about her son's leaving home may have run their course without intervention, or perhaps required only minimal intervention. However, Barbara's increased dependence on Valium delayed resolution of these normal reactions and thus resulted in further disruption of her social and occupational functioning.

Abuse of prescription drugs is further complicated by social acceptance and implied professional sanction. To be sure, there is a small subgroup of people for whom even long-term use of minor tranquilizers and sleeping medications is appropriate. However, the fact that these drugs are legal and prescribed by physicians encourages patients to consider them safe. Consequently, the consideration of dependence occurs only after some dramatic consequence in the environment forces them to seek professional help. In cases such as Barbara's, understandable sympathy on the part of employers, friends, family members can inhibit the recognition of the problem by protecting and "covering" for the person.

REFERENCES

Blackwell, B. Benzodiazepines: Drug abuse and data abuse. *Psychiatric Opinion*, 1979, *16*, 10–37.

Bugental, J. Someone needs to worry: The existential anxiety of responsibility and decision. In G. Belkin (Ed.), *Contemporary psychotherapies*. Chicago: Rand McNally, 1980.

Chowka, P. Pushers in white. *East West Journal*, 1979, *9*, 30–37.

Ellis, A. A note on the treatment of agoraphobics with cognitive modification versus prolonged exposure "in vivo." *Behavior Research and Therapy*, 1979, *17*, 162–164.

Major, L., Murphy, D., Gersohn, E., and Brown, G. The role of plasma amine oxidase, platelet monoamine oxidase, and red cell catechol-O-methyl transferase in severe behavioral reactions to disulfiram. *American Journal of Psychiatry*, 1979, *136*, 717–718.

Mellinger, G., Balter, M., Manheimer, I., and Perry, H. Psychic distress, life crisis, and the use of psychotherapeutic medications. *Archives of General Psychiatry*, 1978, *35*, 1045–1052.

Schuckit, M., and Morrissey, E. Drug abuse among alcoholic women. *American Journal of Psychiatry*, 1979, *136*, 607–611.

4

The Schizophrenic and Paranoid Disorders

Psychosis is the general term for an especially severe form of psychopathology. Psychotic behavior is characterized by perceptual, cognitive, affective, communicative, motor, and motivational disturbances, specifically denoted by a loss of contact with reality. Some psychotic reactions are obviously organic; that is, associated with brain disruption due to physical causes such as diseases of the nervous system, brain tumors or injuries, toxic drug or chemical reactions, or circulation disturbances. These reactions are classified among the previously discussed Organic Disorders and Substance Disorders.

More prevalent are the functional psychoses that do not stem directly from a known physical defect of the brain. There are three major classifications of functional psychoses: Affective, Schizophrenic, and Paranoid. The Affective Psychotic Disorders, which are discussed in the following section, are characterized by extreme fluctuations of mood, with related disturbances in thought and behavior. DSM-III also includes the category "Psychotic Disorder Not Elsewhere Classified," which consists of the Schizophreniform Disorder (schizophrenic symptoms of less than one month duration), the Psychosis (schizophrenic symptoms of less than two weeks duration), the brief reactive Schizoaffective Disorder (where schizophrenic and affective symptoms are both prominent and developed at about the same time), and the Atypical Psychosis.

The primary focus of this section is on the DSM-III diagnostic categories of the Schizophrenic Disorders and the Paranoid Disorders. The major symptoms of schizophrenia involve withdrawal from reality, with flat or inappropriate emotional reactions and marked disturbances in thought processes. Delusions, hallucinations, and stereotyped mannerisms are common associated features.

Schizophrenia has been recognized as a disorder since Morel's (1857) description of a 13-year-old whose intellectual, moral, and physical functions gradually and inexplicably deteriorated over time. Morel used the term *demence precoce* (mental deterioration at an early age); he thought the deterioration was caused by hereditary factors and was virtually irreversible. Several modern theories of the disorder do not differ very much from Morel's views. *Dementia praecox*, the Latin form of Morel's term, was used by Kraeplin (1899) to refer to the rather large class of disorders that have features of mental deterioration beginning early in life. Bleuler (1911) introduced the term *schizophrenia* (split mind) to indicate his belief that the chief characteristics involved a lack of integration between thoughts and emotions and a loss of contact with reality.

There are several different types of schizophrenia. Disorganized Schizophrenia, as is presented in the case of Stephanie, is marked by grossly inappropriate emotional responses and blatantly disturbed thought and behavior patterns. In Paranoid Schizophrenia, as in the case of Perry, the least overtly disturbed form of schizophrenia, disorder is not so extreme, there is usually less premorbid symptomatology, and the disorder typically emerges later in life. This pattern is then contrasted with the case of Lloyd, diagnosed as a Paranoid Personality Disorder. Though disturbed, Lloyd does not show the thought disorder, disorganized behavior, or the hallucinations that are seen in Perry.

Paranoia (a Paranoid Disorder) is characterized by the gradual development of a complex, intricate, and elaborate delusional system. A delusion is a firmly held belief that the individual maintains despite objective evidence to the contrary despite lack of support for it from most other people. The delusional systems in paranoid psychotic reactions are usually based on misinterpretations of actual events. Once this (inaccurate) premise is established, other aspects of the delusional logically follow.

There are three types of delusions: delusions of grandeur, delusions of reference, and delusions of persecution. Persons with delusions of grandeur believe they are some exalted being, such as Jesus Christ or the President. Persons with delusions of reference misconstrue chance events as having a direct relevance to their lifestyle. For instance, thunderstorms may be perceived as messages from God, or such persons may immediately conclude that they are the topic of conversations. Individuals who have delusions of persecution feel they are targets of various conspiracies against them. These delusions are typically developed in this order: reference, grandeur, persecution. First, the individuals develop the belief that they are special and have been singled out for attention by others. They then gradually come to the conclusion that this special attention is the result of admirable and coveted characteristics that only they possess. It is then a short step to believing that others are so jealous and threatened by these qualities that they are spying on, plotting against, and/or planning to eliminate them.

Generally, persons with a Paranoid Disorder are more functional than are those with a Schizophrenic Disorder. Schizophrenia is debilitating in most areas of intellectual, emotional, and psychological functioning. It includes noticeable and pervasive decline from the previous level of functioning. In the Paranoid Disorder, pathological symptoms are more compartmentalized and other functions are preserved. In fact, an extensive interview with a paranoid patient may reveal no marked abnormalities *if* the areas of delusional material are not mentioned.

We now present the first case, Stephanie, in which we see Disorganized Schizophrenia, a particularly severe level of disorder.

REFERENCES

Bleuler, E. *Dementia Praecox oder die Gruppe der Schizophrenia*. Leipzig: Deuticke, 1911.

Kraeplin, E. *Dementia praecox and paraphrenia*, (8th German ed.). R. Barclay and G. Robertson (trans.). Edinburgh: Livingstone, 1919. (Originally published 1899)

Morel, B. *Traite des Degenerescences Physiques, Intellectuelles et Morales*. Paris: Bailliere, 1857.

Disorganized Schizophrenia

The Case of Stephanie   Disorganized Schizophrenia is a chronic form of schizophrenia; it is characterized by poorly integrated delusions and hallucinations, "flat" or bizarre emotions, odd motor patterns, and generally impulsive behavior. Other symptoms may include sudden spontaneous giggling and crying, weird grimacing, odd gestures, and silliness. This form of schizophrenia (labeled "hebephrenic" in DSM-II) involves the most severe personality disorganization and is associated with poor premorbid adjustment, an earlier onset, and a poor prognosis (Meyer, 1982). Such persons have been considered "strange" or "weird" since childhood. When frank psychotic symptoms emerge, it is difficult to get the disorder under control, and first hospitalizations are usually prolonged. It is not unusual for hospital personnel to consider such an individual only partially recovered even though family members report that the person is back to "normal."

The course of Disorganized Schizophrenia is usually chronic and without significant remission. In the overall category of schizophrenia, a schizophrenic who has been released after the first hospitalization has a 50 percent likelihood of returning to hospital status within two years, and that percentage is somewhat higher for the disorganized schizophrenic. Between hospitalizations, their adjustment is marginal and independent living arrangements may not be within their capability. However, overt psychotic symptoms can be sufficiently diminished (and in some cases eliminated) in most cases, so that some of these patients can lead a moderately productive lifestyle. The extent to which treatment can result in a more adequate adjustment outside the hospital is limited by residual schizophrenic characteristics and the extent to which the stress of demands from the environment can be lessened. Support and flexibility in the disorganized schizophrenic's social environment are the most significant variables in lowering readmission rates, as is evident in the case of Stephanie.

Stephanie

Stephanie grew up in the suburbs of a midwestern metropolis, where her parents ran a successful real estate development company. The six children were involved in the family business as soon as they were old enough to be helpful. The young children ran errands and cleaned, while the older children typed and/or assisted in construction after school. As the children grew older, they assumed more responsibilities and began to specialize in the business. At the time of Stephanie's first hospitalization, her three brothers were employed by the company as architect, realtor, and construction supervisor respectively. One of Stephanie's sisters was the firm's accountant and business manager and her husband was the company's attorney. The other sister was the interior decorator. The family was active in social, civic, and political affairs. They took pride in appearing in public as a family and were well regarded in the community.

All indications are that the development of Stephanie's brothers and sisters was normal. As her parents reported: "Each one of them had their quirks and pecularities. All of them went through some stage of rebelling against us, but they always grew out of it, except Stephanie." There were stories of minor crises, such as fluctuations in profits, accidents, poor grades and undesirable boyfriends or girlfriends. On the whole, however, the family reported stable family relationships and positive feelings about one another. At the time of the interview, no members of the immediate family had had any previous contacts with mental health professionals. An aunt on Stephanie's mother's side of the family had shown some bizarre behavior and eventually committed suicide, and a distant paternal cousin had been repeatedly placed in a mental hospital for reasons that were unclear to Stephanie's parents.

According to her parents, Stephanie had been noticeably dif-

ferent from the other children since birth. The birth had been a very difficult one, with a long labor, and Stephanie had to be administered oxygen at one point. She was slighly premature and weighed only 5 lbs., 10 ounces.

She was shy and withdrawn as a child and flatly refused to date as an adolescent. During Stephanie's early childhood, there was an economic recession and her parents were concerned with serious financial problems. During this period, the children became more involved in the business. Her siblings noticed that Stephanie was less capable, but they attributed her lack of response to the fact that she was "spoiled." She was prone to unprovoked tantrums and periods of forgetfulness. However, these behaviors were seen as immature and taken in stride by the family.

By the time Stephanie was ready for junior high school, her family had weathered the economic crunch and moved to an exclusive suburb. At the same time, the oldest daughter, to whom Stephanie had been most attached, left for college. Faced with a new school and the abrupt departure of the only sib she cared for deeply, Stephanie barely left her bedroom for two weeks.

From that point, Stephanie's adjustment was only marginally adequate. Her grades were average and she was friendly with two or three girls. However, Stephanie was very suspicious of boys and began to tell her parents about inappropriate advances by them. These stories were credible at first, then became more exaggerated as the family began to confront Stephanie with evidence to the contrary. At school, Stephanie was regarded as "strange" and "weird." At times, she disrupted class with accusations against male students. Twice she was sent to the principal's office and suspended because of arguments with alleged attackers. After a while, the boys learned to avoid contact with her, and by the eleventh grade these incidents had ceased. As a result, Stephanie's girlfriends began to regard her as a liability with boys and they also avoided her. By her senior year, Stephanie was almost totally isolated. She interacted with few of her classmates and teachers and would not participate in extracurricular activities. After school, Stephanie played alone and did her homework. Her parents reported that Stephanie spent most of her weekends in her room. The family had several school conferences regarding Stephanie's unusual behavior, but they did not seek help for her.

Finally, during the summer after her high school graduation, her mother consulted the family minister. The minister thought that Stephanie was sheltered and overpowered by her successful family. He suggested that Stephanie be sent away to college so that she could experience a measure of independence. Stephanie's parents had some reservations about this "sink-or-swim" method, yet they agreed that some action was necessary. Stephanie did not voice any objections to the plan; she was not enthusiastic about it, either. The family members hoped that this could be the fresh start that Stephanie needed, though there was concern that she might not handle being away from the family very well. Stephanie's mother was the most reluctant and at the last minute decided not to send her. Instead, she enrolled Stephanie in a local private college and obtained space for her in the dormitory.

Stephanie moved back home after three days. Her father became upset and insisted she give the dorm another try. Stephanie returned to the dorm room but quickly settled into a pattern of sleeping at home most nights. Her mother and older sister urged her to stop this, and Stephanie agreed to try. Stephanie became friendly with a few girls in the dorm. However, she called home several times a day, came over for dinner almost daily, and continued to spend weekends with her family.

One Friday night, when Stephanie did not call for a ride home, her parents became encouraged by this apparent adjustment to the dorm. However, in a telephone conversation with her sister the next morning, Stephanie said she was afraid she was being watched by a male student in her history course and was afraid to leave her room. Stephanie called one of her brothers on Sunday and asked him to take her to a service in a fundamental church (to which the family did not belong). The brother pretended to cooperate, then brought Stephanie home. When asked about this unusual request, Stephanie said she was changing religions because the family's traditional church allowed males to sit with females. To placate her, her parents agreed to go to the service with her. Stephanie became very emotional and underwent a dramatic conversion during the service. On the way home, she was unusually verbal and expressed, in great detail, her intent to maintain an impoverished, chaste, and virtuous life. Later at dinner, Stephanie monopolized the conversation, alternating between angry lectures on the moral decay of her peers and elated descriptions of her new lifestyle. These verbalizations became more agitated and inappropriate. Stephanie told her friends at college of her conversion and urged them to follow suit. These friends avoided her, and family members, bored by her incessant phone calls, began to make excuses to avoid her when she called.

At this point, Stephanie started to communicate her ideas in classes. She was so disruptive in one class that the instructor called campus security to escort her out of class. The next day, Stephanie insisted that her English professor was possessed by the devil and was trying to influence her mind through a secret code contained in his lectures. She asked the professor to stop talking so that she could pray for strength. He refused, and Stephanie started a religious dance that precipitated another call to campus security. When they arrived, Stephanie refused to discontinue her ritual until the professor left. Then she alternately attempted to save and seduce the officers. By the time the officers could contain her and escort her to the student health service, Stephanie was incoherent and delusional.

She accused the health center staff of being agents of the devil and having sexual fantasies about her. Stephanie said she was informed of these fantasies by her guardian angel who spoke only to her. Occasionally, she would giggle, shrug, or run to the corner of the room in apparent response to instructions from the guardian angel. The psychiatrist who examined Stephanie diagnosed her condition as Disorganized Schizophrenia, sedated her, and had her transferred to a hospital.

Etiology   A wide variety of etiological factors have been hypothesized as generic in schizophrenia, and there is no doubt that these factors take on differing degrees of importance, depending on the individual case. Although there is substantial disagreement as to the cause of schizophrenia, there are some points on which most theorists tentatively agree. A biological predisposition to schizophrenia, generated by genetic and/or birth disorder factors, is often critical. This predisposition may first show up in academic and social dysfunction that is based on subtle (if detected at all) problems in attending to and processing visual or auditory information (Shakow, 1977; Bernheim & Lewine, 1979; Meyer, 1982). Social learning factors may play a role in generating some of the pathology and undoubtedly contribute to the maintenance and increase in this disorder pattern (Ullmann & Krasner, 1975).

A number of factors predict to the development of schizophrenia (Meyer, 1982). Even though neither of Stephanie's parents were schizophrenic (a major predictor), her aunt was schizophrenic and her cousin probably was also. There were significant problems at her birth, particularly the long labor and temporary loss of oxygen, both of which can result in minor and thus undetected brain damage. As with Stephanie, low IQ and/or birth weight relative to siblings are also predictors.

Stephanie also had the role of "scapegoat" and "odd one" in both her family and peer group. She was eventually rejected by both school peers and teachers and became socially isolated. She moved into a cycle of: 1) isolation and rejection, 2) no social feedback to correct her odd behavior, 3) further isolation, and 4) ultimately bizarre behavior.

Treatment Options   Almost every treatment imaginable has been tried with schizophrenia, none with any respectable number of total cures, and few with any marked impact over time. It is clear that if there is to be any success, there has to be a combination of treatments (for the many areas of disorder), and even here the chances of marked, long-term success are not high. It is particularly important for such persons to have (or to develop) a supportive family and social system to return to after an episode. Also, to the degree that the first episode occurs later in life, and that the person is intelligent and has vocational skills, shows an abrupt onset of disorder, and has a short first stay in the hospital, the prognosis is more positive. The common treatment regimen includes milieu therapy (planned hospital programs) and/or chemotherapy to lessen environmental stress and suppress the psychotic symptomatology. Contrary to some traditional assumptions, milieu therapy while in the hospital is more effective when there is a mixture of both acute and chronic patients (Ellsworth et al., 1979). Also required are individual and family therapy and help toward moving into a more positive family, social, and vocational situation when discharged.

Stephanie's Treatment

This first hospitalization for Stephanie occurred at age nineteen. Treatment within the hospital consisted of chemotherapy (phenothiazines) and milieu therapy (which means the hospital's overall treatment program). After discharge, Stephanie participated in the hospital's day hospital program of group therapy, recreational and occupational therapy, and medication for a period of four to six weeks. Between hospitalizations, Stephanie lived with her parents. They were increasingly involved in her therapy, via family therapy (Framo, 1979), and gradually developed more insight into her disorder and how they had inadvertently contributed to it.

Her family gradually accepted the chronicity of Stephanie's illness, and their support contributed significantly to decreasing the frequency and duration of her hospitalizations. They became very adept at assigning tasks to Stephanie that would increase her feelings of self-worth, with minimal stress and frustration. There were also repeated attempts to provide Stephanie with an employable skill. It soon became apparent that though Stephanie had graduated from high school, her educational achievement was only at the fifth-grade level. Since she had not taken her semester finals at college, she had no college credits. The family tried clerical and cooking training schools as well as sheltered workshop and rehabilitation programs. However, the combination of intellectual and social skills required for successful completion of a viable program was usually beyond Stephanie's capacities. Within a few days, her behavior would become agitated and inappropriate. These behaviors would become more frequent and intense until the agency considered Stephanie too disruptive. Being asked to leave these programs was traumatic to Stephanie and was often the catalyst for deterioration that would result in rehospitalization.

Finally, Stephanie's family decided against further attempts at training and employment. Instead, they asked her to care for her brothers' and sisters' preschool children at her parent's home. Stephanie was adequate as a babysitter and soon had a modest business that also included neighbors' children. Also, Stephanie cleaned, ironed, and sewed for the family. These jobs were well within her skills level and minimized contact with unfamiliar people and novel situations. Still, on two other occasions, Stephanie became disorganized with no apparent precipitant in the environment. She was hospitalized for a short time and then stabilized as an outpatient. She fortunately had a psychiatrist who wanted to avoid the "institutionalization syndrome" (passivity and loss of initiative) that often accompanies long-term institutionalization of any sort.

In addition to familial support and pharmacological treatment, Stephanie's improvement was facilitated by behavior therapy. Both the psychiatric unit and the day-hospital had token economy programs (Lutzker & Martin, 1981; Craighead et al., 1981). Among the goals that were targeted for Stephanie were: 1) decreasing tantrums and excessive emotionality, 2) increasing social skills, and 3) eliminating her near-phobic discomfort with males. In response to the tantrums and excessive emotionality, Stephanie was first asked to remove herself from the group until she was calmer. If this strategy was unsuccessful, she would lose privileges (hierarchically arranged) until she exhibited appropriate behaviors. In order to increase her social skills, Stephanie practiced greetings and small-talk in group therapy and completed series of homework assignments that began with her family and the hospital staff and eventually required her to make telephone inquiries and return merchandise to department stores. Stephanie's response to this program was positive though slow—she was only able to return merchandise to the department store after eighteen months.

Modifying Stephanie's response to males was decidedly more difficult and only partially successful. A desensitization procedure that began with video-taped scenes went fairly well (Lutzker & Martin, 1981). However, when an in vivo phase was initiated, Stephanie's response was extremely variable and emotional. She had to restart the program several times and was eventually successful only in the *practice* in vivo sessions. Stephanie's emotional response to men other than her relatives or therapists did not improve beyond anxious tolerance. Yet, this was an improvement over her previous accusations of sexual advances and the resultant disruptive religious exhortations in public places. Stephanie did make several female friends within the therapeutic milieu and spent time visiting, shopping, and attending movies with them.

Prognosis and Conclusions

Stephanie is now thirty years old. In the eleven years since her first hospitalization, she has been hospitalized on six separate occasions and has spent a combined total of 33 months on a psychiatric unit as an inpatient. In addition, Stephanie has experienced a number of medical problems, some of which were side effects from prolonged use of phenothiazines. She had even begun to show signs of tardive dyskinesia, a typically irreversible side effect of the antischizophrenic drugs. This disorder, which appears about 5 percent of the time (40 percent in the elderly taking these medications for prolonged periods), involves involuntary head and neck movements, particularly grimacing and lip-smacking. Fortunately, her medications were managed quickly enough before the behaviors became irreversible.

Stephanie's prognosis must be considered within the limitations of her chronic and severe pattern of schizophrenia. Phenothiazines are usually helpful in eliminating hallucinations and bizarre behaviors, and these and other major tranquilizers can decrease the high anxiety levels and diminish fearfulness in psychotic patients. Behavioral management and familial support are necessary to develop new social skills and to diminish hostile and otherwise anxiety-provoking elements of the environment. Even so, some characteristics of disorganized schizophrenia often are residual to these factors and affect the long-term prognosis.

First of all, schizophrenics evidence a greater sensitivity to perceptual stimuli that affect cognition, emotional stamina, and speech (Shakow, 1977; Bernheim & Lewine, 1979). This perceptual sensitivity is only partially mediated by medication and therapy. Because external stimulation is often perceived as more vivid and intense, schizophrenic patients are more distractible and vulnerable to stimulus-overload external cues. Unlike psychopaths, who are stimulation-seeking, schizophrenics are stimulation-avoidant. Also, schizophrenics exhibit low frustration tolerance and find problematic situations overwhelming. Thus, they are likely to avoid emotionally charged relationships and prefer familiar and less demanding ones, such as family members, long-standing friendships, and children. These habits persist even after remission.

Secondly, disorganized schizophrenia is typically associated with poor premorbid adjustment and so has a poorer prognosis than do other forms of schizophrenia. As in Stephanie's case, such persons have usually been increasingly withdrawn and marginally adjusted since childhood. Consequently, they typically have fewer cognitive skills and emotional resources with which to cope, even after recovery. In addition, the tendency to avoid and withdraw from problematic and demanding situations further inhibits growth and development.

Finally, disorganized schizophrenics, even after remission, may show residual features that are odd or bizarre and that elicit discomfort in others. Exaggerated mannerisms and unusual facial expressions often prompt employers, coworkers, and schoolmates to label them as strange and to avoid close contact with them. These behaviors are difficult to eliminate because they are seldom under voluntary control and sometimes are even facilitated by the side effects of psychotropic drugs. Anxious responses from others then serve to increase both the perceptual confusion and the withdrawal tendencies, thus furthering the cycle.

Given all of these limitations, Stephanie's prognosis is good as regards living in a supervised situation (her family). She will probably continue to require inpatient care periodically, and she is not likely ever to function completely normally. Because of the support of her family, Stephanie will probably not require extended institutionalization and can be expected to maintain her current level of functioning without significant deterioration. Since she finds it difficult to cope without constancy in the environment, any significant disruption in her now familiar lifestyle could again precipitate withdrawal and a subsequent need for institutional care.

REFERENCES

Bernheim, K., and Lewine, R. *Schizophrenia.* New York: W. W. Norton, 1979.

Craighead, W., Kazdin, A., and Mahoney, M. *Behavior modification.* Boston: Houghton Mifflin, 1981.

Ellsworth, R., Collins, J., Casey, N., Schoonover, R., Hickey, R., Hyer, L., Twenlow, S., and Nesselroade, J. Some characteristics of effective psychiatric treatment programs. *Journal of Consulting and Clinical Psychology,* 1979, *47,* 799–817.

Framo, J. Family therapy and theory. *American Psychologist,* 1979, *34,* 988–992.

Lutzker, J., and Martin, J. *Behavior change.* Monterey, Ca.: Brooks/Cole, 1981.

Meyer, R. *The clinician's handbook.* Boston: Allyn and Bacon, 1982.

Shakow, D. Segmental set. *American Psychologist,* 1977, *32,* 129–139.

Ullmann, L., and Krasner, L. *A psychological approach to abnormal behavior.* Englewood Cliffs, N.J.: Prentice-Hall, 1975.

Paranoid Schizophrenia

The Case of Perry
In order to apply a diagnosis of paranoid schizophrenia, the person must first meet the overall criteria for schizophrenia, which can be fulfilled by any of the following: 1) grossly inappropriate or flat affect, 2) catatonic (rigid) or disorganized behavior, 3) loosening of associations (form of thought disorder), or 4) significant delusions or hallucinations, excluding auditory hallucinations of only one or two words (see Rosenhan, 1973). An active disorder phase must be present, and the schizophrenia must continue for at least six months, which can include prodromal (symptom emergence), active, and residual phases. The disorder is specifically labeled as Paranoid Schizophrenia when the symptom picture is dominated by preoccupation with grandiose or persecutory delusions, delusions of jealousy, or hallucinations with a delusional content.

Several other characteristics typically distinguish the paranoid schizoprenic from other categories of schizophrenia. Paranoid schizophrenia is likely to occur later in life and has a more stable course over time than do other forms. There is also less likelihood of a severe disorganization of personality in paranoid schizophrenics (Gillis & Blevins, 1978; Bernheim & Lewine, 1979; Johnson & Quinlan, 1980). Yet, paranoid schizophrenia is differentiated from other forms of the psychotic paranoid disorders (paranoia, acute paranoid disorder) by the fact that it is the most disorganized paranoid disorder. There are usually a wider variety of delusions, and they are less organized than those found in paranoia and acute paranoid disorder. Gillis and Blevins (1978) find paranoid schizophrenics to be less impaired in their cognitive judgments than are nonparanoid schizophrenics, and others have noted some differences in body build and chemistry.

Perry

Perry was first institutionalized at age thirty-five. He had been picked up by the police, who thought he was drunk. They took him to a detoxification unit associated with one of the local hospitals. It is true that he had been drinking. However, even when his system had obviously been cleared of the alcohol, he still showed very strange behavior patterns. He talked about having been contacted by a variety of alien creatures who would park their space vehicle in the field behind his apartment building. His discussion was not logical, and he often skipped from one thought to another. He said they talked to him "for a real long time about a lot of things." He told different stories at different times about what these discussions focused on. At other times, he indicated a fear that he would be kidnapped by these alien creatures and talked about a variety of ways to keep them from capturing him, including certain bizarre incantations and prayers. At times, he would appear to be very frightened and would report he had just seen one of these "creatures."

As soon as it became clear that alcohol was not his primary problem, he was transferred to the state mental hospital. When his symptoms persisted, he received a diagnosis of Paranoid Schizophrenia. His sister, who said he had always been a bit strange, reported that the odd behaviors had definitely increased in recent months. She took out commitment papers on him, and after an initial observation period, he was committed to the hospital for 60 days.

Perry is a Japanese-American, whose father, a Caucasian, met his Japanese wife-to-be when he was stationed in Japan at the end of World War II. They returned to the States shortly thereafter, and Perry's father took a job as a machinist in a large factory. His mother stayed home until Perry and his sister, two years younger, were old enough to go to school. She then took a job with a power company, first as a clerk, and later she worked up to a supervisory position.

Perry's birth was normal and uncomplicated. He did show some problems in social adjustment in the second grade. Several students delighted in picking on him, apparently responding to his slightly different physical appearance that reflected his Japanese-American ancestry. He became quite sensitive to this and could easily be induced to fight by such teasing. The teasing dropped off in the later grades, though Perry always remained sensitive to any comments in this regard.

Perry's parents were devoted to him and his sister, and they seldom used any form of physical punishment. When Perry did something bad, his father and mother both used shaming techniques as their primary mode of discipline. They apparently felt that if they could induce a humiliation experience, it would prove aversive enough to prevent any repetition of the behavior. Overt expressions of shame and humiliation by Perry were often sufficient to diminish their anger and obtain forgiveness.

Perry did above average work in school, though he was never able to spell effectively. He had an ineffective teacher in the first two grades, who in addition did not like Perry, though it was never clear why this was so. He was always ashamed of his poor performance in this area, especially as there was a glaring discrepancy between his ability in spelling and in other areas, and it was something he could not explain to himself or to others. By the time he was in the sixth grade, he was regularly having his younger sister help him by correcting his spelling in his written assignments.

When Perry was in the eighth grade, his father was crushed and killed by a piece of machinery at work. The damage was so severe that the coffin was closed at the funeral. Perry had always felt close to his father and was very upset for many months after this.

When Perry went to high school, he became interested in radio and electronics and joined a school club that focused on these interests. He socialized regularly with the members of the club, yet had few friends outside of it. He dated only sporadically. He had his first experience with intercourse when he was seventeen, and was basically seduced by the girl.

Perry attended the university for one year but obtained poor grades, largely because he studied very little. He was primarily interested in electronics and did reasonably well when his coursework had even a remote relationship to this area. At the same time, he did poorly in core courses in the humanities, and so dropped out of college at the end of one year. He obtained a job as an assistant to a television repairman and also enrolled in vocational school at night to study electronics. He did well, graduated in the upper half of his class, and obtained a job as a technician in a company that manufactured electronic instruments.

By this time, his sister had married. Though she cared for Perry, they had little contact. Perry had been living in a boarding house since he dropped out of college. He decided to move back in with his mother, and she was happy that he did so as she had been quite lonely.

Perry continued to socialize on occasion with other people whom he met through his interests in electronics and in his job. But he was not active socially. He dated occasionally, though he never became serious with anyone. He periodically had intercourse with girls he dated. Once in a while he would get mildly drunk and pick up one of the local prostitutes for an evening. In the hospital interviews, he verbalized a wish that he had married someone, even though there was little in his history to support this. He seemed content to stay at home with his mother, as she took care of his food and laundry and seldom made any demands on him. She was happy to have him around, and like Perry, she did not have much inclination to socialize.

When Perry was thirty-three, the company he worked for closed the plant. He was offered a job in one of their other plants in another city, but he did not wish to leave, and declined. After a couple of months of unemployment, he obtained a job in a large shop that serviced various electronic instruments. He was not nearly so happy now, as he was much more highly supervised, and he could not use his own initiative as much as he had in his previous job. The pay was also less than he had received, and he did not have a number of his old freedoms, such as a lot of say in what hours he had to work. He also experienced friction with his immediate supervisor. However, this supervisor realized that Perry was an excellent technician, so he never forced their conflict into a confrontation.

Perry became even more reclusive, in part because a number of his friends had moved to work in the plant in the other city. His mother began to develop physical problems, which also put stress on Perry. She was not very self-disclosing as to the extent of her illness, so he had no clear information to lessen his apprehension. He started to spend more time in a small laboratory he had built in the attic of their home, and had told several people he was working on some "new communication inventions." When asked for details about these devices, Perry would simply say that he did not want to give out any secrets that could be used against him. Most people thought he was kidding.

Three weeks before the episode that eventuated in Perry's being hospitalized, his mother was told she had cancer. She told Perry, yet failed to mention any details, or the fact that there was some chance it could be cured. Perry showed little distress when she told him about this, which was surprising in light of his devotion to her,

107

and more importantly, his dependence on her. Perry had typically used alcohol in moderation, but started drinking more after this. He had drunk heavily the night before he was hospitalized, and this loss of control was the last link in the chain that led to full-blown psychotic paranoid break.

Etiology

Several factors in Perry's development contributed to his eventual paranoid adjustment. His Japanese-American background made him an oddity in the almost wholly Caucasian world in which he grew up. Though he did not pose a threat to any of his neighbors and peers, and therefore did not receive consistent hostility, he was quickly aware of the physical differences (and he supposed that this would apply to other areas as well), so it was easy for him to define himself as out of the mainstream.

Another factor in Perry's background that is common in the history of the development of paranoid behavior is the use of shaming techniques by his parents to discipline him. As Kenneth Mark Colby (1977) notes, the paranoid individual learns very early to use "symbol-processing procedures to forestall a threatened unpleasant affect experience of humiliation, detected as shame signals. . . . In preventing humiliation, the procedures use a strategy of blaming others for wronging the self" (p. 56). Shaming techniques particularly predispose an individual to learn to anticipate the possibility of humiliation and thus to engage in numerous mechanisms to protect the ego from this experience.

One major technique used by the paranoid is projection. Projection was initially hypothesized by Freudian theorists, though they were specifically referring to projection of concern about conflict over homosexuality. More recent formulations have pointed out that it is not necessary to hypothesize a homosexual conflict, and indeed some paranoids are overtly homosexual, which directly contradicts this Freudian theory. On the other hand, the Freudian hypothesis of projection has held up well through the years, and it is clear that many of the paranoid's delusions are projections of their own internal ruminations and concerns (Johnson & Quinlan, 1980; Kembler, 1980).

Perry led an essentially isolated existence, and the friends he did have were centered on specific interests. As a result, he had a more restricted information base on how to function in society, so that he was even further isolated. He returned to a dependency relationship with his mother, not only for fulfillment of his physical survival needs, but for simple company as well. He encountered a potential humiliation experience in the loss of his job, and so he protected himself by becoming even further isolated in his own inner world (Colby, 1977). When the threat of the loss of his mother became more real to him than before, his anxiety was markedly increased. His usual defenses of isolation and projection were not sufficient, and as a result he resorted to alcohol to dilute his upset. This also was not sufficient, so he resorted to creating his own world, the delusional system. He was not so severely disturbed and blatantly bizarre as some paranoid schizophrenics are. Yet, his delusions were numerous, and they did not have the clearer focus or organization characteristic of those psychotic individuals diagnosed as either acute paranoid disorder or paranoia.

Treatment Options

Persons with a paranoid disorder of any sort are seldom likely to be involved in treatment unless coerced in some fashion, such as imprisonment, hospitalization, or pressure from a spouse. This is not surprising. Paranoids are suspicious of many, and actually trust few if any people. Also, most therapies, particularly for interpersonal problems, eventually require a degree of self-disclosure and the client's willingness to admit vulnerability. These characteristics are the opposite of some of the inherent qualities that make a person paranoid. Paranoids strongly fear allowing others to see their vulnerabilities and other foibles, as they are then open to a much-feared shame experience or even to attack (especially if they have delusions of persecution) (Colby, 1977; Barrett, 1980). Thus, the critical first step is gaining the trust of the client, as is discussed in Perry's treatment.

Paranoids who are severely disturbed, and thus either dangerous or somewhat disorganized, are likely to be hospitalized. Some clinicians have administered electroconvulsive treatments (ECT) to paranoids, possibly from the therapist's notion that the paranoids will forget the content of their delusions. This treatment has shown little success. First, this lack of success is not surprising since paranoids greatly fear any sense of increased vulnerability and/or loss of control over their self, which is a probable effect of ECT. Secondly, there is not much evidence that ECT is of any therapeutic value, except possibly for acute severe depression, and there is also a high risk of short- and long-term memory loss as well as of brain damage from any continued ECT administration (Friedberg, 1975; Lambourn & Gill, 1978; Squire et al., 1981). The same problems and the lack of positive results have generally been found in the application of psychosurgery to paranoid disorders (Trotter, 1976).

In severe paranoids, particularly paranoid schizophrenics, some chemotherapy strategies have been effective in reducing the more bizarre components. No single drug has emerged as consistently or markedly effective, although some positive results have been obtained with the phenothiazines and with a trifluoperazine-amitriptyline combination.

Direct therapy, based on the theories of John Rosen (1953) and amplified and improved by Karon (1976), attempts to "crash through" the defenses erected by the paranoid. The therapist openly interprets the assumed conflicts of the paranoid, rather than waiting for the clients themselves to formulate the conflict, as a traditional psychodynamic therapist would do. These interpretations, delivered in gut-level language rather than in polite or scientific terminology, usually focus on what are assumed to be the paranoid's major inner conflicts: the areas of sexuality, aggression, and inadequacy.

The irony is that in many cases a therapeutic technique, such as those just described, may reduce the severely disordered behavior, only to find the person now functioning as a Paranoid Personality Disorder (see the next case of Lloyd for characteristics of the personality disorders in general). That is, the person is still suspicious and fearful of vulnerability but can now marshal interpersonal resources to escape (sometimes literally) the treatment situation. It is at this point that the issue of gaining trust, as discussed below, becomes critical.

Perry's Treatment

As is typical for most individuals who are committed to a state hospital, Perry was immediately administered chemotherapy. As noted, the phenothiazines, such as Thorazine, have been helpful with some paranoid schizophrenics, particularly when the person is severely disturbed, anxious, and disorganized in behavior. Though the chemotherapy did diminish Perry's activity level and the overt expression of his delusions, it did not provide any significant cure.

The most critical issue in the treatment of any paranoid disorder is gaining the trust of the client (Barrett, 1980). This is true with any client, but it is doubly important for the paranoid, whose disorder is focused on the issues of trust and fear of loss of control.

In line with the theories of Barrett (1980) and Colby (1977), the social worker who functioned as Perry's therapist at the state hospital tried to understand the meaning of Perry's delusions and to accept them. Yet, at the same time, Barrett (1981) emphasizes that the therapist must maintain his or her own integrity. This requires that the therapist *accept* the paranoid's delusional system while *not participating* in it.

As is typical in this approach, Perry eventually began to question his therapist if she thought that his ideas were reasonable. She attempted to communicate two critical points: first, that she could not really disprove Perry's ideas, in large part because it is almost impossible to prove a negative theorem. At the same time, she also tried to let Perry know that she understood how distressing and frightening it would be to experience the world as he did. She tried to point out any similarities that she could find between her own actual life situations and social history and Perry's. This was an attempt to provide Perry with a frame of reference to which he could orient himself. This was done so that he might begin to evaluate information with a new perspective, and also begin to rely on his therapist's advice and help.

Perry's therapist also attempted, through her own manner and through some bibliotherapy (assigned reading designed to stimulate a therapeutic response) to generate the beginnings of a sense of humor in Perry. Paranoids, somewhat like the compulsive personality disorders, are notoriously lacking in a sense of humor. They cannot take a perspective that many things are not always serious. As a result of this lack of sense of humor, they tend to channel all available information into the serious perspective of their delusional system.

These therapy approaches were successful to a degree with Perry. He eventually began to examine some of his delusional systems with the idea that they might not be totally correct. He did develop a bit of a sense of humor that seemed to help here. Since he had not shown the very disorganized behavior for a long period of time, his prognosis was better than others with the same disorder. When he began to function at a reasonably normal level in the hospital, he was transferred to a half-way house. Strong efforts were made to ensure that he had a job. Efforts were also made to have his sister provide some social support for him. As was seen in the previous case of Stephanie, a supportive family environment is a critical factor in predicting success in staying out of a psychiatric hospital after the person is released.

Conclusions and Outcome
Paranoid ideation is a psychopathological pattern that emerges most severely in the often scattered and varied delusions of paranoid schizophrenia, the more ordered delusional system of the Paranoid Disorders, and then in a more muted (nondelusional) form in the Paranoid Personality Disorder. Fears of vulnerability and avoidance of shame and humiliation, often accompanied by projection, characterize these disorders. Treatment is difficult since the very nature of most treatment approaches (increased self-disclosure and confrontation of the self) are the things the paranoid most fears. Any significant cure depends on the therapist's ability to generate trust in one who is inherently untrusting (Barrett, 1980, 1981).

In Perry's case, he was maintained on medication for one year, which helped reduce his anxiety level. It also helped him sleep, which had been a problem in the weeks before his most severe upset. Perry did return to work, and with the aid of his therapist, he was better able to adjust himself to conditions there. Unfortunately, Perry has never made much progress in the area of socialization. He has stayed out of the hospital for three years now, though he has not always functioned adequately. Of course, the longer he remains out of the hospital, the more positive his chances are for staying out permanently. But the prognosis remains a bit guarded because of his inability to muster the social support systems that develop from adequate socialization skills.

REFERENCES

Barrett, C. Personality (character) disorders. In R. Woody (Ed.), *The encyclopedia of clinical assessment.* San Francisco: Jossey-Bass, 1980.
———. Personal communication, 1981.

Bernheim, K. and Lewine, R. *Schizophrenia.* New York: W. W. Norton, 1979.

Colby, K. Appraisal of four psychological theories of paranoid phenomena. *Journal of Abnormal Psychology,* 1977, *86,* 54–59.

Friedberg, J. Let's stop blasting the brain. *Psychology Today,* 1975, August, 18–26.

Gillis, J., and Blevins, K. Sources of judgmental impairment in paranoid and nonparanoid schizophrenics. *Journal of Abnormal Psychology,* 1978, 87, 587–596.

Johnson, D. and Quinlan, D. Fluid and rigid boundaries of paranoid and nonparanoid schizophrenics on a role-playing task. *Journal of Personality Assessment,* 1980, *44,* 523–531.

Karon, B. The psychoanalysis of schizophrenia. In P. Magero (Ed.) *The construction of madness.* New York: Pergamon, 1976.

Kembler, K. The nosologic validity of paranoia (Simple Delusional Disorder). *Archives of General Psychiatry,* 1980, *37,* 695–706.

Lambourn, J. and Gill, D. A controlled comparison of simulated and real ECT. *British Journal of Psychiatry,* 1978, *133,* 514–519.

Rosen, J. *Direct analysis.* New York: Grune and Stratton, 1953.

Rosenhan, D. On being sane in insane places. *Science,* 1973, *179,* 250–253.

Squire, L., Slater, P., and Miller, P. Retrograde amnesia and bilateral ECT. *Archives of General Psychiatry,* 1981, *38,* 89–95.

Trotter, S. Federal commission ok's psychosurgery. *APA Monitor,* 1976, 7, 4–5.

Paranoid Personality Disorder

The Case of Lloyd The Paranoid Personality Disorder is marked by chronic suspiciousness, emotional detachment and isolation from others, and a tendency to be litigious or even pugnacious under stress. The Personality Disorders are discussed at length in chapter 10 in this book, and the reader is referred to the introduction of that section for a discussion of the general characteristics of those patterns. However, even though this is a Personality Disorder rather than a Paranoid Disorder, the case is presented here because the etiological concepts and treatments dovetail with those presented in the case of Perry. At the same time, the symptomatology, etiological considerations, and outcome do differ, and these contrasts should help to elaborate an overall understanding of the phenomenon of paranoid thinking.

The case reported below, Lloyd, involves a young man for whom being suspicious and blaming others became a lifelong defensive strategy. Not only was the strategy counterproductive, but it also predisposed the social environment to respond to him in a hostile manner. Met with social isolation throughout his childhood and adolescence, Lloyd found enough evidence to support his belief system of his "superiority" and of his jealousy of others. Eventually, his functioning declined, as his paranoid ideation interfered with objective self-evaluation and prohibited personal growth and satisfaction.

Lloyd

Lloyd was an only child whose natural mother died of birth complications when he was three months old. He was mainly cared for by the family's housekeeper until he went to college. When he was three, his father remarried, but Lloyd's relationship with his stepmother was never better than amiable indifference. She was active in church and civic organizations and left the rearing of Lloyd to the housekeeper and his father.

Lloyd's father was a senior executive with a large and competitive business firm. He often discussed his problems and frustrations with work during dinner. He was demanding of his employees and quickly fired them if they did not meet his standards. Also, he was critical of himself and often attributed setbacks in the business to his professional weaknesses. Similar demands were made of Lloyd. His father analyzed all of Lloyd's actions and attributed any instance of less than perfect achievement to Lloyd's weak efforts. His step-mother usually agreed with his father, though she placed no demands on Lloyd. Lloyd's memory of the housekeeper was that she was affectionate toward him and cared for him responsibly. Yet they were not close and Lloyd did not regard her as a parent.

Lloyd did not attend nursery school or kindergarten and became a behavior problem in the first grade. When his teacher corrected his work, he was resentful and angry. On occasion, Lloyd would scream at the teacher, tear his papers, and refuse to work any longer. When his parents were informed of his behavior, they accused the teacher of picking on Lloyd and expecting too much of him. However, they did get Lloyd a tutor, which helped bring him to the level of first graders who had been to kindergarten and/or nursery school. This served to reduce the intensity of Lloyd's response to criticism. Nevertheless, Lloyd's resentment when corrected was noted by each of his elementary and junior high school teachers.

The family, mainly because of their condescending social attitudes, had few close or intimate friends. Lloyd's playmates were carefully screened during his childhood. As he grew older and brought schoolmates home, his father criticized anyone who was not considered "worthwhile." When his parents thought a friend was unacceptable (most of the time), they were rude and later criticized Lloyd for choosing that friend. Aside from compulsory church on Sundays, followed by lunch with the minister and the families of other church leaders, there were few family activities. Lloyd's father and stepmother were socially active with church- and business-related functions, but Lloyd was seldom included in these functions, and he was sent to visit his (natural) maternal grandparents when his parents vacationed each summer.

Since his parents were so selective about his friends, Lloyd felt he had few options among his schoolmates. Apparently taking his father's lead, he was domineering and condescending toward his classmates. They naturally resented Lloyd's constant bragging about his grades and assertions of genius. Also, Lloyd was a self-appointed classroom disciplinarian and could be counted on to report any misbehavior to school authorities. These social problems were brought to his parents' attention, but they criticized the school and assured Lloyd that the other students avoided him because they were jealous of his superior ability. Lloyd internalized these attitudes and used the jealousy explanation to explain his subsequent unsuccessful interactions with his peers. This attitude further generalized to all areas of accomplishment. The fault always lay with unreasonable expectations, unclear instructions, and/or other external circumstances beyond his control.

Needless to say, Lloyd was generally isolated throughout high school and college. Most of his fellow students found him intolerable. Aside from a few superficial lunch and study buddies, Lloyd had almost no contact with his peers by the time he entered high school. He spent most of his time alone in his room—studying or working with his stamp collections. Both activities proved successful for Lloyd. He graduated with honors from high school and college and he developed a regional reputation when he began to exhibit his stamp collections.

After college, Lloyd took a managerial position with the firm for which his father worked. He worked hard and advanced to regional supervisor within three years. At this point, he began dating a young lady of whom his parents approved. They were engaged and married within the year. The marriage was met with more enthusiasm by the parents of the bride and groom than by the newlyweds themselves. Lloyd's wife Ellen was quiet and agreeable though plain and "colorless." Apparently her parents had become concerned that Ellen would not attract a suitable (or timely) husband and were relieved when Lloyd proposed. Lloyd, on the other hand, was flattered by Ellen's uncritical acceptance and minimal expectations of him. The marriage evolved into a nearly platonic and amicable partnership. They did not have children, which resulted more from an unenthusiastic sexual relationship than from any definitive decision.

It was not long before Lloyd realized that his rapidly advancing career had come to a halt. The firm for which he worked was merged with a larger conglomerate, and the positions above were assigned to employees who had been with the conglomerate before the merger. Feeling that he was again the undeserving victim of unfortunate circumstances, Lloyd resigned and took a position with a competitive firm. However, his domineering and critical behavior towards his supervisors had only been tolerated at the first firm because of his father's high position. Lloyd had no such protection in the second job, and created so much resentment among his staff members that he was asked to resign.

Lloyd, who had not experienced a significant failure since first grade, brought suit against the firm, claiming that they had yielded to pressure from the competitive conglomerate to fire him. The suit was quickly dismissed. However, the suit identified Lloyd as a troublemaker and other local firms were now reluctant to hire him. His father was retired by this time and thus unable to use his influence to secure a position for Lloyd. In addition, he criticized Lloyd for not playing the game and accused him of ruining the family's good name.

Lloyd decided to start his own consulting firm and borrowed heavily to establish the business. He did well for a few months, then ran into conflicts with employees and customers. He continually complained of substandard performance and verbally berated clerks, staff members, and even customers on occasion. As a result, there were so many resignations and terminations that the firm became unstable, and then folded. Lloyd's usual externalizations were becoming unacceptable even to Ellen. She pronounced him a failure in life and filed for a separation (with the approval of her parents). Lloyd's parents agreed that he was a failure in life but saw a divorce in the family as an unacceptable social blight. They urged Lloyd to prevent a divorce and criticized him for being unsuccessful. The separation and business failure were financially draining for Lloyd. He declared bankruptcy, moved to another city, and enrolled in dental school. Ellen was keeping in contact with him, and the separation had made both aware of the dependency they had on each other. However, he could not be shaken from the belief that the conglomerate bore him ill will and had ruined his life in his hometown. He hoped he could get a fresh start in another profession and locale over which the conglomerate had no influence.

Lloyd's problems continued in dental school. First, his negative social tendencies did not change, and there were numerous conflicts with instructors, patients, and dental hygienists. Also, Lloyd's manual dexterity was poor. He performed well on written exams, but his practicum evaluations were barely passing. Lloyd, of course, blamed these low evaluations on prejudiced instructors, difficult patients, errors of timekeepers, and so forth. He did graduate from dental school and passed the written licensing exam with honors. However, he could not pass the practical exam in two tries, refused to attempt it again, and so was unable to practice dentistry as an independent professional. Opportunities arose to work under the supervision of a licensed dentist, but Lloyd regarded these posi-

tions as inferior and unacceptable. His reaction to this third failure was extreme rage reactions and sullen anger. He even made some threats of recriminations against several of his dental school professors whom he had especially disliked.

Etiology The dynamics of this case are analogous to those in the previous case of Perry. Just as in that case, the use of shaming techniques (Colby, 1977) as a disciplinary technique was a factor in Lloyd's pathology. However, of far greater import here was the modeling for social isolation and elitism that Lloyd's parents provided, as well as the direct control over friendships that helped to further his isolation. Their own tendency to project failure on to others (again modeled by Lloyd) and their unwillingness to accept any failures or problems in Lloyd similarly made him unwilling to accept these in himself.

After he once started failing, the societal labeling as a "troublemaker" and "difficult person to get along with," combined with the increasing alienation from the few supportive interpersonal relationships he had left (Ellen, his parents) to make him even more vulnerable. He could not tolerate this status, which resulted in anxiety and even more inappropriate expressions of his chronic anger (Barrett, 1980, 1981).

Treatment Ellen, who had been visiting Lloyd on the weekends, became increasingly concerned about his condition. She insisted that he accompany her to see a family physician, which Lloyd only agreed to do after much arguing. The physician prescribed some tranquilizing medication and set Lloyd up for a session with a clinical psychologist in their health maintenance organization.

They had several sessions together, but Lloyd would never allow any trust to develop (Barrett, 1980, 1981). After his anxiety subsided a bit, it became clear that he was only continuing in order to placate Ellen and his parents. The one positive change occurred as a result of the psychologist's referral of Lloyd to a physical therapist to work on his poor manual dexterity. The exercises, combined with some remedial practicum work at the dental school, improved Lloyd's dexterity and he was finally able to pass (though barely) the practical portion of the licensing exam.

He went into practice shortly thereafter. He was able to make an adequate living, though never developed a good practice because of the unattractiveness of his personality. He eventually divorced Ellen and moved to a distant city, possibly in an attempt to distance himself as much as possible from his prior "failures." He became increasingly involved with an extreme right wing political organization. He was once arrested for having an unregistered machine gun and had to pay a heavy fine. His personality never did change much; he lived out his life in this manner and died of a heart attack at age forty-nine. Since there had been no history of heart disease in his family, its appearance here is probably support for the concept that chronically repressed anger can be a major generic factor in heart disease (Friedman & Rosenman, 1959; McClelland, 1979).

Comments The cases of Perry and Lloyd demonstrate the different courses paranoid disorders can take. It is ironic that Perry, who presented an apparently much more severe disorder, eventually made more positive changes. This may have been because the severity of his disorder forced him into a status of vulnerability (thus allowing change), whereas Lloyd was more successful in continuously staying away from moving into a position in which others could break through his system. For the most part, the course of Lloyd's disorder is unfortunately the more probable outcome in the paranoid disorders.

REFERENCES

Barrett, C. Personality (character) disorders. In R. Woody (Ed.) *The encyclopedia of clinical assessment.* San Francisco: Jossey-Bass, 1980.

———. Personal communication, 1981.

Colby, K. Appraisal of four psychological theories of paranoid phenomenon. *Journal of Abnormal Psychology*, 1977, *86*, 54–59.

Friedman, M., and Rosenman, R. Association of specific overt behavior patterns with blood and cardiovascular findings. *Journal of the American Medical Association*, 1959, *169*, 1289–1296.

McClelland, D. Inhibited power motivation and high blood pressure in men. *Journal of Abnormal Psychology*, 1979, *88*, 182–190.

5

The Affective Disorders

The Affective Disorders are broadly defined as primary disturbances of mood and affect. Included among these disorders in the DSM-III are symptom patterns that were formerly labeled as a Depressive Neurosis and even on occasion as a Cyclothymic Personality Disorder. Thus, symptom patterns within this category range from mild to moderate depressive episodes to the psychotic affective reactions.

The major categories are those of Bipolar Disorder, Major Depression, and the specific affective disorders, which include the Cyclothymic Disorder and the Dysthymic Disorder. The Bipolar Disorder, which replaces the traditional term of Manic-Depressive Psychosis, is discussed in the case of Manuel. It should be noted that no category is available for a disorder that has only a manic component (high activity level, grandiosity, and euphoric and/or driven emotionality). It is felt (with supporting though not conclusive data) that such patterns virtually always occur in a history that shows at least some evidence of depression (Nurnberger et al., 1979; Winokur, 1978); thus, the designation as a Bipolar Disorder. The Major Depressive Disorder designates severe, though not usually chronic (in a continuous episode) depression; it is discussed in the case of Deborah, the first case in this section. The other component in this section, the article by Gallagher and Frankel (1980), describes a depression in an older woman, focusing on specific psychological treatment techniques.

The inclusion of the full range of mood disturbances within one diagnostic classification by DSM-III is consistent with the current trend among mental health professionals to consider these disorders along a continuum of affective adjustment. Consequently, differential diagnoses among the subcategories of affective disorders are made in accordance with criteria for intensity and duration, as opposed to traditional conceptualizations that attempted (not always very successfully) to recognize qualitative distinctions.

Normal depression is characterized by a brief period of sadness, grief, or dejection, in which disruption of normal functioning is minimal. Mild disturbances of mood and thought are manifest by apathy, impaired concentration and increased guilt. These reactions are usually responses to discrete environmental events, such as the loss of an important (high stimulus value, though not necessarily loved) other, or disappointments in career, or finances. This depression often requires no treatment and gradually lifts with the passage of time. Moderate episodes are more disruptive to normal functioning and may be associated with distorted cognitions and/or skill deficits that require various psychological therapies. The more severe (and sometimes psychotic) depressive syndrome necessitates a multimodal therapeutic approach, usually including chemotherapy, psychotherapy, and cognitive behavior modification techniques such as those employed in the treatment of Deborah.

REFERENCES

Nurnberger, J., Ruth, S., Dunner, D., and Fieve, R. Unipolar mania: A distinct clinical entity? *American Journal of Psychiatry.* 1979, *136*, 1420–1423.

Winokur, G. Mania-depression: Family studies, genetics, and relation to treatment. In M. Lipton, A. DiMascio, and K. Killiam (Eds.), *Psychopharmocology*. New York: Raven, 1978.

Major Depressive Episode with Melancholia

The Case of Deborah   Depression has been called the "common cold" of psychopathology. At one time or another, most people will become depressed at the loss of or separation from a loved one, or at the failure to achieve a desired goal. Depression has also been observed in individuals exposed to prolonged stress (physical or emotional) and/or chronic frustration. Generally, these depressive episodes are self-limiting and situationally specific. With the passage of time or changes in life circumstances, the person recovers without therapeutic intervention. In contrast to these "normal" or "garden variety" depressive symptoms, the clinical features of major depressive episodes are more debilitating and persistent.

Major depressive episodes are characterized by a generalized slowing down of mental and physical activity, with a gloomy or morbid mood, and with feelings of worthlessness. The psychotic form of depression requires hospitalization and intensive care and is characterized by severe and chronic symptoms along with an associated loss of contact with reality. The speech of psychotically depressed patients is slow, without emotion, and concerned with suffering. Personal and social functioning are severely impaired by a wide range of deviations in thought, mood, and action, such as delusions, hallucinations, and/or bizarre behaviors. Such persons are frequently disoriented with respect to time, place, or personal identity.

During these episodes, patients may attempt suicide and therefore must be carefully watched. Interestingly enough, severely depressed persons present more of a suicide risk as they are on the upswing, since they have more energy available to actuate their plans (Schneidman, 1979).

There appear to be two qualitative types of depression that are mainly distinguished by the presence or absence of precipitating external factors: endogenous and reactive (or exogenous). Endogenous depression is more likely to be primarily caused by such internal factors as biochemical abnormalities and/or genetic predisposition (Nurnberger et al., 1979; Winokur, 1977). Psychomotor retardation, severe mood depression, lack of reactivity to the environment, loss of interest in life, severe insomnia, weight loss, and suicidal tendencies are characteristic features of endogenous depression. The less severe reactive depression is marked by self-pity, inadequate social skills, and the presence of identifiable precipitating stressors. Despite this apparently clear distinction, some symptom patterns evidence both endogenous and reactive features.

Involutional melancholia is the traditional term for a form of extreme depression allegedly characteristic of later life. Winokur (1977) has demonstrated that there is *not necessarily* a greater risk of a depressive episode during this phase than at other times. Rather, it may be that some people become depressed when they undergo the typical self-evaluation of middle adulthood (usually between the ages of 40 and 50). Also "loss," in various forms, is more likely to occur in later life. DSM-III has retained the concept of melancholia, but it has excluded the term *involutional* in light of research findings that depressions in the involutional period are not otherwise distinct from depressive episodes within other life stages (Weissman, 1979).

The term *melancholia*, as used by DSM-III, designates the subtype of depression that is primarily characterized by anhedonia (inability to experience pleasure). It is usually responsive to chemotherapy or cognitive behavior modification techniques (Beck, 1976). Thus, the use of the term corresponds closely to the traditional concept of endogenous depression. In the case of Deborah, reported below, there is a Major Depressive Disorder with melancholia, which includes features of both endogenous and reactive depression.

Deborah
Deborah was hospitalized for a major depressive disorder at age fifty-eight. She had been widowed a year ago, her two daughters resided with their own families in distant states, and none of her relatives

were readily available. She was unskilled occupationally and had never worked outside her home. Before she became depressed, Deborah had been active with civic and charitable organizations. Her husband was a successful businessman, and Deborah had occasionally filled in for sick employees. Her husband sold his business in anticipation of retirement, then died of a heart attack soon after the new owner took possession of the store. Also, Deborah had experienced two mild strokes—one about one year before her husband's death, and another about two months after his funeral. These strokes did not result in permanent damage, and Deborah recovered within a few weeks. Her husband's insurance and the proceeds from the sale of his business allowed Deborah to live comfortably and without debt. However, the standard of living was considerably lower than she had enjoyed when her husband's business was active.

A psychosocial history and psychological examination revealed that Deborah had been very dependent on her husband for almost all of the major decisions in her life. His high income and willingness to take on all of the stressful challenges in their lives were similar to the way her father had treated her. She had been protected all of her life from truly threatening challenges. The inevitable personal losses she experienced were buffered by the supportive family and social systems in which she had always been enmeshed. The only prior time that she had shown any marked depressive symptoms was when her father had died when she was thirty-five years of age. Her involvement with her two children, the doting attention from her husband, and her high activity level in civic affairs kept her from becoming severely disturbed then.

However, in the two years before Deborah's hospitalization, she had experienced two mild strokes, a significant decline in financial status, and the death of her husband after forty years of marriage. This was a series of traumas (or challenges) unmatched in her history, and she had to face it with inadequate coping skills. She was admitted to a mental hospital by her neighbor, who was alarmed by Deborah's deteriorating behavior and obviously depressed mood. Deborah saw herself as useless, worthless, alone, and uncared for. Since she could see no hope for the future, she said she was waiting to die and hoped it would come soon. Her neighbor also reported that Deborah had become lax in her personal hygiene, no longer cleaned her house, and was apparently prone to unprovoked crying jags and irregular sleeping habits.

Though Deborah would not seek professional help on her own, she did not resist the involuntary commitment arranged by her neighbor and family physician. Rather, she saw her institutionalization as a predictable result. She allowed herself to be packed and transported to the hospital, and then she complained constantly that

121

these efforts were futile because she was a hopeless case. Deborah was resigned to what she saw as a set of overwhelming life circumstances and could not at first be convinced that change was possible. Upon admission, Deborah's apathetic acceptance of involuntary hospitalization was so pronounced that the staff physician wondered if she had experienced another stroke. Consequently, her diagnosis was deferred and she was placed under 24-hour observation for three days.

Deborah's behavior during the observation period was apprehensive and agitated, with an intensely depressed mood. She was unable to sleep for more than three hours and did so at irregular intervals. When awake, she would pace the halls while moaning and wringing her hands. When other patients would sympathetically inquire about her distress, Deborah would only become more agitated and continue pacing. Noticeable among her adjustment problems in the hospital were an inability to fall asleep in her room and a tendency to simply lie down in odd spots until someone came to move her. On several occasions, Deborah was found asleep before the television or in another patient's room. Meanwhile, a neurological exam and other tests ruled out the suspected stroke as the cause of her depression. Deborah was given the diagnosis of Major Depressive Disorder with melancholia.

Treatment Options and Etiology

A variety of treatment options are often used for depression. Antidepressant medication, sleep deprivation, electroconvulsive treatments (ECT), and psychosurgery are the most commonly used physical techniques. Psychodynamic therapy to get at the inner conflicts, traditional behavior therapy to get the person functioning again, cognitive behavior modification to deal with the belief systems that create depression, and group therapy to help such clients to develop new social behaviors and test out new concepts and initiatives are the psychological treatments of choice.

The tricyclic antidepressants (such as Tofranil, Elavil, and Sinequan) are the most commonly prescribed medications for depression. The exact action of the tricyclics is unknown, though they do appear to increase the brain's neurotransmitter activity (Baldessarini, 1978). One drawback is that even if they work at all, they do not take effect for up to two to three weeks after they are started. These antidepressants are most appropriate for the severe and endogenous depressive disorders.

Another type of antidepressant is the group of monoamine oxidase (MAO) inhibitors, such as Nardil and Parnate. Depressed patients who respond to tricyclics are generally less likely to respond to MAO inhibitors, and vice versa. MAO inhibitors are more effective with atypical depressions that are characterized by high anxiety, obsessive-compulsive features, concerns about physiological functioning, and increases rather than by decreases in sleep and eating. The action of MAO inhibitors is different from that of tricyclics, as they prevent the metabolism of neurotransmitters following the nerve impulse transmission (Baldessarini, 1978). The MAO inhibitors are less favored overall as they are not as consistently effective and they do produce a higher number of significant side effects.

Even though ECT has shown little value with most disorders (Lambourn & Gill, 1978; Friedburg, 1975), most psychiatrists agree that it can be useful for acute, severe depression. This is particularly so since suicide is often a concern here, and the chemotherapies may not take effect for some time, leaving the person in a high-risk state. There is, however, evidence of significant short- and long-term memory loss, related brain damage, and other negative results from any substantial use of ECT (Friedburg, 1975). The most widely accepted explanation for the effectiveness of ECT is that it changes the amount and availability of neurotransmitter substances (Fink, 1978; Kiloh, 1977).

Sleep deprivation, a simple procedure developed in Europe, is a recent addition to treatments for depression in the United States. It is effective, however, only with that small group of patients who show disturbances in REM sleep patterns. The patient, who is under observation, is kept awake for approximately 40 hours, which apparently regulates the sleep patterns and related levels of neurotransmitter substances back to normal (Gerner et al., 1978). Psychosurgery, an irrevocable treatment choice, has, like ECT, been shown to be consistently effective with only one syndrome, severe depression (Trotter, 1976); but it should only be employed after less risky approaches have been tried.

The demonstrated effectiveness of these biologic treatments is a primary source of support for theories that postulate constitutional abnormalities and/or biologic predispositions as major etiological variables in the development of severe depression. The most widely accepted are the neurochemical theories, which suggest that abnormal levels of certain brain substances (such as neurotransmitters, or histamine) cause depression.

Indeed, the specifics of the neurologic involvement in severe depression remain unclear at this point, and the fact that neurochemical involvement *causes* depression has not been demonstrated. It may be that depressed moods alter neurochemical activity, or that both neurochemical abnormalities *and* depressive episodes are the results of some yet unidentified factor(s). Nevertheless, it is clear that episodes of major depression are *associated with* some type of neurochemical aberration.

There are four types of psychological theories of depression, from which most psychotherapeutic treatments have evolved: psychoanalytic, personality, behavioral, and cognitive. Psychoanalytic treatments involve cathartic expression of alleged unconscious aggression, often related to a significant personal loss in the formative years (Abraham, 1960; Arieti & Bemporad, 1978); the establishment of an intimate therapeutic relationship; and encouraging the depressed person to make use of more adaptive defense mechanisms. Personality theorists focus on specific personality trait distortions, such as low self-esteem, a high propensity for guilt, and fear of competition as causal factors. These variables are considered in the treatment plans, via attempts to restructure the depressed person's personality through individual and group therapy, assertive training, and other such treatments.

Behavioral theories conceive of depression as the result of inadequate levels of positive reinforcement (Ferster, 1965). Thus, the goal in treatment is to increase the frequency and variety of rewarding experiences for the depressed person, for example, through token economies while institutionalized, and later with contracting, family sessions, and so forth. A good example of this approach is seen in the article by Gallagher and Frankel (1980), which appears later in this section. Cognitive theorists have postulated that distorted thinking leads to disturbed moods and have sought to alter the pessimistic attitudes that depressed individuals have toward themselves (Beck, 1976). The cognitive therapist emphasizes a confrontation of those maladaptive belief systems (as in Deborah, "I just can't handle really important tasks all by myself") that generate guilt, low self-esteem, and lack of initiative.

Deborah's Treatment

Tricyclic antidepressants, along with the positive milieu on the ward, were therapeutic for Deborah. Within one week, she evidenced improvement in her personal hygiene, and she began to sleep and eat with increasing regularity. Gradually, Deborah's mood lifted and she participated in more unit activities, such as occupational therapy and recreational outings. In group and individual therapy, Deborah became more verbally expressive about her isolation from other people and her grief over the loss of her husband. By the third week, prominent depressive features (crying jags, disorientation, disturbed sleep, loss of appetite) were no longer observed. Also, in group therapy, Deborah began to relate to other patients and was able to consider problems other than her own. After four weeks, Deborah was discharged from the hospital and referred to a clinical psychologist for psychotherapy. She was continued on low doses of the tricyclic antidepressant for another two months, which was supervised by a consulting psychiatrist on an outpatient basis.

The clinical psychologist treated Deborah with a combination of behavioral and cognitive therapy. The first phase of therapy focused on Deborah's activity level and social contacts. Deborah was encouraged to reestablish the friendships from which she had withdrawn after her husband's death. Further, it became apparent that Deborah's activity level had decreased in part because she believed she might trigger another stroke. Before her first stroke, Deborah was active physically, primarily walking and occasionally swimming. Even though her physician encouraged her here, she continued to fear that any stress might result in a debilitating stroke. Deborah's psychologist gave her readings on the precipitating factors in stroke, the helpful nature of exercise, as well as desensitization training for her fears. Also, Deborah and her therapist negotiated a series of behavioral contracts that required increasing levels of physical activities and social contacts (Lutzker & Martin, 1981). Prior to her depressive episode, Deborah had been involved with several civic organizations, and her return, fortunately, was enthusiastically received.

Deborah's maladaptive belief systems were constantly challenged (Beck, 1976), and she contracted, using the Premack Principle, to increase positive self-verbalizations (Meichenbaum, 1977), such as "I am competent to do any of the things I need to do." The Premack Principle asks the client to follow a high frequency behavior (such as putting a key in the car's ignition) immediately with a low frequency behavior (the new and more positive self-verbalizations). This ultimately increases the habit strength of the new verbalization, which amplifies into more positive behavior and mood. This overall treatment program was successful for Deborah. The results were a generalized mood elevation and the return to a positive level of social functioning.

The prognosis for Deborah is favorable. She has renewed her ties with a supportive social group and is continuing to change her maladaptive beliefs. She reports occasional moments when she has fears of death or a major stroke. However, she has found that these fears are not infrequent events among her peers, and the opportunity to verbalize them with sympathetic friends has been sufficient to this point. She has discontinued the antidepressant medication, and therapy sessions have been reduced to bimonthly visits. These visits are shorter (usually about half an hour) and are mainly designed to allow the therapist to monitor Deborah's mood and lifestyle. It is hoped that this regular monitoring will allow the therapist to identify any prodromal symptoms (early signs of a disorder) and thereby assist Deborah to avoid another episode.

Conclusions and Outcome

Deborah has done well without medication or direct intervention for eight months, and one can be optimistic that she can probably experience the moderate mood fluctuations that often accompany middle and older adulthood without further decompensation. The abrupt onset and reactive components of her disorder, the lack of a prior history of significant depression, and the effective and multimodal treatment she received are important factors in her success.

Depression comes in a variety of symptom and severity patterns. Undoubtedly, both physiological and psychological variables are generic in initiating and maintaining severe depressions, whereas in chronic though milder patterns (Dysthymic Disorder), psychological factors are predominant. Chemotherapy, ECT, sleep deprivation, and psychosurgery can be helpful with severe depressions, especially if combined with milieu control and psychological therapies as some improvement is noted. Cognitive behavior modification and some of the newer psychodynamic approaches have been especially helpful with patterns such as the Dysthymic Disorder.

REFERENCES

Abraham, K. The first pregenital stage of the libido. In *Selected papers on psychoanalysis.* New York: Basic, 1960.

Arieti, S., and Bemporad, J. *Severe and mild depression.* New York: Basic Books, 1978.

Baldessarini, R. Chemotherapy. In A. Nicholi (Ed.), *The Harvard guide to modern psychiatry.* Cambridge, Ma.: Belknap Press, 1978.

Beck, A. *Cognitive therapy and the emotional disorders.* New York: International Universities Press, 1976.

Ferster, C. Classification of behavior pathology. In L. Krasner and L. Ullmann (Eds.), *Research in behavior modification.* New York: Holt, Rinehart and Winston, 1965.

Fink, M. Efficacy and safety of induced seizures (EST) in man. *Comprehensive Psychiatry*, 1978, *19*, 1–18.

Friedburg, J. Let's stop blasting the brain. *Psychology Today*, 1975, August, 18–26.

Gerner, R., Post, R., Goodwin, F., and Buney, W. A comparison of biological correlates and antidepressant effects of sleep deprivation in patients and normals. *Journal of Psychiatric Research.* 1978, *10*, 39–47.

Kiloh, L. The use of electro-convulsive treatment in depressive illness. In G. Burrows (Ed.), *Handbook of studies on depression.* Amsterdam: Excerpta Medico, 1977.

Lambourn, J., and Gill, D. A controlled comparison of simulated and real ECT. *British Journal of Psychiatry*, 1978, *133*, 514–519.

Lutzker, J. and Martin, J. *Behavior change.* Monterey, Ca.: Brooks/Cole, 1981.

Meichenbaum, D. *Cognitive behavior modification.* New York: Plenum, 1977.

Nurnberger, J., Ruth, S., Dunner, D., and Fieve, R. Unipolar mania: A distinct clinical entity? *American Journal of Psychiatry*, 1979, *136*, 1420–1423.

Schneidman, E. Suicidal logic. In W. Sahakian (Ed.), *Psychopathology today.* Itasca, Ill.: Peacock, 1979.

Trotter, S. Federal commission ok's psychosurgery. *APA Monitor*, 1976, 7, 4–5.

Weissman, M. The myth of involutional melancholia. *Journal of American Medical Association*, 1979, *242*, 742–744.

Winokur, G. Unipolar depression. *Archives of General Psychiatry*, 1977, *36*, 47–52.

Bipolar Disorder (Manic-Depressive Psychosis)

The Case of Manuel   That manic and depressive symptoms are components of a single disorder was suspected by Hippocrates (460–377 B.C.) and has remained a consistent assertion. Since that time, unipolar depression has been distinguished from bipolar disorder and is currently thought to result from different etiological factors (Stern & Mendels, 1980; Goodwin, 1977).

The diagnosis of Bipolar Disorder, also referred to as the Bipolar Affective Disorder and Affective Disorder, and formerly termed the Manic-Depressive Psychosis, is made whenever manic features are observed—

regardless of the presence of depressive features. As noted earlier, the former DSM-II subclassifications of 1) manic, 2) depressed, or 3) circular types of bipolar disorder have been abandoned in light of recent evidence that virtually all individuals with primary manic features have evidenced depressive symptoms at some point (Nurnberger et al., 1979; Winokur, 1969). Thus, only depression is considered a unipolar disorder.

The range of behaviors that typify mania are broad and most commonly include 1) hyperactive motor behavior, 2) variable irritability and/or euphoria, and 3) a speeding up of thought processes, called a "flight of ideas." Manic speech is typically loud, rapid, and difficult to understand. When the mood is expansive, manics take on many tasks (seldom completing them), avoid sleep, and easily ramble into lengthy monologues about their personal plans, worth, and power. When the mood becomes more irritable, they are quick to complain and engage in hostile tirades.

Psychotic manic reactions involve grandiose delusions, bizarre and impulsive behavior, transient hallucinations and explosiveness, and as such, these reactions may be confused with schizophrenic episodes. However, whereas schizophrenics (and schizoaffectives) are distracted by *internal* thoughts and ideas, manics are distracted by *external* stimuli that often go unnoticed by others. Also, whereas schizophrenics (and schizoaffectives) tend to avoid any true relationships with others during an active phase, manics are typically profoundly open to contact with other people (NIMH Staff, 1977).

Though the onset of discrete manic episodes may be sudden, the disorder has a generally slow onset in many cases, and as with Manuel, the person's life history evidences preliminary symptoms in childhood or adolescence that at some point become more intense and debilitating.

Manuel
Manuel was hospitalized for a psychotic manic episode when he was thirty-three years old. Six weeks before the emergency admission, he had begun exhibiting mild hypomanic symptoms: taking up several new hobbies, treating coworkers to expensive lunches, buying drinks for everyone in bars, and challenging his friends to tennis matches with exorbitant wagers. His wife reported being initially pleased with these actions since Manuel had been depressed and withdrawn for several previous weeks. Further, Manuel had been described by his friends and relatives as "moody and unpredictable" since childhood. But this time, Manuel's expansive mood escalated, and his behavior became so inappropriate that his wife asked the police to locate him so that he could be hospitalized. She became concerned when she found a letter from him explaining that he was moving to a hotel to write his memoirs. The letter was lengthy, unsigned, and ended abruptly in the middle of a sentence.

The police had some difficulty locating Manuel. He was eventually found in the city park reciting and writing his life's story for a crowd of encouraging teenagers. He could not be persuaded to accompany the officers willingly and was restrained with handcuffs. He became agitated and verbally obscene, so the police bound his feet and gagged his mouth. When Manuel arrived at the emergency room, he was strongly sedated and transferred to the psychiatric unit for observation.

Manuel's wife, Alicia, was interviewed the next day, and his behavior on the unit was closely observed. Alicia reported that Manuel was a high school mathematics teacher who at night was working toward his masters degree in accounting. Alicia was a former keypunch operator who had stopped working three years earlier when their son was born. They had become engaged in junior high school and married as soon as Manuel (who was a year younger) had finished high school.

Throughout elementary and high school, Manuel had received above average grades, lettered in track, and was sports editor for the school newspaper. He was popular with his peers, although he was perceived as moody and quick tempered. In high school, he and Alicia settled into a social circle with three other couples with whom they continue to socialize almost exclusively. Manuel attended college and found part-time sales jobs until he received his bachelors degree. After graduation from college, he taught high school and Alicia became pregnant with their first child, a daughter, and Alicia was six-months pregnant at the time of Manuel's hospitalization.

Alicia was able to give detailed information about Manuel's life history since they had been next door neighbors as children. Manuel was the only child of parents described as loving and hard-working. His father was self-employed as an electrician, and his mother taught high school business courses. Alicia was aware of a maternal aunt who had committed suicide and also thought that a couple of Manuel's cousins (on his mother's side) were "strange."

Although Alicia described her husband as moody, easily provoked to anger, and somewhat impulsive, she thought their marriage was close and successful. Her perception was that although Manuel was difficult to live with at times, he was otherwise loving, responsible, and attentive toward his family. Alicia noted that he had been depressed about his grades, though this was not an unusual event for him, as he was always disappointed with less than superior performance. According to Alicia, Manuel usually "snapped out of it" within a few days and began to plan for the next semester. However, this latest depression had lasted for many weeks and was replaced with the hypomanic behavior described earlier.

After the onset of the switch out of the depression, Manuel's *activity level rapidly increased and his behavior became less inhibited and more inappropriate. The students reported Manuel's sudden outbursts and tangential lectures to the principal, and he dismissed Manuel for drunkenness. That afternoon, Manuel came home with a new sports car and a diamond necklace for his wife. He announced that the loss of his job was a sign that he should go into business for himself and "make millions." His behavior continued to escalate and his wife could not persuade him to seek any professional help. Instead, he insisted that he had never felt better, and argued with his wife for not having faith in his ability to succeed. He also invested their savings in an expensive office building and contracted for extensive renovations in preparation for his new business. He began to tell rambling stories of his childhood to his children and friends and then decided to write his memoirs while the office building was being remodeled.*

Manuel's behavior on the psychiatric unit was similar to Alicia's descriptions. He continued to recite and write his memoirs for other patients, though he now claimed that these were the "words of God spoken through Manuel." He engaged in several shouting matches with patients who questioned the truth of his stories. Efforts to interview or test Manuel were futile because he would only discuss the "new gospel" and his future wealth, which had been promised him in return for spreading the "Gospel according to Manuel."

Treatment Options

Treatment for severe manic disorders is usually within an inpatient setting, with a focus on chemotherapy. After the intensity of the episode has subsided, supportive psychotherapy, social skills training, and assistance with legal and vocational problems are often necessary to help the person readjust both interpersonally and occupationally. Milder hypomanic disorders can often be managed with outpatient chemotherapy and/or psychotherapy, and psychotherapy is considered the treatment of choice for the Cyclothymic Disorder—a nonpsychotic affective disorder characterized by rapid mood swings.

The evidence in support of biological cause theories of the bipolar disorder suggests that it very probably has a genetic base. The genetic concept is based on the observation that the disorder affects more members of some families than others (Winokur, 1978; Klerman, 1978), and on the fact that there is a single, effective biological method for treating bipolar mood disorders—lithium (Lipton, 1978; NIMH Staff, 1977). Lithium, an alkaline metal found in mineral rocks and salt water, has been used as a mineral water cure for various problems since the second century A.D. Lithium relieves the symptoms of acute manic episodes at about a 75 percent effectiveness rate (Lipton, 1978; NIMH Staff, 1977) and also acts for some as a prophylactic agent against recurrent manic episodes.

Unfortunately, patients with bipolar disorder are notorious for medical noncompliance (Goodwin, 1977; Jamison et al., 1979). Between 35 and 50 percent of patients on lithium maintenance 1) complain of side effects, some of which can be quite serious (Davis et al., 1981), 2) object to having their moods controlled by medication, and/or 3) resent the implication of chronic illness symbolized by regular drug use (Jamison et al., 1979). In Manuel's case, noncompliance was a minor problem that his wife successfully influenced. However, as noted, there were consequent residual problems in his employment and financial status.

Manuel's Treatment

Based on Manuel's behavior on the inpatient unit and in the emergency room, and on the interview with Alicia, the diagnosis Bipolar Disorder-Manic, with psychotic features, was given, and he was started on lithium carbonate (a salt of lithium). The effects of lithium usually take several days to manifest fully in the patient's mood and behavior, so sedative medications are often used initially, and then gradually decreased until the desired blood level of lithium has been attained. Manuel was responsive to the lithium, and was discharged after three weeks with a prescription for lithium, psychotherapy, and regular appointments for medication monitoring. Eventually, he was able to return to his teaching position (after a letter from his therapist explained the disorder, which prompted the principal to remove the "drunkenness" episode from Manuel's personnel records). The therapist also referred Manuel and Alicia to an attorney who was able to sell the office building, car, and diamond necklace, and settle the debts that Manuel had incurred during this episode. For the past two years, Manuel was maintained on lithium. Because of the potentially severe side effects of lithium (Davis et al., 1981), he is now trying to manage without medication and has been relatively successful. It is probable, however, that he will manifest similar episodes at some future point, and he and Alicia have been cautioned to return for a resumption of the treatment if he begins to show the preliminary signs again.

Comment

The relationship between psychosocial stressors and episodes of mania or depression is often obvious for first episodes; subsequent episodes, however, can occur without apparent precipitants. Also, the predisposing factors, other than family history, for the development of the bipolar disorder have not been clearly identified. In Manuel's case, there is evidence of an increasingly stressful lifestyle for a person with marginal frustration tolerance. Perhaps the biologic predisposition combines with the more demanding developmental tasks of late adolescence and young adulthood to explain the typically later onset (late 20s to early 30s) of the bipolar disorder, as is seen in Manuel. It is also possible that the moodiness, quick temper, and unpredictable behavior of Manuel's childhood and adolescence were too clearly reinforced by task avoidance and/or maternal attention and affection. Fortunately, the combination of the lithium therapy, psychotherapy, legal and social interventions, and Alicia's support allowed a positive outcome in Manuel's case.

REFERENCES

Davis, B., Pfefferbaum, A., Krutzik, S., and Davis, K. Lithium's effect on parathyroid hormone. *American Journal of Psychiatry*, 1981, *138*, 489–492.

Goodwin, F. Diagnosis of affective disorders. In M. Jarvik (Ed.), *Psychopharmacology in the practice of medicine*. New York: Appleton-Century-Crofts, 1977.

Jamison, K., Gerner, R., and Goodwin, F. Patient and physician attitude toward lithium: Relationships to compliance. *Archives of General Psychiatry*, 1979, *36*, 866–869.

Klerman, G. Longterm treatment of affective disorders. In M. Lipton, A. DiMascio, & K. Killiam (Eds.), *Psychopharmacology*, New York: Raven, 1978.

Lipton, M. Lithium: Developments in basic and clinical research. *American Journal of Psychiatry*, 1978, *135*, 1059–1061.

NIMH Staff. *Lithium in the Treatment of Mood Disorders*. Rockville, Md.: National Institute of Mental Health, 1977.

Nurnberger, J., Ruth, S., Dunner, D., & Fieve, R. Unipolar mania: A distinct clinical entity? *American Journal of Psychiatry*, 1979, *136*, 1420–1423.

Stern, S., and Mendels, J. Affective disorders. In A. Kazdin, A. Bellak, M. Hersen (Eds.), *New Perspectives in abnormal psychology*. New York: Oxford, 1980.

Winokur, G. Genetic principles in the clarification of clinical issues in affective disorders. In A. Mandell & A. Mandell (Eds.), *Psychochemical research in Man*. New York: 1969.

Winokur, G. Mania-depression: Family studies, genetics, and relation to treatment. In M. Lipton, A. DiMascio, & K. Killiam (Eds.), *Psychopharmacology*. New York: Raven, 1978.

Depression in an Older Adult

The Case of Mrs. A   The following article (Gallagher & Frankel, 1980) describes treatment techniques oriented toward controlling depressive behavior in an older adult, especially where this depression is not the result of an organic dysfunction. In fact, there are no evident traumas leading to the depression in this older woman. Rather, it appears as if she has gradually moved out of the sources of enjoyment and reinforcement in her life.

Even though depression can be generated by hormonal changes, as well as by significant trauma, any process that results in a loss of reinforcement sources, whether abrupt or gradual, also results in depressive behaviors, particularly those marked by slowed motor behaviors and withdrawal from social interactions. At the same time, the ensuing depression and accompanying complaints may be used to manipulate others, as we see in Mrs. A's case. She becomes a focal point in the family's interactions, a reaction to her expressed belief that she was no longer relevant to the family. Her depression has moved her back into being the focus of concern. The treatment therefore attempts to render these manipulations irrelevant and at the same time tries to increase meaningful behaviors for her, such as by teaching the grandchildren how to interact with her. As she moved into a higher rate of interaction with them, she developed a greater sense of meaning, which seemed to be the critical factor in this particular case of depression. Gallagher and Frankel (1980) are adept at describing the psychotherapy technique that focuses on manipulative interactions between people, a technique particularly associated with the work of Jay Haley (1963). This therapy has proven to be particularly useful in dealing with groups that have meaningful relationships with each other, as in families and marital couples.

Depression in (An) Older Adult(s): A Moderate Structuralist Viewpoint

Dolores Gallagher and A. Steven Frankel

The Client

Mrs. A, a 74-year-old white woman, was brought to a therapist by her married daughter, Mrs. B. The daughter explained that her mother had been depressed for some time. Her mood had not changed for several years, and Mrs. B brought her mother in because she could find no way to cheer her up, despite the fact that Mrs. A had a few friends and lived close enough to her family to spend at least one or two weekends per month with them. Mrs. A was also reported to keep busy by going with groups of older adults to plays, museums, and the like.

Mrs. A had worked part-time from her husband's death (she was then 55) until she was 65, when she was forced to retire, due to her company's mandatory retirement policy. She had remained active and in good physical health after her retirement, but when she reached the age of 70 or 71, she began to become depressed. Her daughter and son-in-law were financially successful, and even though Mrs. A herself was not facing financial difficulties, they provided money for her to take trips, and bought her special gifts that were out of her price range. Her family physician felt that Mrs. A

From: Gallagher, D., and Frankel, H. Depression in (an) older adult(s): A moderate structuralist viewpoint. *Psychotherapy: Theory, Research and Practice*, 1980, *17*, 101–104. Reprinted by permission of *Psychotheraphy: Theory, Research and Practice*.

was not organically depressed, and recommended psychological intervention within six months of the onset of the depression. The family felt that she would soon come out of it, and waited until they finally realized that it would not lift by itself.

The therapist felt that adequate understanding and treatment could not be provided without a full grasp of how the family interacted together, despite Mrs. B's comments. It was thus decided to interview Mrs. A's entire family, including her daughter, son-in-law, younger (by two years) sister, and two grandchildren. During the interview the following interactions were noted:

1. *Mrs. B. seemed both worried about and angry with her mother. She repeatedly attempted to get her mother to talk about what was "bothering" her, but became increasingly frustrated as Mrs. A indicated that she didn't know what was wrong. Mrs. B would respond to these remarks by looking over at her husband, but she made no comments to him.*

2. *Mr. B said little directly to Mrs. A. His comments were directed toward the therapist, and were primarily about the ways in which the family had tried to help Mrs. A over the years. He diverted his gaze away from his wife whenever she looked at him.*

3. *Mrs. A's sister sat next to Mrs. A. She would frequently hold Mrs. A's hand and cry. She repeatedly tried to comfort Mrs. A by indicating that it was probably natural "to feel a little down" as one gets older. With each utterance of this nature, Mrs. B glared at her aunt until finally the aunt looked at Mrs. B and said: "I know you don't like it when I say things like that, but you'll see. It is natural to feel down when you get older. I feel down myself, but I just don't let it show.*

4. *Mrs. A's grandchildren played by themselves in a corner of the room. At several points during the interview, they would pick up a toy and bring it over to show their grandmother. Mrs. B would intercept them and send them back to the corner, with the injunction: "Don't bother Grandma, can't you see that she's upset?".*

5. *Mrs. A was depressed in mood. She frequently stated that she really wasn't all that bad off, and that she didn't want her family to make a big thing of it. She stated that the family interview was taking up too much of the therapist's time, and offered to "forget the whole thing."*

Relevant Literature Depression is a common problem at all ages, but recent reports suggest that it is most prevalent in the young and the old. While rates for women are consistently higher than for men, the incidence of depression in older men is rising (Gurland, 1976; Weissman & Klerman, 1977; Zung, 1967). These findings, along with the increasing interest in understanding and treating the problems of older adults, suggest a growing need for theory, research, and clinical approaches that bear on depression in the older adult.

In Akiskal and McKinney's (1975) review of depression research, few of the 10 conceptual models currently used to account for depression include interpersonal positions, in which symptoms are approached either in terms of interpersonal utility or interpersonal message value. (It should be noted here that the depressive phenomena of current interest are not those which might be called "endogenous," "psychotic," "senile," "manic-depressive," or "with organic brain syndrome".) With some exceptions (Beck, 1967, 1976; Lewinsohn et al., 1976), few research studies report success in treatment of depression, and many practitioners view it as a self-limiting condition that will improve substantially with the passage of time.

A Structural Approach

Introduction. Structural approaches to pathology and change have been around for some time (see e.g., Haley, 1963), but have only recently begun to break into psychology's "mainstream" (see Lazarus, 1977). Simply put, structuralists see symptoms as messages within interpersonal communications systems or networks. These networks are said to be governed or to reflect a set of rules (see Minuchin, 1974; Watzlawick et al., 1967) which describe, define, and delimit the behaviors which occur within the system. Structural therapists attempt to tease out (but not out loud) the rules governing any given system and then promote change by modifying the structure and process of the system. Rule changes are thus believed to be accompanied by changes in interpersonal messages, and therefore an occasion exists for a removal of symptoms (since symptoms are themselves messages) (see Watzlawick et al., 1974).

As Haley (1977) points out, the structural model is not seen as a model of human behavior in general (although there is some apparent disagreement within the structuralist ranks on this issue), as much as it is an heuristic for particular symptoms in particular contexts (see Bateson, 1972; Sluzki & Ransom, 1976). Thus, for us to talk about the model's application to "depression in older adults" might be somewhat less warranted than our talking about the model's application to a given case. Nonetheless, we believe that the way of thinking offered by the structural model is helpful for many aspects of psychological dysfunction, and we therefore trust that the reader will generalize beyond the present case to other cases of this type.

While a complete statement of the model is not within the scope of the present paper, the part of it dealing with communicational rules deserves some elaboration, as it bears directly on the problem of depression. Watzlawick et al. (1967) describe two rule structures which have received considerable attention by structuralists; symmetry and complementarity. First described by Bateson (1935), symmetrical interactions are characterized by two partners behaving as mirror images of each other (e.g., A boasts, then B boasts louder, then A boasts still louder). Complementary interactions are characterized by one partner "yielding" to another (e.g., A boasts, then B praises A).

Basic communicational rules such as symmetry and complementarity may be overlaid with other rules, such that the descriptive power of the model is both complicated and enriched. For example, "a third type of relationship has been suggested—'metacomplementary'—in which A lets or forces B to take charge of him" (Watzlawick et al., 1967, p. 69).

From a moderate structuralist position (e.g., one which sees certain communicational rules as descriptive of a given individual's relationships over time), "depressives" are seen as people who show a repeated tendency to engage in metacomplementary behavior, characterized by seeking others to support and encourage them, but becoming more depressed as those efforts repeatedly fail. Clinicians often label such behavior as "passive-aggressive," "passive-dependent," but these labels have not led to particular fruitful therapeutic interventions, and have led to a virtual absence of research. Some examples, however, of successful structural interventions have been described (see e.g., Watzlawick et al., 1974, p. 34; Minuchin, 1974, pp. 158–188).

Further, metacomplementary interactions are paradoxical in nature, in that two messages are sent, but the messages are conflictual in nature (e.g., I am unhappy—my unhappiness is not to be taken seriously). By behaving paradoxically, depressed individuals perpetuate their depression, and render ineffective all of those who try to help. The depressed individual is thus an active participant in a homeostatic network that serves to maintain the depression (see Hoffman, 1971).

Beyond the individual. But paradoxical interactions are interactions. That is, they are not characteristics of individuals, but rather are characteristics of interpersonal systems. Thus, an attempt to understand (and change) metacomplementary (in this case, depressive) interactions calls for an examination of the ways in which broad and complex interpersonal systems are themselves characterized by paradoxes. The understanding of the relationship between aging and depression must therefore include more than limited reinforcers, death instincts, social isolation, and cognitive dissonance.

It is interesting to note that while depression tends to increase with age (Gurland, 1976; Weissman & Klerman, 1977; Zung, 1967), older people are less likely to seek treatment than are their younger counterparts (Goldfarb, 1974). At the level of individual report, older people indicate that depressed feelings are associated with the approach of death, physical and mental incapacitation, absence of personal and vocational value to their families and communities, etc. Further, they report feelings of futility with regard to attempts, on their parts or on the parts of others, to remedy the circumstances. Often they appear resigned to their depression.

At a broader level, they receive many messages that their own impressions are in fact accurate; that there is nothing to be done about it; that they should accept their condition and not complain about it. In communicational terms, person A (society, family, and friends) sends the paradoxical messages, "It's sensible to be depressed, so why be depressed about it?" Person B (the older adult) responds with the paradoxical, "I'm complaining about my situation, but since that's the way it's supposed to be, don't take me seriously—don't consider my complaint a complaint."

It is not surprising that older adults are under-represented among the population receiving psychological treatment for depression. To ask for help would be to complain about things that are not (by "agreement" between the individual and the broader interpersonal network) reasonable to complain about. Thus, older people are by and large an active part of a system which renders them distressed, and which makes complaining about that distress illegitimate—a paradoxical communication pattern.

The Client(s)   At the end of the first session, everyone agreed that the family should do whatever it could to help Mrs. A feel better. The therapist thus assigned the family the following tasks:

1. Since the grandchildren "obviously" upset Mrs. A, they were to be taught how to interact with her. Mr. B was to be the instructor, since he had grown up with a grandmother in his home, and thus was an expert on these matters. Thus, Mrs. A was to visit her family with some frequency, and during the visits, Mr. B was to supervise the children's play with Mrs. A. Mrs. B was to absent herself from the home on these occasions.
2. Mrs. A's sister was to watch Mr. B teach his children how to interact with their grandmother, and report to Mrs. B concerning their mutual progress.
3. At the next family meeting, Mrs. B was to report the results of the task to the therapist (after Haley, 1977).

At the next meeting, Mrs. A's mood was improved. During most of the session, she played with her grandchildren and talked to her sister while Mrs. B watched with her husband and a co-therapist from behind a one-way mirror (after Minuchin, 1974). At the end of this session, Mr. and Mrs. B discussed the possibility of Mrs. A staying with the children while the Bs went off on a weekend. They were concerned about whether she could handle the "pressure" for a weekend, but agreed to have Mrs. A and her sister inform them when there was mutual agreement that Mrs. A was "ready" for the task.

At a six-month follow-up, Mrs. A's mood was considerably improved. She indicated that she had her "ups and downs," but that she was generally pleased with the way things had been going. She had stayed with her grandchildren three times during the six-month period, had talked with her daughter less than before treatment, and remained active with her friends and outside interests.

Conclusions   Each case must, of course, be considered on its own, with appropriate interventions developed and utilized. We suggest that the structural approach offers a helpful way to view problems like Mrs. A's and the many people like her when they don't involve intact family structures. Our point is that the metacomplementary interaction pattern may be found with many older (and younger, for that matter) depressed people, and that regardless of whether one does individual, group or family therapy, a recognition of the pattern offers a variety of treatment alternatives that may be obscured in other models. The clinician who does individual therapy, in particular, must attend to the pattern so as to avoid taking the position that society and family so often take with such people—that there is plenty to complain about, and since there's nothing to be done about it but to "experience" it, why complain?

REFERENCES

Akiskal, H. McKinney, W. Overview of research in depression. *Archives of General Psychiatry*, 32, 285–304, 1975.

Bateson, G. Culture contact and schizmogenesis. *Man*, 35, 178–183, 1935.

Bateson, G. *Steps to an ecology of mind*. New York: Ballantine, 1972.

Beck, A. *Depression*. New York: Harper & Row, 1967.

Beck, A. *Cognitive therapy and the emotional disorder*. New York: International Universities Press, 1976.

Goldfarb, A. Masked depression in the elderly. In S. Lease (Ed.), *Masked Depression*. New York: Aronson, 1974.

Gurland, B. The comparative frequency of depression in various age groups, *Journal of Gerontology*, 31, 283–292, 1976.

Haley, J. *Strategies of psychotherapy*. New York: Grune & Stratton, 1963.

Haley, J. *Problem-solving therapy*. San Francisco: Jossey-Bass, 1977.

Hoffman, L. Deviation-amplifying process in natural groups. In J. Haley (Ed.), *Changing families*. New York: Grune & Stratton, 1971.

Lazarus, A. Has behavior therapy outlived its usefulness? *American Psychologist*, 32, 550–555, 1977.

Lewinsohn, P., Biglan, A. & Zeiss, A. Behavioral treatment of depression. In P. Davidson (Ed.), *The behavioral management of anxiety, depression, and pain*. New York: Brunner-Mazel, 1976.

Minuchin, S. *Families and family therapy*. Cambridge: Harvard University Press, 1974.

Sluzki, C. & Ransom, D. *Double Bind*. New York: Grune & Stratton, 1976.

Watzlawick, P., Beavin, J. & Jackson, D. *Pragmatics of human communication*. New York: Norton, 1967.

Watzlawick, P., Weakland, J. & Fisch, R. *Change.* New York: Norton, 1974.

Weissman, M. & Klerman, G. Sex differences in the epidemiology of depression. *Archives of general psychiatry,* 34, 98–111, 1977.

Zung, W. Factors influencing the self-rating depression scale. *Archives of general psychiatry,* 16, 543–547, 1967.

Comment The case of Mrs. A is an example of exogenous (or reactive) depression, which is frequently observed in older adults. Reactive depressions are often precipitated by loss in the family, social, or work environment, and in older adults are commonly related to loneliness, loss of occupational status, and/or the person's reaction to declining physical and cognitive capacities. Most older widows and widowers develop primary symptoms of depression within a few months of the spouse's death. However, in most of these cases, the depressive episodes are self-limiting and disappear within a few months without intervention. Close family ties and the opportunity to develop substitute interpersonal bonds (through children, grandchildren, siblings, friends, remarriage) are variables that distinguish the time-limited depressions and those which require intervention.

The rapid response of Mrs. A. to relatively minimal intervention illustrates the extent to which mood and self-esteem can be successfully altered with environmental modifications. Mrs. A. had been unable to develop a sense of purpose and involvement in her daughter's family, except through complaints about her loneliness and depression. The essence of treatment was to teach the family new ways of interacting and to formulate a strategy to increase the attention and affection for Mrs. A through appropriate channels. Once these goals were achieved, the depression lifted.

The Anxiety Disorders

In the Anxiety Disorders, anxiety is either rather consistently experienced or at least occurs when the person attempts to master the symptoms. Generally, this category replaces the former Neuroses category, which included disorders in which anxiety was presumed to be "controlled unconsciously and automatically by conversion, displacement and various other psychological mechanisms" (DSM-III, p. 39). The reason for the change was the lack of empirical support for this latter traditional conceptualization. Disorders in which anxiety is not a manifest feature have now been classified elsewhere (for example, as somatoform, dissociative, and affective disorders). Further, some disorders formerly referred to as transient situational disturbances are now included among the Anxiety Disorders in the posttraumatic stress disorder category. Thus, three categories are within the general class of Anxiety Disorders: Phobic disorders, Anxiety states, and Posttraumatic stress disorders.

The essential feature of the Phobic disorders is a consistent and irrational fear of a specific object or situation that results in a strong desire to avoid the phobic stimulus. The individual recognizes that the fear is an overreaction to the actual danger. The three types of phobia are agoraphobia, social phobia, and simple phobia. Agoraphobia, as seen in the case of Agnes in this section, is a fear of being left alone or finding oneself in public places from which escape might be difficult and/or help unavailable in case of sudden incapacitation. In a social phobia, people fear and avoid situations in which they might be open to scrutiny by others. They are afraid of being embarrassed and often avoid such situations as public speaking or being called on in class. The simple phobia diagnosis is a residual category of DSM-III and is often referred to as a specific phobia. The phobic stimulus is an object or situation *other* than being alone or of public humiliation or embarrassment (for example, a white rat in the classic case of Peter, the case presented first in this section). The simple phobia is the most common Phobic disorder; agoraphobics are likely to be more severely disturbed.

There are three Anxiety states: Panic disorder, Generalized anxiety disorder, and Obsessive compulsive disorder. In a Panic disorder, the person experiences at least three unpredictable panic attacks within a three-week period (not resulting from heavy physical exertion or true actual threats to life). The sudden panic attacks involve anxiety or even terror and are accompanied by four physical manifestations such as palpitations, chest discomfort, unsteady feelings, trembling, and so forth. The generalized anxiety disorder is characterized by consistent physiologically experienced anxiety of at least one month's duration in an adult who does not present a primary syndrome manifesting phobias, panic attacks, obsessions, or compulsions. The diagnostic emphasis is on muscle tension, apprehension, and autonomic overreactivity. The obsessive-compulsive disorder, discussed in detail in the upcoming case history of Bess, is a relatively common and debilitating disorder that is often difficult to treat. This disorder probably fits least well in the overall category of the Anxiety Disorders since actual anxiety is often not observed. However, most observers agree that anxiety was at least at some point generic to the obsessions and/or compulsions.

The Posttraumatic stress disorders are reactions to psychologically traumatic events that are generally beyond the range of normal human experiences and that would elicit symptoms in most people (for example, rape or assault, kidnapping, military combat, and disasters). The characteristic response involves reexperiencing the traumatic event, depressive and/or withdrawal responses, and a variety of autonomic symptoms. Simple bereavement or upset about marital or business problems are considered to be normal experiences and unlikely precipitants of Posttraumatic stress disorders. The two subtypes of Posttraumatic stress disorders are acute, and chronic or delayed. In the acute subtype, the onset of symptoms occurs within six months of the upsetting event and duration of symptoms is less than six months. In the chronic or delayed subtype, symptoms persist for at least six months (chronic) and/or the onset of symptoms is at least six months after the trauma (delayed). These latter patterns have been commonly noted in veterans of combat in Vietnam and are described in the case of the "Postman" in this section.

The first case in this section is the classic case of Peter, a simple phobia, as described by Mary Cover Jones (1924).

REFERENCE

American Psychiatric Association. *Diagnostic and Statistical Manual of Mental Disorders (DSM-III)*, 3rd ed. Washington, D.C.: American Psychiatric Association, 1980.

A Laboratory Study of Fear

The Case of Peter The concept of a phobia is basic to this section. For this reason, the first case presented is the classic case of Peter, authored by Mary Cover Jones. Watson and Watson (1921), in the only study referenced by Jones, had already demonstrated that a phobia could be created under laboratory conditions. Jones logically follows through to the next stage, and certainly a more immediately useful step, of demonstrating how a phobia can be eliminated under controlled conditions.

Jones does note that even though Peter is cured of his phobia, further psychological disorder is probable, given his home conditions. For this reason, there is now more attention to follow-up assessments of a cure and toward efforts at prevention and the development of positive habits. In any case, it is tribute to her that the gist of her technique is still used in treating phobias today, especially if the phobia is relatively mild and simple.

A Laboratory Study of Fear: The Case of Peter

Mary Cover Jones

As part of a genetic study of emotions, a number of children were observed in order to determine the most effective methods of removing fear responses.

The case of Peter illustrates how a fear may be removed under laboratory conditions. His case was selected from a number of others for the following reasons:

1. Progress in combating the fear reactions was so marked that many of the details of the process could be observed easily.
2. It was possible to continue the study over a period of more than three months.
3. The notes of a running diary show the characteristics of a healthy, normal, interesting child, well adjusted, except for his exaggerated fear reactions. A few descriptive notes show something of his personality:

Remarkably active, easily interested, capable of prolonged endeavor. . . . A favorite with the children as well as with the nurses and matrons. . . . Peter has a healthy passion for possessions. Everything that he lays his hands on is his. As this is frequently disputed by some other child, there are occasional violent scenes of protest. These disturbances are not more frequent than might be expected in a three-year-old, in view of the fact that he is continually forced to adjust to a large group of children, nor are they more marked in Peter's case than in others of his age. Peter's IQ at the age of two years and ten months was 102 on

From: Jones, Mary Cover. A laboratory study of fear: The case of Peter. *Pedagogical Seminary* and *Journal of Genetic Psychology*, 1924, *31*, 308–315. Reprinted by permission of the Journal Press.

the Kuhlmann Revision of the Binet. At the same time he passed five of the three-year tests on the Stanford Revision. In initiative and constructive ability, however, he is superior to his companions of the same mental age.

4. This case is a sequel to one recently contributed by Dr. Watson and furnished supplementary material of interest in a genetic study of emotions. Dr. Watson's case illustrated how a fear could be produced experimentally under laboratory conditions (Watson & Watson, 1921). A brief review follows: Albert, eleven months of age, was an infant with a phlegmatic disposition, afraid of nothing "under the sun" except a loud sound made by striking a steel bar. This made him cry. By striking the bar at the same time that Albert touched a white rat, the fear was transferred to the white rat. After seven combined stimulations, rat and sound, Albert not only became greatly disturbed at the sight of a rat, but this fear had spread to include a white rabbit, cotton wool, a fur coat, and the experimenter's hair. It did not transfer to his wooden blocks and other objects very dissimilar to the rat.

In referring to this case, Dr. Watson says, "We have shown experimentally that when you condition a child to show fear of an animal, this fear transfers or spreads in such a way that without separate conditioning he becomes afraid of many animals. If you take any one of these objects producing fear and uncondition, will fear of the other objects in the series disappear at the same time? That is, will the unconditioning spread without further training to other stimuli?"

Dr. Watson intended to continue the study of Albert in an attempt to answer this question, but Albert was removed from the hospital and the series of observations was discontinued.

About three years later this case, which seemed almost to be Albert grown a bit older, was discovered in our laboratory.

Peter was two years and ten months old when we began to study him. He was afraid of a white rat, and this fear extended to a rabbit, a fur coat, a feather, cotton wool, etc., but not to wooden blocks and similar toys. An abridgment of the first laboratory notes on Peter reads as follows:

> Peter was put in a crib in a play room and immediately became absorbed in his toys. A white rat was introduced into the crib from behind. (The experimenter was behind a screen). At sight of the rat, Peter screamed and fell flat on his back in a paroxysm of fear. The stimulus was removed, and Peter was taken out of the crib and put into a chair. Barbara was brought to the crib and the white rat introduced as before. She exhibited no fear but picked the rat up in her hand. Peter sat quietly watching Barbara and the rat. A string of beads belonging to Peter had been left in the crib. Whenever the rat touched a part of the string he would say "my beads" in a complaining voice, although he made no objections when Barbara touched them. Invited to get down from the chair, he shook his head, fear not yet subsided. Twenty-five minutes elapsed before he was ready to play about freely.

The next day his reactions to the following situations and objects were noted:

Play room and crib	Selected toys, got into crib without protest
White ball rolled in	Picked it up and held it
Fur rug hung over crib	Cried until it was removed
Fur coat hung over crib	Cried until it was removed
Cotton	Whimpered, withdrew, cried
Hat with feathers	Cried
Blue woolly sweater	Looked, turned away, no fear
White toy rabbit of rough cloth	No interest, no fear
Wooden doll	No interest, no fear

This case made it possible for the experiment to continue where Dr. Watson had left off. The first problem was that of "unconditioning" a fear response to an animal, and the second, that of determining whether unconditioning to one stimulus spreads without further training to other stimuli.

From the test situations which were used to reveal fears, it was found that Peter showed even more marked fear responses to the rabbit than to the rat. It was decided to use the rabbit for unconditioning and to proceed as follows: Each day Peter and three other children were brought to the laboratory for a play period. The other children were selected carefully because of their entirely fearless attitude toward the rabbit and because of their satisfactory adjustments in general. The rabbit was always present during a part of the play period. From time to time Peter was brought in alone so that his reactions could be observed and progress noted.

From reading over the notes for each session it was apparent that there had been improvement by more or less regular steps from almost complete terror at sight of the rabbit to a completely positive response with no signs of disturbance. New situations requiring closer contact with the rabbit had been gradually introduced and the degree to which these situations were avoided, tolerated, or welcomed, at each experimental session, gave the measure of improvement. Analysis of the notes on Peter's reactions indicated the following progressive steps in his degrees of toleration:

A. Rabbit anywhere in the room in a cage causes fear reactions.
B. Rabbit 12 feet away in cage tolerated.
C. Rabbit 4 feet away in cage tolerated.
D. Rabbit 3 feet away in cage tolerated.
E. Rabbit close in cage tolerated.
F. Rabbit free in room tolerated.
G. Rabbit touched when experimenter holds it.
H. Rabbit touched when free in room.

I.   Rabbit defied by spitting at it, throwing things at it, imitating it.

J.   Rabbit allowed on tray of high chair.

K.   Squats in defenseless position beside rabbit.

L.   Helps experimenter to carry rabbit to its cage.

M.   Holds rabbit on lap.

N.   Stays alone in room with rabbit.

O.   Allows rabbit in play pen with him.

P.   Fondles rabbit affectionately.

Q.   Lets rabbit nibble his fingers.

These "degrees of toleration" merely represented the stages in which improvement occurred. They did not give any indications of the intervals between steps, nor of the plateaus, relapses, and sudden gains which were actually evident. To show these features a curve was drawn by using the seventeen steps given above as the Y axis of a chart and the experimental sessions as the X axis. The units are not equal on either axis, as the "degrees of toleration" have merely been set down as they appeared from consideration of the laboratory notes with no attempt to evaluate the steps. Likewise the experimental sessions were not equidistant in time. Peter was seen twice daily for a period and thence only once a day. At one point illness and quarantine interrupted the experiments for two months.

The question arose as to whether or not the points which indicated progress to the experimenter represented real advance and not merely idiosyncratic reactions of the subject. The "tolerance series" as indicated by the experimenter was presented in random order to six graduate students and instructors in psychology to be arranged so as to indicate increase in tolerance, in their judgment. An average correlation of .70 with the experimenter's arrangement was found for the six ratings. This indicates that the experimenter was justified from an a priori point of view in designating the steps to be progressive stages.

The first seven periods show how Peter progressed from a great fear of the rabbit to a tranquil indifference and even a voluntary pat on the rabbit's back when others were setting the example. The notes for the seventh period read:

> Laurel, Mary, Arthur, Peter playing together in the laboratory. Experimenter put rabbit down on floor. Arthur said, "Peter doesn't cry when he sees the rabbit come out." Peter, "No." He was a little concerned as to whether or not the rabbit would eat his kiddie car. Laurel and Mary stroked the rabbit and chattered away excitedly. Peter walked over, touched the rabbit on the back, exulting, "I touched him on the end."

At this period Peter was taken to the hospital with scarlet fever. He did not return for two months, and he showed a significant level of fear reaction when he returned. This was easily explained by the nurse who brought Peter from the hospital. As they were entering a taxi door at the hospital, a large dog, running past, jumped at them. Both Peter and the nurse were very much frightened, Peter so much that he lay back in the taxi pale and quiet, and the nurse debated whether or not to return him to the hospital. This seemed reason enough for his precipitate descent back to the original fear level. Being threatened by a large dog when ill and in a strange place and being with an adult who also showed fear, was a terrifying situation against which our training could not have fortified him.

At this point we began another method of treatment, that of "direct conditioning." Peter was seated in a high chair and given food which he liked. The experimenter brought the rabbit in a wire cage as close as she could without arousing a response which would interfere with the eating. Through the presence of the pleasant stimulus (food) whenever the rabbit was shown, the fear was eliminated gradually in favor of a positive response. Occasionally also, other children were brought in to help with the "unconditioning." These facts are of interest in following the charted progress. The first decided rise was due to the presence of another child who influenced Peter's reaction. The notes for this day read:

> Lawrence and Peter sitting near together in their high chairs eating candy. Rabbit in cage put down twelve feet away. Peter began to cry. Lawrence said, "Oh, rabbit." Clambered down, ran over and looked in the cage at him. Peter followed close and watched.

The next two decided rises occurred on the day when a student assistant, Dr. S., was present. Peter was very fond of Dr. S. whom he insisted was his "papa." Although Dr. S. did not directly influence Peter by any overt suggestions, it may be that having him there contributed to Peter's general feeling of well being and thus indirectly affected his reactions. The fourth rise was, like the first, due to the influence of another child. Notes for the twenty-first session read:

> Peter with candy in high chair. Experimenter brought rabbit and sat down in front of the tray with it. Peter cried out, "I don't want him," and withdrew. Rabbit was given to another child sitting near to hold. His holding the rabbit served as a powerful suggestion; Peter wanted the rabbit on his lap, and held it for an instant.

The decided drop was caused by a slight scratch when Peter was helping to carry the rabbit to his cage. The rapid ascent following shows how quickly he regained lost ground.

In one of our last sessions, Peter showed no fear although another child was present who showed marked disturbance at sight of the rabbit.

An attempt was made from time to time to see what verbal organization accompanied this process of "unconditioning." Upon Peter's return from the hospital, the following conversation took place:

E: (experimenter): What do you do upstairs, Peter? (The laboratory was upstairs.)

P: I see my brother. Take me up to see my brother.

E: What else will you see?

P: Blocks.

Peter's reference to blocks indicated a definite memory as he played with blocks only in the laboratory. No further response of any significance could be elicited. In the laboratory two days later (he had seen the rabbit once in the meantime), he said suddenly, "Beads can't bite me, beads can only look at me." Toward the end of the training an occasional "I like the rabbit," was all the language he had to parallel the changed emotional organization.

Early in the experiment an attempt was made to get some measure of the visceral changes accompanying Peter's fear reactions. On one occasion Dr. S. determined Peter's blood pressure outside the laboratory and again later, in the laboratory while he was in a state of much anxiety caused by the rabbit's being held close to him by the experimenter. The diastolic blood pressure changed from 65 to 80 on this occasion. Peter was taken to the infirmary the next day for the routine physical examination and developed there a suspicion of medical instruments which made it inadvisable to proceed with this phase of the work.

Peter has gone home to a difficult environment but the experimenter is still in touch with him. He showed in the last interview, as on the later portions of the chart, a genuine fondness for the rabbit. What has happened to the fear of the other objects? The fear of the cotton, the fur coat, feathers, was entirely absent at our last interview. He looked at them, handled them, and immediately turned to something which interested him more. The reaction to the rats, and the fur rug with the stuffed head was greatly modified and improved. While he did not show the fondness for these that was apparent with the rabbit, he had made a fair adjustment. For example, Peter would pick up the tin box containing frogs or rats and carry it around the room. When requested, he picked up the fur rug and carried it to the experimenter.

What would Peter do if confronted by a strange animal? At the last interview the experimenter presented a mouse and a tangled mass of angleworms. At first sight, Peter showed slight distress reactions and moved away, but before the period was over he was carrying the worms about and watching the mouse with undisturbed interest. By "unconditioning" Peter to the rabbit, he has apparently been helped to overcome many superfluous fears, some completely, some to a less degree. His tolerance of strange animals and unfamiliar situations has apparently increased.

The study is still incomplete. Peter's fear of the animals which were shown him was probably not a directly conditioned fear. It is unlikely that he had ever had any experience with white rats, for example. Where the fear originated and with what stimulus, is not known. Nor is it known what Peter

146

would do if he were again confronted with the original fear situation. All of the fears which were "unconditioned" were transferred fears, and it has not yet been learned whether or not the primary fear can be eliminated by training the transfers.

Another matter which must be left to speculation is the future welfare of the subject. His "home" consists of one furnished room which is occupied by his mother and father, a brother of nine years and himself. Since the death of an older sister, he is the recipient of most of the unwise affection of his parents. His brother appears to bear him a grudge because of this favoritism, as might be expected. Peter hears continually, "Ben is so bad and so dumb, but Peter is so good and so smart!" His mother is a highly emotional individual who can not get through an interview, however brief, without a display of tears. She is totally incapable of providing a home on the $25 a week which her husband steadily earns. In an attempt to control Peter she resorts to frequent fear suggestions. "Come in Peter, someone wants to steal you." To her erratic resorts to discipline, Peter reacts with temper tantrums. He was denied a summer in the country because his father "forgets he's tired when he has Peter around." Surely a discouraging outlook for Peter.

But the recent development of psychological studies of young children and the growing tendency to carry the knowledge gained in the psychological laboratories into the home and school induce us to predict a more wholesome treatment of a future generation of Peters.

REFERENCE

Watson, J. B., & Watson, R. R. Studies in infant psychology. *Scientific Monthly*, 1921.

Comment Jones's article is a precursor to the major behavioral techniques for the control of anxiety. Her method of bringing the feared object closer and closer (either physically or in the imagination), while the anxiety level is controlled, eventually evolved into one of the first systematized behavioral techniques, that of systematic desensitization (SDT) (Wolpe, 1958). Jones's first measure of change in Peter was that he tolerated the close presence of the white rat; although, of course, he could have been paralyzed with fear. However, he did report "I like the rabbit" (an early form of self-report data), and his blood pressure readings suggested the absence of anxiety.

REFERENCE

Wolpe, J. *Psychotherapy by reciprocal inhibition.* Stanford, Ca.: Stanford University Press, 1958.

Agoraphobia

The Case of Agnes The primary symptom in agoraphobia is an irrational fear of leaving one's home and its immediate surroundings. Agoraphobics often insist that friends or family members accompany them when they leave their "safe" area. As a result, they eventually become tiresome and thus aversive to those around them, which of course compounds the disorder. Agoraphobia is quite common and is considered to be the most severe of the phobic disorders (Chambless & Goldstein, 1980).

Phobic disorders generally consist of knowingly irrational and unreasonable fears of an object or situation, along with the accompanying secondary avoidance behaviors. In agoraphobia, these avoidance behaviors focus on situations in which one might be left alone or be unable to attain help from others if some catastrophe were to occur (Sinnott et al., 1981). Agoraphobia is more frequently diagnosed in women, especially those who are in their late teens and early twenties. Sometimes the age of onset is much later, as is the case when a woman who has been an active housewife all her life becomes agoraphobic in response to the "empty nest" syndrome; that is, her children leave home and she needs to develop a new lifestyle.

In the DSM–III, Agoraphobia is defined as the persistent avoidance of any situation, particularly being alone, where people fear they could not be helped or reach help in the event of an "emergency."

Agnes

Agnes is a thin, reasonably attractive forty-three-year-old Caucasian female who was brought to the community mental health center in the eastern seaboard city in which she lived. Her twenty-two-year-old daughter brought her to the clinic, stating that Agnes was driving her crazy with requests that she accompany her everywhere. Agnes reports that she has experienced agoraphobic symptoms off and on during the last seven years, but the intensity has increased substantially in the last six months. Even when not experiencing agoraphobia, she shows at least a moderate level of tension and anxiety.

For the past four years, Agnes has also suffered with what she refers to as "heart disease." She has often taken herself to a cardiologist, complaining of rapid or irregular heartbeats. The physician always reassured her that he saw no pathology and stated he felt that it was probably a result of anxiety and tension. He advised her to exercise regularly and prescribed tranquilizers for any severe episodes of anxiety. Agnes occasionally uses the tranquilizers, but not to any significant extent. It is interesting that she has never ex-

perienced any of the symptoms at home, even though she does rather heavy housework without any assistance.

The agoraphobic pattern took a severe turn for the worse six months ago during the middle of winter, while Agnes was visiting her daughter. Her daughter had taken her own child to a movie, leaving Agnes alone in their home. There had been a severe snowstorm the day before. It was difficult for cars to get about, and Agnes became fearful that she was isolated. She tried to call her sister who lives in a nearby city, only to find that the phone was dead. At this point, she began to panic, noticed her heart beating rapidly, and thought she was going to have a heart attack. When Agnes's daughter eventually came home after the movie and some shopping, Agnes was extremely distraught. She was lying on the couch crying and moaning and had started to drink to try to lose consciousness. After her daughter had returned, Agnes continued to drink, and with the added reassurance of her daughter, she managed to fall asleep. When she awakened, she felt better and refused to seek help for her fears. In the last six months, she has had other similar experiences of near panic at the thought of being alone.

Agnes's husband, who is a sales representative for a national manufacturing company, spends a lot of time on the road. When he is home, he refuses to listen to Agnes's complaints. But the problem is not as apparent then, since Agnes relaxes considerably when her husband accompanies her on outings. Even though she can acknowledge that her behaviors are absurd and not warranted by demands in her environment, Agnes is still compelled to perform within this pattern. Naturally, there is an accompanying level of depression, since she has a sense of helplessness about controlling the events of her world. In that sense, she reflects the phenomenon referred to as "learned helplessness" (Klee & Meyer, 1979).

Agnes did not have a difficult or unhappy childhood. Her father was very authoritarian and discouraged rebellion in his children, though he was otherwise warm and affectionate with them. Her mother was passive and submissive and manifested mild agoraphobia herself though she would never have been allowed to seek professional help for her condition.

Agnes's father had a moderate drinking problem and was particularly prone to whip Agnes's older brother when he was intoxicated. This older brother was the one family member who was overtly rebellious and independent.

Throughout her school years, Agnes was described as a "good student" and as "teacher's pet." She did have one or two girl friends with whom she could talk to about her worries, but she was not active socially. She did not participate in school activities and was not *very outgoing with other students. Because Agnes was somewhat plain in appearance, she was not "pulled out" of her withdrawal by any males who might have shown some interest. When free of school and school work, she assisted her mother in domestic duties.*

Following high school graduation, Agnes took a job as a secretary with hopes of saving money for college. She did not make enough at first, and had to remain at home. When she was twenty years of age, she met her husband at a church gathering, and they were married within the year. She continued her work as a secretary in order to help him finish his last year of college. Her husband was stable and undemonstrative and, like her father, was a bit authoritarian. Agnes thus found it easy to become passive and dependent in response to him. She continued to long for a college degree, but never really made any efforts to pursue it. After the birth of her daughter, she had another pregnancy, which ended in a miscarriage. This upset her so much that she refused to think of becoming pregnant again. Throughout the early years of her marriage, Agnes was stable in her functioning and only occasionally showed nervousness or anxiety. Yet, as noted above, in recent years she has shown increased problems.

Etiology A number of factors in Agnes's background make it understandable that she would eventually develop an agoraphobic response. First, she had always been timid and shy; it is probable that genetic temperament factors at least partially influenced her development in this pattern. But the pattern was also greatly facilitated by her parents. Her father was clear in what types of behaviors he expected. He did not want any rebellious behaviors, particularly from his daughter, and was quick to suppress any show of such behavior. On the other hand, he was affectionate, and his affection was clearly reserved for times when deference to his authority was apparent. Agnes's mother was a classic model for agoraphobic behavior. She was deferent and passive, and at the same time showed anxiety coping patterns that had an agoraphobic quality to them. She also kept Agnes involved in domestic activities through late adolescence, which did not encourage her to experiment with new and independent roles.

Agnes's lack of physical attractiveness precluded being drawn out of her developing withdrawal patterns by attention from males, and her lack of social or athletic interests reinforced her lack of attention from peers. When Agnes eventually married, her husband's similarity to her father's authoritarianism facilitated the promotion of passive and dependent behaviors. Even though she hoped someday to return to college and develop a career, she never made any efforts to bring this to fruition. It is probable that her husband would have quashed this desire.

Agnes's miscarriage was her first panic-like response, but it was controlled by the structure of the hospital and the sedative medication she received. The miscarriage was a tremendous threat, since it was in the area of child caring that she had found her primary source of self-definition. She carried a fear of reexperiencing this panic, and as a result avoided future pregnancies while throwing herself into the care of her home and daughter. It is interesting that while Agnes's husband demanded passivity in his wife, he allowed and reinforced independent and even masculine behaviors in his daughter. Such behaviors provided him with a companion in fishing and golf, skills his wife had never considered developing. This allowed the daughter to escape the cycle that had been passed to Agnes from her mother and probably from other women in the family history before her. Her daughter's independence, however, stressed Agnes because it threatened her own sense of being needed. As her daughter became more independent, Agnes became more liable to anxiety, which then channelled into agoraphobic responses. The heart palpitations and slight arrythymias that naturally accompany anxiety in many individuals provided her with another focus for her anxiety. However, she was not *classically* hypochondriacal (Meister, 1980) since she did not seek out a variety of physicians to look at her symptoms, she did not present a wide variety of symptoms, and in general she attended to the comments and advice of her physician.

Once she had experienced a true panic reaction, she was then sensitized to anticipate a fear of helplessness, a very frightening feeling. As a result, she engineered a wide variety of behaviors to keep her from reexperiencing a panic. The patterns she developed were initially successful, since remaining at home kept her calm. But such a pattern requires giving up much in the world, including the support of her husband and daughter, who increasingly found her behaviors tedious and irritating. As this occurred, she became more isolated, thus coming closer in actuality to the feeling of being alone emotionally and to the consequent panic she feared so much (Sinnott et al., 1981).

Treatment Options

A number of treatments are potentially useful in dealing with agoraphobia. The specific diagnosis that Agnes received was agoraphobia with panic attacks. Incidentally, it should be noted that some of her behaviors might also have suggested the diagnosis of Avoidant Personality Disorder. But there is very little concern about the symptoms in the avoidant personality. The person may be socially isolated and passive, yet seems unconcerned about this behavior and evidences little desire to change it.

Systematic Desensitization (SDT) is commonly used with a wide variety of phobias. SDT can be adapted to group treatment and does not require a substantial number of sessions. It is particularly effective for simple, discrete phobias (Wolpe, 1981; Foa et al., 1980).

If the SDT is done in a group, the experience has the added advantage of providing real-life modeling from the other members of the group. As agoraphobics move through SDT, they may often concomitantly need assertive training. The passivity and timidity common to agoraphobia make assertive training a helpful adjunct. Certain of the tranquilizing drugs, such as propranolol and phenelzine, can aid in controlling the panic attacks associated with the agoraphobia. These drugs are most helpful for individuals who do not initially respond to SDT intervention. The use of drugs, however, has problems of side effects and presents an implicit message that these persons cannot do much to help themselves.

Occasionally, other symptomatology surfaces after the behavioral treatments have dealt with the specific referral symptom. This is not an indication of symptom substitution. In most instances, the other pathology has always been there. When the more debilitating primary symptoms are relieved, the person can turn his or her attention to other problems. Marital problems and secondary gain patterns especially occur with agoraphobia (Sinnott et al., 1981). For example, Agnes's controlling response toward her daughter is this kind of side effect. Insight-oriented psychotherapy can be helpful in breaking the dependence roles that so often interfere with the agoraphobic's development of new responses.

One of the most effective techniques for agoraphobia is implosion therapy, or flooding (Chambless & Goldstein, 1979).

The Treatment of Agnes

Implosion therapy attempts to maximize one's anxiety, whereas SDT attempts to keep it at a minimal state while the person gradually confronts the feared stimuli. Implosion therapy, or flooding, thus is ideal for agoraphobics such as Agnes since she already shows a moderate ongoing level of anxiety. Implosion therapists attempt to maximize anxiety and yet keep the person in continued confrontation with the feared stimuli so that the anxiety peaks, or in the language of the behaviorist, "extinguishes." A cognitive explanation for the extinction phenomenon asserts that the person has simply discovered that the expected catastrophic events do not occur, even under maximal stimulus conditions. As a result, they become aware that there is nothing that warrants their extreme fear and they gain an increased sense of control.

Agnes was sheduled for an open-ended implosion session—one that did not have a built-in time limit. This type of session is standard since it is difficult to predict how long it will take the anxiety to peak. Agnes was asked to imagine different variations of her greatest fears—such as being left alone, being helpless, and going into a panic. The therapist then continually used graphic and vivid language throughout the session to maximize the images in Agnes's imagination. Agnes had been told ahead of time that this technique would bring on anxiety, but she had to commit herself to stay with it, with the assurance that the therapist would be there with her. She did so, and even when the scenes produced intense anxiety, she continued to hold the scenes in her imagination. If she had not done so, the result would have been counter-productive rather than simply neutral. The following excerpt is from the dialogue used in her first treatment session:

Therapist: Agnes, keep imagining the scenes just like you have been doing —you're doing very well. I want you to imagine yourself at your daughter's house. It is a cold bleak day. The wind is howling and all of a sudden the electricity goes out. Imagine that intensely. You rush to the phone and pick it up only to realize the phone is also dead. Now you realize that with the electricity off, the furnace will not turn on and it is gradually getting much colder.

Agnes: I'm scared, I don't want to see that. Can't we stop?

Therapist: No, remember you must go on and keep these images in your mind. You're feeling colder. It's getting darker and now your heart starts to beat wildly. It's not beating right. You can feel it going wrong. You're really scared now and you know that no one's coming back home.

This type of suggestion, along with suggestions concerning being abandoned as an old person, a lonely death, or having another miscarriage, were suggested throughout the three sessions it took for Agnes to begin to be able to face her fear and make some new and positive steps. Her anxiety peaked and extinguished several times in those three sessions, as it is not just one peak and extinction phase that is usually required. Once Agnes began to feel more confident, she was included in group therapy and also had a few marital therapy sessions with her husband. She recovered significantly over a period of five months. Though over the years she is likely to have occasional return bouts of at least a mild form of the agoraphobia, her increasing confidence and positive behaviors predict that she will be able to bounce back and handle those situations.

Comment   Agoraphobia literally means "fear of open spaces." However, the person with agoraphobia may eventually develop an intense fear of any situation outside home—particularly when alone. Agoraphobics often present related fears of dying, fainting, disease, and panic attacks without assistance. Also, more than any other phobic disorder, agoraphobia is associated with other behavior problems, such as exhaustion, tension, obsessive thoughts, headaches, and/or depersonalization. Generally, this disorder has more in common with panic disorders than with the other phobic disorders, which tend to be monosymptomatic, and therefore difficult to treat (Chambless & Goldstein, 1980).

In Agnes's case, the following factors contributed to her debilitating agoraphobia: 1) a probable temperamental predisposition toward excessive organismic arousal to stress; 2) her mother's modeling of mild agoraphobic symptoms; and 3) her father's contingent affection. Against these historical factors, Agnes's response to the miscarriage in her second pregnancy was her first experience with extreme anxiety. She was frightened by the magnitude of her experienced distress and immediately decided to avoid (with certainty) another experience of overwhelming helplessness by refusing to become pregnant again. The typical mild anxiety that pervades the agoraphobic's life between panic episodes was exacerbated in Agnes's case by her own daughter's independence, which threatened Agnes's sense of being needed. These variables combined with Agnes's limited social development and resulted in an inability to cope with her loneliness and anxiety, except through increased withdrawal and fearfulness. Her family's impatience with Agnes's symptoms increased her isolation and encouraged her manipulation of her daughter's affection.

The immediate focus of treatment was Agnes's excessive anxiety, which was successfully treated with implosion therapy. Agnes's anxiety level was allowed to escalate beyond her previous tolerance level so that it would "extinguish" and she could see that her fearfulness was unwarranted. Afterwards, Agnes's social skills deficits and dependence were treated through group and marital therapy. The prognosis for Agnes is favorable, although mild agoraphobic episodes are predicted if unusual psychosocial stress occurs. To the extent that she acquires more adaptive coping responses to stress and effective strategies for decreasing anxiety-provoking events, she can be expected to maintain adequate social functioning and independence. However, she is not so likely to attain fully normal and positive functioning as are persons with a simple or social phobia.

REFERENCES

Chambless, D., and Goldstein, A. The treatment of agoraphobia. In A. Goldstein and E. Foa (Eds.), *Handbook of behavioral interventions.* New York: Wiley, 1980.

Foa, E., Steketee, G., and Ascher, L. Systematic desensitization. In A. Goldstein and E. Foa (Eds.), *Handbook of behavioral interventions.* New York: Wiley, 1980.

Klee, S., and Meyer, R. Prevention of learned helplessness in humans. *Journal of Consulting and Clinical Psychology*, 1979, 47, 411–412.

Meister, R. *Hypochondria.* New York: Taplinger, 1980.

Sinnott, A., Jones, B., and Fordham, A. Agoraphobia: A situational analysis. *Journal of Clinical Psychology*, 1981, 37, 123–127.

Wolpe, J. Behavior therapy versus psychoanalysis: Therapeutic and social implications. *American Psychologist*, 1981, 36, 159–164.

The Obsessive-Compulsive Disorder

The Case of Bess The major diagnostic criterion for the obsessive-compulsive disorder is the presence of persistent and repeated obsessions (images, thoughts, or impulses that are experienced by the individual as a product of an external source apart from personal volition) and/or compulsions, commonly defined as ritual behaviors, such as counting behaviors, repetitive checking of the body, or hand washing, again characterized by a lack of volition. Although the obsessive-compulsive disorder is listed as one of the anxiety disorders in DSM–III, the direct experience of anxiety is not so clearly evident as it is in the other anxiety disorders, where simple observation makes it obvious that the person is suffering anxiety. Rather, in this disorder, the person avoids anxiety by cooperating with obsessions and compulsions. Anxiety is experienced when the person attempts to resist these behaviors. Even though obsessive-compulsive patterns are at least initially recognized as irrational by the person performing them, the individual seldom goes into a panic experience or becomes blatantly upset in the face of bothersome stimuli (Foa & Tillmanns, 1980).

These obsessive-compulsive behaviors are seen as ego-alien, as foreign to one's personality disorder. In the latter category, the behaviors are ego-syntonic; that is, they are not viewed by such persons as in conflict with the essential aspects of their personality.

The obsessive-compulsive disorder has traditionally been thought to be relatively rare, at least as compared to the other anxiety disorders (Gardner, 1965). However, this could be because of a lower rate of reporting the behavior; analogously, people with this disorder control their anxiety better than do other anxiety disorders, such as agoraphobics, so they would feel less pressure to seek treatment. Obsessive compulsives tend to be more intelligent and from a higher social economic class than do other neurotics. This characteristic makes sense, since the minor variants of this disorder, such as meticulousness and persistence, are efficient and productive, particularly in a society that is so immersed in the idea of external achievement (Rachman, 1980).

The diagnostic criteria also include the individual's recognition of the senselessness of the behavior, stress when attempting to change the behavior, and difficulty functioning within a normal given role and in various social situations. Although ritualistic behavior often occurs in schizophrenia, the behavior is delusional rather than ego-alien.

Bess

Bess is an attractive twenty-seven-year-old upper middle-class woman. She lives by herself in a well-kept apartment in one of the best sections in town. Yet, she has few friends, and social activities play a small role in her life. Most evenings, she works rather late and then comes home, fixes her own dinner, and reads or watches television until she gets ready to fall asleep. Frequently, she needs alcohol and a sleeping pill to get to sleep. She is an only child; her parents were divorced when she was ten-years-old. She was primarily raised by her demanding mother, and had sporadic contact with her father. Bess is a successful accountant for a large manufacturing

*firm and spends a lot of time with her work. She is very perfec-
tionistic, but of course this is generally functional in accounting.*

*Bess's mother often expressed her love for her and spent a
great deal of time with her. At times, it was as if she had no other
activities in her world that could give her a sense of meaning. Yet,
Bess does not recall the time with her mother as filled with warmth
or fun. Rather, her mother focused on activities in which Bess could
"improve herself." She was constantly setting up lessons for Bess to
take, and they would usually fight over whether or not Bess was
really trying hard enough at these lessons. When home, her mother
consistently emphasized the virtues of cleanliness and neatness.
There was a lot of struggle between them over these issues. Her
mother would constantly nag her for not having the things in her
room "in order." Bess would work at this task when she was ordered
to do so, but the minute her mother took her attention away, Bess
would allow things to get disorderly. Her mother continually emphasized to her that this attitude would hurt "when she got older,"
yet she never made it clear how it would hurt her.*

*Her mother showed an inordinate concern about cleanliness.
She would make sure that Bess washed her hands thoroughly each
time that Bess went to the bathroom or for any reason touched
herself in the genital area. Her mother was especially repulsed by
the smell of the bathroom and had a variety of deodorants and in-
cense candles available to counteract these odors. Anything rotten or
dirty was lumped into this category and immediately received efforts
toward cleaning and deodorizing.*

*Like most individuals, Bess had times as a child when she felt
unhappy. When she expressed these feelings to her mother, she
would immediately try to talk Bess out of the feelings. Her major
point seemed to be "I love you so much, and spend so much time
with you, so how can you be unhappy." If Bess further expressed her
unhappiness, it would quite clearly upset her mother.*

*Bess enjoyed visiting her father, who lived in a nearby city.
He was more relaxed about the world, though he had not been very
successful and had moved through a series of jobs. He was generally
a happy person and attended to Bess when she was there, though he
seldom kept in contact when she was absent. Her mother was never
happy when Bess went to see her father and subverted this contact
whenever possible. She never failed to take the chance to point out
to Bess how her father's "laziness" had brought him nothing from
the world and implied that he did not support them the way he
should.*

*Though Bess in various ways resisted her mother at home, she
lived out her mother's value system in school. She worked very hard
and was meticulous in her preparation of assignments. Because she*

was higher than average intellectually, she consistently succeeded in school. At the same time, she was seen as a "do-gooder" and was not popular with her peers. She did not get involved in class activities and spent most of her time preparing her lessons and then doing chores around the house.

She also was quite active in the Methodist religion, in which her mother raised her. This was generally a positive experience for her, though there were occasions when she became very upset about whether she "had been saved" or whether she was a "sinner." The upset usually passed quickly as Bess pushed herself further into her school work or into any activity prescribed by her church for dealing with these concerns. As Bess moved into late adolescence, she became more and more beset by erotic fantasies. She was never totally sure whether this was against the rules of her church, but she supposed it was. Bess would try to control these fantasies by getting involved in repetitive tasks or other kinds of activities that distracted her attention. She particularly became a fan of crossword puzzles and jigsaw puzzles. These would occupy her for hours, and her mother was happy to buy her the most complex puzzles available. But occasionally the erotic fantasies arose at a time when Bess had few defenses available, and she would then engage in orgiastic bouts of masturbating.

Bess had surprisingly little difficulty interacting with males on a friendship basis. Yet, she never seemed to know how to deal with the romantic and sexual issues. As a result, she seldom dated anyone for any length of time. She did become enamored of a boy at a nearby college when she was a senior in high school. He constantly pressed her for sex, and she would refuse. However, one night she gave in when they had been drinking too much at a party. They then had sex virtually every day for a couple of weeks, at which time Bess began to fear pregnancy. It turned out her fears were well founded, to the horror of her mother when she was told. She immediately arranged an abortion, and never really allowed Bess to think out whether this was what she wanted. After the abortion, she took Bess on a trip to Europe, during which time she strictly chaperoned her. When they returned, the boyfriend had found another lover, as Bess's mother had hoped.

Bess slipped into the role of the "top student," received many honors, and then easily moved into the consequent role of "up-and-coming young career woman." Her involvement in her job absorbed most of her time, and it was clear that she was a rising star in the firm she worked for. Bess continued to have vague anxieties about dating, marriage, and having a family, and other related issues. She handled these anxieties by throwing herself even harder into her work. At the same time, however, she began to experience symptoms that focused around the issue of cleanliness, a pattern not dissimilar from her mother's.

This concern with cleanliness gradually evolved into a thorough going cleansing ritual, which was usually set off by her touching of her genital or anal area. In this ritual, Bess would first remove all of her clothing in a preestablished sequence. She would lay out each article of clothing at specific spots on her bed, and examine each one for any indications of "contamination." She would then thoroughly scrub her body, starting at her feet and working meticulously up to the top of her head, using certain washcloths for certain areas of her body. Any articles of clothing that appeared to have been "contaminated" were thrown into the laundry. Clean clothing was put in the spots that were vacant. She would then dress herself in the opposite order from which she took the clothes off. If there were any deviations from this order, or if Bess began to wonder if she might have missed some contamination, she would go through the entire sequence again. It was not rare for her to do this four or five times in a row on certain evenings.

As time passed, she began developing a variety of other rituals and obsessive thoughts, usually related to using the toilet, sexual issues, or the encountering of possible "contamination in public places." As her circle of rituals widened, her functioning became more impaired. She was aware of the absurdity of these behaviors, but at the same time felt compelled to go through with them and did not constantly question them. Finally, the behaviors began to intrude on her ability to carry out her work, the one remaining source of meaning and satisfaction in her world. It was then that she referred herself for help.

Etiology One of Freud's primary views of obsessive-compulsive individuals was that these persons were still functioning at the anal-sadistic stage of development and that conflicts over toilet training were critical in their development. This theory has some "face validity" (or apparent truth) in many cases, including Bess's. However, these common concerns about dirt related to toilet training could occur simply because this is one of the first arenas in which parent and child struggle for control of the relationship. It is also usually the first period in which whole sequences of parental behavior are integrated and modeled by the developing child. Hence, it is easy for these types of concerns to become the content of obsessive-compulsive features. It is also clear that these issues are not relevant to a substantial number of obsessive compulsives.

Obsessive compulsives usually model much of their behavior from parents, who are typically "repressors." Repressors are sensitive to the "discomfort of anxiety" (Ellis, 1979) and as a result develop numerous coping patterns to avoid that discomfort. Even though obsessive compulsives do not often report experiencing much present anxiety, they usually manifest it on physiological measures and psychological tests (Rachman, 1980; Meyer, 1982). A common defense against anxiety for the obsessive compulsive is the use of "intellectualization" (talking around the core issue of a conflict in order to avoid its gut level impact). This pattern is effective in many areas, such as school and work. But when it is used to deal with anxiety, it is not effective in the long run.

Bess's development shows most of these factors. Her mother was a thoroughgoing model for obsessive-compulsive behavior, and Bess had no significant access to other models. Her mother was also adept at inculcating guilt, and in addition voided any of Bess's attempts to dissipate her conflicts by voicing and sharing her concerns and upset. Bess's pattern of religious involvement furthered the development of guilt, and, as is common with most adolescents, sexual concerns provided a ready focus for the conflicts.

The rituals that the obsessive compulsive develops serve to distract the individual from fully confronting the experience of anxiety or the feeling of a loss of control. Bess had long ago learned that involvement in academic subjects not only brought her inherent rewards, but at the same time served to distract her from her conflicts and impulses. She feared that if she gave in to the unacceptable impulses, she could not control her behavior. As a result, she often vacillated between overcontrol of impulses and constant indulgence, as was evident in her masturbatory patterns. Like many obsessive compulsives, Bess feared that if she let down her guard and followed her impulses, that she might never regain control, and "control" is important to obsessive compulsives. Hence, any activities that served to distract her were welcomed. Her obsessive interest in crossword and jigsaw puzzles is an instance of an individual's trying to distract oneself in activities that are often pleasant accompaniments to a full life. Her ritual cleansing was another way of distracting herself from the void of meaning in her world and from the anxiety that was always at the edge of her awareness. Yet, as she most feared, she gradually lost control of these patterns and they began to dominate her world even to the point of interfering with the area that had always provided meaning and satisfaction to her—her work.

Treatment Options   A wide variety of treatments have traditionally been applied to the obsessive-compulsive personality. In actuality, none has achieved spectacular success, since this is one of the most difficult neurotic disorders to treat. This difficulty is probably because the conflicts and anxiety have already been well covered over by the obsessive-compulsive patterns. Also, such individuals seem to fear the passivity (that is, loss of control) implied by the "patient role."

Psychoanalysis has had some success with the obsessive-compulsive personality. However, the danger with this technique is that the obsessive-compulsive individual has had a long history of using intellectualization as a defense mechanism (Rabin, 1968), and the technique of free association in psychoanalysis easily lends itself to the abuse of intellectualization. Only if the therapist can skillfully keep the client away from this pattern can psychoanalysis be helpful.

Psychosurgery has had a traditional though unverified reputation of being successful in some cases of obsessive compulsive disorder. But more recent research reviewed by Trotter (1976) suggests that in actuality it is seldom effective. Medication has occasionally been useful in allaying some of the underlying anxiety while the therapist tries to break through the defensive patterns, but in and of itself has not really been significantly helpful.

Several behavioral techniques have been helpful. Implosion therapy, or flooding, a technique described in some detail in the case history on agoraphobia (Stampfl & Lewis, 1967) has occasionally been used. The difficulty here with the technique is that obsessive compulsives are usually so well defended that it is hard to get them actually to maximize their anxiety and experience the peak of the conflict, which is theoretically required. For that reason, most therapists do not choose to use implosion therapy with obsessive compulsives.

A second technique that has been of help is "thought stopping." In this technique, presented in more detail in the case history of Randy, the transvestite, the therapist teaches the client to use a verbal command (such as Stop!) to interrupt the obsessive thoughts or compulsive behaviors as soon as they emerge into awareness. A third technique, not unlike thought stopping, is referred to as Covert Assertion. Here, the client is taught to make a strong positive statement that declares that he or she refuses to proceed with the compelling dictates of the obsessions or compulsions. This statement, often in the form of a declarative sentence, is first asserted out loud with the therapist and is eventually used subvocally any time an obsessive compulsive impulse emerges (Cautela & Wall, 1980).

The fourth technique is Covert Modeling. The client and therapist together construct an imaginary scene in which the client encounters the obsessive or compulsive condition. The client and therapist then also construct an appropriate nonpathological way of countering and dissipating the strength of the obsessive compulsive mechanism (Cautela & Wall, 1980).

In various combinations, these behavioral techniques, particularly those that act to prevent the response early in the sequence (Rachman, 1980), have proven to be as effective as any approach for this most difficult syndrome to change.

Bess's Therapy   Bess's therapist chose to start the treatment with thought stopping (Meyer, 1982). She first asked Bess to let the obsessions just flow freely, and to raise her hand to let the therapist know when she was doing so. Some time after Bess had raised her hand, the therapist shouted "Stop," and then asked Bess to examine her consciousness. Naturally, the train of obsessions had been disrupted. They did this several times, and then the therapist asked Bess herself to shout "Stop" whenever she felt herself in the midst of these obsessions. She was then asked to practice this in her own natural world as well and was given a small portable shock unit to amplify the effect. Whenever Bess shouted "Stop" to herself, she also gave herself a moderately painful electric shock from this unit that she had strapped inconspicuously under her dress. This thought-stopping demonstrated to Bess that her obsessions could actually be controlled. In that sense, it was the basis on which her therapist could train her in new, positive behaviors (Ost et al., 1981).

Bess and her therapist then used the technique of Covert Modeling. They developed an imaginary scene during which, as the feelings of contamination arose, Bess visualized herself first laughing at the concerns. She then visualized herself handling some of the contaminated garments, or even touching herself in the genital or anal area while laughing and seeing herself as confident in the situation. These images were practiced in the therapy hour. She was then instructed always to follow up any thought stopping with the Covert Modeling.

She also contracted with her therapist that if she did not respond as instructed, she was to penalize herself by performing one task from a list of odious (to her) chores that she had composed with her therapist. This list included such things as eating some undesirable foods for supper or unplugging her television set for the entire night. Likewise, each time she had successfully carried out her therapy practices for an entire day, she was allowed to reinforce this by choosing from a list of pleasant activities that they had also constructed, such as attending a very expensive movie, or getting "the works" at her beauty salon.

Together, these techniques helped Bess substantially diminish the obsessive compulsive patterns within four months. She and the therapist also continued to work on the void of positive activities in Bess's life. She was in therapy for approximately two years before she achieved what she considers to be an adequate success. Even so, at various points in the ensuing years, Bess occasionally experienced a re-emergence of the concerns that she had experienced (Rachman, 1980). On one occasion, she did return for several therapy sessions in order to work these through, though she was usually able to deal with any residual patterns by the skills she had learned in the original therapy sessions, plus training in new skills to cope with these impulses (Emmelkamp et al., 1980).

Comment   The obsessive-compulsive disorder is at least initially experienced as a distressing loss of control over one's thoughts and actions and is usually somewhat incapacitating because it interferes with other behaviors and patterns (Emmelkamp et al., 1980; Rachman, 1980). As in Bess's case, the primary goal of treatment is to get such persons to suspend these actions long enough to find out that the dreaded outcomes (usually vaguely conceptualized) will not occur—for example, by the thought-stopping technique that was successful with Bess's compulsions. Another technique that has been successful with compulsive behavior is response prevention. Response prevention involves temporarily blocking the compulsive response so that extinction can occur; for example, dismantling the faucets in order to prevent compulsive hand washing.

Bess was able to diminish her obsessive-compulsive patterns to a substantial degree within four months. Unfortunately, she had developed obsessive-compulsive behaviors over an extended period of time and in response to numerous situations before they became troublesome enough for her to seek professional help. The resulting deficits in social skills and emotional responsiveness required considerable therapeutic attention; thus, her therapy lasted for two years. Even then, obsessive thoughts and compulsive actions are fairly probable respones for her under stress, and minor patterns still occasionally reappear. They will decrease in frequency and intensity as Bess's emotional adjustment and social skills improve.

REFERENCES

Cautela, J., and Wall., C. Covert conditioning in clinical practice. In A. Goldstein and E. Foa (Eds.), *Handbook of behavioral interventions.* New York: Wiley, 1980.

Ellis, A. A note on the treatment of agoraphobics with cognitive modification versus prolonged exposure "in vivo." *Behavior Research and Therapy*, 1979, *17*, 162–164.

Emmelkamp, R., Van Der Helm, M., Van Zanten, B., and Plochg, I. Treatment of obsessive-compulsive patients. *Behavior Research and Therapy*, 1980, *18*, 61–66.

Foa, E., and Tillmanns, A. The treatment of obsessive-compulsive neurosis. In A. Goldstein and E. Foa (Eds.), *Handbook of behavioral interventions.* New York: Wiley, 1980.

Gardner, E. The role of the classification system in outpatient psychiatry. In M. Katz, J. Cole, and W. Barton (Eds.), *The Role and Methodology in Psychiatry and Psychopathology.* Washington, D.C.: U.S. Public Health Service, 1965.

Meyer, R. *The Clinician's Handbook.* Boston: Allyn and Bacon, 1982.

Ost, L., Verremalm, A., and Johansson, J. Individual response patterns and the effects of different behavioral methods in the treatment of social phobia. *Behavior Research and Therapy*, 1981, *19*, 1–16.

Rabin, A. (Ed.). *Projective techniques in personality assessment.* New York: Springer, 1968.

Rachman, S. *Obsessions and compulsions.* Englewood Cliffs, N.J.: Prentice-Hall, 1980.

Stampfl, T., and Lewis, D. Essentials of implosive therapy: A learning theory based psychodynamic behavior therapy. *Journal of Abnormal Psychology*, 1967, *72*, 496–503.

Trotter, S. Federal commission on psychosurgery. *APA Monitor*, 1976, *7*, 4–5.

Posttraumatic Stress Disorder

The Case of Ryan the "Postman" The Posttraumatic Stress Disorder is a maladaptive reaction to a psychologically traumatic event that is usually considered to be outside the average range of human experience, and as such, would seriously distress most people. Its characteristic symptomatology involves: a) the reexperiencing of the traumatic event, b) a reduction of involvement with the external world (a kind of "psychic numbing"), and c) various related autonomic, cognitive, and/or emotional symptoms. The traumatic event, such as military combat or a natural disaster, is usually reexperienced in recurring dreams (often nightmares), persistent memories, and/or dissociative states. The distancing from the external world is commonly seen in lessened affect, decreased interest in activities formerly found to be interesting, and/or detachment from others. Additional symptoms include sleep disruption, hyperalertness, guilt over survival, memory or attention disturbance, and avoidance of stimuli that might arouse memories of the traumatic event.

The disorder is sublabeled *acute* if symptomatology both occurs within six months after the stressor and lasts only six months. It is considered *delayed* if symptoms develop more than six months after the event, and *chronic* if they last longer than six months. The impairment suffered as a result of the disorder ranges widely in severity, with preexisting personality characteristics apparently influencing both etiology and severity of reaction.

This disorder should not be confused with the Adjustment Disorder, a disorder also involving a maladaptive reaction to a stressor. In the Adjustment Disorder, the stressor is usually less severe, more common, and is not vividly reexperienced. The Posttraumatic Stress Disorder category was a late addition to DSM-III, a recognition of the consistant maladaptive reaction processes that follow exposure to atypical and severe stress. The conflict in Vietnam, and its subsequent effects on the participants, particularly played a major role in the recognition of this syndrome.

Ryan, the "Postman"

Ryan, known by his friends in the army as "The Postman," was a twenty-one-year-old Caucasian, first seen by staff psychologists at the Veterans Administration hospital in the fall of 1970. At that time, he quietly stated that he was seeking help at the "request" of his fiancée, who had threatened to break off their engagement unless he did so.

A check into his background revealed that he had been honorably discharged from the army the previous summer following a tour of duty in Vietnam. He had been reserved and aloof on his return home, and his family and friends had simply assumed this was a natural reaction to readjustment to civilian life, noting that he was obviously happy to be home.

163

About a month after his return, to no one's surprise, he announced his engagement to his high school sweetheart. However, he did raise a few eyebrows by taking a job at a local factory instead of returning to college to obtain his degree in forestry, which had been his lifelong dream. He seemed dissatisfied with the job from the beginning. He worked lethargically, grew irritable at the slightest frustration, and remained detached from his fellow workers. It was also about this time that he experienced his first panic-filled dissociative state.

His roommate, an old friend with whom he shared an apartment, recalled that one night, after a particularly rough day at work, Ryan had fallen into a light sleep in a chair while watching television. After turning off the television, his roommate walked across the room to lock the front door. Just as he shoved home the bolt of the dead lock, Ryan awakened and hit the ground yelling something unintelligible. His eyes were wide open, as he rapidly scanned the room. He appeared to be having difficulty breathing, was trembling, and was sweating profusely. After calming down somewhat, he complained of dizziness and "feeling odd," and swore his roommate to secrecy concerning the incident.

Ryan recalled that in the days following that first incident, his irritability and anger grew even worse and he began to have nightmares. The only people with whom he retained even a semblance of closeness were his family and fiancée, and even those relationships lacked their characteristic warmth and spontaneity. In an attempt to break him out of an ever-increasing depression, his fiancée finally convinced him to join her and his grandfather in a quiet stroll through some of the woods on his parents' property. This was a formerly enjoyable activity, but on his return home, he had up to that point declined to go along.

Ryan remembered that during the walk, after some initial apprehension, he had actually felt relaxed for the first time in a long while. However, when a helicopter suddenly flew over, he dropped to a crouched position, frantically scanning the woods and shouting orders. After getting him back to the house, his grandfather and fiancée watched helplessly as he broke down crying, admitting that this had been the second such occurrence. It was at this point that his fiancée responded to his objections to seeking help with the threat of a terminating their engagement.

Ryan's History Ryan was the oldest of two boys and a girl raised in a small town, fifteen miles outside a large northwestern city. His father was a physician who was already forty when Ryan was born, and his mother, eight years younger than his father, dedicated all of her time to her firm though protective upbringing of the children. The family was of "good stock," and serious illness or death were unfamiliar to Ryan as he grew up.

He was polite, bright, and happy as a young boy, and while he enjoyed the company of other people, he also loved being by himself on occasion, particularly outdoors. The family owned several hundred acres, and he spent many weekend afternoons in the woods with his favorite grandfather, who taught him how to hunt and to appreciate nature. Ryan also proved to be quite athletic; and although he lettered in high school basketball and baseball, he never developed an interest in football, somewhat in respect for his mother's worry that it was "too violent."

By the summer of 1968, Ryan was nineteen years old, standing 6 feet tall and weighing 175 pounds. He had grown into a rather independent, yet surprisingly sensitive young man, with an easy-going laugh and a sparkle in his eyes. Though friendly to everyone, he considered himself to have only two or three close friends, along with his steady girlfriend, whom he had dated since his sophomore year in high school. A good student, he had just finished his first year at a state university working toward a degree in forestry when he received his draft notice. Though at the time of his draft lottery he felt that his number was in the "safe" range, he had not anticipated the sharp escalation of United States involvement in Vietnam in 1968. Although understandably unhappy about the two-year interruption in his life plans, he nonetheless accepted the notice as a responsibility he had to fulfill.

Following a tearful farewell and what seemed to him to be a whirlwind training period, Ryan found himself in an Army Ranger unit operating in the Central Highlands of Vietnam. He was a member of a six-man squad that would spend anywhere from four to twelve weeks at a time out in the field. Their mission was to make contact with enemy forces, at which point they would engage the enemy or else radio their position for an air strike and fall back. His initial job, as was that of most men newly rotated into such a squad, was radio operator. This position was "inherited" by most newcomers due to 1) the weight and cumbersomeness of the radio, and 2) the danger involved in carrying it, since the enemy would naturally make a high priority of knocking it out to prevent notification of their position.

Two other positions usually "inherited" were those of the "point" and "slack" men. These two men would walk approximately 15 yards ahead of the other four, with the point man in the lead checking the ground for booby traps, while the slack man followed close behind scanning the cover immediately ahead for any hint of "Charlie." It was the position of "point" for which Ryan was being groomed, due in part to the recognition of his skills in the field previously developed by his grandfather. It was also around this time that he was no longer known as Ryan, but rather as "The Postman," a nickname resulting from the quantity of mail he would receive from home, most of which he would carry into the field in his helmet.

In writing home, the Postman found it extremely difficult to find the right words to express his experiences, though words such as scared, cold, hot, wet, and lonely certainly applied. However, one word seemed to sum up the totality of the whole experience: *waiting*. The very nature of the job dictated that something was going to happen, yet there was absolutely no way of knowing *when* it would occur. Compound this with the added knowledge of the "point" man that if he missed as much as one small clue his next step could be his last, and one can begin to understand the Postman's experience. However, as the Postman tried to explain in his letters, and as did probably thousands of others like him, one had to live through it to understand the nature of combat in Vietnam.

The only bright spot in his ordeal, if there was such a thing, was a friendship that developed with Winston, a fellow draftee who had been rotated into the squad shortly after the Postman's own arrival. Even though the friendship was based on their mutual respect for nature, it was the rather unusual way in which their respective interests in nature proved complementary that made the relationship special. For while the Postman had all the instincts and knowledge of a pathfinder, Winston's specialty was in the area of botany, his major in college. They seemed to enter into almost a mutual information exchange when time allowed, each teaching the other their complementary knowledge.

Unfortunately, this ad hoc nature seminar had an unhappy ending about two weeks after Winston succeeded the Postman at "point." Possibly some aspect of the Southeast Asian flora caught Winston's eye when he should have been concentrating on the ground ahead. The Postman never had a chance to find out; both Winston and the "slack" man were blown apart by a grenade boobytrap.

The Postman's withdrawal from reality following the death of his friend proved extensive enough to warrant his temporary removal from his squad for treatment of "combat fatigue." The application of the crisis intervention principles of *immediacy, proximity,* and *expectancy* (discussed later in this case) had drastically improved the success rate of the treatment of "combat fatigue" in Vietnam. In fact, the Postman was back with his squad within a week, though his sparkle and spontaneity were gone.

Following his return, the Postman kept himself rather distanced from other squad members. In addition, he strongly objected to anyone other than himself taking the position of "point" for the remaining five months of his tour of duty, even as it approached its end, a time when most men understandably became very protective of themselves. As a tribute to his skill, however, his squad experienced no death or injury related to booby traps during this period.

Etiological Factors   Several key factors were involved in the Postman's development of a Post-traumatic Stress Disorder, the most obvious of which was the nature of the stressor. Military combat has long been recognized as an extremely stressful experience, and combat in Vietnam proved to be even more so due to the guerrilla-style "hit and run" fighting. There were no "front lines" behind which one was safe. Death could come from an unseen sniper, a booby-trapped trail, and even from "innocent" women and children. This was particularly true of action in the field, with survival literally depending on hyperalertness. Such an attitude had to be maintained virtually twenty-four hours a day, for anywhere from thirty to ninety days at a time, particularly in such positions as "point" and "slack."

There was also a certain trade-off in the Vietnam conflict regarding the rotation system that was used. The policy of rotation after twelve months of duty was a factor in the decrease in cases of combat exhaustion during that conflict, apparently as a result of the establishment of a DEROS (date of expected return from overseas), recognized by the service as a clear point at which the stress would cease. However, at the same time, the system usually had men returning home within forty-eight to seventy-two hours of the end of their tour of duty, offering them little in the way of "decompression" from their traumatic experience.

Experience with posttraumatic stress suggests that "decompression" is a natural and necessary process for many individuals following such an extreme stressor (Figley, 1981). Decompression involves a gradual "coming to grips" with the traumatic event and the eventual acceptance and integration of the experience into the self. As with civilian disasters, this process often necessitates a rehashing of the experience, a process which many returning servicemen find almost impossible to go through, for several reasons. First of all, the system of rotation was highly individualized in the sense that a soldier rarely returned home with his buddies, a situation in which common experiences could at least be shared and discussed. Secondly, the swiftness of the return allowed little time for adjustment to the inevitable cultural shock generated by moving from the pressures of jungle warfare back into the alternative pressures of a highly technological society. In addition, far from the respect and gratitude expected, many returning veterans were aghast at finding themselves bearing the hostility generated by the nation's growing dissatisfaction with the war effort. Rather than offering the supportive environment so necessary and listening to the horrors these men had experienced, people were rejecting or at best chose to ignore these veterans. With no outlet for their pent up frustrations, anxieties, problems of conscience, and emotional confusion, it is small wonder that many such veterans (both men and women) developed, and continue to develop, problems in adjusting to civilian life (Figley, 1981).

As acknowledged in DSM-III, predisposing characteristics of the person may play a role in the development of a Posttraumatic Stress Disorder. This often refers to the existence of prior psychopathology. However, in the Postman's case, any predisposing "weakness" probably came from the absence of any emotional or stress "inoculation" in his life history; for example, no threatening illness, his rather protected upbringing by somewhat older parents, and the small size of his hometown. Thus, when confronted with the extreme stress of warfare in Vietnam, he lacked a substantial arsenal of adaptive coping methods that might have been learned from lesser stressors and that would have served to prepare him for response to later stress.

Lacking this psychological toughness, the Postman's already pressed defenses had been overwhelmed by the horror of seeing a close friend blown to bits. This shock to his unprotected system was so severe that it forced a temporary "shutdown" of reality processing, with consequent development of an extremely "thick" emotional insulation. Such a defense was probably furthered to a degree by his already introspective nature. The cost of such protection was the suppression of all of his feelings and emotions arising from the incident, particularly the guilt. For not only did he experience the common "survivor's" guilt of "why him and not me?" but he also felt that his own skills should not have let something like that happen. This feeling was reinforced when his guilt-induced claim to the "point" resulted in no further casualties for the remainder of his tour. Thus, he agonized, if he had never originally relinquished that position, the deaths would never have occurred.

Even though such feelings were initially kept out of consciousness, the Postman's return to the intimate relationships with his family and fiancée created problems. The emotional base and depth of those relationships slowly wore through his tough insulation. The return of feelings also meant the return of painful memories. As they slipped closer to consciousness, such strong cues as the sound of a helicopter or a metallic sound similar to the click of rifle bolt elicited the hidden emotions.

Treatment   The principles of crisis intervention noted earlier that have been employed in cases of "combat exhaustion" in the field also provide an excellent framework within which to treat posttraumatic stress syndromes. In this case, *immediacy* refers to the early detection and treatment of the disorder, with an emphasis on returning individuals to their typical life situations as quickly as possible. *Proximity* emphasizes the need to treat them in their ongoing world by avoiding hospitalization. Lastly, *expectancy* is the communication of the therapist that while their reaction is quite normal, it still does not excuse them from functioning adequately; the "sick role" is not reinforced (Meyer, 1982).

Within this framework, the particular symptomatology of a specific case can be treated by a variety of methods. For example, an individual may be taught a *controlled relaxation response* through Progressive Relaxation, Autogenic Training, or any other form of systematized relaxation training, to treat both acute panic attacks and a chronic state of autonomic arousal (McPherson et al., 1980). In the case of the latter, the concomitant use of biofeedback has also proven helpful. In some cases, the prescribing of tranquilizing medication to be taken "as needed" serves to give the individual a feeling of control while learning other techniques, though any indications of potential for substance abuse place limitations on this practice.

If such clients can be convinced to work on the relaxation training in a group setting, they become aware that others share the problem and they may also begin to discuss the problems in a quasi-group therapy fashion. This discussion facilitates later entry into actual group therapy, where they may come into greater contact with the sources of anxiety. Specific fears or phobias that then surface can be treated by such methods as systematic desensitization (SDT) (Wolpe, 1981).

An overall supportive atmosphere of warmth, understanding, and whatever empathy is possible is also important. Since the environment to which these individuals return should be similarly supportive, sessions with family and friends can be beneficial in helping them to understand the nature of the problem and the role they can play in successful readjustment (Figley, 1981). Such a resource played a valuable role in the development of Ryan's treatment plan; (he refused to be called by his nickname after returning home).

Treatment of Ryan An alert staff member at the VA hospital to which Ryan originally inquired about help noted his strong attachment to both his father and grandfather, so he referred Ryan to a rather "fatherly" therapist. True to the hunch, rapport was easily established despite the somewhat coercive nature of the referral. After some trust was developed, Ryan was induced to attend weekly "rap sessions" held for veterans at the hospital, which, although painful, did help him to face the memories that he had for so long attempted to suppress.

Both processes emphasized the recognition that the disorder was an understandable reaction and that the resulting anxieties had to be approached and dealt with if a desired level of adjustment was ever to be attained (Greist et al., 1980). Ryan's specific focus eventually turned to his guilt over the circumstances of his friend's death, a guilt that permeated the memory of everything associated with his Vietnam experience. The therapies allowed him to realize that despite the injustice of the deaths, he himself had not failed in any responsibility to the two men killed. The effectiveness of his relaxation training also played an important role here in dealing with the generalized anxiety that had resulted from the guilt. Such anxiety is problematic in many cases of a Posttraumatic Stress Disorder, as it often remains despite the recognition of its irrationality.

Another focus of attention at this point were the cues that had apparently triggered his dissociative states. Discovering these to be the sounds of a helicopter or a metallic click similar to the click of a rifle bolt, a systematic desensitization technique (SDT) was employed (Wolpe, 1958). Ryan was urged to use a controlled relaxation response in handling his fears and anxieties associated with the particular sound through the progressive stages of: 1) imagining the sound in different situations, 2) listening to a recording of the sound, and 3) eventually having in vivo experiences with the source of the sound. This last stage consisted of an actual ride in an army helicopter and several sessions of having a rifle randomly bolt loaded and fired near him. Therapy could not entirely eliminate a fear response to these cues (Mineka, 1979), but it did extinguish their ability to elicit a dissociative state. Just as importantly, it showed Ryan a method by which he could adaptively handle such anxiety when it occurred.

Another resource that played a vital role throughout his treatment and subsequent recovery was the supportive, caring atmosphere provided by his family and fiancée. Involved from the beginning, they attended several sessions, both with and without Ryan, in an effort to gain more of an understanding of the problems he faced and to learn what role they could play in his recovery. This served to revive the former intimacy of their relationships with Ryan and also taught them how to be supportive without reinforcing the "sick role."

Conclusions The tremendous amount of change inherent in modern society has furthered the possibility of experiencing an event sufficient to generate a Posttraumatic Stress Disorder. As with the Adjustment Disorder, the use of the intervention principles of 1) immediacy, 2) proximity, and 3) expectancy is helpful, but they also need to be bolstered by techniques that allow a catharsis, such as the rap sessions in which Ryan participated. It is also important that the victim be helped back into a network of support systems (such as family) and begin to orient toward the future with new plans and hopes.

For example, at the point of formal therapy termination, Ryan was making plans for marriage and a return to school to finish his degree in forestry. However, he did realize that the traumas he had experienced would likely haunt him to a degree, possibly for the rest of his life. Thus, he was going to continue to make the rap sessions as needed. Yet, he now felt he had faced and conquered the worst times and sensed that he had the family support and coping skills to maintain and further his positive adjustment.

REFERENCES

Figley, C. Working on a theory of what it takes to survive. *APA Monitor*, 1981, *12(3)*, 9.

Greist, J., Marks, I., Berlin, F., Gournay, K., and Noshirvani, H. Avoidance versus confrontation of fear. *Behavior Therapy*, 1980, *11*, 1–14.

McPherson, F., Brougham, L., and McLaren, S. Maintenance of improvement in agoraphobic patients treated by behavioral methods—a four year follow-up. *Behavior Research and Therapy*, 1980, *18*, 150–152.

Meyer, S. *The clinician's handbook*. Boston: Allyn and Bacon, 1982.

Mineka, S. The role of fear in theories of avoidance learning, flooding, and extinction. *Psychological Bulletin*, 1979, *86*, 985–1011.

Wolpe, J. *Psychotherapy by reciprocal inhibition.* Stanford, Ca.: Stanford University Press, 1958.

———. Behavior therapy versus psychoanalysis: Therapeutic and social implications. *American Psychologist.* 1981, 36, 159–164.

7

The Factitious, Somatoform, and Dissociative Disorders

Factitious means not genuine or real and refers to symptoms that are under the *voluntary* control of the individual. At first glance, this condition may sound like malingering. The difference is that in a Factitious Disorder, the goal or reinforcement sought is not obvious or inherent in the apparent facts of the situation, as it is, for example, in a person who fakes psychotic behavior in an attempt to buttress an insanity defense in a criminal charge. Instead, the motivation is understandable only within that person's individual psychology; for example, gaining a sense of being nurtured and cared for when being in a hospital. These factitious patterns have been traditionally confused with the conversion disorders; but in the DSM-III somatoform disorders, the symptoms are *not* under voluntary control.

Factitious disorders are rare. According to Spitzer, Forman, and Nee (1979), the factitious disorder is the most difficult DSM-III category to diagnose, as is evident in the first case in this section, Stewart McIlroy. When diagnosticians do become aware of what they perceive as deception, they are inclined to diagnose the person as an antisocial personality disorder instead of as a factitious disorder. Factitious disorders are chronic, and it is thought that the pattern is more common in males. This may only reflect a more ready acceptance of verbalizations of sickness from females; thus the diagnostician would be less inclined to label the behavior as a factitious disorder in females.

The factitious disorders are subdivided into (1) Factitious Disorder with Psychological Symptoms and (2) Chronic Factitious Disorder with

Physical Symptoms, the latter often referred to in the literature as the Munchausen Syndrome. In the factitious psychological syndrome, the symptoms are mental rather than physical, and as a result they are often less well defined.

The Munchausen Syndrome, termed Chronic Factitious Disorder with Physical Symptoms in DSM-III, was named after Baron Von Munchausen, an eighteenth century German equivalent of America's Paul Bunyan, both of whom are associated with tales of exaggeration. The range of symptomatology is limited only by the imagination and the degree of sophistication about medical information. Some experience with hospitals or medical situations, either through previous hospitalizations or knowledge from family members who were involved in the medical profession, can contribute to this disorder. The most severe victim of the Munchausen Syndrome may be our first case here, Stewart McIlroy; he stayed in 68 different hospitals (with at least 207 separate admissions) in England, Scotland, Ireland, and Wales.

Persons with Somatoform Disorders, like the factitious disorders, manifest complaints and symptoms of apparent physical illness for which there are no demonstrable organic findings to support a physical diagnosis. Thus, diagnosis of somatoform disorder is made when there is good reason to believe that the person has little or no control over the production of symptoms. Whereas the factitious disorders are more commen in men, the somatoform disorders occur more frequently in women.

There are four major subcategories of the somatoform disorders: Somatization Disorder, Conversion Disorder, Psychogenic Pain Disorder, and Hypochondriasis. The Somatization Disorder is a chronic disorder with multiple symptoms and complaints, usually presented in a vague fashion. The Conversion Disorder focuses on a specific symptom or two that are suggestive of a physical disorder, yet which, on closer examination, primarily reflect a psychological issue, either as a reflection of symbolic conflict or from the attainment of secondary gain. Psychogenic Pain Disorder, which is the subject of our second case study, Eugene, is functionally a conversion disorder that refers specifically to psychologically induced pain states. Hypochondriasis is the consistent overresponse to and concern about normal and/or insignificant bodily changes, in spite of expert reassurance that there is no reason for concern.

The Dissociative Disorders, a number of which were traditionally referred to in the DSM-III as the Hysterical Neuroses, Dissociative Type, are characterized by a sudden disruption or alteration of the normally integrated functions of consciousness. This disturbance is almost always temporary, though it may wax and wane, particularly in Amnesia and Fugue.

The various subcategories of the Dissociative Disorders are: Psychogenic Amnesia, which is an acute disturbance of memory function; Psychogenic Fugue (in the third case here, Bernice), which is a sudden disruption of one's sense of identity, usually accompanied by travel away from home; Multiple Personality (as in the famous movie *Three Faces of Eve*), which is the domination of the person's consciousness by two or more separate personalities; and the Depersonalization Disorder (the last case in this section, Elenrae), in which there is a disturbance in the experience of the "self," resulting in the sense of reality's being temporarily distorted.

It can be argued that the depersonalization disorder, also referred to as the depersonalization neurosis, is not appropriately included in this general category, as there is no substantial memory disturbance. Yet there is a significant disturbance, albeit often temporary, in the sense of reality, and thus the identity is certainly affected.

REFERENCE

Spitzer, R., Forman, J., and Nee, J. DSM-III field trials: Initial interrater diagnostic reliability. *American Journal of Psychiatry*, 1979, *136*, 815–817.

McIlroy Was Here. Or Was He?

C. A. Pallis and A. N. Bamji

It is now over a year since we last heard of Mr. McIlroy, and we must presume him dead. With him has passed an era. His brilliant career spanned the entire life of our National Health Service, and it is improbable that we shall ever see the like of him again. In his day he baffled, entertained, fooled, and infuriated the medical and nursing staff of many hospitals. Numerous neurologists must have made his acquaintance, and many physicians from overseas may remember him from difficult hours spent in his company in various British casualty departments. How much Mr. McIlroy cost the health services both here and in Eire will remain a matter of conjecture. The sum must run into six, possibly seven figures.

Case History
Stewart McIlroy may have been born in County Donegal in 1915. His early life was uneventful. In 1944 he was admitted several times to the City Hospital, Belfast, with a left-knee injury that failed to heal. In 1947 "Convict McIlroy" was transferred from HM Prison, Belfast, to Purdysburn Mental Hospital, where he spent five years before beginning his peregrinations. London attracted him. In 1954, Charing Cross Hospital admitted him with a left pneumothorax, sustained (so he claimed) during the reduction of a dislocated shoulder under local anaesthesia at another London teaching hospital. Later

From: Pallis, C., and Bamji, A. McIlroy was here or was he? *British Medical Journal*, 1979, *1*, 973–975. Reprinted by permission.

that year neurological symptoms made their appearance. These were dramatic, consisting of recurrent episodes of headache, photophobia, neck stiffness, and left hemiplegia. Subarachnoid haemorrhage was repeatedly diagnosed but never confirmed, numerous lumbar punctures yielding clear fluid. Surprisingly, many carotid angiograms were performed, all of them proving normal. Palpation of the skull, on the rare occasions it was carried out, showed the presence of burrholes. He often demanded large doses of analgesics, and was referred for psychiatric treatment more than once during the next seven years. In this period he seemed to have developed neurological signs suggestive (to some observers) of syringomyelia. Others thought he had a chronic neuropathy with functional sensory loss over the trunk. In 1961, after several episodes of dysphagia, dysphonia, and "acute respiratory failure" (for which emergency tracheotomy was performed), he acquired a permanent tracheotomy, we think in Doncaster.

In 1965, he suffered his first attack of severe abdominal pain. This symptom was to lead to many further hospital admissions. Dozens of barium swallows, meals, and enemas (and at least four laparotomies) failed to disclose a cause for his pain. His scarred abdomen, meanwhile, remained a monument to current investigative enthusiasms, if not to modern powers of discrimination. Under the strain of continued ill health, and by now with an expanding experience of hospital practice, he began to complain of chest pain. This was intermittently diagnosed as angina and worsened progressively. Recurrent chest pain, with or without recurrent episodes of hemiparesis or recurrent acute abdomen or both, led to many further emergency admissions. In 1975, after an admission for chest pain, he developed acute retention of urine. A transurethral prostatectomy was performed.

In 1976, he was admitted to the City Hospital, Belfast—an old favourite—because he had fallen and fractured his right femur. Pinning proved unsuccessful, and later he underwent total hip replacement in London, at St. Mary's Hospital, Praed Street. But we are now near the end of our story, for after a few more admissions to various hospitals he made a brief appearance at the Belfast City Hospital, and then disappeared.

Diagnosis As most readers will have guessed (and many more will know) many of Mr. McIlroy's symptoms were fraudulent. The bare bones of the case described do scant justice to his skill and success as a peregrinating patient. All of his acute symptoms and signs were faked, with the exception of his fractured femur and the possible exception of his retention of urine. He had, of course, Munchausen's syndrome. Our persistent inquiries, now spreading over

175

several years, have shown that since 1944 he had been a patient in at least 68 hospitals. We have documented 207 admissions, and there is strong circumstantial evidence for at least another ten. This makes him the longest followed-up patient with Munchausen's syndrome ever recorded. It was at least a year after we began our researches that we discovered that his story had been reported in 1960, but, hardly surprisingly that interesting account is very incomplete. The report clearly shows, however, how McIlroy would sometimes help the doctors find the "relevant" physical signs they were seeking. A history taken in 1960 suggested that he had served in the armed forces, but subsequent checking shows this to be false. Another hospital record led us to believe that he had been in the RAF, until we discovered that two sets of notes had been combined. The genuine ex-serviceman had died several years before.

We don't know McIlroy's real name and age for certain. His relatives, or so he was fond of recounting, had all met violent deaths at the hands of Republican "bombers" and gunmen. This discourages us from seeking to confirm which of his surnames and eight Christian names were genuine. His sister, we might add, "died" at least three different deaths, on seven different occasions. Whenever afflicted with his recurrent aphonia he would write out his history. Practice makes perfect and he had refined this to a great art. His symptoms would first be described separately. Latterly, as one set approached the point of exposure, he would switch to another. When a showdown seemed imminent he would depart with speed, his hemiplegic or paraplegic disabilities miraculously receding. In all, he discharged himself on 133 occasions.

As befits someone with such a wide hospital experience—and who had been "taught on" so many times—McIlroy had acquired a remarkable grasp of medical terminology: so much so that we suggest that in addition to Asher's "laparotomophilimigrans" he suffered from "neurologica sophistica." His success owed much to his minimal signs of organic neurological disorder, with slight wasting of the intrinsic musculature of the left hand, areflexia of the arms, and dissociated suspended sensory loss over the upper trunk and arms.

We know that McIlroy spent well over ten of the last 34 years in hospitals. Probably during the remaining two decades he had similar domiciles: we just don't have the records. But quite apart from bed and board, he cost the taxpayer dear in investigations and operative procedures. There was always evidence of recent venepuncture, and his numerous scars bore witness of laparotomies and orthopaedic procedures, the details of which are unknown to us. In 1965, after admission to the City Hospital in Belfast, because of difficulty managing his gastrostomy tube, laparotomy showed an enteroanastomosis between two jejunal loops, and that the "gastrostomy" was in fact a jejunostomy. His medical career antedated the widespread use of CAT scanning. He therefore underwent at least 48 lumbar punctures and three air encephalograms, not to mention myelography. Radiographs of his skull had shown burrholes since the early stages of his career. The number of ordinary x-ray examinations and blood tests must run into hundreds if not thousands.

We hope this obituary is premature. It was once said that old patients with Munchausen's syndrome were like old soldiers: they never died but faded away. Stewart McIlroy taught many lessons to those who were deceived, not least being the lesson that we are not always the astute physicians we should like to believe.

Postscript Munchausen's syndrome has been much discussed since Asher first described it.[1] The difficulty of arranging psychiatric treatment is well known: the patients will not stay long voluntarily, and it is usually impossible to justify detention under the sections of the Mental Health Act.[2] The concept of a general register has been rejected as unethical, and the black book kept in casualty departments is circumvented if (a) a new name is used and (b) the symptoms are convincing—and they usually are, especially if there is a genuine underlying medical condition.[3]

Our thanks are due to the many physicians and medical records staff who replied to our requests for information during the past four years.

REFERENCES

1. Asher, R., *Lancet*, 1951, *1*, 339.
2. Blackwell, P., *Guy's Hospital Reports*, 1965, *114*, 257.
3. Unfug, H. V., *Journal of the American Medical Association*, 1977, *238*, 2265.

Comment Pallis and Bamji go on to enumerate Mr. McIlroy's physical signs (16) and the number of known hospital admissions (over 200 in 68 hospitals and 5 countries). Though the Munchausen syndrome is rather rare, instances of factitious physical symptoms have been consistently reported since Asher's original description in 1951. Bursten (1965) listed the following as major features of the syndrome:

1. Dramatic presentation of one or more physical complaints.
2. "Pseudological fastastica" (dramatic, exaggerated intriguing accounts of physical illness).
3. Using several hospitals and physicians in different geographical areas.

The prevalence of Munchausen syndrome and factitious disorders with *psychological* symptoms are difficult to determine. With the Munchausen syndrome, incidence rates are affected by problems in recognizing the disorder and by the transient lifestyles of persons with chronic forms of the disorder.

177

Cheng and Hummel (1978) list the following disorders as ones from which the Muchausen syndrome must be distinguished: hospital addiction, malingering, hysteria, drug addiction, multiple surgery, and acute psychosocial crisis.

As mentioned earlier, factitious disorders are motivated by the person's desire to assume the patient role, and an allied diagnosis of some form of personality disorder is usually appropriate. Such patients generally respond to psychiatric referrals with hostility and criticisms of their physicians' competence. Patients with factitious psychological symptoms present an elaborate and varied symptom pattern, usually with evidence of minimal motivation to relinquish these symptoms. This latter disorder pattern, although generally recognized among professionals in inpatient treatment settings, has received little empirical attention and may occur more frequently than suspected. Some authors have suggested that episodes of factitious psychological symptoms are commonly overlooked or misdiagnosed when symptoms of another psychological disorder are present (Sussman & Hyler, 1980; Hyler & Spitzer, 1978).

REFERENCES

Asher, R. Munchausen's syndrome. *Lancet*, 1951, *1*, 339–341.

Bursten, B. On Munchausen's syndrome. *Archives of General Psychiatry*, 1965, *13*, 261–168.

Cheng, L., and Hummel L. The Munchausen syndrome as a psychiatric condition. *British Journal of Psychiatry*, 1978, *133*, 20–21.

Hyler, S., and Spitzer, R. Hysteria split asunder. *American Journal of Psychiatry*, 1978, *135*, 1500–1504.

Sussman, N., and Hyler, S. Factitious disorders. In Kaplan, H., Freedman, A. & Sadock, B. *Comprehensive textbook of psychiatry* (3rd ed.). Baltimore: Williams & Wilkins, 1980.

Psychogenic Pain Disorder

The Case of Eugene   The pattern described in this case is diagnosed as a Psychogenic Pain Disorder, a new category in DSM III. It is functionally a subcategory of the Conversion Disorder category, in which the focus is primarily on pain. Similar to other Conversion Disorders (for example, hysterical rather than physiological paralysis of a limb), there is no actual physical disorder. Yet the person consciously believes that there is a physiological disorder.

Other types of Conversion disorders, as opposed to a Psychogenic Pain Disorder, occurred more commonly in Freud's time. For example, a common pattern then was "glove anesthesia." People with this symptom complained of paralysis and numbness, roughly in the area a glove would cover. However, such a disorder is not at all correlated with the actual nerve distribution pattern in the hand. As a result, this disorder was seen less as a more sophisticated awareness of this disorder developed in both physicians and potential patients. On the other hand, chronic and vague pain offers a more difficult diagnostic challenge and is not so easily confronted as "not real" (Fordyce, 1979; Hanback & Revelle, 1978). Thus, the incidence of Psychogenic Pain Disorder has risen as that of Conversion Disorder has decreased.

Eugene

Eugene, who is forty-five years old, had recently retired from the Navy when his surgeon referred him to the VA hospital's chronic pain clinic. Eugene had undergone surgery nine months ago for a back injury sustained in an automobile accident. He had experienced intense pain immediately following the surgery and was continued on heavy dosages of barbiturates for three weeks. This was much longer than the usual few days, and the surgeon became concerned about the possibility of addiction. Eugene was discharged from the hospital with over-the-counter analgesics. He was told that physical recovery was usually associated with some degree of pain, which would gradually decrease with time. Though Eugene reported a decrease in pain intensity, he said that it was never totally absent. Further, Eugene reported that the pain was sporadically (once or twice per month) so debilitating that he would be confined to bed for two or three days. The surgeon had prescribed stronger analgesics, exercise, physical therapy, bed rest, and diet changes—all to no avail. In his referral letter, Eugene's surgeon stated that medical evidence indicated normal postoperative recovery and that the medical staff could find no anatomical basis for Eugene's pain. The surgeon suggested that Eugene be accepted for a program based on three of the major psychological treatments offered by the chronic pain clinic: biofeedback training, operant conditioning, and/or hypnosis.

Etiology Eugene was given a comprehensive psychological test battery and an extensive interview to determine the psychological parameters of his pain experiences. One striking piece of evidence that Eugene's pain was psychogenic was the presence of an invalid family "model" who enjoyed considerable

179

respect and attention from relatives. Eugene's father had suffered a major stroke at age forty-seven, was forced to retire from a service career, and was semi-invalid for the next twenty-five years. Eugene remembered that his mother was very solicitous of his father's health and encouraged her children to appreciate him while he was alive. Eugene's mother was careful that his father should never be alone, and Eugene remembers sitting with him while his mother shopped or attended church. Eugene, the only son, enjoyed those times with his father and admired the courage and good spirits maintained by his father throughout his extended illness. Thus, Eugene grew up with a slightly different concept of physical dysfunction than do most people. He felt his father had a pleasant life and was deeply cared for by family members.

Further, Eugene's wife, Dorothy, had unwittingly encouraged his symptoms by responding to his illness in the same manner as her mother-in-law had responded to Eugene's father. Though Dorothy had been active in her own career as a hairdresser, she decreased her hours after Eugene's accident and only worked when one of their four children could stay with him. However, when Eugene was confined to bed, Dorothy insisted that she be the one to stay home with him, thus reinforcing his pattern (Craighead et al., 1981). Though Eugene's retirement plans preceded the accident, he was forced to abandon his second career plans to consult for a shipbuilding firm.

In addition to the increased attention of his wife, there were signs of other secondary gains for Eugene's back pain. There were indications of suggestibility, need for dependency, and depression in his test profiles (Fordyce, 1979), with several references to the difficulties of parenting in response to both test items and the interviewer's questions. When asked if these findings were related, Eugene expressed strong disappointment with his children's lifestyles and career choices. Eugene was disappointed that none of his children had graduated from college or participated in the military. Also, Eugene especially disliked his one son-in-law and objected to the live-in-friends. Further, when Dorothy asked one of the children to sit with their father, that child almost always came alone. Dorothy had instructed the children to avoid upsetting their father by sticking to neutral ground in conversations. Also, Eugene enjoyed playing games such as Scrabble or Monopoly or watching television with his children on these visits. Eugene obviously relished the advantages of these arrangements. Indeed, according to his wife, familial conflict was greatly reduced by Eugene's "inability" to participate in the larger family gatherings.

Thus, Eugene's chronic and occasionally debilitating back pain allowed him to: 1) follow his father's model for acquiring affection through illness; 2) avoid noxious contact with the romantic partners chosen by his children; and 3) maintain the illusion of a unified family by regular pleasant visits from his otherwise disappointing children. These and other psychological factors such as depression, suggestibility (Fordyce, 1979), need for dependent relationships, a predisposition toward pain experiences (Hanback

& Revelle, 1978), along with the negative results of medical tests, confirmed the suspicion of Eugene's surgeon that Eugene's pain was a Somatoform Disorder, specifically a Psychogenic Pain Disorder. Malingering and Factitious disorders were ruled out because Eugene did not appear to have voluntary control over his symptoms. In the DSM-III somatoform disorders, such persons do not feel as if they control the production of the symptoms. They sincerely believe their symptoms are real and serious, and initially they react negatively to any suggestion of psychological involvement.

Treatment Options

The major treatment options include confrontation-insight therapy (Bugental, 1980), behavior modification (Craighead et al., 1981), hypnosis (Cheek, 1965), and biofeedback (Fordyce, 1979). The role of insight psychotherapy with psychogenic pain sufferers involves encouraging them to acknowledge psychological involvement and personal responsibility for their symptoms. Biofeedback has an analogous role with some patients—providing the person with a sense of control over the symptoms. Some psychologists have used biofeedback as a successful treatment with chronic pain, *regardless* of evidence of psychological involvement (Fordyce, 1979). Also, the relaxation component of biofeedback training can be helpful in reducing the anxiety and distress reported by many persons with psychogenic pain disorder.

Unfortunately, most sufferers of psychogenic pain disorder do not easily accept referrals for psychological treatment. Rather, they continually seek medical prescriptions and treatments. Such patients eventually become at risk for iatrogenic complications and unrecognized true physical disorders. Multiple surgeries and chronic use of pain relievers can eventually harm the person's general health and can generate numerous serious side effects (Cheek, 1965; Fordyce, 1979). Further, the chronic complaints of persons with psychogenic pain can mask symptoms of actual illness (Fordyce, 1979). It is not unusual for physicians to habituate to these complaints and automatically prescribe pain relievers without re-examining the person. Consequently, by the time actual physical disorders are noticed, they have become rather advanced and may require extraordinary treatments.

Eugene's Treatment

Eugene's cooperation with the chronic pain clinic's extensive evaluation was facilitated by two coincidental environmental events. Firstly, Eugene was surprised when his surgeon clearly stated that he had exhausted the medical treatments available for his symptoms. Thus, he felt the clinic was his last chance for successful treatment. Secondly, his wife had had a mild stroke a few weeks earlier and he felt as if he ought to help care for her. These events, in addition to serving as powerful motivators for cooperation, reduced the opportunities for the secondary gains for the back pain discussed above. Indeed, the back pain was now quite burdensome in some instances. Eugene's therapist was also developing a treatment plan for Eugene that combined behavior modification and post-hypnotic suggestions.

First of all, Eugene and his wife were asked to come to a feedback session. A feedback session is a meeting with clients (and appropriate others) in which results of psychological evaluations and recommendations for treatment are discussed. The clinical formulation of the dynamics of Eugene's pain and the maintaining behaviors on Dorothy's part were directly presented along with the treatment plan. Eugene and Dorothy generally agreed with the formulation, but said they had not thought about their interactions in the same way as the psychologist. At this point, the psychologist explained that he also thought Eugene's problems had originated in actual physical pain, but that his condition had been aggravated by the presence of secondary gains, which were detailed and eventually accepted. The psychologist thought that Eugene had gradually associated back pain with support in the environment, and at this point, illness was his only strategy for eliciting affection from his family. Suggesting that Eugene try other ways to relate to family members, the psychologist asked Eugene to contract for at least one such effort per day and agree to a series of hypnosis sessions.

Hypnosis has long been considered an effective treatment for conversion symptoms (physical symptoms with presumed psychological etiology) (Cheek, 1965). There is considerable controversy about the operative variable(s) in hypnosis with conversion symptoms. Some dynamic theorists have attributed the relief of symptoms to the direct communication with the person's unconscious mind during the hypnotic state (Cheek, 1965). Others have pointed out that the hypnotic state itself can facilitate the patient's acceptance of the therapist's instructions and advice (Meyer, 1982). From either perspective, post-hypnotic suggestions have been successful with such psychogenic dysfunctions as amnesia, paralysis, blindness, and pain. Eugene was given the suggestion that he would be increasingly bored talking about his back pain and that he would rather engage in various pleasant activities than give in to it. The therapist also suggested that the intensity of Eugene's pain would gradually decrease and he would be symptom free within three weeks.

At the same time, Dorothy agreed to stop Eugene's patterns by ignoring his remarks about his pain and also to support him when his conversation or behavior was more appropriate (Craighead et al., 1981). The couple had some ideas about situations they could enjoy together and that they could prefer to their former patient/nurse roles. Also, Eugene thought he could try to be more tolerant of his children's romantic friends. Eugene negotiated a series of contracts with the therapist for extending individual invitations to each of his children within the next week for lunch, dinner, shopping, fishing, or whatever was agreeable to both. Also, Eugene and Dorothy planned a dinner in their home to celebrate the approaching wedding anniversary of their daughter and son-in-law.

Eugene was seen for eight sessions. The second through sixth sessions involved repetitions of the hypnotic suggestions and negotiating contracts for appropriate affective strategies for Eugene's lifestyle. He reported a noticeable decrease in the frequency and intensity of pain over the first week. By the fifth week, Eugene reported that he had had ten consecutive pain-free days and that he had required no pain medication for more than four weeks. Interestingly enough, Dorothy reported that her recovery from her stroke had been accelerated by the increased family harmony and by her decision to de-emphasize her discomfort in her conversations with Eugene. Though Dorothy's motivation had been to make it easier for Eugene to fulfill his contracts, she found that her own pain was less noticeable when she concentrated on some other conversation topic. Eugene continued to be symptom free at one-, three-, and six-month follow-up sessions. He resumed his plans to consult part-time with the ship-building company, and Dorothy returned to regular part-time hours as a hairdresser. Eugene continued to complain about the new spouses of his children. However, once he had two grandchildren on the way, one of whom was to be named after him, he found the marriages easier to tolerate.

Conclusions The Psychogenic Pain Disorder has received increased attention in the last couple of decades, in large part because of the recognition that there is a group of disorders that are neither the result of actual physical insult nor malingering (Cheek, 1965; Fordyce, 1979). This disorder can be facilitated by an actual experience with a similar illness or by modeling of a significant other for such a disorder, as well as by personality traits such as depression, suggestibility, the need to be dependent in relationships, and a propensity for pain sensations (Cheek, 1965; Hanback & Revelle, 1979; Fordyce, 1979).

Many people with this disorder do not make a particularly good recovery, but Eugene's prognosis is favorable. He has made a successful adjustment to the semi-retired lifestyle that he and his wife share. Further, he has developed and utilized a set of more appropriate strategies for eliciting affection from his wife and children. It is probable that successful treatment for Eugene was primarily a function of his strong motivation for change. Barber (1978) has suggested that post-hypnotic suggestions allow the conversion patient to "save face" in the surrender of symptoms when they are no longer useful or functional in the person's lifestyle.

Yet, many persons with psychogenic pain do develop a more chronic disorder before recognition of psychological involvement and the subsequent referral for psychotherapy occurs. In these cases, such persons may have experienced multiple surgical and evaluation procedures at considerable financial and emotional costs. Further, the longer they experience psychogenic pain, the more likely they are to experience generalization; that is, the experience of pain becomes associated with a variety of situations in which the person seeks to avoid unpleasant events or to manipulate affection from others. Thus, the resultant complex reinforcement systems may render any future successful intervention improbable.

REFERENCES

Barber, T. *Hypnosis and psychosomatics: A collection of reference material.* San Francisco: Proseminar Institute. 1978.

Bugental, J. Someone needs to worry: The existential anxiety of responsibility and decision. In G. Belkin (Ed.), *Contemporary psychotherapies.* Chicago: Rand McNally, 1980.

Cheek, D. Emotional factors in persistent pain states. *The American Journal of Clinical Hypnosis,* 1965, 8, 100–110.

Craighead, W., Kazdin, A., and Mahoney, M. *Behavior modification.* Boston: Houghton Mifflin, 1981.

Fordyce, W. Use of the MMPI in the assessment of chronic pain. In J. Butcher, G. Dahlstrom, M. Gynther, and W. Schofield (Eds.), *Clinical notes on the MMPI.* Nutley, N.J.: Roche, 1979.

Hanback, J. and Revelle, W. Arousal and perceptual sensitivity in hypochondriacs. *Journal of Abnormal Psychology,* 1978, 87, 523–530.

Meyer, R. *The clinician's handbook.* Boston: Allyn and Bacon, 1982.

Psychogenic Fugue

The essential feature of psychogenic fugue is the assumption of a new identity by a person who has rather suddenly and unexpectedly wandered from home. Such persons are unable to recall their past and develop an entirely new identity, lifestyle, and social group. Generally, the clinical picture is one of an immature and highly suggestible person who feels that there is no other escape from an intolerable situation. Though the causal variables of psychogenic fugue have yet to be clearly delineated, DSM-III lists heavy alcohol use and severe psychosocial stress as predisposing factors. The disorder is relatively rare, though incidence rates tend to increase during war time and following natural disasters. Psychogenic fugue differs from psychogenic amnesia in that amnesia victims seldom travel and do not establish a new identity; and from multiple personality, in which there is more than one distinct personality.

Basic behaviors are preserved in the psychogenic fugue. Amnesia is highly selective: only material that is related to the intolerable situation is forgotten. The person typically maintains past personal habits and does not evidence typical symptoms of emotional disturbance. Aside from the memory disturbance (albeit dramatic), there is no cognitive impairment. Further, the individual manages to avoid "discovery" for impressive lengths of time, as did Bernice in the following case.

The Case of Bernice

Jules Masserman

Repression may be seen in many of the minor aberrations of daily living; we "forget" unpleasant occurrences, unwanted information or the names of people we don't like—phenomena which Freud described as the psychopathology of everyday life. Similarly, analytic theory holds that the loss of infantile and childhood memories is due less to temporal fading to overlay by later experiences than to defensive repression of the poignant frustrations and disillusionments of early life. Thus, many apparently "forgotten" occurrences in childhood may be recollected if their accompanying anxiety is temporarily or permanently relieved by nepenthic, or narcotic drugs, hypnosis, the permissiveness of "free associations," or merely the reassuring receptiveness of a sympathetic listener. Conversely, severe motivational stresses may again require repressions of such sweeping thoroughness and intensity that entire configurations of behavior may be obliterated in space or time. Examples of such reactions may be seen in the functional amnesias, in which large segments of experience are repressed while more acceptable patterns are retained in a dissociated "fugue state." Morton Prince regarded patients showing such phenomena as split or multiple personalities, since their behavior in one state seemed to differ so completely from that in another; however, it is probable that each "personality" merely represented a more or less independently integrated set of behavior patterns that, for predominantly unconscious reasons, best suited the patient for the duration of the fugue. An illustration of this type of reaction is the following:

Case 3. Repression: fugue state
Bernice L—, a forty-two-year old housewife, was brought to the hospital by her family who stated that the patient had disappeared from her home four years previously, and had recently been identified and returned from R—, a small town over a thousand miles away. On rejoining her parents, husband and children she had at first appeared highly perturbed, anxious and indecisive. Soon, however, she had begun to insist that she really had never seen them before, that her name was not Bernice L—, but Rose P—, and that it was all a case of mistaken identity; further, she threatened that if she were not returned to her home in R— immediately, she would

From: Masserman, J. *Principles of Dynamic Psychiatry*. Philadelphia: W. B. Saunders, 1961, pp. 35–37. Reprinted by permission of W. B. Saunders Company.

sue all concerned for conspiracy and illegal detainment. Under treatment the patient slowly formed an adequate working rapport with the psychiatrist, consented to various ancillary anamnestic procedures such as Amytal interviews and hypnosis, and eventually dissipated her amnesias sufficently to furnish the following history:

Bernice was raised by fanatically religious parents, who despite their evangelical church work and moralistic pretenses, accused each other of infidelity so frequently that the patient often questioned her own legitimacy. Instead of divorcing each other, the parents had vented their mutual hostility upon the patient in a tyrannically prohibitive upbringing. In the troubled loneliness of her early years, Bernice became deeply attached to her older sister and together they found some security and comfort; unfortunately, the sister died when the patient was seventeen and left her depressed and inconsolable. At her parents' edict, Bernice then entered the University of A— and studied assiduously to prepare herself for the life of a "Missionary Sister." During her second semester at the University, she was assigned to room with an attractive, warm-hearted and gifted girl, Rose P—, who tactfully guided the patient to new interests, introduced her to various friendships and encouraged her to develop her neglected talent as a pianist. Bernice became as devoted to her companion as she had formerly been to her sister, and was for a time relatively happy. In her junior year, however, Rose P— became engaged to a young dentist, and the couple would frequently take the patient with them to act as a chaperone on week-end trips. Predictably, the patient fell "madly in love" with Rose P—'s fiance, and spent days of doubt and remorse over her incompatible allegiances and jealousies. The young man, however, paid little attention to his fiancee's shy and awkward roommate, married Rose P— and took her to live with him in Canada. The patient reacted with a severe depression and left the university because she "did not deserve to be a Sister in God"; however, at her family's insistence, she returned, took her degree and entered a final preparatory school to qualify her for a foreign assignment.

On completion of these studies, and in further expiation for what she now called her previous "sin of jealous coveting," she entered into a loveless marriage with a man designated by her parents as a "worthy partner in her work," and spent six unhappy years in missionary outposts in Burma and China. The couple, with their two children, then returned to the United States and settled in the parsonage of a small midwest town. Bernice's life as a minister's wife, however, grew less and less bearable as her husband became increasingly preoccupied with the affairs of his church, and as the many prohibitions of the village (e.g., against movies and plays, most recreations, politically liberal opinions and even secular music) began to stifle her with greater weight from year to year. During this time the patient became increasingly prone to be quiet, hazily glorifying reminiscences about the only relatively happy period she had known—her first two years in college with her friend, Rose P—; these years, in her day-dreaming, gradually came to represent all possible contentment. When the patient was thirty-seven years of age, the sickness and death of her younger, musically talented and favorite child culminated her frustrations and disappointments. The next day the patient disappeared from home without explanation or trace, and her whereabouts, despite frantic search, remained unknown to her family for the next four years.

Under therapy, the patient recollected that, after a dimly remembered journey by a devious route, she finally reached R—, the college town of her youth. She insisted that she had lost all conscious knowledge of her true identity and previous life except that she thought her name was Rose P—. Under this name she had begun to earn a living playing and teaching the piano, and was so rapidly successful that within two years she was the assistant director of the local conservatory of music. Intuitively, she chose friends who would not be curious about her past, which to her remained a "mysterious blank," and eventually established a new social identity which removed the need for introspections and ruminations. Thus Bernice lived for four years as Rose P— until the almost inevitable happened; she was recognized by a girlhood acquaintance who had known both her and Rose P— in their college years. The patient at first sincerely and vigorously denied this identification, resisted her removal to Chicago where her husband was now a prominent minister, and failed to acknowledge either him or her family until her psychiatric treatment penetrated her amnesia. Fortunately, her husband proved sympathetic and cooperative, and the patient eventually readjusted to a fuller life with a more understanding as well as devoted spouse under happily changed circumstances.

Comment This case history illustrates many dynamisms, but outstanding is the patient's use of repression as a means of escaping a mode of living that was no longer tolerable. Denied was her unwanted existence as Mrs. Bernice L—, the unhappy wife, and substituted was an identification with an intensely desired way of life personified by Rose P—, the loved and successful sister surrogate. Without conscious recognition of either the fact or the dynamics of this wishful transfiguration, the patient had therefore changed her identity and for four years followed the dictates of desires and fantasies long repressed but insistently recurrent. However, the "new" personality was not really novel, but consisted rather in certain unconsciously selected, isolated and recombined patterns of the old. Significant, for instance, is the fact that despite proposals from acceptable men, in her identity as the spinster, Rose P—, she neither married again nor permitted herself any form of direct sex expression, since bigamy or unfaithfulness, conscious or not, would have been untenable. Nevertheless, when she was returned to her family, her fears of punishment for her desertion of them again induced severe anxiety and renewed denials, and the transition back to being Bernice L— became stable only when new and predominantly satisfactory readjustments were attained.

Repressed impulses, however, only rarely cause as drastic and sweeping a revision of personality adaptations as occurred in the fugue state illustrated above; instead, if sufficient outlets are available, they are ordinarily channeled into patterns of behavior more acceptable to the current social group and thereby more advantageous to the individual. Thus, had Bernice L— found a new sister-substitute in her parish who, perhaps even in the guise of close fellowship in the church, could have satisfied her needs for dependent alliances, or had she been allowed expression of her esthetic longings in music or art, or had she been permitted to find vicarious gratification in the anticipated success of her pretty and talented daughter, a complete amnestic break with her mundane, inhibited, small-town existence might not have become necessary. Such modes of adaptation, however minimal, are generally accepted and keep many of our otherwise inexplicable social customs and institutions going. [End of excerpt from Masserman]

Discussion   The case of Bernice L. illustrates how successful one can be in exchanging identities. Bernice lived under an assumed identity for four years despite the extensive search efforts of her family. Masserman discusses the preservation of Bernice's moral values within the context of unconscious guidance and uses the defense mechanism of repression to explain her selective amnesia. Though they would use other terms and would diminish the role of the unconscious, certain conceptualizations by humanistic and behavioral theorists are similar to Masserman's psychoanalytic interpretation. Generally, the three orientations agree that such individuals are unable to tolerate perceived prohibitive and restrictive forces in a previous lifestyle and as a result escape to an identity in which they can practice greater personal autonomy. For psychoanalysis, this move is regressive and unconsciously motivated. For humanists, such persons embark on the only available route to self-actualization (Bugental, 1980). For behaviorists, they escape a punitive environment and move to a situation in which reinforcers are more accessible (Lutzker & Martin, 1981). As may be evident from Bernice's case, discovery of true identity in psychogenic fugue is rare—and then often accidental. Fugue patients rarely spontaneously remit and generally respond to discovery with hostility and denial. It is possible that the incidence rate is much higher than current estimates; a significant number of individuals could be leading prolonged lives with different identities.

The dissociative states in general seem to be the result of active interference processes. Flight, amnesia, and/or new identities are apparently motivated by the person's desire to block personal disappointments, conflicts, or anxiety from recognition. The individual's memory and awareness remain intact—but are subdued. Coe et al. (1976) have found that dissociated material is recoverable under hypnosis. However, for cases of dissociative fugue, the person's dissociated history is rarely apparent, and hypnosis is not attempted. Once such persons go away from home and establish a new identity, it is highly unlikely that they will come to the attention of professionals during the fugue state.

After discovery or spontaneous recovery of memory, the primary focus of treatment involves helping such persons return to their original lifestyle, and then maintain that adjustment in the long run (Karoly & Steffan, 1981). As with Bernice, the conflicts that precipitated the fugue state may continue to cause problems for them after their return. Another focus of treatment for a person who has recently returned from fugue is facilitating the person's memory for events *during* the fugue state. Kisker (1964) reported the case of a gentleman whose memory spontaneously returned after a six-year fugue. Ironically, the events that had occurred during the six-year wandering were then totally forgotten. Situations such as these probably result from an unsuccessful resolution during fugue states of conflicts that are similar to those that precipitated the original flight.

REFERENCES

Bugental, J. Someone needs to worry: The existential anxiety of responsibility and decision. In G. Belkin (Ed.), *Contemporary psychotherapies*. Chicago: Rand McNally, 1980.

Coe, W., Basden, D., and Graham, C. Posthypnotic amnesia: Suggestions of an active process in dissociative phenomena. *Journal of Abnormal Psychology*, 1976, *85*, 418–421.

Karoly, P., and Steffan, J. *Improving the long-term effects of psychotherapy: Models of durable outcome*. New York: Gardner, 1981.

Kisker, G. *The disorganized personality*. New York: McGraw-Hill, 1964.

Lutzker, J., and Martin, J. *Behavior change*. Monterey, Ca.: Brooks/Cole, 1981.

Depersonalization Disorder

The Case of Elenrae Depersonalization is a state in which a person's sense of personal identity is disrupted. Sometimes the person has the definite impression of being some-

189

one else. More frequently, such persons experience a vague sense that the self is different or at a distance. Changes in sensation, size, and location of extremities are frequently reported. Generally, they feel that their place in the physical environment has been changed. The result is a pervasive sense of change, confusion, and/or loss (Kirshner, 1973). The disturbance is usually temporary, with sharp onset and gradual recovery. Since such experiences are not that uncommon, especially in adolescents, a formal diagnosis is applied only when an episode is disruptive of vocational or social functioning.

The Depersonalization Disorder was included among the dissociative disorders because it does include a change in the integrative functions of identity. There has been some controversy regarding the extent to which depersonalization constitutes a true dissociative disorder. This disorder differs from the other dissociative disorders in that significant memory disturbances are absent. It is generally agreed, though, that there are dissociative features; and (memory disturbance aside) the symptomology and course of the depersonalization disorders are more consistent with dissociative disorders than with other categories. The symptom of depersonalization does occur in several other disorders, such as schizophrenia, mood disorders, and alcohol and drug disorders. Thus, the DSM-III requires that the diagnosis of depersonalization disorder be made only when depersonalization is the major presenting symptom.

The young person who is engaging in the typical reassessment of values and search for identity is naturally vulnerable to this disorder when confronted with unusually stressful and/or traumatic life events (Kirshner, 1973). Thus, it is most frequently seen with adolescents and young adults. The case reported below is a vivid example of the process by which a normal development task of adolescence (solidifying gender and sex-role identity) becomes an overwhelming task for a young girl and precipitates episodes of depersonalization.

Elenrae

Elenrae, a twenty-one-year-old college senior, came to the emergency room one November night about 2 A.M. and asked to be admitted, stating she was afraid she was losing her mind. She was quite agitated and disoriented, complaining that she felt as if she couldn't keep her mind and body together. She was admitted and sedated. The next morning, Elenrae gave the following account of experiences to the intake social worker who interviewed her:

It all started this past summer at a camp for girls where I taught swimming. I had worked there every summer since high school. I had always enjoyed working there and looked forward to returning—but this summer was different. The first day, I met Risa, who taught horseback riding there. We were immediately attracted to one another and quickly became really close. After each class, she would find me and we would make plans for that evening, usually to do some drinking. Then we began doing some dope, probably too much, as I started needing help getting upstairs at the end of the night. And Risa always tried to arrange it so it would just be us two. At first I didn't think anything of it, but after a while I began to wonder. Then, too, it seemed like she became jealous when anyone else talked with me—or at least that's what I felt.

Well, one night about three weeks after camp started, we were out and had been drinking a lot, and she began to say strange things. Things that girls don't usually say to one another. She told me how beautiful she thought I was, and that there was something she wanted to ask me but the time wasn't right. All along, I felt she was sizing me up and that somehow I met her standards. As I tried to figure out what it all meant, I began to suspect she was gay. Then I thought no—not one of my friends. You see, I've never been around any homosexuals before. I never even thought about them very much. I always figured it didn't involve me, so they can do whatever they want. Risa didn't say any more, so I let it go and we went on back to camp.

It got to the point that Risa was cutting me off from everyone else. She came and got me out of bed each morning, sat next to me at every meal, and waited for me after classes. I thought it was a bit strange, yet deep inside I liked it. And I liked the idea of having the upper hand but not giving her what she wanted. See, she would almost ask me something (I think I always knew what it was), and then I would change the subject or something to make her be quiet. I mentioned to one of my friends that I thought Risa was gay, and she didn't believe me. Still, somehow I think I always knew.

Well, one night about a month or so after that night she said all those strange things, we were sitting out on a dam drinking beer. Risa turned and looked at me and I got this sick feeling inside me. I knew I was about to know for sure if she was gay. She told me that she couldn't put it off any longer; and that I would probably freak out but she had to tell me anyway. She looked at me and said, "Elenrae, I want you." I really didn't know how to handle it, so I managed to mumble something about there being nothing wrong with the way she felt or anything, but I didn't feel the same way. I told her she was only a friend to me and there could never be anything more between us.

Really, I wasn't sure about what to say or how to feel. She told me she knew I would ignore her from then on—since she had exposed herself. I really didn't want to do that. I mean, I like her, you know. So, I didn't say anything to her—and that was my big mistake! When we talked again, she said it only had to be for fifteen days. Then we could go our separate ways. The reason for the fifteen days was because that was when camp would be over.

Well, my boyfriend was coming to camp that weekend. So she had given me a choice—her or him! At first I thought I could deal with it, though in the back of my mind, it began to mess me up. I got so confused about who I was and what I wanted, I began to feel like I wasn't anybody. Like I really didn't exist at all—physically. I started looking in mirrors and pinching myself—to make sure I was still there. For two days before he came, I didn't go to my swimming classes because I didn't feel like I could control my arms and legs. They felt so numb.

Then my boyfriend came and we had a great time together. I forgot about Risa altogether. I felt like I loved him even more by the time he left. I was feeling alive, and sure of myself. Risa came and found me right after he left. She asked me how I felt about my boyfriend and how I felt about her. Well, I started getting confused so I told her I didn't want to talk about it and let's just have a drink. I drank a lot because I was trying to get it off my mind. But she continued to pressure me for an answer and I got confused again. So, I drank more and more.

This went on for about a week. The only way I could tell Risa I couldn't be her lover was to drown myself in alcohol. Then she would get mad and storm off. I would go after her, apologize, and tell her I would think about it some more. I never really told her I would be her lover; I just kept putting her off. I couldn't decide what I wanted to do because I couldn't think. I would get so confused that I felt like I was watching myself and couldn't control anything I was doing. Finally, I wrote my boyfriend that I thought it would be best to call things off because I wanted to think things out more. I didn't write or call my parents or friends back home. It got so I couldn't teach swimming classes because my arms and legs felt disconnected from the rest of me. So I told the camp director I was sick and went home. I didn't tell Risa I was leaving. I just left.

When I got home, I started seeing my boyfriend again. I felt better and was sure again of who I was and what I wanted. The fall term started and I still hadn't heard from or talked with Risa. I didn't think about her much anymore and figured she had found someone else.

Then last night she called me and told me how much she missed me and how she had never loved anyone as much as me. She asked me to come live with her, and said she was willing to take the consequences. I completely freaked out, screamed at her to leave me alone, and hung up on her. Then I couldn't get to sleep because I couldn't stop thinking about her. I started imagining being with her and then I would think about my boyfriend. I got confused again and felt like my mind and body were no longer attached. Then I started to panic because I was afraid I was losing my mind. That's when I called a taxi and came here.

Etiology   Psychodynamic theorists have traditionally suggested that repression of unacceptable impulses is a major factor in dissociative experiences (Kiersch, 1962). This would fit with Elenrae (whose name is fitting, as later in the treatment she commented that she always had a funny feeling about having a single name made up of two names). She could discuss the issue of homosexuality at an intellectual level and could theoretically consider the possibility for Risa and herself. However, any gut-level (maybe the wrong level) upsurge of these feelings would trigger anxiety, which generated the dissociative experiences of confusion about her "self" and a loss of coordination in her legs.

At the same time, those theorists with a behavioral orientation have pointed out how more recent experiences can be a model for the dissociative experience. Munich (1977) presents the case of an adolescent girl who developed dissociative experiences in the face of unacceptable feelings of hostile anger toward her mother and incestuous feelings about her father.

Munich notes that a prior mild delirium experienced when she was stung by a bee more than likely served as the model for the dissociative experience. Experiences generated by alcohol or drug intoxication are a common model here, which would fit with Elenrae's history.

Treatment

Fortunately, this disorder usually remits under placement in a controlled and positive structure, such as hospitalization, or other means of control over stimuli and experiences. Providing information that such experiences are not an indication of serious abnormality is also very helpful. This was a primary technique in the treatment of the rash of "LSD flashbacks" in the 1960s (which were conditioned anxiety responses rather any actual physiological disorder generated by the LSD). Psychotherapy, with a focus on coming to terms with the suppressed feelings, is also usually necessary. This can be complemented by specific techniques such as assertiveness training, and SDT, depending on the individual case (Kirshner, 1973; Munich, 1977; Craighead et al., 1981).

Elenrae's Treatment

Elenrae responded well to her brief hospitalization. She reported feeling better after relating her story, as up until that point she had not felt comfortable confiding in anyone. Since there were no subsequent depersonalization episodes during hospitalization, Elenrae was discharged after four days of observation and was referred to the university counseling center for follow-up therapy.

Elenrae's counselor felt that she might benefit from a weekly women's group in addition to individual therapy. Elenrae found the women's group helpful in clarifying the boundaries of intimacy between heterosexual women. Some of the women were gay and Elenrae learned to relate to them without becoming confused about her own sexual identity.

The course of individual therapy was more painful for Elenrae. It became apparent that several issues required attention. First of all, they worked to help her decrease her use of drugs and alcohol. The loss of consciousness in these experiences is often a precursor for a depersonalization experience. Secondly, it became clear that Elenrae was undecided about a vocation and fearful of graduating from college. She was in recreation and education, yet not particularly enthusiastic about teaching. She said she would be happier in business but thought she was not bright enough. Also, her boyfriend was graduating at the same time and wanted them to start planning their wedding. Elenrae had dated this young man throughout high school and college. Her experience with other men was limited since she had had no other serious relationships. She thought she loved her boyfriend, yet wanted more experience. Also, Elenrae was concerned that they had settled into a routine of taking one another for granted. There were other less prominent issues; for example, Elenrae wanted to lose ten pounds, get along better with her roommate, and improve her study habits.

The most debilitating issue, however, was Elenrae's problem-solving style. Actually, the major focus of therapy involved helping her develop a problem-solving style. Elenrae was in the habit of ignoring problems and hoping they would go away. She discovered that her reluctance to face problems was as much a precipitant of the depersonalization episodes as the gender identity issue. Unfortunately, the tendency to depersonalization would release her from tension and anxiety by essentially allowing her to escape from situations, so that whenever therapy became difficult she would depersonalize. The therapist was initially accepting of these episodes and would discontinue the session so that Elenrae could recover. But the third time, the therapist merely continued the session in silence until the usual stopping point. Elenrae found this very disconcerting and expressed her anger with the therapist in the next session. The therapist responded by suggesting that Elenrae attempt to keep on task by talking out loud about the distraction pull she was experiencing. This was effective in keeping her on task (Meichenbaum, 1977).

Elenrae agreed to learn deep muscle relaxation and to employ the technique whenever she began to depersonalize (Craighead et al., 1981). This plan was effective, and the number of depersonalization episodes gradually decreased. Also, Elenrae began to resolve other issues. She did her student teaching in the winter quarter. The experience was a good one, and Elenrae accepted a job as a high school physical education instructor. She decided that she had been exclusive with her boyfriend because she was afraid of new relationships. She talked this over with her boyfriend and discovered he had similar feelings. They decided to postpone their engagement but to continue seeing one another along with other people.

Conclusions While depersonalization experiences are not unusual in adolescence, they can lead to serious life disruption unless controlled. They do respond effectively to therapy, especially if the person can be helped to gain access to the previously unacceptable feelings and impulses. Experiences that produce distortion in the sense of self, such as drug episodes, promote susceptibility to dissociative experiences in those persons whose ego is somewhat fragile or in a state of flux, as in adolescence or "change of life."

Interestingly enough, Elenrae's other problems abated without intervention. Her grades improved, as did her relationship with her roommate. Also, she lost ten pounds without much effort. Apparently, these areas had been affected by Elenrae's general confusion and anxiety. When she resolved the major issues, she was able to increase her concentration, be more pleasant with her roommate, and attend to her diet.

REFERENCES

Craighead, W., Kazdin, A., and Mahoney, M. *Behavior modification*. Boston: Houghton Mifflin, 1981.

Kiersch, T. Amnesia: A clinical study of 98 cases. *American Journal of Psychiatry*, 1962, *119*, 57–60.

Kirshner, L. Dissociative reactions: An historical review and clinical study. *Acta Psychiatrica Scandinavia*, 1973, *49*, 498–511.

Meichenbaum, D. *Cognitive behavior modification*. New York: Plenum, 1977.

Munich, R. Depersonalization in a female adolescent. *International Journal of Psychoanalytic Psychotherapy*, 1977, *6*, 187–197.

The Psychosexual Disorders

The Psychosexual Disorders include syndromes in which psychological factors are assumed to be of major etiological significance in the development of disrupted or deviant sexual behaviors. They include the Gender Disorders, Paraphilias, and the Psychosexual Dysfunctions. If the disorders of sexual functioning are caused solely by organic factors (a fairly rare occurrence), a psychosexual disorder diagnosis is not made—even though there may be psychological consequences. The Gender Disorders are marked by felt incongruence between the actual physical sexual apparatus and gender identity. If these concerns have continuously existed for more than two years in an adult, are not due to schizophrenia or a genetic disorder, and the person strongly desires to alter the genital structure and live as the opposite sex, it is labeled Transsexualism. Otherwise, the diagnosis is either Gender Identity Disorder of Childhood or Atypical Gender Identity Disorder.

In the Paraphilias, sexual arousal by unusual objects or situations may interfere with the individual's capacity for reciprocal affectionate sexual activity. The specific diagnoses are made in accordance with the nature of arousing stimuli; for example, transvestism, pedophilia, voyeurism, sexual sadism. The essential feature of the Psychosexual Dysfunctions is inhibition in the appetitive or psychophysiological changes that accompany the complete sexual response cycle. Inhibitions in the response cycle may occur in one or more of the following phases: appetitive, excitement, orgasm, resolution. Finally, there is the class of Other Psychosexual Disorders that includes Ego-dystonic Homosexuality and psychosexual disorders not elsewhere classified. Ego-dystonic Homosexuality is applicable only when a sustained pattern of overt homosexual arousal has been a persistent source of distress for a person who has an internalized desire to acquire or increase heterosexual arousal.

The expanded DSM-III category of Psychosexual Disorders is indicative of the continuing attitude change toward the description and treatment of sexual problems. Before Freud, sexuality was not discussed in polite society and was attributed to superstition, sin, or to presumed genetic defects in most medical treatises. Freudian theory brought sexual dysfunctions into more open consideration, even though he attributed them to unconscious childhood conflicts that could be resolved only through psychoanalysis.

Current thinking generally regards psychosexual disorders to be the result of faulty psychosexual adjustment and learning and to be affected in certain cases by genetic and temperament variables. Thus, they are considered responsive to a variety of treatment approaches, such as operant and classical conditioning, biofeedback, hypnosis, and/or sexual reassignment surgery. Outcome studies using these techniques have been generally encouraging, especially for the sexual dysfunctions (Masters & Johnson, 1970; Zeiss et al., 1977; Levine, 1979), also for the gender disorders (Rekers, 1977; Rosen et al., 1978), and to a lesser degree for the paraphilias (Meyer & Freeman, 1977; Hendrix & Meyer, 1976; Cox, 1980).

REFERENCES

Cox, D. Exhibitionism: An overview. In D. Cox and R. Daitzman (Eds.), *Exhibitionism*. New York: Garland STPM, 1980.

Hendrix, M., and Meyer, R. Toward more comprehensive and durable client changes: A case report. *Psychotherapy: Theory, Research and Practice*, 1976, *13*, 263–266.

Levine, S. Barriers to the attainment of ejaculatory control. *Medical Aspects of Human Sexuality*, 1979, *13*, 32–56.

Masters, W., and Johnson, V. *Human sexual inadequacy*, Boston: Little, Brown, 1970.

Meyer, R., and Freeman, W. A social episode model of human sexual behavior. *Journal of Homosexuality*, 1977, *2*, 123–131.

Rekers, G. Atypical gender development and psychosocial adjustment. *Journal of Applied Behavior Analysis*, 1977, *10*, 559–571.

Rosen, A., Rekers, G., and Bentler P. Ethical issues in the treatment of children. *Journal of Social Issues*, 1978, *34*.

Zeiss, A., Rosen, G., and Zeiss, R. Orgasm during intercourse: A treatment strategy for women. *Journal of Consulting and Clinical Psychology*, 1977, *45*, 891–895.

Transvestism

The Case of Randy   Transvestism is classified in the DSM-III as one of the Paraphilias, which is the DSM-III designation for the older term of *sexual deviation*. The term

Paraphilia is used because it apparently is felt to have fewer inherent connotations of sinfulness and disorder; the term also is used in order to emphasize that most sexual behaviors are on a continuum with normal behaviors. The concept of deviance is thought to introduce an unnecessary distancing from normal sexual experiences. Transvestism is defined in the DSM-III as recurrent and persistent cross-dressing that is initiated for the purpose of sexual arousal and that eventually becomes habitual. The transvestite experiences intense frustration when external circumstances interfere with cross-dressing.

The disorder is relatively rare and more predominant in males than females. Most individuals who have been involved in transvestism have cross-dressed by the age of ten, and usually much younger (Rekers, 1977). These individuals usually are married, so this status is likely to generate additional anxiety and depression. Most cross-dressing starts out as a partial phenomenon, but it is likely to generalize to the point at which the person feels compelled to dress fully as a woman and occasionally to behave as a female in public.

Transvestism is commonly confused with transsexualism (Rekers, 1977; Meyer, 1982). The major difference is that transsexualism is considered to be a gender identity disorder whereas transvestism is a paraphilia or sexual deviation. Transsexuals truly feel as if they should be the other sex. In fact, most transsexuals feel so strongly that they have been trapped in the wrong body that they actively pursue surgical alterations. The transvestite, however, does not have compelling desires to participate in sex change surgery. Rather, even though they seek sexual arousal through cross-dressing, they maintain identity with their biological gender.

Randy

Randy, a handsome thirty-eight-year-old black, came to his first appointment at the mental health center with his wife. She was obviously more upset than he was at the time of referral, and she clearly had initiated the idea to come to the center. With some prodding, Randy finally said that he was a transvestite and that he wished to change this. His assertion that he wished to change was not completely convincing, as it was evident that his wife had played a major role in his making that statement.

This was a second marriage for Randy. Even though he had been a transvestite throughout the five years of this marriage, only recently had his wife become aware of Randy's unusual sexual interests. Randy admitted that he had been careless in the last several months. As a result, his wife found certain clothes that led her to an initial erroneous conclusion that Randy was having a standard extramarital affair. Randy's first mistake was that he left a small make-up kit in his clothes pocket, which his wife found when she

*picked up the coat to take to the cleaners. He was able to provide
her with a story that she reluctantly accepted. But she then acciden-
tally discovered a suitcase of "change clothes" in the back of his car.
She again assumed that this was evidence that he was seeing another
woman and she became very irate and confronted him with the
evidence.*

*Randy then felt he had no other option left except to explain
his behavior. When he did so, it was clear that he had upset his wife
much more than if he had told her that he had been having an affair. She said she was not only shocked, but also ashamed and embarrassed, and she insisted that he get help as soon as possible. Although Randy had not been as concerned about the behavior, he
realized that he did feel committed to his wife, that he loved her,
and that this had hurt her intensely. As a result, he stated that he
would make an effort to change.*

Social History   In many cases of transvestism, it is not clear as to how the cross-dressing first
started and became reinforced. Fortunately, in Randy's case, certain known
variables make his inclination towards transvestism more understandable.

Until the age of two, Randy's mother and father raised him in a normal fashion. However, when Randy was two, his mother contracted a rare
respiratory disease, which required her to leave the area and go to a special
hospital. Randy's father felt that his wife deeply needed him near her, and
also that he could not adequately care for Randy at the same time. Randy's
father had a sister whom he trusted could raise Randy adequately, so Randy
moved to the home of his aunt. She was a forty-five-year-old woman who
had lived alone ever since a short and traumatic marriage that she had
entered into when she was eighteen years old. Since that time, she had
worked as a legal secretary and had lived a quiet and reclusive life. Though
she was devoted to her younger brother, Randy's father, in general she was
relatively hostile toward men, and had seldom dated since her divorce many
years ago.

As might be expected, she really had little sense of what child rearing
entailed. When Randy inadvertently picked up some of her shoes and put
them on, she saw no problem with this, and indeed thought this was
humorous and cute. Randy responded to this reinforcement by trying on
other articles of her clothing, and she accepted this behavior as long as he
only did it in the house.

At times she would let Randy dress up and and they would have tea
parties. She even took pictures of Randy in his feminine dress to put in an
album. The basic problem was that she really had no idea of how to deal
with a little boy and had no interest herself in the activities that are interesting to most young boys.

Randy's mother died when Randy was four years old. His father took

199

a job as traveling salesman and decided to let Randy continue living with his aunt. Randy's father eventually took a more lucrative job as a sales representative and was not required to travel as extensively. When Randy was nine, his father remarried and brought Randy to live with him and his new wife. The cross-dressing naturally ceased for a time as the usual stimuli that elicited it were now absent. However, his new step-mother once allowed Randy to put on one of her dresses, and she also thought it was very cute. Then, some time after this she discovered Randy going through her lingerie drawer, and on another occasion she discovered him wearing a pair of her underwear. When she reported the incidents to Randy's father, he became very upset and whipped Randy. When they discovered him doing it again, Randy's father and step-mother attempted a homemade version of the therapeutic technique called "negative practice." That is, they forced Randy to dress entirely in women's clothing and wear them for the duration of the day. However, they did not realize that he went into a high state of sexual arousal and masturbated several times during that day. Randy did at least get the message that his parents disapproved of this behavior, and as a result he became secretive about it.

On the surface he showed a rather normal adolescence. He participated in many school activities in high school, and in particular became so skilled in tennis that he was elected team captain. He dated occasionally, and in all overt respects seemed to be relatively normal. However, in his secret life, he would often steal or buy women's clothes and wear them while by himself in a woods near their house, or he would wear them when he knew his parents would not be around. He now consistently masturbated to orgasm when he wore the clothes.

Randy continued to date fairly regularly throughout high school and college. These were social rather than sexual events for him, and on those few occasions when he did become sexually involved, he would use fantasies of cross-dressing to initiate and maintain his arousal.

He first married when he was twenty-three years old, and the marriage lasted about two years. He was only able to experience sexual arousal with his wife when he fantasized being in women's clothes. They did not have sex often, though it was reasonably satisfactory to both when they did. He tried on occasion to give his wife some hints about his interests, but she did not respond. Further, he became aware from her cues that unusual or "kinky" sexual behavior would be upsetting for her. They had few mutual interests and eventually little affection for each other. The divorce seemed inevitable and was not remarkably distressing for either party.

After the divorce, there was a noticeable increase in Randy's transvestite behavior. Though he had attained a fine job with an insurance firm, he would occasionally go off on vacation and spend most of the time dressing up in women's clothes and masturbating. Also, he found a club in a nearby metropolitan area that catered to transvestites. Individuals would openly share fantasies about their behavior and would go about the club dressed in women's clothes doing a number of behaviors that any member of a normal club would consider typical, such as having dinner and dancing. Randy managed to keep this aspect of his world separate enough so that it did not interfere with his work or other social behaviors. He met his second wife through his work. They had a number of mutual interests and both were somewhat lonely, so after a short courtship they married.

Etiology   Traditional theories have emphasized the denial of masculinity and castration anxiety as critical in the development of transvestism, but the relevant social learning theory is somewhat more applicable to Randy's case. At a very early juncture in Randy's life, cross-dressing received much attention from the "Significant Other" in his world, who at that time was his aunt. She was also the major figure from whom Randy could model behaviors. As a result, Randy was involved almost exclusively in a traditionally feminine world with few other real options to consider. Also, the attention and approval he received from his aunt for cross-dressing were particularly reinforcing (Rekers, 1977; Rosen et al., 1978).

This attention continued when he returned to live with his father and new step-mother, at least for a short period of time. Their later attempt to frustrate this behavior by having him dress up totally as a female and keep the clothes on all day unfortunately backfired. Their idea was not that bad, however. Negative practice is effective in certain conditions, but it needs to be carefully monitored and must be done in such a way that the experience is clearly aversive. Most parents are not going to be adequately sophisticated psychologically to carry this through. A professional consultation at this point could have turned things around (Rekers, 1977). Randy went underground with his behavior and his parents, of course, were relieved not to see any evidence of it anymore, as it ended much upset and embarrassment for them. The behavior waxed and waned throughout the rest of Randy's life. It was most prominent when Randy was experiencing frustration in other interpersonal areas of his life, or when he simply had more options to practice the transvestism.

As is seen in Randy's case, transvestism is a variation of fetishism, particularly from a social learning theory view (Meyer & Freeman, 1977; Meyer, 1982). A specific object or behavior becomes associated with social reinforcement and/or sexual reinforcement at an early period. Continued pairing of the behavior with sexual reinforcement, often accidental on the first few occasions, or engendered by another person such as a playmate, further reinforces the pattern. The person then begins practicing it habitually, and it becomes crystallized.

Treatment   The clinician asked to treat a transsexual might consider a referral for transsexual surgery, but such an option would be irrelevant for the transvestite who does not really consider himself to be of the other sex. Actually, whether even a transsexual should also undergo this surgery remains a controversial issue among professionals. Some argue that it is unnecessary, and that with counseling and the passage of time, the transsexual individual can lose the compulsion to change sex. On the other hand, there is some evidence that transsexual surgery is effective in making a certain subgroup of individuals happier and more satisfied with their life situation (Pauly, 1968; Money & Wiedeking, 1980).

The most effective method for changing any pattern of sexual behavior to another one has been that of aversive conditioning (Meyer & Freeman, 1977; Meyer, 1982). It was initially used for changing the sexual preference of the homosexual individual, then was expanded into dealing with the wide variety of disordered sexual behaviors. In Randy's case, it was decided to employ the therapy technique of "thought stopping" before using the aversive technique, as it was felt this would enhance the total effectiveness of the treatment program.

During the thought-stopping phase, Randy was asked to envision a scene in which he was cross-dressing. When he was able to develop this pattern of thoughts adequately, he was asked to signal to the therapist that he had done so. His therapist then shouted "Stop," and asked Randy if the thoughts had been interrupted. Usually, the thoughts would be interrupted by the startle response. Thus, the client learns that these patterns are not as compelling as they seem. Randy was instructed to use thought stopping when he found himself considering cross-dressing outside the therapy session. For example, if the thoughts came unwittingly, Randy was asked to shout "Stop," or to say it to himself. Thought stopping has proven to be effective with this type of behavior, though it was originally developed for the more inclusive concept of obsessive thoughts. In that sense, the fantasies in a paraphilia can be seen as having obsessive components (see the earlier case of Bess).

The second phase of Randy's treatment was the aversion therapy. Randy was asked to sit in a chair in front of a standard movie screen and was hooked up with electrodes to a shock unit. Independent of the shock unit, a piece of rubber tubing was placed around his penis. It measures the degree of blood flow to the penis. Randy was shown a series of slides, some of which depicted scenes that would be arousing to a transvestite. Others were of normal heterosexual behavior or of a nude person of the other sex, in this case Randy's wife, to whom he wished to increase his sexual attraction. A slide of a transvestite scene, preferably a slide from pornographic material Randy might have already used to gain arousal, was placed on the screen. Randy was told that he could keep the picture on as long as he wished, but that he would receive an increasingly strong electrical shock as he did. When he eventually asked the therapist to take the picture away, this turned the shock off and a scene of either normal heterosexual behavior or a picture of his wife was flashed on the screen. The rationale here is that the cessation of shock is a reinforcing event, so the aim was to pair the reinforcement with the desired sexual behavior (Meyer & Freeman, 1977; Sturgis & Adams, 1978).

When Randy began to notice a change in his sexual preference, which occurred after three half-hour sessions of aversive conditioning and thought stopping, he was asked to participate in controlled masturbatory training. He was told that when he masturbated he was to force himself to imagine desired scenes, such as sex with his wife, at the time of orgasm. Also, he was to try to introduce these scenes in his mind as early as possible in the masturbation sequence. At first, he needed the transvestite scenes to obtain arousal, but gradually he was able to replace these scenes earlier and earlier with imagined scenes of sexual behavior with his wife. In that way, the reinforcement from his sexual arousal and orgasm increased the future arousal of these new images, and hopefully this would generalize to his wife in actuality, and it did.

Naturally enough, there had been some disruption of his marital situation. So Randy and his wife also participated in marital therapy (Framo, 1979) and had several sessions in sexual instructions along the lines that Masters and Johnson (1970, 1979) suggest. These sessions helped to enhance their long-term relationship. All indications are that Randy's change was thorough and without regression to the transvestite pattern. It is true that in other such cases there might well be a regression on occasion to the earlier behaviors, and booster treatments at that time would be necessary.

Comment   Because transvestites are secretive about their behavior and usually cross-dress in private, many are never seen by professionals. Although impersonating the opposite sex is sometimes illegal, cross-dressing is not considered a serious offense and arrests are seldom made. When a transvestite is arrested or otherwise discovered (as with Randy's wife), then incarceration is usually recommended. Some wives of transvestites are accepting of the cross-dressing, are willing to accompany their husbands on public outings while they are cross-dressed, and are adapting sexually to that pattern. But, as noted in this case, the usual effect of cross-dressing is marital strain, leading to divorce. For cases for which cross-dressing is a focus of treatment, behavioral techniques supplemented by psychotherapy and social skills training have been generally successful.

REFERENCES

Framo, J. Family theory and therapy. *American Psychologist*, 1979, 34, 988–992.

Masters, W., and Johnson. V. *Human sexual inadequacy.* Boston: Little, Brown, 1970.

————. *Homosexuality in perspective.* Boston: Little, Brown, 1979.

Meyer, R. *The clinician's handbook.* Boston: Allyn and Bacon, 1982.

Meyer, R., and Freeman, W. A social episode model of human sexual behavior. *Journal of Homosexuality*, 1977, *2*, 123–131.

Money, J., and Wiedeking, C. Gender identity/normal role differentiation and its transpositions. In B. Worman (Ed.), *Handbook of Human Sexuality.* Englewood Cliffs, N.J.: Prentice-Hall, 1980.

Pauly, I. The current status of the change of sex operation. *Journal of Nervous and Mental Disease*, 1968, *147*, 460–471.

Rekers, G. Atypical gender development and psychosocial adjustment. *Journal of Applied Behavior Analysis*, 1977, *10*, 559–571.

Rosen, A., Rekers, G., and Bentler, P. Ethical issues in the treatment of children. *Journal of Social Issues*, 1978, *34*.

Sturgis, E., and Adams, H. The right to treatment: Issues in the treatment of homosexuality. *Journal of Consulting and Clinical Psychology*, 1978, *46*, 165–169.

Autocastration

The Case of Mr. A Autocastration (removing one's own testicles and/or penis) is a rare event. Occasionally, it has been mistakenly viewed as a desire to change sexual identity. A strong-felt need to change one's anatomical sex combined with a strong identification with the opposite sex is labeled Transsexualism, which is listed as a gender disorder in DSM-III. In screening candidates for transsexual surgery, the clinician has to be concerned about individuals who seek this change for pathological reasons. For example, some candidates for this type of surgery may have delusions, such as Mr. A does, that their sexual apparatus is the cause of their problems. Thus, they hope to remove the problems by removing the offending body part. As the authors of this case note, autocastration can also have a suicidal component. They feel that here it was a kind of compromise with the suicidal impulses, though certainly a costly one. There are other types of slow or partial suicide; for example, people who drink or smoke to excess just after being told by a physician that they must cut down on these patterns because of developing heart disease. Yet, few patterns are as dramatic or as shocking as autocastration.

A Case Study of Autocastration

Roman Pabis, Masood A. Mirza, and Seymour Tozman

Although transsexual surgery has received considerable attention, autocastration remains a rarity (1, 2). Self-castration is usually performed in a state of psychotic confusion, except for those few men throughout history who castrated themselves for religious reasons (2, 3). Our case report describes a man with minimal psychotic confusion, although elements of psychotic depression were evident, who committed autocastration in a premeditated and carefully thought out manner, possibly as a substitute for suicide.

Case Report

Mr. A, a 29-year-old man, was admitted to our hospital emergency room after excising his scrotum and testes with a kitchen knife. He committed autocastration while immersed in the ocean because, he alleged, the ocean "was cool and would act as an anesthetic." He then returned home and handed his testicles to his mother. Apparently, he felt that at his birth "she had half died," and he intended to give back to her the life she had given him at birth. His mother flushed the testicles down the toilet and promptly called an ambulance. Mr. A's act was not impulsive; he had previously consulted a surgeon about an orchidectomy, but the surgeon refused to perform the operation.

While in the hospital, and receiving psychiatric treatment, Mr. A's anxiety and depression diminished and many of his delusions vanished. He exhibited no regrets about his drastic act and seemed, in fact, relieved. He was particularly happy about losing some of his facial hair because the hairs "multiply and germinate and are dirty." In the following months his facial hair grew back (with compensating adrenal testosterone production), and he again exhibited accelerating agitation, although he responded well to psychiatric support. Mr. A is now considering a testicular prothesis but has no interest in a transsexual procedure.

During his childhood Mr. A exhibited behavioral problems severe enough for him to spend 10 years in a class for emotionally disturbed children. Despite emotional difficulties he finished high school satisfactorily. At age 17 he withdrew from social activities and at his parents' prodding, he consulted a psychiatrist who felt that Mr. A was suffering from psychotic depression. At this time Mr. A also reported a frequent visual percept that things were "getting smaller and farther away" (micropsia and teleopsia), and he had a long standing delusion that masturbating was "draining my brain of nuclear material." Masturbation aggravated his guilt and shame and, consequently, his anxiety. During this time he sought prostitutes and demanded humiliating, sado-masochistic acts. He also engaged in homosexual prostitution assuming a passive, masochistic role. He always insisted however, that he was heterosexual and that his homosexual acts were committed only for money.

His sexual activities compounded his feelings of guilt, anxiety, and depression until suicide seemed the only solution. He chose autocastration instead, an act which was less final than suicide but which would destroy the object of his guilt—his genitals, specifically his testicles, which represented his germinative capacity, his progeny, and his future self.

Discussion We think Mr. A's autocastration was either a substitute for suicide or a focal suicide as described by Menninger (4) rather than the result of transsexual sex misidentification or dissatisfaction with his masculinity. Mr. A was driven to commit his act while under a sustained and mounting sexual tension, which he could not understand. In fact, he developed an elaborate delusional system to explain his unusual state of tension. His sharp decrease in sexual drive and anxiety after autocastration suggest the possibility that the male hormone testosterone might be related to development of such tension.

REFERENCES

1. Haberman, M. and Michael, R. Autocastration in transsexualism. *American Journal of Psychiatry*, 1979, *136*, 347–348.
2. Lowy, J. and DePriest, M. Three cases of genital self-surgery and their relationship to transsexualism. *Journal of Sex Research*, 1976, *12*, 283–294.
3. Cleugh, J. *Love Locked Out.* New York: Crown Publishers, 1955.
4. Menninger, K. *Man Against Himself.* New York: Harcourt Brace and World, 1938.

Comment Autocastration occurs rarely and is almost always associated with emotional disturbance. The belief that one's genitals are a "source of evil" or otherwise undesirable occasionally accompanies the delusions of paranoia or the confused associations of schizophrenia. In this regard, this article presents dramatic confirmation of the point that fantasies that may at first seem to be suggestive of transsexualism can instead indicate unrelated though severe psychopathlogy. The radical and irrevocable nature of transsexual surgery requires that a significant psychological screening procedure be administered before surgery is allowed (Jayaram et al., 1978; Strassberg et al., 1979).

REFERENCES

Jayaram, B., Stuteville, D. and Bush, I. Complications and undesirable results of sex-reassignment surgery in male to female transsexuals. *Archives of Sexual Behavior*, 1978, *4*, 337–345.

Strassberg, D., Roback, H., Cunningham J., McKee, E., and Larson, P. Psychopathology in self-identified female-to-male transsexuals, homosexuals, and heterosexuals. *Archives of Sexual Behavior*, 1979, 8, 491–496.

Exhibitionism

The Case of Roger We will shortly be presenting an article published in 1976 in which Dr. Mitch Hendrix and the senior author of this book outlined a multimodal treatment approach for exhibitionism. The article shows how a variety of different treatment techniques can be blended into a treatment package designed for a specific problem. It is additionally important since exhibitionism is one of the most common sexual deviations in our society. Since the article does not go into the DSM-III considerations and does not give many details of Roger's background, we will provide some introductory material here before presenting the article.

Diagnostic Considerations Exhibitionism is the exposing of one's genitals to a stranger in order to obtain sexual arousal. The arousal occurs immediately or shortly after the exposure, and ordinarily the exposure is the only sexual encounter that the individual seeks at the time. It is listed in DSM-III as a paraphilia, and it is said to only occur in males. Exhibitionists show a particularly high recidivism rate; more than 20 percent get rearrested for the same offense (Cox, 1980).

Smith and Meyer (1980) have detailed four different personality types that are usually found in exhibitionism. In the Unaware type, the act is simply a secondary result of such disorders as extreme alcohol intoxication or mental retardation. The Characterological type is similar to the rapist in that there is a strong element of hostility in the behavior. The shock expressed by the victim is one of the primary reinforcements. Few exhibitionists are dangerous (estimates range from about 1 to 10 percent); those who are almost always come from this personality type. The Impulsive exhibitionist is tense and sexually confused, and the behavior is an impulsive response to upset and anxiety.

The last pattern, the Inadequate type, which is the pattern that best fits Roger, is also somewhat obsessional in nature. In addition, this type is relatively shy and introverted and does not have good social relations, particularly with the opposite sex. Though there often is some anger towards women in this type, the exhibitionistic behavior is at the same time a pathetic attempt at ego affirmation, such that there is even hope for later social and/or sexual contact with the victim.

Roger: Social History Data
The important features of this particular selection are the treatment issues. Yet, certain aspects of Roger's earlier development should be

mentioned because they are consistent with the observations noted in other exhibitionists.

Like many exhibitionists, Roger did not have a consistent and positive relationship with a father or father-substitute. Roger's father abandoned the family when Roger was about seven years old. He has only vague memories of his father, none of which are positive. Roger is an only child. Following the abandonment by his father, Roger's mother reacted to the demands of the single parent role by becoming overprotective and dominating. Though she did not directly reinforce any effeminate behavior in Roger, she always emphasized "dangers" in the world and generally made conservative decisions about any potential risks that Roger might encounter. As a result, Roger feared risking, not only in physical activities, but in interpersonal areas as well.

He did have friends as he grew up, some of whom were close to him, though he never effectively interacted with women. He was seduced when he was twelve years old by a sixteen-year-old cousin. She made Roger disrobe in front of her, played with him until he had an erection, and then masturbated him to orgasm while she also fondled herself. On later occasions she had Roger attempt penetration, though this never led to a satisfying sexual experience for either of them.

Roger began to date with regularity when he entered his senior year in high school. He had intercourse on two occasions during that year, but neither was particularly satisfying to either himself or his partner. He reported that he got more enjoyment out of masturbating in front of his partner than he did actually having intercourse with her, though he always insisted that he wished he enjoyed intercourse more.

The first occasion when he exhibited himself occurred in his junior year in high school when he encountered two younger girls in a field near his school. He had been urinating and did not see the girl until they were very close. He turned and the girls looked, screamed, and ran away. Roger reports he became terribly aroused, and when he came home that evening, he masturbated several times with the images of exhibiting himself. He tried to repeat the pattern regularly, often using the ploy of pretending to be urinating into bushes at spots where he knew women would pass by. In one sense, this was a wise choice. The victim was always in the bind of deciding whether or not the exhibitionism had been intentional or accidental, and for that reason there was seldom a report to the police. But Roger is a bright individual, and knew the risks he was taking. When he came very close to being caught, he referred himself to the psychological training clinic where he went to school.

Now we will present the material from the article, as it details an extensive multimodal therapy approach.

REFERENCES

Cox, D. Exhibitionism: An overview. In D. Cox and R. Daitzman (Eds.) *Exhibitionism.* Garland STPM, 1980.

Smith, S. and Meyer, R. Workings between the legal system and the therapist. In D. Cox and R. Daitzman (Eds.) *Exhibitionism.* Garland STPM, 1980.

Toward More Comprehensive
and Durable Client Changes:
A Case Report

E. Mitchell Hendrix and Robert G. Meyer

Case Study

Roger, a self-referred undergraduate in his mid-twenties, had been sexually exposing himself to females five to seven times weekly for several weeks, and this was the most intense the problem behavior had been in its seven-year history. He estimated his total number of exposures to be between six and seven hundred. Incredibly, he was not criminally apprehended. Roger's exhibitionism occurred in his military service, where he received brief inpatient treatment and was said to have paranoid schizophrenic tendencies. Most recently, when the threat of being caught or the likelihood that he would be seen by persons other than the target individual was too high, he would yell obscenities or show female pornographic materials. On occasion, he aggressively grabbed his victim as he exposed himself and spoke obscenely to her. At referral, Roger was doing quite well academically and seemed fundamentally intact, yet the deviant and schizoid quality of his interpersonal behavior warranted intervention.

Although aversive conditioning techniques might have been considered apropos, the current authors* felt that a more comprehensive approach was warranted. Further exploratory sessions with the client revealed a history of adequate heterosexual functioning apart from his exhibitionism. Very active sexually since puberty, Roger had had a brief marriage and a series of interpersonally superficial sexual partnerships.

Roger was seen for 32 sessions within a six-month period. The problem was first re-conceptualized as an inappropriate response to heterosexual stimuli rather than sexual deviancy. A very goal-directed and hard-driving individual, Roger could trace sources of tension to his busy schedule, his relationship with his current girlfriend,

From: Hendrix, E., and Meyer, R. Toward more comprehensive and durable client changes: A case report. *Psychotherapy: Theory, Research and Practice*, 1976, *13*(3), 263–266. Reprinted by permission of *Psychotherapy: Theory, Research and Practice.*

*The first author served as therapist in consultation with the second author.

and to his work. He felt that exposing himself and later masturbating provided him momentary release of frustration and "time
out" from tension, although guilt feelings typically followed. Hence,
the next step involved progressive relaxation training in the office as
a self-control technique and a means of interrupting tension-building
response sequences.

He was then given cassette tapes of the relaxation instructions
and asked to practice frequently on his own, at the same time recording the time of relaxation and degree of experienced calmness.
Autogenic training was later used as an adjunct. Roger was asked
immediately to keep a daily log of his sexual behavior, describing in
appropriate detail the precipitating conditions and results of both
desirable and undesirable sexual responses. Consonant with Goldfried and Trier (1974), self-control was emphasized as the rationale
for use of relaxation approaches, the home practice, and the record
keeping.

Another aspect of treatment involved desensitization to several hierarchies of interactions with females. Key dimensions were
imagined females' attractiveness, dress, ages and interpersonal styles,
as well as the extent of imagined interaction. Cognitive restructuring
was also employed in an attempt to have the client broaden his
range of expected positive outcomes.

In-session work was complemented by in vivo desensitization
and practice in interpersonal interactions in a manner similar to that
described by Arkowitz (1974). On several occasions the therapist accompanied Roger to interaction settings such as the campus snack
shop. There they jointly analyzed situations and discussed interactions as the client conversed with other students, particularly females. His perceptions of other persons' styles were examined and
alternative perceptions were proposed by both client and therapist.
An additional homework assignment asked Roger to monitor the frequency, nature, and degree of satisfaction of his interactions with
others. Behavioral contracts were then negotiated which called for
him to interact with others with increasing frequency, and progress
was monitored.

A technical matter to be dealt with was that Roger had
typically only felt the urge to expose himself if he was further than
10 feet from the target female. If he found himself within that
radius, he did not lose sexual interest, but he was disinclined to act
inappropriately. With close monitoring, a technique which combined general relaxation and self-instructions to be calm and behave
cordially was designed and implemented. In vivo use of this technique, coupled with desensitization to approaching attractive
females, eventually enabled Roger to interact much more frequently
with women. He reported a corresponding decrease in both his felt

hostility and the urge to expose himself. Positive coping imagery was also used during therapy meetings and by Roger when he practiced relaxation on his own. His developing ease in the company of attractive females allowed him to elicit more and more positive responses from them.

Roger's high rate (almost daily) of indecent exposure declined dramatically shortly after the onset of therapy, but he continued to occasionally expose himself. He was trained to analyze situations in which the opportunity for exhibitionism was great and to administer subvocal self-instructions on how to deal with these temptations. Initially, the strategy was to have him masturbate from seclusion (a response already in his repertoire) instead of actually exposing himself. Later, when it was clear that this response had supplanted the indecent exposure, he worked on fixing the sexual image in his mind and removing himself to a more private setting to masturbate. Finally, he was able to either delay responding to sexual stimuli, or to respond in a more socially appropriate manner, e.g., engaging the female in a conversation. This succession of graded steps seemed to be a major facet of the treatment. At each step, associated fears were extinguished as new skills were developed.

Because it was expected that temptations would sometimes override Roger's self-control abilities, a provision was made for him to call the therapist at the Clinic or at his home, or to stop by the office during periods of difficulty. This variant of delay therapy (Meyer, 1973) offered support and served to interrupt the exhibitionistic response chain.

At Roger's request, an attempt was made to enhance his sexual attraction to his current girlfriend. The therapist suggested that Roger substitute an enticing sexual image of his girlfriend for whatever fantasies he might be imagining during masturbation. At first the substitution was made just before ejaculation. Gradually the substitution was made earlier and earlier. Correspondingly, some suggestions from the work of Masters and Johnson were offered to enhance actual sexual relations with his girlfriend. Assertive training at this point also proved helpful. Feedback from Roger indicated success.

Interspersed among Roger's periods of tension were feelings of pessimism and depression, and he would speak in the bitter tones of a cynic. Experiential focusing (Gendlin, 1969) invariably related these feelings to the avoidance of practical decisions which he needed to make. Later in therapy, Roger was well aware of this trap and worked to confront issues in his life more squarely. Another technique involved replaying sections of earlier therapy tapes. For instance, when he occasionally became discouraged and cynical about the treatment, the therapist played back Roger's earlier com-

ments in which he expressed pride in his progress and in himself.
Much of the last few sessions was then spent listing alternative
courses of career action for Roger's immediate future.

Discussion The authors attribute much of Roger's success to his self-instructing progressively more acceptable sexual and social responses. Meichenbaum and Cameron (1974) have written that "when the standard behavior therapy procedures (are) augmented with a self-instructional package, greater treatment efficacy, more generalization and greater persistence of treatment effects [are obtainable]" (p. 103). The results of helping Roger talk to himself in more adaptive ways were definitely supportive of this claim and point to the need for clients to experience and enhance perceptions of self-control.

At the time this report was prepared, Roger had not exposed himself for at least three months. Rather, during the last therapy meetings and at follow-ups he continued to present evidence that he was actively seeking heterosexual relationships, was optimistic about his potential, and was experiencing enhanced self-esteem and self-control.

Active follow-up of Roger's posttreatment maintenance is underway. For the present, informal monthly checks will be made of his adjustment. While trying to avoid building in failure expectancies or enhancing dependency, the therapist assured Roger that additional treatment sessions would be available in the unlikely event the problem recurred.

In summation, a presenting problem which might have been dealt with primarily (if not exclusively) via aversive conditioning, was handled here with a melange of techniques. Over the course of a six-month active interaction between client and therapist the following techniques were selectively applied: extensive historical interviewing and client expression of feeling; progressive relaxation (with home practice); autogenic training; self-monitoring and record-keeping; environmental manipulation; assertive training; self-instruction; operant and respondent shaping procedures; desensitization (with in vivo exercises); cognitive restructuring; client-therapist meetings in real world settings; behavioral rehearsal; imagery; delay therapy; Masters and Johnson techniques; experiential focusing; joint review of transcripts of previous therapy sessions; active follow-up agreements. These techniques were not applied mechanistically, but rather in the context of a helping relationship marked by mutual respect and commitment to honesty and responsibility. Roger's complex of new skills and behaviors continues to appear more adaptive and durable.

REFERENCES

Arkowitz, H. Desensitization as a self-control procedure: A case report. *Psychotherapy: Theory, Research and Practice*, 1974, *11*, 172–174.

Gendlin, E. T. Focusing. *Psychotherapy: Theory, Research and Practice*, 1969, *6*, 4–15.

Goldfried, M. R., and Trier, C. S. Effectiveness of relaxation as an active coping skill. *Journal of Abnormal Psychology*, 1974, *83*, 348–355.

Meichenbaum, D., and Cameron, R. The clinical potential of modifying what clients say to themselves. *Psychotherapy: Theory, Research, and Practice*, 1974, *11*, 103–117.

Meyer, R. G. Delay therapy: Two case reports. *Behavior Therapy*, 1973, *4*, 709–711.

Psychosexual Dysfunction (Impotence)

The Case of Tim   Psychosexual Dysfunction with Inhibited Sexual Excitement is the DSM-III terminology for the syndromes commonly referred to as impotence and frigidity. Throughout this case history, we will use the term *impotence*, yet note that there is general pejorative connotation to these terms. That is, impotence suggests general personality inadequacy and a weakness of character. The standard term for female psychosexual dysfunction, *frigidity*, in turn suggests a lack of emotional warmth. But there is no evidence that these implied traits occur more commonly in individuals who experience these problems. It is interesting that the weakness in the male and the coldness in the female suggested by these terms are the exact opposites of the characteristics most clearly prescribed in the sex roles of our society—competence for males and sensitivity and warmth for females.

The sexual response cycle is typically thought to be composed of four stages: (1) appetitive, (2) excitement, (3) orgasm, and (4) resolution. Psychosexual dysfunction pertains primarily to the second stage, the excitement stage (Meyer & Freeman, 1977).

The DSM-III characterizes impotence as a recurrent and persistent inhibition of sexual excitement during sexual behavior, manifested by a partial or complete failure to obtain and maintain erection until the sexual act is completed. This definition assumes that the clinician has already judged that the individual engages in sexual activity that is adequate in duration, intensity, and focus. The fact that the term is *psychosexual dysfunction* points out that we are not talking about a disorder caused exclusively by organic factors, such as a spinal tumor, nor are we talking about sexual disorder that is the direct result of a more primary and severe psychiatric syndrome, as for example, from severe and acute anxiety disorder.

In practice, one has to be rather arbitrary in assigning a label of psychosexual dysfunction. Masters and Johnson (1970) arbitrarily define it as a clinical problem if there are failures in 25 percent of the attempts at intercourse. Also, in most cases, total "erectile dysfunction" (the common term in the research literature) is fairly rare, and typically suggests a biological cause. More often than not, the dysfunction is partial. An erection occurs, but it does not persist long enough to provide satisfaction for the partner or for one's own orgasm to occur (Masters & Johnson, 1970).

Tim

After suffering silently for some time, as is typical in this syndrome, Tim went to his personal physician asking for treatment of impotence. The physician referred him to a specialist, who through a careful medical examination ruled out the various physical and endocrinological factors that can affect impotence. Tim's testosterone level was appropriate, and there was no evidence of severe diabetes or of a circulatory disorder. These are the most common physical causes of impotence. Though Tim's testosterone level was not abnormally low, it was slightly below average, so a urologist first administered testosterone to see if this might have a positive effect. There was no relief for Tim. The urologist then attempted to use a placebo, on the assumption that the suggestion could increase Tim's hope and effect a cure. This also was not successful. The urologist then referred Tim to a clinical psychologist who specialized in the treatment of the sexual dysfunctions.

The clinical psychologist listened at length to Tim's story of his background, as a preparation for initiating appropriate psychological treatment.

Tim is thirty-three years old, college educated, and makes a very good first impression. He is physically handsome and in good shape physically, reflecting his prior occupation as a professional baseball player. He also dresses well, keeps himself well groomed, and relates to others with apparent warmth and interest.

Though he recently has been promoted to assistant vice president in the bank in which he works, the general impression he gives is that he is neither strikingly successful nor interested in his work. Also, in spite of his good first impression, it is quickly evident that he is moderately anxious most of the time. On several occasions, he had trouble articulating some of his concerns and he needed to get up and move about on occasion in the interview.

From his description of his parents, his mother seems to be best described as passive and pious, and his father as authoritarian and perfectionistic. Tim describes his upbringing as "standard middle-class Catholicism." Tim still attends church on occasion, but is clearly not committed at any great depth to a religious orientation. The most important focus in his world still seems to be his relationship to sports. One of his most vivid early memories is of playing in a baseball game as a very young boy, possibly age three or four, and receiving the cheers of his mother and father as he ran from base to base. Yet, his parents were extremely demanding in the area of sports, in particular his father, but also his mother in a more subtle fashion.

His positive early images of his participation in sports are clouded by several other memories of his father's role in his early feelings about sports. His father coached the Little League team on which he played, and would often harangue him if he made any errors, particularly any mental errors. His father was also demanding of the other children on the team, but certainly hollered more at Tim when he made an error, possibly to avoid any accusations of favoritism. It was only when Tim performed competently that his father showed any positive response at all, and, of course, in the early years such moments were not common. Tim's father also demanded a great deal of off-the-field discipline and practice from him. Though it may have taken some fun out of growing up, Tim still refers to it as "a necessary evil that allowed me to develop the skills I needed later."

The most disturbing aspect of his parents' attitudes in this area is that they still so highly value his life in sports, even though his professional career is over, due to an injury from which Tim did not recover well. Both of his parents still fixate on his role as a professional baseball player and often refer to his achievements in their discussions of him with family and friends, even though he makes his discomfort apparent when they do so. They seem to have stopped seeing him as a developing person, and rather wish to retain their image of him as the successful and applauded athlete.

Tim has one sibling, Jack, a brother three years younger than he is. Tim's brother never showed much interest in sports, yet won the respect of his parents, sometimes grudgingly because of his accomplishments in academic areas. Surprisingly enough, Tim's parents allowed Jack to pursue an interest in music, possibly because they felt their needs in the sports area would be filled by Tim. Jack never really related well to their father, but generally avoided hassles of any real dimension. He was clearly their mother's child, while Tim received most of the attention from the father.

Tim himself was rather ambivalent about his inability to function any longer as a professional baseball player. His career was first curtailed when he injured his foot sliding into a base. He returned and played earlier than he probably should have, before the foot was fully healed. He favored it slightly, which caused a subtle change in his pitching motion, eventually leading to a chronically sore arm. The orthopedic surgeon he consulted told him that he had strained the arm such that it would never return to full functioning. His manager made it clear that Tim would have to work back to an effective approach by first performing again in the minor leagues. Since Tim felt he could work in other areas, he quit rather than return to the transient existence of a minor league baseball player.

Several things made his demise as a baseball player particularly painful to him and his parents. First, he had not made it to the big leagues until he was twenty-nine years old, having spent many more years in the minor leagues than is typical. It also appeared that before the injuries he had been on the edge of true stardom. He had started to win consistently, and there was no reason to believe this would not continue. He also had the prospect of being on a team that made it to a championship. His injury curtailed this not only for himself, but for the team as well.

It was particularly galling to Tim when some sportswriters suggested that he did not have the courage to "stick with it" and make a success of his baseball career after the injury. The implication was that he did not have enough personal courage to make the required sacrifices to generate a comeback.

Tim married his first wife when he was a junior in college, just as he had moved into a star role on the college baseball team. She was a freshman at the university, and obviously enjoyed the moderate degree of glamour that surrounded Tim at that time. They married after a short courtship and had a child almost immediately. Then it began to dawn on them that they had few mutual interests, as well as totally different views on child rearing. Though he indicated there were no episodes of impotence in the marriage, their sexual life was sporadic at best. She began an affair with an attorney at the office where she worked, and eventually left Tim to marry him. When her new husband obtained a job with a prestigious firm in a distant city, she took Tim's child with her and went with him. Tim still manages to see his son, now eleven years old, with moderate regularity, but the distance and the early separation have prohibited the development of a strong relationship. In recent years, Tim has dated Pam, a woman with whom he had initially enjoyed a satisfying sexual relationship. She moved in with him a year and a half ago, six months before he made the final decision not to continue with his baseball career. It is clear that Pam never saw Tim's career in sports as something she valued highly.

Tim has never been very clear as to whether or not he "loves Pam." Sexual attraction was a major part of their early courtship, and they had a very active sex life in the first several months of their dating. Though Pam did not seem to respond specifically to his baseball career, Tim's overall athletic appearance was a strong factor in her initial attraction to him. They have talked of marriage on numerous occasions, but neither has come to feel confident about making that type of commitment. In the meantime, Tim's parents

216

have been upset about the fact that Pam and Tim are living together without having been married, and they never mention Pam to any of their friends.

Tim personally links the first occasions of impotence with worries generated by criticisms of sportswriters about his alleged lack of desire to make a comeback. He remembers the first incident as occurring on a night when he had been drinking heavily, in large part because he had been upset by reading an article noting how his absence had probably cost his former team a shot at the championship. He had also been feeling uncertain at that time about the permanence of his relationship with Pam. These factors together resulted in a distracted and apprehensive mental set. When he became aware that he did not have a full erection, he became even more anxious, thus deflating what erection he had obtained. Though Pam was not overtly critical at the time, she also had not been very supportive, possibly because of her own ambivalence about the relationship. In any case, Tim saw this as a humiliating experience and naturally anticipated, at least unconsciously, repeats of such a performance in the future. This expectation brought on anxiety, and Tim continued having problems obtaining or maintaining an erection.

Though Tim was raised with prohibitions against virtually all types of sexual behavior, he did not take his religious views seriously at a conscious level. He had been taught to masturbate by an older male friend. In high school, he engaged in much fondling and petting with Barbara, the first girl he really dated with any consistency. But he had his first experience of intercourse with Carolyn, a good friend of Barbara's. It had been enjoyable, though in the early stages it had been very anxiety-provoking. It occurred in the living room of Carolyn's home, and just as they got started, Carolyn's father called down and asked if anyone was there, scaring Tim and temporarily deflating his erection. But his high drive level at that time came to his rescue, and they went on to finish.

Etiology   As noted, Tim received a complete physical examination; the typical physical causes that can sometimes generate impotence, such as spinal cord tumors and circulatory difficulties, were ruled out. Also, he spent an evening at the university sleep lab. The tests indicated that he did show nocturnal penile tumescence, referred to as either erections while sleeping or NPT's. NPT's commonly occur in normal individuals during the REM stage of sleep, the stage usually associated with dreaming. It has been found that men with physically based impotence seldom show NPT's, whereas those with primarily psychological impotence show normal NPT's (Fisher et al., 1979).

Several factors that emerged in the psychological evaluation contributed to the impotence. Like his father, Tim had a strong need to control the environment around him and felt threatened if changes occurred that he did not control. The divorce, the problems with his baseball career, and the ambivalence about his present girlfriend all suggested a loss of control to Tim and in turn generated anxiety. The impotence provided a practical focus point for the more vague feelings of anxiety. But his focus on the sexual concerns created what Masters and Johnson (1970) have termed "performance anxiety." Under performance anxiety, persons take on a spectator role in the sexual act rather than letting themselves fully enjoy the pleasures of the response.

As far as the specific instance that set off the impotence, Tim had experienced fatigue that day and had also overindulged in alcohol, a common factor when individuals first experience impotence. Also, it is important to note that even though his early sexual experiences usually had been successful, they were often associated with a significant level of anxiety.

Over and above his obsessive features, which generate a high need to control events, other characteristics would predict the impotence. Tim revealed that he perceived Pam as moving more heavily into the women's liberation movement than he would like. She had openly begun to discuss her need to "fulfill her own needs." She had begun to do a lot more flirting while in his general vicinity, a behavior he allowed himself but frowned on in Pam. She had also made some innuendos that Tim had not really worked hard to recover fully from his injury. As a result of all these developments, Tim began to perceive Pam as threatening his self-esteem. When he then experienced the impotence with her, these developing beliefs were strongly reinforced.

Residual guilt from his rather strict Catholic upbringing was also a factor with Tim. He had verbalized some concern about being divorced and now living with another woman, since he was still attempting to maintain a standard role in a church that forbade such behavior. Also, as Welch and Kartub (1978) found, the incidence of impotence is highest in societies in which sexual restrictiveness is highest. In particular, a higher rate of impotence is likely if the society has had a restrictive belief system, and also if it is now rapidly moving toward a more liberal value system.

Treatment There are a number of treatment options here; the choice in large part depends on whether or not a physical cause is present (Tucker, 1981). For example, administration of a hormone, testosterone, is common, but since Tim's testosterone level was only slighly below average to start with, it was unlikely this would provide a cure.

In some individuals, prosthetic devices have been used (usually, but not always with a physical cause). The Smith-Carrion penile prosthesis is simply two silicone sponges that are implanted surgically in the corpora cavernosa, the two parts of the penis that normally engorge with blood when the male has an erection. This device has several problems. First, orgasm does not always occur, and secondly, there is a permanent erection (this may not seem like a problem for some individuals, but at the very least it does cause embarrassment). Thirdly, and most importantly, certain urological diagnostic procedures are rendered virtually impossible because of the perpetual erection (Meyer, 1982).

As an alternative, the Scott prosthesis, a hydraulic system, can be used. A bulb, which has been implanted in the abdomen or scrotum, inflates the sacs of the corpora cavernosa when it is pressed. A second compression of the bulb deflates the erection. This device has the problems of any mechanical instrument that is implanted in the body, such as possible rejection biologically. It also is an expensive procedure. Prosthetic devices would not be appropriate for Tim since the probabilities were high that the disorder could be cured with the less radical and intrusive psychological techniques.

Tim's actual treatment first involved several sessions with the psychologists to clarify his feelings about the relationship with his girlfriend, the guilt about sex he experienced at a less-than-conscious level, and his perfectionistic needs. Tim gradually felt more confident of his relationship with Pam, and he asked her to participate in the latter part of the treatment program with him.

This phase of treatment proceeded along the lines suggested by Masters and Johnson (1970); they suggest that it is important to have a partner during the treatment. Because this partner is someone to whom the person will return after the treatment, a sexual surrogate is a poor choice for predicting successful outcome (Meyer & Freeman, 1977).

The therapist emphasized to Tim and Pam that they were to focus on the pleasures of fondling and petting, and for a period of time they were admonished not to proceed into intercourse. When they were doing well with this, and also were becoming strongly aroused, the therapist suggested that they proceed to intercourse, but not attempt to reach orgasm. Eventually, as their arousal continued to be very high, intercourse was allowed and was successful. The therapist obviously attempts to minimize the performance anxiety by restricting the options. Since they had been specifically admonished not to go to orgasm there was no need to be concerned about performance. This phase of the treatment lasted five weeks, at the end of which Tim and Pam were having satisfactory sexual relationships, and at a higher rate than even before the impotence started. Other areas of their relationship continued to improve as they clarified the meaning and impact of their communications, and a year after the treatment they got married. The marriage helped with Tim's relationship with his parents, but he needed to work on clarifying his dependency on their approval. During some follow-up therapy sessions, he was able to distance himself from this need, while retaining a caring relationship for them.

An interesting sidelight was that Pam reported she was much happier now that Tim was accepting his own passivity and could allow himself to let go of the dominant role on occasion, not just in sexuality, but in their relationship as a whole. Eventually Tim enrolled in some refresher courses related to his work and also took up a course in painting. It was an interest he had always had in the back of his mind but had never really developed, probably because he feared the implications of femininity and passivity that he saw as associated with it. All of these changes helped his self-esteem, which, in turn, allowed him to initiate new behaviors, thus creating a positive cycle, the antithesis of the negative cycle often seen in psychopathology.

Comment   Not surprisingly, most men are reluctant to report impotence. Thus, actual rates are difficult to determine. Situational anxiety, especially fear of failure, manifest in the spectator attitude mentioned earlier, is often the critical factor. The person becomes so involved in critically evaluating his performance that he cannot participate in love-making without feeling self-conscious. Typical sources of anxiety that negatively affect sustained erection include worry over penis size, fear of contagious disease, fear of partner's pregnancy, and ambivalence toward the sexual partner (as was the case with Tim). Also, levels of alcohol consumption are associated with decreased sexual arousal in males.

    As with depression and anxiety, psychogenic sexual dysfunction is often time limited. Isolated episodes of impotence may occur in response to important vocational demands, prolonged abstinence (due to illness or separation), and/or following vasectomies. The majority of these symptoms disappear without intervention as the impact of external stress subsides. On the other hand, chronic and prolonged impotence can cause a marital relationship to deteriorate and generally results in lowered self-esteem. In Tim's case, it was first necessary to clarify his feelings about Pam and his relationship with her. Once the anxiety about the relationship had lessened, Tim could ask Pam to assist him in the program of systematic desensitization and sensate focusing. The effectiveness of this approach and the resulting improvement in the overall relationship are consistently reported findings.

REFERENCES

Fisher, C., Schiavi, R., Edwards, A., Davis, D., Reitman, N., and Fine, V. Evaluation of nocturnal penile tumescence in the differential diagnosis of sexual impotence: A quantitative study. *Archives of General Psychiatry*, 1979, *36*, 431–437.

Masters, W., and Johnson, V. *Human sexual inadequacy.* Boston: Little, Brown, 1970.

Meyer, R. *The clinician's handbook*. Boston: Allyn and Bacon, 1982.

Meyer, R, and Freeman, W. A social episode model of human sexual behavior. *Journal of Homosexuality*, 1977, 2, 123–131.

Tucker, D. Lateral brain function, emotion, and conceptualization. *Psychological Bulletin*, 1981, 89, 19–46.

Welch, M, and Kartub, P. Socio-cultural correlates of incidence of impotence: A cross-cultural study. *The Journal of Sex Research*, 1978, 14, 218–230.

Female Psychosexual Dysfunction

The Case of Virginia

As with males, the traditional term for female psychosexual dysfunction in the DSM-III is Psychosexual Dysfunction with Inhibited Sexual Excitement. In this case, the symptoms include both frigidity and vaginismus. As the case developed, it became apparent that vaginismus had to be dealt with first. Vaginismus is a condition in which the vaginal musculature goes into intense involuntary spasms, primarily in the bulbocavernosus muscle, and also in the levator ani muscles. As a result, intercourse is impossible, or is accompanied by extreme pain (dyspareunia) (Cox & Meyer, 1978). Vaginismus is not necessarily associated with sexual inhibition or orgastic problems, though it often is, as we see in Virginia's case (Masters & Johnson, 1970).

Virginia

Virginia had suffered with her problems most of her life, and indeed had seldom had any satisfactory sexual experiences. Yet she waited until three years after she had been married to report her difficulties to her gynecologist. This lag in reporting such difficulties is not uncommon in the sexual disorders. Virginia's gynecologist gave her a thorough physical examination, which revealed severe vaginismus, but no physical cause was found. This is not uncommon, since vaginismus and frigidity are often unrelated to physical disorder. The gynecologist then referred Virginia to a clinic that specialized in the treatment of sexual disorders. Virginia's husband was also referred to the clinic since it was quite clear that he also had some disturbance in the sexual area.

Virginia, who is twenty-three years old, is reasonably attractive and pleasant interpersonally. She was initially interviewed alone, during which time she talked about her childhood and adolescence as well as her present concerns. Virginia's family had lived a middle-class existence in a small northwestern town, and her early life would best be described as stable and quiet. Her father was a generally quiet and passive individual who nevertheless occa-

sionally indulged in strong outbursts of anger if Virginia or her younger brother would upset him for any length of time. Virginia describes her mother as a rather saintly individual who was always warm and supportive. At the same time, there was a repressive atmosphere in the home as regards sexuality. Both her father and mother avoided discussing it, and Virginia learned most of what she knew about sexual matters from her friends in school. Her mother did attempt to discuss menstruation with her, but generally communicated the feeling that it was an inherently painful event and something that she ought not discuss publicly. Virginia naturally assumed that the whole issue was shameful; in part, this attitude contributed to the substantial pain she experienced during her menarche. Virginia would often skip school and stay in bed during the first day of her menstruation, and was grouchy and irritable throughout her period.

Though Virginia's father was nominally a Roman Catholic, he did not practice his religion. Her mother, however, was devoted to her fundamentalist religion, often working many hours with several Protestant organizations. She made sure that Virginia and her brother were raised in her faith. Virginia rebelled against this in late adolescence by simply refusing to go to church, and gradually drifted away from most of the tenets of her religion. But the admonitions that the expression of sexuality outside of marriage was wrong stayed in the back of her mind and caused her to experience guilt and anxiety on occasion. She began to masturbate regularly when she was sixteen years old, and for quite a while felt very guilty about it. She had little difficulty experiencing orgasm in masturbation.

Virginia had not been allowed to date until she was fifteen, and only then when she was with a large group of individuals who were chaperoned to and from whatever event was going on. She was allowed to date individually when she was seventeen years old. Yet, because she was rather quiet and unassuming and because she did not run in the more active groups in her school, she had few dates. Her first romantic interest was a boy named Bill, who was also very passive and did not push her toward any sexual experience. After they had dated approximately one year, they were petting rather heavily. On one of these occasions, Bill inserted his finger in Virginia's vagina and she experienced an orgasm. The spontaneity and intensity of the orgasm scared her, and she became very upset with Bill. They soon ceased dating and Virginia was relatively inactive in this area until she met David, her husband-to-be.

After graduation from high school, Virginia enrolled in a dental hygiene training program at the local community college. As she was nearing completion of her program, she met David, who was an assistant librarian at the college. She was primarily attracted to him because he seemed "older and wiser" than most of the other men she knew. David was mild mannered and passive, and even after they had dated for several months, they were still only giving each other a goodnight kiss. They married after about one year of dating, and even at this point had not done much sexually except mild petting.

Three months before they were married, Virginia developed a vaginal infection and experienced a virtual panic, fearing that she may somehow have contracted a venereal disease. She went to a gynecologist who was competent medically, but did not have much of a bedside manner. He was a bit rough in the examination. He was also slightly sarcastic in telling her that she had no venereal disease and that he could not see why she worried about it, given her sexual history. Virginia came away from the situation shaken and upset and vowed never to go back to him.

Virginia and David's wedding went happily except for an uncomfortable moment when her mother attempted to give her a last minute lesson about sexuality. The most positive thing she could say was that although it would probably hurt the first several times, it "wouldn't be that bad."

As is common when both parties have had little sexual experience, the honeymoon was a disaster. David's apparent maturity and wisdom did not extend into the area of sexuality. Virginia took the strategy that if she just remained quiet and passive, he would know what to do. David's role by default as the wiser and more experienced person propelled him into taking initiatives, even though he knew little about what to do. He attempted penetration after only minimal foreplay, and before Virginia had any vaginal lubrication. Virginia's vaginal muscles spasmed almost immediately, causing her intense pain. She screamed and David withdrew right away, very confused as to what he did to cause the pain. They were both so distraught by this event that they did not attempt intercourse again until the third night of the honeymoon. Virginia again had intense pain. This time she attempted to endure the pain, but it was clear to David that it was distressing her and he withdrew, soon losing his erection. They were both upset and embarrassed about the situation and avoided any further attempt at intercourse during the honeymoon.

Since that time they have only attempted intercourse approximately once or twice a month, usually with the same accompanying problems. Never have they been able to continue intercourse to the point that either of them experienced orgasm. They eventually began to engage in mutual masturbation, yet both felt this was "not real sex," and they both reported being dissatisfied.

Virginia did not seek help for several reasons. She was too distressed with the idea of returning to the gynecologist who had been sarcastic and rough with her, and she feared repeating that experience with another gynecologist. Also, she was quite embarrassed and hoped that her mother's prophecy that it would gradually be all right would come true. After three years, the couple began to experience other problems in their relationship, in large part because of their inability to communicate. Also, it was very hard for them to find a way to express affection without having to consider the possibility of intercourse, which by this time they avoided at all costs. Virginia went to the phone book and simply sorted through to a name she somehow felt comfortable with, and made an appointment. Fortunately, this random selection led her to a gynecologist who was understanding of and empathetic with her situation.

Etiology   Virginia's background is not atypical for a woman with vaginismus. She is not significantly pathological psychologically, though she does have a background that induced a substantial amount of sexual guilt and repression. Not only was she made to feel that sexuality was sinful, but even more importantly, she felt that it was shameful and dirty. In addition, she had little accurate sexual information provided for her as she grew up and had to resort to information she received from her friends, most of whom were equally uninformed. As a result, many of her general beliefs about sexuality crystallized around inaccurate information.

Consequently, Virginia basically rejected her bodily experiences; she saw them as intrusive and as a cue for anxiety. Though she was able to masturbate to orgasm, she experienced much guilt in the process.

The traumatic gynecological examination that she experienced shortly before her marriage also unfortunately contributed to her problem. Again, this is not uncommon. Many women with vaginismus fear gynecological examinations, and if there is any insensitivity on the part of the gynecologist, the trauma increases the potential for vaginismus (Tollison & Adams, 1979).

The other major contributing factor was her husband's inexperience in sexuality. Any normal woman would likely experience some pain if penetration was attempted before any real lubrication had begun. Their mutual inexperience led them to attempt this, which exaggerated the pain experience already initiated by her own expectancies and prior experiences. Her mother's admonition that her initial sexual experiences would cause her pain led her to believe that the severe pain she experienced was a normal response. As a result, she did not immediately seek treatment and unfortunately she and her husband then indulged in the repeated trials that reinforced the vaginal spasm sequence. Spasms became conditioned responses to all of the attempts at intercourse. From that perspective, vaginismus can be seen as a phobic response. It is an irrational anxiety that occurs in response to anticipated vaginal penetration. Anxiety and muscular spasms then naturally occur. The spasms cause intense pain, which naturally furthers the strength of the phobic response.

Treatment The specific treatment for vaginismus is a fairly straightforward procedure. It involves the use of dilators, graduated in size, which are inserted into the vagina until the vagina relaxes. The next larger catheter is inserted in the next session. Masters and Johnson (1970) recommend that the male partner participate in the insertion of the catheters, and also suggest that he witness any pelvic examinations that occur in an effort to help dispel any irrational fears he may have developed. It particularly reassures him that the vaginismus is not a direct response to his efforts at intercourse. Masters and Johnson (1970) report a success rate of 100 percent with simple vaginismus using this technique. However, as in most cases, Virginia's vaginismus is confounded by other sexual problems.

Virginia and her husband participated in some simple education sessions about sexual matters. They were then taught the technique of sensate focusing, in which emphasis is placed on focusing on the sensations from a sexual experience. Sensate focus is commonly used to treat impotence and frigidity, but in this case, its main function may have been to alleviate guilt and the couple's inhibitions about explorations in the sexual area.

After they had shown progress in this regard, they then moved on to the use of the dilators (Tollison & Adams, 1979). The use of dilators can be considered as analogous to systematic desensitization therapy, such that the phobic anxiety that caused the spasm is confronted with an in vivo stimulus —that is, with something that is to be inserted directly into the vagina. The therapeutic effect occurs because the person is kept relaxed and comfortable so that the spasms ultimately subside (Cox & Meyer, 1978).

The first dilator is very small. Her husband handled the dilator during insertion while Virginia guided his hand. Larger dilators are used as the muscle spasms decrease each time, and ultimately the husband guides the dilator himself. The largest dilators, which are about the size of the erect penis, are kept in place for several hours. It may take five to six weeks of treatment with the dilators before actual intercourse is attempted. Virginia and her husband proved very responsive to this technique, and in four weeks they were able to have intercourse.

Concomitant with the use of the dilators, Virginia was taught the use of the "squeeze technique" since her husband had been experiencing occasional premature ejaculation. The squeeze technique has been highly effective in helping the partner delay ejaculation, thus prolonging intercourse.

Virginia was taught first to manipulate her husband's penis to a full erection and then to place her thumb on the frenulum (on the underside of the front of the penis) with her first two fingers on opposite sides at the top of the penis, one on each side of the ridge which separates the shaft from the glans. By squeezing hard at this point for about three seconds the urge to ejaculate is substantially lessened, and some of the erection is also lost. At first, this procedure may be repeated every half minute or so, with gradually greater time periods interspersed (Masters and Johnson, 1970; Levine, 1979).

When they were first allowed to have intercourse, Virginia first used the largest dilator for a long enough period of time to allow her vagina to relax fully. Before David inserted his penis, she employed the squeeze technique a couple of times and then straddled him in the female superior coital position. This position allowed her more control plus the ability to pull away if she began to have spasms again. If the spasms did recur, then they returned to working with the dilators until she again felt comfortable. At first, both remained motionless for a long period of time as they both became used to the penis being in the vagina. Then David was allowed to thrust enough to maintain his erection and obtain some sexual pleasure, but it was emphasized to him to keep his movement very slow. Gradually, the speed of thrusting is increased, the time of insertion is increased, and different sexual positions are attempted. When they show control throughout these variations, progression to orgasm is allowed.

Virginia and David were highly motivated, not only reflecting their desire mutually to enjoy their sexual experience, but also because of their deep caring for each other and the desire to make a good marriage. The combination of therapies took approximately three months. Consistent with the work of Masters and Johnson (1970), it was very successful. They are now enjoying sex consistently, and although Virginia first had difficulty reaching orgasm in intercourse, she now does so with increasing regularity. It is highly probable that the success they attained will continue.

Comment   As with Virginia, the person is physiologically capable of adequate sexual performance in most cases of sexual dysfunction. Most sexual dysfunction occurs when psychological factors exert an inhibitory action over what is normally a series of reflexive responses. Virginia's inexperience and certain beliefs (possibly distorted) from her religious training resulted in anxiety and inhibited excitement on the occasion of her first attempt at intercourse. The predictably inadequate lubrication resulted in painful muscle spasms, which in turn generalized as a classically conditioned response to subsequent penetration attempts. The unfortunate encounter with the first gynecologist and her husband's inexperienced sexual performance strengthened Virginia's anxiety about intercourse, thereby worsening the problem. The use of a series of vaginal dilators, which successively approximate the size of an erect penis, was a successful treatment for her vaginismus, as it has been in most cases (Tollison & Adams, 1979). It usually needs to be supplemented by therapy to repair the damaged interpersonal interactions in the marriage, as well as probable self-esteem problems.

REFERENCES

Cox, D., and Meyer, R. Behavioral treatment parameters with primary dysmenor-rhea. *Journal of Behavior Medicine*, 1978, *1*.

Levine, S. Barriers to the attainment of ejaculatory control. *Medical Aspects of Human Sexuality*, 1979, *13*, 32–56.

Masters, W., and Johnson, V. *Human sexual inadequacy*. Boston: Little, Brown, 1970.

Tollison, C., and Adams, H. *Sexual disorders*. New York: Gardner, 1979.

Disorders of Impulse Control

The extent to which an individual is in command of and can control fleeting urges to violate social rules is always an important consideration when evaluating emotional development. It is expected that young children will often find behavioral control difficult, but one is expected to achieve increasing mastery as socialization proceeds. Inadequate impulse control is symptomatic of a wide range of disorders, including alcoholism, obsessive-compulsive disorder, exhibitionism, pyromania. Thus, the category of impulse control disorders could be so extensive and inclusive as to be meaningless. As a result, disorders in which an absence of impulse control is only a component are classified in accordance with other symptoms (eating disorders, substance abuse, and paraphilias, for example). However, there are at least five disorders for which poor impulse control is the primary feature and that are not elsewhere classified: pathological gambling, kleptomania, pyromania, intermittent explosive disorder, and isolated explosive disorder.

Pathological gambling is characterized by chronic and irresistible urges to gamble, with consequent negative effects on the individual's personal, family, and/or vocational endeavors, as is evident in Gary's case. The case of Clare demonstrates the essential feature of kleptomania, a recurring inability to resist impulses to steal things for reasons other than their usefulness or monetary value. In pyromania, the individual cannot resist impulses to set fires and is powerfully fascinated by burning fires. The explosive disorders are marked by incidents of inability to control aggression, resulting in serious attacks on others or destruction of property. The isolated and intermittent explosive disorders are designated simply as to whether there were one or more aggressive episodes.

In all of the disorders of impulse control, a compelling impulse accompanied by a rising sense of tension is experienced. It may or may not be premeditated and/or consciously resisted. Then, when the act is committed, there is a sense of release, which may even be so intense as to be described as pleasurable or euphoric.

Pathological Gambling

The Case of Gary Pathological gambling, as a specific disorder, was not included in DSM-I and DSM-II. Its inclusion in DSM-III as a disorder of impulse control is indicative of changing attitudes toward gambling as a behavioral problem. Traditionally, the compulsive gambler has been perceived as an immature and irresponsible person who merely needed to exercise greater will power. Also, as with alcohol and food, the addictive potential of gambling has recently received considerable attention. Therapeutic programs and self-help groups for habitual gamblers are becoming increasingly available.

The essential features of compulsive gambling closely parallel the general class of addictive disorders. First, the consistent and progressive failure to resist gambling impulses and the frequent increase in gambling activity under stress are disruptive to the victim's family and work. The individual quickly enters the classic "downward spiral" experienced by victims of other addictions. Gambling produces stress in interpersonal relationships, which results in more gambling, resulting in greater stress, and so on. The gambler becomes preoccupied with winning and eventually creates insurmountable debts and intolerable absentee records at work. Thus, financial crime such as forgery or embezzlement are frequently seen as associated features.

Unfortunately, compulsive gamblers are slow to realize the compulsive nature of their activities and seldom enter therapy early on a voluntary basis. The following case illustrates that by the time therapeutic contact is established, the individual's situation has greatly deteriorated and a complex array of related problems also require attention (Bolen & Boyd, 1968).

Gary
Gary was born in a small midwestern town. He was the youngest of three boys. When Gary was five, his father, a career Army officer, was killed in a Korean War battle. Gary's mother was able to supplement the small annuity by substitute teaching and did not remarry. She was very religious and insisted that all the children attend church regularly. However, this was the only restriction she could manage to place on their behavior, and all three boys were repeatedly in trouble.

The only consistent male influence in Gary's life was his uncle Howie. Howie was a good natured sort, and was known around town as "lazy" and "only out for a good time." He liked to bet on the horses, would bring the boys to the track with him, and was always talking about how a "long shot" or "sure thing" was going to come through. The implication to the boys was always that instant wealth was just around the corner, even though Howie never did make it around the corner.

When Gary was sixteen, he left home to work with a home insulation crew for the summer. Instead of returning in the fall, he decided to remain with the crew and enjoy the "good life." Gary recalls the two years spent with the insulation crew as "the best time in my life." He was accepted by the other men and included in their weekend evening drinking sessions. Also, Gary became sexually active at this time—finding himself charming and attractive to most women.

When the company discontinued the home insulation project, Gary joined the Navy. The screening tests given during basic training indicated that Gary was capable of college work. He was placed in a preparatory course for the GED and given a college scholarship when he excelled on the exam. Gary was accepted in a large university and made good grades his first year. During that year, he became involved with a student religious group and made an attempt to conform to his image of a good person. Also, during this same year, he met Joyce, who was active in the religious organization. Gary was convinced that she could help him become the good Christian he thought he should be.

As Gary was beginning his second year, the university discontinued the program that sponsored active military students. He was sent to a small private school whose student body was primarily comprised of active military students. Here Gary fell in with the prevailing lifestyle, which was very similar to that of the home insulation work crew—lots of drinking parties. There were also numerous poker games, and Gary learned to play well. Soon he was sending large sums of money to Joyce, who started a savings account for their future house and furniture. Afraid that Joyce would disapprove of gambling, Gary told her he earned the money by being an evangelist in a college crusade.

Gary began to spend more time playing poker and less time studying. He now began to experience a strong build up of excitement before the game and only felt a release of "satisfaction" after a long bout of gambling. His grades fell, though he managed to graduate on time with a degree in mechanical engineering. He and Joyce were married and moved to Germany for active duty. He kept his continued gambling hidden from Joyce for about two years. This was accomplished mainly by "swearing off" for a few weeks and covering his losses by surplus duty. But the gambling became even more compulsive, and the bets became larger. When asked to account for checks written for cash and frequent withdrawals from savings, Gary would become defensive and accuse Joyce of distrust and nagging. Joyce became convinced Gary was keeping a mistress, and she returned to the states. Gary's response was severe depression and increased gambling. He acquired thousands of dollars of debt to loan sharks. Unable to earn the money gambling, and unable to use his military check because it was sent to Joyce, Gary began forging checks. Upon discovery, the navy held a court martial and Gary was dishonorably discharged.

When he returned to the States, Gary confessed everything to Joyce and went through another brief period of conformity. He resumed his religious activities and took a job teaching mechanical engineering in a private technical college. He and Joyce bought a new home and furniture with the money Joyce had saved. However, after about one year, Gary became "bored" with teaching, began to move from job to job, and resumed gambling. The marital relationship deteriorated. Joyce became more rigid about religion and Gary became more compulsive about gambling. They had many arguments about cashed checks and missed church meetings. Gary would promise to do better and "swear off" for brief periods. But the reform periods became shorter and the arguments more frequent. Eventually, Joyce spent most of her time involved in church activities and Gary spent most of his time in poker games. Gary developed a reputation as an unreliable employee and was unable to find any decent jobs. Joyce began working with the church nursery school program to help supplement Gary's unemployment check.

Gary continued to gamble and covered his bets by "running" for other betters at the horse races. He would accept the money for friends but would use their money for poker stakes. If they lost, he would simply report that, and hope he could cover any winnings with the money from his own bets. Of course, Gary's success with this scheme was short-lived, and he was unable to cover all the winnings. This once resulted in several fractured ribs on behalf of a "friend."

Meanwhile, Joyce developed a relationship with the director of the church nursery school. The relationship was platonic at first because Joyce remained committed to her religious beliefs. Divorce was unacceptable, and she felt Gary's misbehavior could not release her from her vows of fidelity. But Joyce was lonely, the nursery school director was understanding, and Gary was distant. An affair evolved and Joyce became pregnant. There was no possibility of convincing Gary that he was the father since there had been no sexual relationship for almost a year. He began drinking heavily, gambling more, and feeling more depressed. One night after a particularly heated argument during which Joyce rejected Gary's insistence on an abortion, he tried to kill himself by driving his car into a tree.

Gary was thrown from the car unharmed but was hospitalized for severe depression. He was thoroughly convinced that he was a failure and was upset that he was unsuccessful even in suicide.

Etiology   Unfortunately, very little systematic research has been done with pathological gamblers and the causal factors are not yet fully understood. Freudian theorists assert that guilt-generated masochism sows the seed for the later compulsive gambling, but the specific pattern of gambling behavior appears to be a learned response that is highly resistant to extinction. The acquisition of the response is not that complex. Most games of chance are easily learned, and "getting something for nothing" is powerful reinforcement. Of course, many people enjoy an occasional bingo game or afternoon at the horseraces without losing control.

However, in pathological gambling, wagering generalizes very quickly, in part abetted by the high level of stimulation-seeking needs in such persons (Zuckerman et al., 1980). Before long, gambling becomes the most probable response to a wide variety of situations. Gambling becomes the way to solve financial problems, is an outlet for anger and anxiety, a distraction from depression, and the vehicle to celebrate accomplishment. Eventually, for the compulsive gambler, there is no situation for which gambling is inappropriate or ineffective, and the tension build up and tension release sequence become accentuated. It works—gamblers report feeling more confident and "alive" as a result of gambling activities. Many report that the rest of their life is "boring." These "positive" results have sufficient power of immediate gratification to override the long-term disadvantages and problems.

For Gary, it seems that training in the ability to delay reinforcement was noticeably absent in his home environment. Even before he began to gamble, there is evidence of his attraction for immediate pleasure without consideration for ultimate outcomes. The model for attempts at instant gratification through gambling was provided by his Uncle Howie. Also, like many other pathological gamblers, Gary has a stimulation-seeking and extroverted personality, had no real model for "saving" in childhood, and had lost a parent before the age of sixteen (Zuckerman et al., 1980; Bolen & Boyd, 1968; Meyer, 1982).

While in school, Gary was repeatedly punished for truancy and misbehavior, yet did not learn to resist those momentary impulses to "act out." Thus, Gary's background, along with his immaturity and lack of judgment in childhood and adolescence, rendered him a likely candidate for some kind of addictive disorder.

In addition, Gary evidenced considerable confusion regarding the nature of success in life. He vacillated between the strict religious principles heard about in church, yet vaguely longed to fulfill the hedonistic lifestyle he has led. He was unable to arrive at a comfortable integration of these forces or to choose between them (Kohut, 1977). Instead, he retained both elements in his adult life—Joyce and gambling. Perceiving Joyce and gambling as incompatible, Gary began to alternate his attention and allegiance. Thus, several abrupt changes in Gary's lifestyle are evident. He tried to commit himself to the religious and moral character, then threw the entire thing over for poker parties and drinking sprees, with later remorse and depression. Gary's lack of any real success in all his major life pursuits—engineering, marriage, gambling, even suicide—only furthered the negative cycle.

Treatment   Gary's response to milieu therapy and antidepressants during hospitalization was slow. He did not eat for several days, refused visitors, and generally failed to respond to staff or to other patients. When Gary did communicate, he verbalized considerable self-deprecation, guilt, and the desire to die. He was placed on suicide precautions, with an emphasis on limiting his access to lethal means (Boor, 1981), and he made no attempts. Gradually, Gary made progress and his depression lifted. He was discharged to an out-patient clinic and a position as manager-trainee of an electronics sales firm. Gary insisted his gambling had brought sufficient suffering and misery that he was finished forever. He resolved to return to Joyce, accept her child, and resume his church activities.

The treatment plan of the out-patient clinic included individual and group therapy for Gary, weekly marital therapy with Gary and Joyce, and covert sensitization and aversion therapy for the control of the specific gambling behaviors (Cotler, 1970). Initially, Gary's progress in therapy was excellent. He talked freely about his gambling and openly admitted that he had enjoyed the stimulation and excitement of gambling more than the religious life he had attempted several times. He began to examine his ambivalent feelings toward his marriage and to explore the role Joyce had played in his fantasy of the moral husband. His therapist was beginning to revise her initially guarded prognosis when Gary encountered two setback events.

First, he became friends with another gambler at work, and then Joyce decided to divorce him to marry the nursery school director. It is possible that Gary might have made it past either one of these obstacles. Both proved too much for him, and he resumed gambling. For several months, Gary was back on the downward spiral. He lost his job and two subsequent ones, had his collarbone broken by a loan shark, and was arrested for forging checks. He was sentenced to one year in prison and three years of probation.

Prison was a very painful experience for Gary, but it was also a most enlightening one. He was assigned to a therapist for individual therapy and showed some substantive progress. As a result, it was decided that he was eligible for early release to a halfway house.

Gary's continuation on release was contingent on 1) regularly participating in Gamblers Anonymous (a group organized in 1957 along the lines of Alcoholics Anonymous) and 2) finding a job. He was guided into a series of social and physical outlets for his high level of stimulation seeking (Zuckerman et al., 1980). With the help of the halfway house, Gary found a job as lab assistant with an electronic factory. He responded well to the support and encouragement of Gamblers Anonymous and moved out of the halfway house. Also, Gary began to participate in a community church program with less intensity and desperation. Three years later, Gary continues to abstain from gambling. He has been promoted to supervisor in the electronics factory and remains active with Gamblers Anonymous.

Comment   Although opportunities for gambling are currently available in most areas, recent and pending states' legislation to legalize gambling will increase both recreational and pathological gambling. Most people will be able to restrict gambling activities to occasional and moderate investments. For others, however, risking something valuable in situations with uncertain outcomes becomes a compelling and uncontrolled response to an increasing range of emotional cues. Bolen and Boyd (1968) have suggested that compulsive gamblers are less likely to stop gambling when they are losing than when they are ahead, while recreational gamblers, who are more interested in diversion, relaxation, and winning, stop quickly to limit their losses. Bolen and Boyd suggest that this difference represents the crucial sign in addictive gambling. In any case, learning to suppress the overall impulse to gamble is important in any change (Seager, 1970).

The deteriorating social and occupational adjustment is usually the reason that compulsive gamblers come to the attention of psychologists (Eadington, 1976). In Gary's case, the immediate problem was his severe depression and sense of failure. Once the depression had lifted and Gary's marital situation was resolved, treatment was focused on increasing social skills and resolving his conflicting expectations of adulthood. Finally, Gary's adjustment without gambling was facilitated by the support of Gamblers Anonymous and satisfactory employment. The prognosis for Gary's continued abstinence from gambling is reasonably positive, inasmuch as he has evidenced abstinence for more than two years and appears to have developed a more adaptive lifestyle.

REFERENCES

Bolen, D., and Boyd, W. Gambling and the gambler: A review and preliminary findings. *Archives of General Psychiatry*, 1968, *18*, 617–629.

Boor, M. Methods of suicide and applications for suicide prevention. *Journal of Clinical Psychology*, 1981, *37*, 70–75.

Cotler, S. The use of differential behavioral techniques in treating a case of compulsive gambling. *Behavior Research and Therapy*, 1970, *8*, 273–285.

Eadington, W. (Ed.). *Gambling and society.* Springfield, Ill.: Charles C Thomas, 1976.

Kohut, H. *The restoration of the self.* New York: International University Press, 1977.

Meyer, R. *The clinician's handbook.* Boston: Allyn and Bacon, 1982.

Seager, C. Treatment of compulsive gamblers by electrical aversion. *British Journal of Psychiatry*, 1970, *117*, 545–553.

Zuckerman, M., Buchsbaum, M., and Murphy, D. Sensation seeking and its biological correlates. *Psychological Bulletin*, 1980, *88*, 187–214.

Kleptomania

The Case of Clare

Kleptomania refers to a recurrent inability to resist the impulse to steal. It is important to note that the motivation for the stealing in kleptomania is not the value of or the need for the article. It is to gain the strong feelings of gratification that occur with the release of tension that the act brings in such an individual. These acts are seldom accompanied by significant preplanning, are primarily impulsive in nature, and are seldom carried out with assistance from others.

Although kleptomaniacs (and the use of the subterm *mania* is unfortunate) may have problems in interpersonal relationships, their general personality functioning is likely to be within the normal range. Kleptomania can begin as early as the first school years, and it is likely to be chronic without some kind of direct intervention. Anxiety and depression, as well as guilt over the fear of being apprehended, may accompany this condition.

Stealing is a common behavior in our society (Farrington & Knight, 1980). Statistics on shoplifting compounded annually by the United States Department of Commerce indicate that about one out of every twelve shoppers is a shoplifter, but that only about one shoplifter in thirty-five is apprehended. Some 145 million instances of shoplifting occur annually. It is important to note, however, that only an extremely small proportion of shoplifters suffer from kleptomania. Most shoplifters are stealing in order to get something they want for free. Also, a substantial proportion of shoplifting occurs in isolated acts and the person does not repeat the behavior very often. Thirdly, a great many people, particularly adolescents, shoplift in a group to gain peer acceptance. This third condition, however, can act as a catalyst for later kleptomania (West & Farrington, 1977).

Since this disorder is not necessarily accompanied by significant pathology, or by clear-cut childhood syndromes, we will not detail our case history as much as we do with other cases in this book. But it is worthwhile to examine this pattern, particularly as it can be compared to the antisocial personality disorder case.

Clare

Clare is a bright and attractive young woman of twenty-eight who has an interesting and responsible position in an advertising firm in the large western city in which she grew up. She first talked about her problem with a minister whom she met at a book club she attended monthly, and he referred her to a private psychologist.

Clare reports that she had been compulsively stealing off and on since she was thirteen years old. She had never sought treatment before, but several recent events had heightened her fear of being apprehended. On these occasions, Clare was sure that she had been seen stealing by other customers and began to realize that she had been very lucky never to have been caught yet. Also, one day when she was out browsing in a department store on her lunch hour with one of her coworkers, she compulsively stole a pair of stockings and she is afraid that the coworker saw her take them. She knows that if she is ever caught and prosecuted it will mean losing her job, and most certainly the blemish on her record would hurt her in any number of ways.

Clare's description of her emotional responses during the stealing behavior fits the classic kleptomania pattern. She first experiences an intense state of nervousness and general tension, which gradually crystallizes into an irresistible impulse to take some specific object. She tries to resist the impulse, but generally stays within the immediate range of the object, almost as if she enjoys a further tension buildup. Eventually, she steals the object, at which time she experiences a release of tension and a feeling of satisfaction. Though on a milder scale, her verbal description of these events sounds very much like a description of the buildup and release of tension in orgasm.

Though Clare does use some of the items she steals, many others that she takes go unused. For example, she had accumulated a larger supply of women's cosmetics than she could ever hope to use in the next ten years. Also, for some reason, possibly the ease with which she has been able to steal them, she has accumulated a boxful of men's jewelry, such as cuff links. Clare reports that she is not really limited to any subgroup of items in her stealing but responds primarily to her impulses by going into the nearest store and meandering about until the act takes place.

Clare had a basically normal childhood and says that she was happy at this time in her life. She did very well in school and received much attention for this. Her parents both loved their children

*(Clare is the second oldest of four children), though at the same time
they did not show much physical affection or direct attention to any
one child for very long. Many family activities occurred, such as pic-
nics and fishing trips. But seldom did either her mother or father attend for long to any one individual child, with the possible exception
of her older sister. This probably occurred because the older sister
did have that period of time when she was the only child, and as a
result the parents were used to responding to her individually.*

*When Clare was approximately nine years old, she began to
steal money on occasion from her mother's purse. She used the
money to buy candy and other small items at a local small grocery
store. When her parents found out about this, they became very
distressed and sat down with Clare and had a long talk about the
moral issues involved and how people would not trust her any
longer. But they did not really punish her, nor did they have her
make any meaningful restitution for the acts she committed. As she
reflects on this, Clare feels that her parents' concern came mostly
from the potential embarrassment that could occur if she began to
steal outside the home. She continued to steal occasionally and
became more sophisticated about the whole situation, so that her
parents rarely caught her. When they did, they only repeated the
same moral prohibitions, without forcing any means of restitution on
her. When she was ten, Clare attempted to steal candy from the
local grocery store, but was easily apprehended. The woman who
ran the store reported to Clare's parents. This time, they severely
spanked her, and followed the spanking with a repeat of the discussion of the moral issues involved.*

*From this point, Clare only stole occasionally until she was
approximately thirteen years old. She then began associating with
four other girls who would occasionally take "stealing trips" to
downtown stores. This was not an everyday occurrence, but it was
common enough to become a ritual behavior in their social interactions together. They would go downtown, and each of them would
try to steal a specific object that was predetermined before they
went into the store. They did this off and on for several years, and
amazingly, only one girl was ever caught. She feigned great distress
at this time, stating that she had never done anything like this
before, and carried off a very emotional scene. The storekeeper
responded sympathetically and did not report the event either to the
police or parents.*

*Clare did exceptionally well academically in high school and
enrolled in a premed program at the university. She did reasonably
well during her first year, and the stealing behavior had ceased
when she came to college. In her sophomore year, she had trouble
with two courses and received low grades. She realized that she was*

not likely to be accepted into medical school. Coincidentally, she had the first disappointing love affair of her life.

During high school years, she dated regularly, yet never developed any long-term romantic involvement that had any deep meaning for her. However, she met another student in her first year at the university with whom she fell deeply in love. They dated seriously for the latter part of her first year and into the second year, but then he gradually became bored with the relationship and dropped her for another girl. She had sexual intercourse with him, the first time for her, and she had rationalized it by saying that she thought they would some day get married. When they broke up, she at first had a great deal of guilt about this, to add to her general disappointment.

It was at this point that Clare began occasionally stealing again, and now she was doing it alone. She would experience a buildup of apprehension and then found relief when she would proceed to shoplift an item successfully. During this period of time, she was extremely careful as to how she went about it. She usually chose small stores that had only one proprietor, so the risk was low.

After graduation from the university, she took a glorified secretarial job in an advertising firm. Through her job, she met a man whom she dated for about four months, after which time they somewhat impulsively married. The marriage lasted for two years. It was clear from the start that her choice had been a bad one, as her husband was sexually inadequate most of the time and also had a drug problem. Clare ended up supporting him, and when it became apparent that he was not really going to change his behavior, she left him. But she had always believed that "marriage is forever," and so the divorce caused her a great deal of hurt. She threw herself more forcefully into her job, and her intelligence and hard work won her a promotion into a position that was a stepping stone to executive rank.

Subsequent to divorce, Clare had a series of intense romantic involvements, but she was very fearful of making any new commitments. When she was not involved in a relationship, she was prone to anxiety and depression, and it was at these times that she was drawn to the stealing behavior. As she quipped, "I'm still looking for Mr. Goodbar," but as she also noted later, "at times I'm pretty scared that I'll find him."

Etiology   Clare is reflective of most kleptomaniacs in that there is no remarkable history of pathology in childhood, nor any significant problems as regards thought disorder, consistent neurotic behavior, or psychopathy. The evolution of her kleptomania occurred in several gradual phases.

Phase one occurred when she was approximately nine years old. It was marked by behaviors common to many children. She stole money that she found easily available, and like most of these children, she was caught. But in her case, this originally utilitarian pattern was reinforced by the parental interest and a lack of effective punishment. As noted, there was much caring in her family, yet little individualized attention to any one child. The stealing gained her the individual attention. Though it did have negative costs, these were not strong enough to void the reinforcement of her pattern.

She moved into phase two when the stealing not only reflected the reinforcement but, in addition, became a channel for hostility toward her parents. She saw their hypocrisy, and in addition was developing clearer anger feelings over not getting any individual attention from them. Her stealing behavior was a lashing out at them, and at the same time again forced them to attend more individually to her.

The next phase in this evolution is a common one in the background of kleptomaniacs. She became involved in a peer group that integrated stealing into their social rituals. It was a necessary behavior to gain acceptance in this particular subgroup. Clare was happy with these girls, got along well with them, and enjoyed many activities with them, only one of which was the stealing behavior. It is interesting that at this point she only stole while she was with her friends.

The fourth and final phase in the evolution of her pattern occurred when she moved from her peer stealing back to individual stealing. The stealing alleviated some of the anxiety and boredom she was experiencing as she went through the trials and tribulations that occur in most people's lives. The disappointment in the failure of her first true romantic attachment came close on the heels of her realization that she would not be able to fulfill her long-sought goal of entering medical school. So, she had a lot of self-evaluation to do (Kohut, 1977), which generated anxiety and depression. There is also evidence that these feelings combined with her ambivalent resolution of her sexual needs. At periods of time, she would behave rather promiscuously, and at other times she would return to a more restrained pattern. In any case, when there was any buildup of general tension in her, the stealing behavior would distract her and in that sense also give her a thrill and a feeling of satisfaction. Though Clare saw the behavior as ego-alien, she usually could no longer restrain herself.

In this sense, kleptomania is not dissimilar to chronic obesity. In chronic obesity, the buildup of anxiety (or almost any emotion) becomes a discriminative cue for overeating. It is as if the individual cannot sort out the meaning of emotional cues. In the case of Clare's kleptomania, a buildup of any tension was channeled into a cue for stealing behavior. For this reason, she often stole articles that were of no real use to her. It was the act itself that was reinforcing, not the objects that were gained.

The realization eventually hit home that this behavior put her at risk for enjoying other areas in her life. One could even speculate that she became more careless in her recent stealing behavior from unconscious motivation to shock herself with the realization of the risks that she was posing for herself. In the last incident before referral, the presence of her coworker was a concrete reminder that her job, which was her one positive source of self-esteem, could be lost if she were apprehended. As a result, she then sought treatment.

Treatment

As with most of the habit disorders, the treatment must first focus on the specific behavior itself and then later attend to any ancillary issues, such as accompanying anxiety, depression, and/or interpersonal difficulties. Eliminating the problematic habit behavior is particularly crucial in Clare's case, in which there is a potential legal difficulty if she continues in it. There has not been much attention in the research to the elimination of kleptomania; the treatment rendered Clare reflects most of the work that has been done.

The first phase of Clare's treatment used an aversive conditioning procedure similar to that used by Kellam (1969) to cure another chronic kleptomaniac. Clare was asked to simulate her entire shoplifting sequence in a room that was made up as much as possible to look like a store. The procedure was videotaped, and Clare was asked to amplify this in her imagination as strongly as she could while the videotape was being replayed. At critical decision points, she was administered a very painful electric shock, which acts to suppress the behavior. To strengthen this effect, Clare was asked occasionally to imagine herself in a shoplifting sequence at various times outside the treatment hour, and she was asked to hold her breath until discomfort occurred. This discomfort, like the electric shock, acts as an aversive cue to help suppress the behavior. A small portable electric shock unit could have been used as an alternative to asking her to hold her breath (Lutzker & Martin, 1981).

Once Clare felt she was gaining control over the stealing impulse, she was asked to go to various stores in which she had stolen. She was asked first to respond to any stealing impulses with the "holding the breath" technique. If the impulse could not be suppressed by this approach, she was then slowly and deliberately to pick up a fragile item, such as a vase, and then deliberately drop it on the floor near a number of customers. The idea was to generate as much disturbance and embarrassment as possible. She was to stay around as long as possible while the item was being cleaned up, and insist on paying for the item. This action interrupts the compulsive sequence and also pairs the impulse with actual unpleasant and embarrassing consequences of an in vivo situation. Over a period of six weeks, the intense application of this three-stage aversive procedure (shock with the simulated video tape, the discomfort of breath holding while imagining the sequence, and generating the embarrassment while in the actual store) suppressed Clare's desire to go through a shoplifting sequence. She could comfortably go into stores, and though she occasionally felt a twinge of the old impulse, she was able to avoid ruminating about it or feeling compelled to carry it out.

Concomitantly with the aversive approach, she was taught control of a relaxation technique in order gradually to dissipate some of her ongoing anxiety. It was hypothesized that anxiety and other emotions were channelled into the impulse to steal, hence it is worthwhile not only to suppress the specific problem behavior itself, but also to lessen the anxiety that generated it. She responded well to the relaxation training and did report a gradual lessening of anxiety. She was also seen in psychotherapy weekly for six sessions, during which she clarified some of her interpersonal conflicts.

Clare did shoplift three different times during the first two weeks of this combined treatment approach. But as she gained control of the relaxation response and as the aversive technique took effect, she was able to avoid the stealing behavior altogether. The changes were then solidified by her gaining more awareness of how she mishandled certain areas and also by dissipating some of the feelings that had accumulated around past events in her life. Clare was followed up by her therapist for two years, and there was no recurrence up to that time.

Comment   Clare's case is one in which compulsive stealing became a conditioned emotional response to depression and distress. Her initial stealing from her parents could have remained one of those isolated episodes of misbehavior that characterize the development of most people. The reaction of Clare's parents was only mildly negative, and she was subsequently strongly influenced by the pressures of her peers. Afterward, Clare's period of abstinence in college from stealing was interrupted by her depression when her first romantic relationship ended. At this point, Clare's stealing became part of her standard response to emotional distress.

It seems appropriate to consider Clare's stealing habit a gradually acquired strategy for alleviating anxiety and depression. Her build up in anxiety and/or depression became discriminative cues for stealing. The only negative consequences for stealing were Clare's own guilt (mild) and self-deprecation. These reactions then ironically produced greater anxiety and increased stealing. The initial phase of Clare's treatment involved interrupting the downard spiral characteristic of compulsive behaviors (see the earlier case of Bess). In Clare's case, aversive conditioning was also helpful (Kellam, 1969). Afterwards, Clare learned more adaptive stress responses via relaxation training (Lutzker & Martin, 1981) and clarified her interpersonal conflicts through insight therapy (Kohut, 1977).

REFERENCES

Farrington, D., and Knight, B. Four sides of stealing as a risky decision. In P. Lipsitt and B. Sales (Eds.), *New directions in psycholegal research.* New York: Van Nostrand Reinhold, 1980.

241

Kellam, A. Shoplifting treated by aversion to a film. *Behavior Research and Therapy*, 1969, 7, 125–127.

Kohut, H. *The restoration of the self*. New York: International University Press, 1977.

Lutzker, J., and Martin, J. *Behavior change*. Monterey, Ca.: Brooks/Cole, 1981.

West, D., and Farrington, D. *The delinquent way of life*. London: Heinemann, 1977.

10

The Personality Disorders

Common to most definitions of personality is an emphasis on the individual's most enduring traits, that is, on those recurring perceptions and behaviors that are exhibited in a wide range of important social and personal contexts and that are most useful in predicting future behavior. To say that people have an habitual way of dealing with the world is not to say that they are exhibiting pathological behavior. In fact, most people have developed customary and comfortable patterns of interacting with the environment. In the personality disorders, however, these patterns (or personality traits) evidence a rigidity and destructive interpersonal results that make them counteradaptive.

The personality disorders are common patterns. People with a personality disorder are not typically as disturbed or as concerned by their behavior as are friends and relatives. Such people see these particular personality traits as ego-syntonic, that is, as consistent with their self-perception. Thus, persons with personality disorders are more likely to be brought to the attention of professionals by other people than by themselves, such as by spouses, relatives, or the criminal justice system.

Recognizing that addicted and sexually disordered persons (included as personality disorders in the DSM-II) do not necessarily suffer from associated psychopathology, DSM-III excluded these disorders from the category of personality disorders and classified them elsewhere. Also, the hysterical personality was changed to the histrionic personality, and the cyclothymic personality was reclassified as an affective disorder. Explosive, obsessive-compulsive, asthenic, and inadequate personalities were dropped from DSM-II, and six new personality disorders were added. The present eleven personality disorders are listed below in the "appearance clusters" suggested by DSM-III.

243

1. *Disorders that appear odd or eccentric*
   Paranoid: hyperalert, suspicious, litigious, and authoritarian.
   Schizoid: asocial "loners," not "schizophrenic-like."
   Schizotypal: "schizophrenic-like," but no hallucinations or delusions.
2. *Disorders that appear dramatic, emotional, or erratic*
   Histrionic: emotionally flamboyant and dramatic, though shallow.
   Narcissistic: chronically inflated sense of self-worth.
   Antisocial: chronic antisocial patterns, does not learn from experience.
   Borderline: irritable, anxious, sporadically aggressive and emotionally
       unstable.
3. *Disorders that appear anxious or fearful*
   Avoidant: shy and inhibited, afraid to "risk" relationships.
   Dependent: seeks dependent relationships; naïve, yet suspicious.
   Compulsive: controlled, formal, perfectionistic; "workaholics without
       warmth."
   Passive-Aggressive: passively resistant through stubbornness, ineffi-
       ciency, or *threatened* aggression.

The personality disorders are coded on Axis II in DSM-III, which allows the unfortunate implication that the personality disorders are not "clinical" syndromes, but rather are behavorial and psychosocial conditions, and thus are "less important." Though DSM-III does not always disallow these diagnoses in children, the diagnosis of a personality disorder in a person under eighteen is discouraged. In fact, these are critically important disorders patterns, and are often generic to more "dramatic" and "severe" psychopathology. By definition, these patterns begin to emerge in childhood or adolescence. DSM-III presents the following corresponding relationships between certain personality disorders and certain of the Disorders usually First Evident in Infancy, Childhood, or Adolescence:

Disorders in Childhood or Adolescence	Personality Disorders
Schizoid	Schizoid
Avoidant	Avoidant
Conduct	Antisocial
Oppositional	Passive-Aggressive
Identity	Borderline

The cases in this section were chosen to demonstrate the most important personality disorders. The histrionic and passive-aggressive personality disorders, described in the cases of Hilde and Patsy respectively, are common patterns; they are often critical to the development of marital and family distress, as well as to eventual personal unhappiness because of negative social feedback. The antisocial personality disorder, the case of Andy, exemplifies what is the most common personality disorder and certainly the most socially destructive pattern.

From: Meyer, R.C. + Osborne, Y.V.H. (Eds.)
Case Studies in abnormal Behavior (1982).

The Histrionic Personality Disorder

The Case of Hilde

The DSM-III category of histrionic personality disorder had traditionally been known as the "hysterical personality." This latter term has now been discarded in the DSM-III since *hysterical* wrongly implies that it is a disorder that parallels the symptom picture of what has previously been labeled as the hysterical neurosis. This term *(hysterical neurosis)* has also been changed in DSM-III to help in eliminating this confusion.

The specific criteria that mark the histrionic personality disorder include dramatic and intense emotional expressions, efforts to gain the center of attention, and shallow, insincere, and disrupted interpersonal relationships. Such people are likely to overreact emotionally, even in everyday situations. They have superficial interpersonal relationships, though they easily verbalize the platitudes of intense relationships, and they are inclined toward suicide gestures as a manipulation of others. Vanity and self-absorption are common traits. In that sense, histrionic individuals parallel the narcissistic personality disorder (Lasch, 1978).

Histrionic personalities appear to be empathic and socially perceptive, so that they easily elicit new relationships. Since they then turn out to be emotionally insensitive, and with little depth of insight into their own role in relationships, they are likely to avoid any blame for the inevitable problems in the relationships. In this fashion, they are closer to the defense mechanism of paranoid patterns. Histrionic individuals are often flirtatious and seductive sexually, though there is little payoff if one follows these cues (Barrett, 1980). The behavior of the histrionic personality resembles the traditional concepts of ultrafemininity, so for that reason it is more common in females than in males. Indeed, the Greek root of the term is *hustera*, meaning uterus.

Since denial is such a common approach to conflict in this pattern, intellectual accomplishment, relative to potential, is often limited, and there is a de-emphasis on analytic thought. As a result, histrionic individuals tend to be gullible and impressionable. Somatic complaints such as "spells of weakness" and headaches are typical. The histrionic individual is commonly encountered in clinical practice (Gardner, 1965).

Hilde

Hilde is a forty-two-year-old homemaker who sought help from her family physician for a combination of complaints, including headaches, mild depression, and marital difficulties. The family physician had attempted to treat her with quick reassurance and Valium. When these proved ineffective, he referred her to a private psychiatrist. Hilde, still quite attractive, obviously spent a great deal of time on grooming and her personal appearance. She was cooperative in the initial interview with the psychiatrist, though at times she rambled so much that he had to bring her back to the subject at hand. As one listened to her, it became apparent that she had not really reflected in any depth on the issues that she discussed and was only pumping out information much as a computer would. She showed a significant amount of affect during the interview, but it was often exaggerated in response to the content she was discussing at the time. She delighted in giving extensive historical descriptions of her past life, again without much insight as to how these had any causal role in her present distress.

In fact, many of the descriptions she gave appeared to be more for the purpose of impressing her therapist than in order to come to grips with her problems. When confronted with any irrelevancies in her stories, she first adopted a cute and charming manner, and if this proved ineffective in persuading her psychiatrist to change topics, she then became petulant and irritated.

When she described her present difficulties, she was always inclined to ascribe the responsibility to some person or situation other than herself. She stated that her husband was indifferent to her and added that she suspected he had been seduced by one of the secretaries in his office. This situation, along with a "lot of stress in my life" were given as the reason for the headaches and depression. When pressed for more details, she found it hard to describe interactions with her husband in any meaningful detail.

A parallel interview with her husband revealed that he felt he "had simply become tired of dealing with her." He admitted that his original attraction to Hilde was for her social status, her "liveliness," and her physical attractiveness. Over the years, it became clear that her liveliness was not the exuberance and love of life of an integrated personality, but simply a chronic flamboyance and intensity that was often misplaced. Her physical attractiveness was naturally declining, and she was spending inordinate amounts of time and money attempting to keep it up. Her husband was able to admit that when he had married her he had been reserved and inhibited. He was a competent and hard-working individual but had had little experience with the more enjoyable aspects of life. He viewed Hilde as his ticket to a new life. Now that he had established himself on his own, and had both matured and loosened up emotionally, he had simply grown tired of her childish and superficial manner. As he put it, "I still care for her and I don't want to hurt her, but I'm just not interested in putting up with all of this stuff too much longer."

It is interesting that when Hilde was asked about her children, she immediately responded that they were both "wonderful." They were now fourteen and sixteen years old, and Hilde's descriptions of them suggested that they were exceptionally bright and happy children. She was adamant about this, saying "they are *doing fine, and it's my problems that I want to deal with here." Unfortunately, her husband's descriptions of the situation did suggest that both children showed patterns analogous to Hilde's. They were both spoiled, and the oldest boy in particular had some difficulties keeping up with his schoolwork. He also had become a bit of a loner because of his dramatic and intense behaviors, a pattern that male peers are particularly likely to reject.*

Hilde was raised as the prized child of a moderately wealthy family. Her father owned a successful grain and feed operation. Her mother was active socially, joining virtually every socially prominent activity that occurred in the city. She did not have much time for Hilde, yet delighted in showing her off to guests. Hilde was one of those individuals who is born with many gifts. She had potential for high intellectual achievement, easily adapted to all the social graces, and was almost stunningly beautiful. The sad part is that the family provided few if any rewards for high achievements in the intellectual area. Hilde was expected to get decent grades, but there was no incentive for high grades, and the family often made fun of others in the town who were "intellectual snobs." Hilde's beauty was obviously prized, and she was taught many ways to maximize her attractiveness.

Her beauty and the response it received from friends in her parents' social circle also provided her with more than simple attention. Her mother delighted in having her stay up and greet guests at their parties, something she never consistently allowed Hilde's brothers and sisters to do. Also, Hilde soon discovered that if she misbehaved, a charmingly presented "I'm sorry" to her father usually voided any necessity for punishment.

As Hilde moved into adolescence, she developed a wide circle of friends, though it is interesting that she never maintained any one relationship for very long. Her beauty, social grace, and high status in the community made it easy for her to flit about like a princess among her court. Males came to her as bees come to a flower. She had a reputation for being loose sexually, though it is clear this was based on hopes and rumor rather than on actual behavior.

Throughout high school, she was active as a cheerleader and as an organizer of class dances and parties. She was usually elected to be class secretary and once was the class vice-president. No one ever considered her as a candidate for class president, and she herself would not have cared for the position. She had little trouble with her course work; though she seldom spent much time preparing, she usually obtained B's and C's, with an occasional A. Hilde remembers her junior high and high school years as "the happiest time of my life," an assessment that is probably accurate.

Hilde's college years were not unlike her high school years, except that some notes of discord began to creep in. She had to work harder to obtain the moderate grades she had always been pleased with, and she was not always able to carry through with the required effort, particularly since she was wrapped up in sorority activities and cheerleading. She dated many people, though rarely did she allow dating to get to the point of a sexual experience. When it did happen, it was more to try it out than as a result of any strong desires on her part. She occasionally experienced orgasm during foreplay, though never during intercourse.

After college, she took a job in a woman's clothing store whose clientele was primarily the rich and fashionable. One of her customers subtly introduced Hilde to her son, Steve, a young attorney with one of the most prestigious firms in the region. He courted Hilde in whirlwind fashion. They went out almost every night, usually attending the many parties to which they were both invited. Each was enraptured by the other, and they were married five months after they met. Both families had mild objections to the short courtship. However, since each was from "a good family," no strong objections were lodged.

Over the years, Steve's practice developed rapidly. He not only had the advantage of being with an excellent firm, but was in addition both intelligent and hard working. Hilde meanwhile moved into many social activities, though occasionally abruptly finding that they demanded more than charm and attractiveness. In spite of her best efforts, her beauty is naturally fading, and the bloom has worn off the romance that impelled them into marriage. She and Steve seldom do anything together that involves a meaningful interaction. Most of the time he is absorbed in his work, and they only go out together on ritual social occasions. They seldom have sex together, and usually only after Steve has drunk a bit too much at a party. There is not much conflict in the marriage; there is not much of anything else, either.

Etiology   One of the original explanations for this disorder, by the Greek physician-philosopher Hippocrates, held that the unfruitful womb became angry and wandered about the body, causing hysteria. As is obvious, Hippocrates thought the disorder only occurred in women, a conception that has since proven to be inaccurate. Freud saw conflict over the expression of sexual impulses as critical. Interestingly enough, both Hippocrates and Freud prescribed marriage as the cure. Since marriage would provide a legitimate outlet for sexual desires, in some cases this medicine might be effective (though the side effects might be more than many would wish to risk). Yet, in Hilde's case marriage exaggerated the problem instead of curing it.

Her background has a number of factors that would facilitate the development of a histrionic personality disorder. Hilde's mother showed little interest in her, except on those rare occasions when she wished to show Hilde off, in essence responding to her as an object. It is common that a lack of consistent maternal attention can produce intense strivings for paternal attention as a replacement, particularly in the female child, and this appears to have been the case with Hilde. Though her father obviously cared for her, he had little time available to attend to her. As a result, he, too, responded primarily to the superficial aspects of her being.

In addition, both parents allowed Hilde to use her charm and physical attractiveness as an excuse for not fulfilling the responsibilities that are expected of most children. Hilde came to learn that a charmingly put "I'm sorry" would suffice as a consequence of misbehavior. So she never learned to see her personality and decisions as the responsible agents in the problems she naturally encountered. As she grew up, other people would often give her the same allowance, though not to the degree her parents did. The inability to examine and respond effectively to the long-term consequences of her behavior was never reinforced and developed in Hilde (Bugental, 1980).

As a result, Hilde made a wide range of friendships, but none with any real depth. They were oriented around social activities but involved little self-disclosure or sharing of personal vulnerabilities. Similarly, her parents never openly manifested their own personal vulnerability. They always put forth an optimistic and cheerful facade, even when it was apparent that they were having problems in their own lives.

It is most unfortunate that Hilde's potential for intellectual competence and analytic thinking withered in the face of the type of reinforcement she received from her family. The high level of attention to her physical attractiveness and social skills stood her in good stead during her adolescence. Physical attractiveness naturally decreases with age and does not carry one through the intricacies of any long-term relationship. Analogously, she had long ago learned to see her sexuality as a means of interpersonal manipulation and was never able to focus on the achievement of mutual intimacy and pleasure. It is as if she saw her responsibility ending at the point the male showed initiative behaviors toward her (Barrett, 1980).

Her husband Steve came from a family that emphasized status, hard work, and vocational achievement. Hilde appeared to him as a guide to a new world, one in which pleasure, intimacy, and social activity were paramount. It was only when their whirlwind courtship, extravagant wedding, and expensive honeymoon were well behind them that the bloom went off the relationship. He gradually recognized the lack of depth in their relationship, and when he attempted to talk this out with Hilde, she became upset. She accused him of not loving her and even occasionally accused him of having another woman. She also responded by trying to make herself even more attractive, at the same time realizing her physical beauty was naturally decreasing. She did not age gracefully and Steve even began to think of her as "pathetic" in this regard. Their meager sexual life dissipated even further. He eventually did start to see other women. Since he still cared for Hilde in a platonic way, he attempted to keep these affairs from her, and did so rather successfully.

By this time, Hilde's father had become a kind of patriarch in the area. He was a man of great wealth and still enjoyed indulging his favorite and most beautiful daughter. Hilde emotionally moved back toward her family, though like Steve, she kept up the facade of the marriage. She also became depressed on occasion, and periodically drank too much. The cycle spiraled, as if at some level of consciousness she realized her own role in her problems, as well as her inadequacy to deal with them.

Treatment   A number of possible treatments were considered for Hilde. The first and most difficult task is to gain her trust. In that regard, several sessions were held in which the therapist adopted a posture not unlike that employed with the paranoid individual. He listened to Hilde's discussion with empathy, yet at the same time wistfully or bemusingly offered other alternative explanations for her behavior. He did not confront her directly, as it had been her life-long pattern to run away from any confrontation (Greist et al., 1980).

As the trust developed, other therapeutic modes were tried in order to help her defenses gradually lessen. In that regard, bibliotherapy, or the reading of certain prescribed books, was used. She was asked to read various novels and plays that portrayed individuals who had grown up feeling as if they were appreciated for external rather than any ongoing essential personality factors. Of course, some of these individuals had developed coping strategies that were not unlike Hilde's. The work of Tennessee Williams, Edward Albee, and Jean Genet convey these concepts quite well. She was then asked to write her own poetry or short stories that focused on characters who developed similar defenses. This led eventually to the use of role playing. Her therapist would take the role of Hilde's mother, for example, and Hilde would play herself in some typical childhood interaction. It is also effective to role-play the opposite roles, so Hilde would play her mother and the therapist would play Hilde as a child. This role playing was expanded to include interactions with her father, her husband, and some of her friends (Yablonsky, 1976).

Unfortunately, at approximately this time Hilde's husband told her that he had fallen in love with another woman and wanted a divorce. He refused to consider marital therapy, said that his decision had functionally been made long ago, and that he had only waited to find a woman with whom he could really become involved. Hilde made a mild suicide gesture, overdosing on a small bottle of aspirin. She obviously did not want to kill herself (Boor, 1981), but in line with her dramatic behavior patterns, she

250

had hoped to reverse her husband's decision in this manner. It was unsuccessful, and she and her therapist worked through this situation, again using the role playing.

At this time, it was recommended to Hilde that she also enter group therapy. Her first reactions were that "those people won't understand me," and "I don't have really bad problems like they do." After the therapist was able to work through her defensiveness in this regard, she asked Hilde to commit to go to at least three sessions. It was agreed that if she felt as if she could not continue after that, she could leave the group. Hilde made the contract and went for the three sessions. Fortunately, the group was supportive of her, something she needed at this point, particularly because of the divorce. It is also ironically probable that Hilde enjoyed this forum, in which she could dramatically replay many of the events in her life. She started to attend the group regularly and began to improve in her ability to confront the responsibility she had for the events that happened in her life. She felt she could stop seeing her individual therapist, though at her last contact with her, Hilde was still struggling substantially with the problems of her world. For one thing, her defensive view that her children did not have problems had dissolved. She became aware that they needed much more attention from her and that they also would need professional intervention for some emotional problems. The prognosis for continued improvement in Hilde is good. However, it should be noted that the prognosis for most histrionic personality disorders is not so positive, since their defenses are strong and well learned and unfortunately often continue to be at least partially reinforced by some of the people around them (Barrett, 1980).

Comment   The diagnosis of an histrionic personality disorder is associated with behavior that is overly reactive and intensely expressed. Interpersonal relationships are particularly impaired, primarily due to others' perceptions (usually accurate) of the person as shallow, superficial, and insincere. Persons with histrionic personalities are typically attractive and charming; they thus initiate friendships and romantic involvements quickly. However, the rule in these relationships is similar to the course of Hilde's marriage. Once the initial attraction inevitably subsides, the histrionic person is unable to develop sustaining intimacy and to participate in a reciprocal relationship (Chodoff, 1974). The impression one gets in clinical observations is that such persons have adopted a role (usually ultrafeminine) in relating to others that is compelling in presentation, though eventually disappointing because there is no authenticity in these relationships (Meissner, 1981).

The higher incidence of histrionic personality disorders among women can be attributed to the close parallel between diagnostic criteria for the disorder and features of the traditional stereotype of the female role (Barrett, 1980; Hyler & Spitzer, 1978). In some ways, however, the personality disorders in general, and the histrionic personality in particular, are social epiphenomena. Among others, Price and Bouffard (1974) suggest that whether or not a person who meets the diagnostic criteria for a personality disorder will be seen as truly abnormal depends on the context in which the behavior is observed.

Perhaps, then, the earlier prescriptions of marriage for "hysterical patients" were somewhat successful because histrionic features were more consistent with the social expectations of "traditional" married women and mothers. Indeed, excessive emotionality, intense involvements, and superficial (yet manipulative) concern with "serious" endeavors (such as scholastic achievement, political issues, and finances) have until recently been considered desirable traits and were characteristic of a number of popular heroines—including Scarlett O'Hara of *Gone with the Wind* and Meggie of *The Thornbirds*. However, as is evident with Hilde, marriage is a successful strategy for persons with a histrionic personality disorder only while the expectations of spouses are consistent with the stereotype of an attractive though naïve spousal role. Most mates find that the initial glamour of such an individual soon fades and becomes tedious.

REFERENCES

Barrett, C. Personality (character) disorders. In R. Woody (Ed.), *The encyclopedia of clinical assessment*. San Francisco: Jossey-Bass, 1980.

Boor, M. Methods of suicide and implications for suicide prevention. *Journal of Clinical Psychology*, 1981, 37, 70–75.

Bugental, J. Someone needs to worry: The existential anxiety of responsibility and decision. In G. Belkin (Ed.), *Contemporary psychotherapies*. Chicago: Rand McNally, 1980.

Chodoff, P. The diagnosis of hysteria: An overview. *American Journal of Psychiatry*, 1974, 131, 1073–1078.

Gardner, E. The role of the classification system in outpatient psychiatry. In M. Katz, J. Cole, and W. Barton (Eds.), *The role and methodology in psychiatry and psychothology*. Washington, D.C.: U.S. Public Health Service, 1965.

Greist, J., Marks, I., Berlin, F., Gournay, K., and Noshirvani, H. Avoidance versus confrontation of fear. *Behavior Therapy*, 1980, 11, 1–14.

Hyler, S., and Spitzer, R. Hysteria split asunder. *American Journal of Psychiatry*, 1978, 135, 1500–1504.

Lasch, C. *The culture of narcissism*. New York: W. W. Norton, 1978.

Meissner, W. A note on narcissim. *Psychoanalytic Quarterly*, 1981, 50, 77–87.

Price, R., and Bouffard, D. Behavioral appropriateness and situational constraints as dimensions of social behavior. *Journal of Personality and Social Psychology*, 1974, 30, 579–586.

Yablonsky, L. *Psychodrama: Resolving emotional problems through role-playing*. New York: Basic Books, 1976.

The Antisocial Personality Disorder

The Case of Andy

The essential characteristic of the antisocial personality disorder is the chronic manifestation of the antisocial behavior; that is, behavior that in some form violates another's rights. These individuals are amoral, impulsive, narcissistic, and are unable to delay gratification or deal effectively with authority figures. There is a heightened need for environmental stimulation, as well as a lack of response to standard societal control procedures, such as punishment. The chronicity of the pattern is reflected in their inability to profit from experience. Much of the material about this disorder is discussed in Meyer (1980, 1982) and will not be repetitively referenced here.

The DSM-III specifies that the person be over the age of eighteen in order to receive this diagnosis. Yet it is quite clear that the behavior patterns associated with this disorder are almost always evident before the age of fifteen. When an individual does display these behaviors prior to age eighteen, the diagnostic label of *conduct disorder* is given. The DSM-III requires evidence of the pattern before age fifteen (truancy and/or delinquency, for example) and persistent and varied manifestations after eighteen in marital, vocational, moral, or criminal disorder patterns.

There has been far more research on the antisocial personality than any other personality disorder, both because it is commonly encountered and because the cost to society is high from these individuals. There are good data (Gray & Hutchinson, 1964) to show that diagnosticians find this concept to be a meaningful one and also that this category is more reliably diagnosed than virtually any other psychiatric diagnostic category (Spitzer et al., 1967).

Evolution of The Term

The term *antisocial personality* has evolved from a number of traditional terms that are still in use, such as *psychopathic* and *sociopathic personalities*. Even Pinel began to conceptualize this category with his term *manie sans delire*. However, it was not until late in the nineteenth century that the term *psychopath* first appeared.

The first DSM (DSM-I), the *Diagnostic Statistical Manual* published in 1952 by the American Psychiatric Association, clouded the issue by substituting the term *sociopathic personality* to cover those behavior patterns that had been traditionally included in the term *psychopath*. The term *sociopathic* was used to emphasize the environmental factors that at that time were felt to generate the disorder. The confusion was heightened by the 1968 revision of the Diagnostic and Statistical Manual (DSM-II), as neither term was included. Instead, the new term used was *antisocial personality*. One semantic problem with this term is that many people feel it contains an inherent implication of specifically criminal behavior. Thus, it may not be clear to some whether or not a formal indictment or conviction is required for the diagnosis. What is required is evidence of a chronic pattern of violating other people's rights, in particular as manifested through the four criteria mentioned earlier.

Andy

Andy, age twenty-two, was first seen by mental health personnel when he was routinely referred to the psychiatric clinic of a state prison by the screening unit of that institution. He had been incarcerated for auto theft and simple assault. At age twenty, he had been convicted of grand larceny but had been given probation.

Andy also had a substantial list of offenses stemming from when he was a juvenile, including auto theft, assault with a deadly weapon, and sexual misconduct. He had been accused of rape, but the girl's prior arrests as a prostitute and the lack of witnesses resulted in the lesser charge. Andy's childhood had been a tumultuous one. He was the second of two children, his brother being a year and a half older than he. His father abandoned the family two years after Andy's birth, and though Andy has a general idea where his father lives, he has never had any contact with him. His mother worked as a waitress, though on occasion she accepted "dates" for sexual purposes that she made at the restaurant. In general, she lived on the fringes of society.

She seemed to care about her two boys and gave them as much attention as was possible, given her lifestyle. Yet, on occasion, the frustrations of her world became too much for her, and she would beat them rather brutally. This typically occurred when she became frustrated and confused as to how to cope with the discipline problems that naturally emerge from having two active boys.

She would periodically drown her frustrations in alcohol, and it was at these times that she was especially prone to beat them. As she grew older and they gradually left her care, she developed a sense of being unimportant to any one, and the alcoholism increased substantially.

Andy was born prematurely during the early part of his mother's eighth month of pregnancy. There were mild complications in the delivery, and Andy experienced a period of anoxia (lack of oxygen to the brain). Though there was no evidence at the time of any resultant gross brain damage, Andy's later performance in school would be consistent with that type of occurrence. Andy was able to walk unaided at fifteen months of age, which is average, but he did not speak words adequately until he was two and a half years old, which is later than average. Toilet training was started shortly after Andy was one year old and was completed about a year and a half later, though he continued to wet the bed periodically until he was seven years old.

In addition to the occasional severe spankings he received from his mother, Andy also had been severely beaten by one of his mother's boyfriends. This beating included substantial blows to the head; when they took Andy to the hospital, they told the physician that Andy had fallen down the steps. The issue of child abuse was investigated, but there was no definite proof, and Andy did not implicate the boyfriend.

Andy had been placed in day care since he was two and a half years old, and he made an adequate adjustment there. When he was enrolled in school, he seemed to do well in tasks that involved manual dexterity but could not deal with reading or spelling. He was soon placed in a remedial reading group and never did catch up in this area. When one fails at reading, one naturally has difficulty with many other subjects that depend on it, and this was so with Andy.

In school, Andy exhibited a short attention span and a restlessness that soon crystallized into a classic pattern of hyperactivity. Attentional difficulties resulted in academic problems. Andy's tolerance for frustration was so low that when he was teased by anyone he would lash out aggressively. Disciplinary efforts by his teachers were almost totally ineffective.

He was similarly disruptive in his neighborhood. He would fight with younger children, sometimes brutally kicking them. On one occasion, an older boy in the neighborhood had beaten up both Andy and his brother. The next day, Andy sprayed a can of lighter fluid over his adversary's pet dog and set it afire. He showed no concern in response to the garish scene that ensued.

It is common for someone like Andy to become negative toward school in general. He did so, and began to run away from school. At first, he would just go home and play. Then, when truant officers began to look for him there, he would stay out on the streets of the city finding different things to entertain him. He started to get in trouble as he engaged in mild shoplifting and vandalism.

He also began to run with a gang of boys, and though he had many social contacts, it was clear that he had no deep friendships or loyalties. This gang was constantly in trouble, and it was with the gang that Andy was usually picked up by the police during his juvenile years.

His mother attempted to set limits for him and explained the ethical issues of stealing. Yet, it was clear that in her own life she had few limits that she followed, and that she commonly accepted gifts (often of stolen property) from her various lovers and customers. She also was extremely inconsistent in enforcing the rules she laid down, so that neither of the boys paid much attention to them. Andy's older brother also belonged to this gang. When Andy was sixteen years old, his brother and three other boys robbed a service station. In the ensuing resistance they killed the attendant. Andy's brother was sentenced to prison for murder in the first degree and faces the prospect of a long stay there.

As Andy moved into middle adolescence, he was constantly in front of juvenile authorities and spent these years going from juvenile detention centers to home and back. Andy's behavior in the juvenile centers was marked by good relations with individuals he could manipulate and indifferent or bad relationships with those he could not. When he was home, he was out in the streets most of the time and would often get into fights with his mother's lover of the moment.

At the age of eighteen, he was fortunate to get a job as a hospital orderly through the intercession of his juvenile worker. He seemed to do well there because he liked his fellow workers, was earning some money, and because it was was active work. But after about a year, he was caught stealing drugs from the hospital dispensary and was fired. He had never had a history of prolonged substance abuse. He apparently broke in and took the drugs simply to give them to several of his present associates.

Andy had been introduced to masturbation by his older brother when he was about twelve years old. He was having sexual intercourse when he was fifteen, mostly with girls associated with the gang he ran with. Though he eventually had women whom he each in turn called "his woman," there was never much evidence of any committed or even particularly affectionate relationships. For a short period of time, Andy pimped for one of his girlfriends, then found the role distasteful and stopped. As he moved into early adulthood, he lived with a series of different women. He showed little evidence of committed behavior while he lived with them and no concern or remorse about breaking off any of the relationships. When he turned twenty, he was living with a woman who worked as a maid in the hospital where he had worked. During that time, he was arrested for assault. His girlfriend used most of her savings to pay a lawyer who was able to have Andy acquitted on a technicality. As soon as the incident was over, Andy left her holding the bill for the lawyer's fee.

Like most inmates, Andy verbalized innocence of all charges when he was first interviewed at the clinic. He also said that he was interested in treatment. Of course, virtually all inmates quickly learn to show an interest in any self-improvement program and try to get as many of them as possible on their record. There was little evidence that Andy had any real interest in changing himself, but a variety of treatment options were developed nonetheless.

Etiology   Andy's history certainly makes him a prime candidate for developing into an antisocial personality. Even his premature birth probably caused some minimal brain dysfunction that could further inhibit the development of behavioral controls. The mild hyperactivity that he showed throughout his early school years has been linked in some individuals to brain dysfunction from anoxia at birth, and hyperactivity is a major predictor toward later criminal behavior and/or schizophrenic behavior. This is not to say that all hyperactives develop this way, but there is a significant correlation (Safer, 1976).

In addition to this biological factor, Andy had a number of environmental conditions that would make the probability of an antisocial personality disorder quite high. First, the absence of any consistent father figure during his childhood and adolescence gave him no real model for appropriate behavior. The only available models were the casual lovers who drifted through his mother's world, and they had few positive qualities to emulate. When he became old enough to become associated with a gang, it provided further negative role models.

The brutal spankings that he received from his mother, as well as the occasional beatings from one of her boyfriends, certainly reinforced the use of aggression as a coping behavior. Anxiety and upset became discriminative cues for aggression.

In addition to the severe beatings, which primarily reflected his mother's ignorance and frustration over how to cope with her role, her inconsistent discipline and her hypocrisy about verbalized values cemented the development of the antisocial pattern. It was clear to both Andy and his brother that she was saying these things because she thought that she should do so, but that she did not adhere to them herself.

If Andy had been bright, he might have become involved in school activities and received the reinforcements that could have attracted him into more appropriate behavior patterns, and also thereby opening him up to the influence of teachers as surrogate fathers. Unfortunately, his intellectual abilities were below average, particularly in the verbal areas such as reading. So he received little reinforcement here. School quickly became aversive for him. He started running away, and easily drifted into delinquent behaviors.

Andy never was able to establish lasting or affectionate relationships with his peers. He seemed to associate with them as a form of status and security and through them found the high environmental stimulation he seemed to need. When he moved into early adulthood, he was not able to establish any committed relationships with women or any pattern of adult responsibility. He maintained contact with these women primarily to have an available sexual outlet. Though it does appear that Andy's mother wanted to care for him and did love him, her manner and lifestyle prohibited this attitude coming through very clearly, leading to his thoroughgoing egocentricity.

Treatment Options

A variety of treatment possibilities have been suggested as appropriate for the antisocial personality disorder. Some have advocated psychosurgery, but it has not been markedly successful here (Trotter, 1976). It is unrealistic to assume that specific lesions are going to eradicate the complex and long-standing patterns of behavior that mark this disorder. Drug treatments, such as with the phenothiazines or fluphenazine decanoate, have been of help in some cases. The positive feature of the fluphenazine treatment is that if desired, it can be administered by injection only once every several days. Most antisocial personalities are not particularly likely to follow through with the ritual of taking a prescription drug several times a day. Some antisocial personalities under treatment with these long-acting tranquilizers do become calmer. However, these drugs have significant side effects that must be considered in making the long-term prescriptions that are required.

In treating the antisocial personality, the major problem is getting the person involved in the treatment (Yochelson & Samenow, 1976). Most have no interest in changing their behavior and are only in a treatment program because they have been forced to do so by circumstances, as we see in Andy's case. This kind of motivation can lead to bizarre behavior.

When the senior author was associated with the psychiatric clinic of the Southern Michigan State Prison at Jackson, many inmates used to join the Alcoholics Anonymous program. It later turned out that many of them had never been alcoholics or even had a drinking problem. They just wanted the apparent change in behavior to show up on their record as if they had participated in an additional necessary treatment program. These same individuals were likely to show up at chapel services every Sunday, but spent most of their time reading the paper and playing cards. Their goal was to get their name on the roll to show that they had attended chapel.

Some ingenious attempts have been made to get the antisocial personality disorder involved in treatment. Some treatment programs have paid antisocial personalities to come to talk into a tape recorder, allegedly in order for the program to obtain sociological background data on such a population. Several of the individuals who originally participated for the money became so involved in this process that they were willing to continue even after the pay stopped.

Andy's Treatment

Andy was first confronted with his self-defeating failure patterns. These confronting statements were made in strong language over four different sessions. This technique is not unlike the Reality Therapy of William Glasser and also incorporates some notions of the work of Yochelson and Samenow (1976). These latter authors have reported success with a therapy in which they confront antisocial personalities with their lies and failure patterns. The effort is to "enhance their self-disgust" and maneuver them into participating in attempts to change their behavior.

After this stage, the treatment consisted of the applying of various ego building techniques. In general, these techniques attempt to stimulate new interests and behaviors that could improve confidence. In Andy's case, enrollment in skills that tapped his good visual motor skills were emphasized, rather than continuing to push participation in standard academic subjects that focused so much on reading ability. In addition, there was an attempt to improve his object perception and to improve his ability to evaluate his motivations and feelings. He also received training in empathy, training in developing alternate plans of behavior through mental imagery and symbolism, and efforts to change his beliefs through such techniques as Rational Emotive Therapy (Ellis, 1973).

One exercise that helped Andy develop some much needed empathy involved looking at various pictures of individuals who were interacting with each other and then asking him to say what he thought each person in the pictures was experiencing. At first, Andy was clumsy with this technique. Then he began to develop a wider range of options. His initial descriptions were of physical events; only later could he move into conceptualizing the more complex emotional aspects that people might be experiencing. A variety of exercises were provided in which mental imagery and symbolism were required to plan out later responses to different crisis situations. Andy was given feedback on the validity of his strategies and was also taught some of the self-verbalization techniques of Meichenbaum (1977).

It has been found that individuals such as Andy surprisingly have a very negative self-image. This image is evident in the way they talk about themselves to themselves. They are encouraged to state things more positively in their self-vocalizations about themselves. Lastly, Andy was taught to develop interests in areas that would provide him higher levels of environmental stimulation. This included increased participation in traditional athletic activities, dancing, and any other behavior that required a physically active response to a high level stimulation. It has been found that antisocial personalities are very stimulation-seeking individuals (Quay, 1965; Zuckerman et al., 1980); if their environment does not provide enough stimulation, they will seek it through deviant behaviors.

Andy was seen in the prison clinic for a period of nine months, during which time he showed a significant improvement. Unfortunately, he still had several years to serve on his sentence, and during that period he did regress from his positive changes, probably as a result of having to live in a prison environment that long. An attempt was made to get him involved in treatment again several months before he was due to be released. However, he continually missed his appointments and clearly no longer had much interest in participating.

Andy left the state shortly after being released from prison, which violated his parole requirements. He was apprehended and convicted two years later in connection with an attempted robbery. Some antisocial personalities are changed as a result of treatment, and some change as a result of simply aging ("burn out"); the great majority, however, are not changed by their environment or by treatment techniques. It is likely that Andy will continue in this pattern until age robs him of the ability or interest to act out against the environment.

Comment   Considerable effort has been extended toward clarifying the nature of the antisocial personality disorder. To date, attempts to isolate etiological variables and to identify factors related to successful treatment outcomes have yielded generally unclear data. The symptom pattern of the antisocial personality is one of the more consistently perceived of the personality disorders (Gray & Hutchinson, 1964; Spitzer et al., 1967; Smith, 1978). Descriptions in both clinical reports and empirical studies have characterized the person with an antisocial personality disorder as selfish, irresponsible, unable to learn from experience, impulsive, and lacking in guilt (Meyer, 1980, 1982).

The essence of the numerous treatment strategies that have been implemented (with varying effectiveness) with the antisocial personality disorder has been aimed toward developing internal controls over behavior. As evidenced by Andy's case, psychotherapy is difficult because such persons exhibit minimal anxiety, are poorly (or inappropriately) motivated to change, and/or have difficulty perceiving their role in problems with social and occupational adjustment. However, when a trusting relationship can be established within a setting with strong external controls (such as a correction facility), progress toward socialization can be accomplished. Unfortunately, in Andy's case, the prison environment eventually had a negative effect on his progress because of his extended stay there.

A critical issue in understanding and treating persons with antisocial personality disorders has to do with the prediction of violent and otherwise criminal behavior. Heilbrun (1979) has suggested that violent and impulsive criminal acting-out results from a combination of antisocial traits and lower intelligence. Heilbrun found that evidence of violent crimes was greater for persons with high levels of psychopathy and low levels of intelligence than for other combinations of the two variables. It is unclear at this point whether intelligence mutes the characteristic impulsivity of the antisocial personality or simply helps the individual avoid discovery by legal authorities.

REFERENCES

Ellis, A. *Humanistic psychotherapy: The rational emotive approach.* New York: McGraw-Hill, 1973.

Gray, H., and Hutchinson, H. The psychopathic personality: A survey of Canadian psychiatrists' opinion. *Canadian Psychiatric Association Journal*, 1964, 9, 450–461.

Heilbrun, A. Psychopathy and violent crime. *Journal of Consulting and Clinical Psychology*, 1979, *47*, 517–524.

Meichenbaum, D. *Cognitive-behavior modification*, New York: Plenum, 1977.

Meyer, R. The antisocial personality. In R. Woody (Ed.), *The encyclopedia of clinical assessment*. San Francisco: Jossey-Bass, 1980.

——. *The clinician's handbook*. Boston: Allyn and Bacon, 1982.

Quay, H. Psychopathic personality as pathological stimulation seeking. *American Journal of Psychiatry*, 1965, *122*, 180–183.

Safer, D. *Hyperactive children: Diagnosis and management.* Baltimore: University Park Press, 1976.

Smith, R. *The psychopath in society.* New York: Academic Press, 1978.

Spitzer, R., Cohen, J., Fliess, J., and Endicott, J. Quantification of agreement in psychiatric diagnosis: A new approach. *Archives of General Psychiatry*, 1967, *17*, 83–87.

Trotter, S. Federal commission ok's psychosurgery. *APA Monitor*, 1976, *7*, 4–5.

Yochelson, S., and Samenow, S. *The criminal mind.* New York: Jason Aaronson, 1976.

Zuckerman, M., Buchsbaum, M., and Murphy, D. Sensation seeking and its biological correlates. *Psychological Bulletin*, 1980, *88*, 187–214.

The Passive-Aggressive Personality Disorder

The Case of Patsy   Even though the passive-aggressive personality disorder is a commonly encountered clinical pattern (Gardner, 1965), there was a strong question of whether it would be included in the DSM-III. It was apparently felt that this pattern did not have as clear-cut criteria as other patterns hopefully do, and that in many cases individuals who demonstrate this pattern could be fitted into other categories without much trouble. Also, there is not much research literature dealing with this pattern. Although clinicians find the term useful (Gardner, 1965), few people have developed operational criteria that can be researched and replicated. Yet, since it is a common pattern in clinical practice, and one that people are likely to encounter in everyday interactions, we thought it would be worthwhile to include a passive-aggressive personality case history in this text.

The core features of this personality disorder are indirectly expressed resistance and hostility in the face of common environmental demands for adequate performance and behavior. There is hostility toward others, though the passive-aggressive denies this hostility and may even act insulted when confronted with it. The relevant behaviors may be either aggressive or passive, and actual physical aggression seldom occurs (Barrett, 1980).

This resistance is expressed through such indirect behaviors as stubbornness, intentional inefficiency, deliberate forgetfulness, and procrastination. These individuals resent and oppose any demands, however reasonable, that are placed on them. They carry around moderately high levels of anxiety and aggression as well as a negative self-image, and they lack the ability to assert themselves appropriately in the face of authority. They usually first come to the attention of clinicians because of problems in a family or work situation.

Most parents have experienced their children's pushing them to the limits of their ability to control their anger. Passive-aggressive individuals similarly become acutely sensitive to the limits of the people with whom they interact; they are consistently able to move up to that point and not go beyond it. They appear to take the rules set up by others and effectively turn them around to immobilize the more dominant individuals who made the rules.

Patsy

Patsy, a twenty-four-year-old married woman, is a housewife in a small southern town. She and her husband have been married for six years, and they have a five-year-old daughter. Both Patsy and her husband feel the marriage has become "stuck in a rut," and both admit they are unhappy with the prospect of continuing in this situation. They also comment that this has been so for the last three years, yet they have not been able to respond to it effectively by themselves. Her husband, Art, feels that over the last year Patsy has too often complained about his drinking (which is a problem behavior), has accused him of not loving her and of running around with other women (which he says is not true), and of not loving their daughter enough (which he also states is not the case).

It is not uncommon for the passive-aggressive person to make accusations that are extremely difficult to defend. The mistake is accepting the challenge of defending oneself in the first place. In this case, Art was not sophisticated enough to avoid the initial challenge and then found himself unable to produce any exact proof to refute her accusations. As soon as there is a response to the content of the question, there is a functional admission that there may be some truth to the accusation.

Art also responded to the content of the question rather than to the basic premise, and in doing so he allowed the "burden of proof" to shift to him from Patsy, who made the accusations. Passive-aggressive individuals are usually a bit more sophisticated psychologically than the partners on whom they depend. At the same time, they are fearful of asserting their personality, and they use their psychological sophistication to gain a form of control in the relationship (Barrett, 1980).

Patsy's childhood history was reasonably normal. She grew up in an intact family and was generally loved by both of her parents. However, the family was a large one; Patsy was the fourth of six children. As a result, she became somewhat lost in the crowd. This could have promoted independent behaviors, as one had to stand out from the group in some way to gain any attention, but two things operated against this. The first was Patsy's father. Though he loved his children, he could not stand any behaviors that threatened his authority, particularly from his female children. In addition, he would virtually go berserk in the face of their tantrums or extended crying and upset. All the children quickly learned that any such behavior could drive him into a rage, and the consequent cost of a brutal spanking was not worth the benefit. As a result, Patsy learned to obtain attention through passivity, but passivity that necessarily had a degree of uniqueness and assertiveness to it.

A second factor that promoted the pattern was her mother's passivity, which operated as a model, particularly for the female children. Patsy's mother was adept at using sick behaviors and guilt-inducing behaviors to control her husband. He would not tolerate any direct confrontation with the demands that he made upon his wife. He believed that his word was law and that he had the ultimate right to avoid or uphold any decision made in the household, a right he often exercised. But Patsy's mother learned that he could be controlled through a variety of behaviors. "Sick" behaviors were particularly effective. Patsy's mother would occasionally have fainting spells, which always seemed to occur in a way that changed the direction of a family decision.

For example, on one occasion, Patsy's father wished the family to spend their vacation with him at a fishing camp. Patsy's mother much preferred that he go alone, and also that she stay home with the children so that she could then entertain her own mother and sister during that vacation period. Patsy's father adamantly refused to accept this option, and stated that everyone would accompany him to the fishing camp. Patsy's mother immediately began having a series of headaches and fainting spells. She sought advice from the old family physician whom she had consulted since childhood. He was impressed by the symptoms, but had no idea what was causing them, so he gave her a prescription for a mild sedative that he hoped would calm her down. His response legitimized the behavior and put Patsy's father in an untenable situation. Though he was demanding, he could not reasonably ask his sick wife to go with him into the wilderness, and so she obtained her way. At other times, she would use her religious beliefs to maneuver her husband. He always wished that she would join him in his drinking bouts at home, which though infrequent, were something that he indulged in mightily when he did. She refused, usually saying that she had to go to work at the church, or visit some sick people at the hospital. Again, this was more than he could operate against.

Patsy learned to use similar behaviors and even had a short period of anorexia. This behavior never earned her the formal diagnostic term of Anorexia Nervosa, in part because the pattern was not extended over a significant period of time, and secondly, because the family never took Patsy to a clinician for it. (See the earlier case of Anna, regarding anorexia nervosa.) The anorexic pattern was not unlike Patsy's mother's behavior when she controlled her husband by the fainting spells. Patsy's anorexia came about when her father had begun to criticize her school performance. Patsy had been falling behind in several subjects. The anorexia put her in the position of being a "sick person" and muted her father's upset and at the same time gained a degree of positive attention from him, a rarity for Patsy.

Patsy's father had always been restrictive toward the children about staying out at night. Patsy maneuvered around this by joining a number of church and school activities that required her presence in the evenings. Her father was in the bind that he could not criticize her for these "good" involvements in church and school, and yet it allowed her to get around his proscriptions against staying out at night. In that sense, she was able to void one set of his rules by appealing to a higher order set of values to which he also adhered.

Patsy's youngest brother, the baby of the family, had come as a "surprise" sixteen years after Patsy had been born. Though Patsy's mother verbalized much upset about his late arrival, it became clear that she was not unhappy about it. It kept her in the role of the housewife and allowed her to exist in patterns that she had learned were effective in controlling her husband. Patsy, on the other hand, was increasingly called on to take on the duties of surrogate mother. This role was onerous to her, as it came a time when she was attempting to break away from family restrictions.

Patsy solved the dilemma, again without confronting it directly, by getting into a new situation that indirectly removed her from the problem. She got married shortly after her eighteenth birthday. Though her father protested vehemently that she was too young, Patsy was of legal age and so she and Art were able to elope. They called the family after they had been married and presented their "fait accompli." Though her father was quite upset, there was little he could do at this point. Like her mother, she soon solidified her role by getting pregnant.

However, her strong need to escape, combined with her youth and relative lack of experience with males, produced a bad judgment regarding a marital partner for her. Though a reasonably good provider, Art has almost no interests outside of going to work, coming home and drinking beer while watching television, and occasionally going fishing with some friends. So Patsy was brought into a relationship that was similar to the ones she had in her own family. Also, like Patsy's father, Art believed that he should make all the decisions about the family and he also felt that he had a right to abuse Patsy physically if she overtly resisted. Naturally, she continued using the patterns she had learned so well in her own family, so that she did retain a degree of control over her destiny.

Yet this was not a satisfactory arrangement to either partner, and the upset increased when Patsy was influenced by a woman's consciousness raising group at her church. She began to assert herself more directly with Art, and he retaliated with verbal and physical abuse, resulting in the referral.

Further Etiological Considerations

A number of the causes of Patsy's pathology have been embedded in the prior case description. But let us now recapitulate some of the causes of passive-aggressive behavior. Her position as fourth of six children made it difficult for her to gain attention from her parents, something all children seek. By the time the parents had dealt with the more aggressive and traditional demands of the older children, there was not much time for the younger children, and Patsy never really had the "baby of the family" role that inherently brings extra attention. Aggressive and/or delinquent behavior is a usual reaction to such a situation. But her mother provided a role model of passivity, and in addition, the traditional expectations for a female child do not promote aggressive and/or delinquent behaviors. Possibly of greater importance, independence and aggression were seen as inappropriate behaviors by her father; he reacted swiftly and brutally to such behaviors. So any tendencies that Patsy might have had in this regard were quickly suppressed. Rather, she learned to adopt the patterns that had been successful for her mother. Sick behaviors, especially suicide gestures (Shneidman, 1979), are effective in maneuvering people because it is hard to question them as an excuse in our society. Similarly, engaging in activities associated with school and church is something that was hard for her father to criticize. Yet, these activities allowed her to escape from his demands, at least at various periods of time. When it became clear that she was going to be put in the role of surrogate mother, she needed an escape; the legally prescribed role of leaving the family when one gets married was an obvious choice for her. The fact that she made the choice without due reflection on the real potential of the relationship is not uncommon for persons moving into early marriages.

It is important to note that the child who learns to push up to the limits of parental control has the potential for adopting passive-aggressive behaviors. This pattern fitted well with the style of Patsy's family situation, yet it was costly in terms of achieving optimal personality development and in preparing her to live effectively with many types of people. When she realized that she had married into the same situation, she became quite depressed, then resorted to more aggressive behaviors, which disrupted the "stability" that she and Art had evolved. This is not surprising, since most of the personality disorders are likely to cause problems when they are transferred out of original family situations and into intimate, consistent-contact relationships such as marriage (Barrett, 1980).

An excellent literary description of this pattern from a different perspective is found in *The Good Soldier Schweik* (Hasek, 1930). Like the modern-day cartoon character Beetle Bailey, Schweik continually frustrates his superiors' orders by following them in a simplistic fashion to their logical endpoint. So the strategy (not in reality a conscious behavior) is to place others (usually people depended on) in a situation that forces them either to give up the demands they have made or else to violate their own rules. As a result, the other person is immobilized and has no rational reason or overt act that justifies retaliation (Barrett, 1980). Patsy was particularly adept at putting her father in this situation.

Treatment It would be natural to consider marital therapy for Patsy and Art (Framo, 1979). This possibility was explored, but it soon became apparent that neither wanted to continue the marriage. Both realized they were dia-metrically opposed as regards interests and visions of what they hoped to achieve in life, and they decided to obtain a divorce.

Patsy wished to continue in her woman's consciousness raising group, and in this vein it was recommended that she engage in a behavioral treatment program of Assertiveness Training. Patsy was asked to bring up anger-inducing situations in her world to which she usually responded passively. This was not hard for her to do since such situations were the preponderance of her behavior patterns. As she brought up each situation, her therapist asked her to detail the events that occurred. It soon became apparent that Patsy was not really aware of many aspects of these situations, so she was asked to keep a diary. When she began to monitor her situations more effec-tively, her therapist asked her to think of ways in which she could have in-teracted differently.

Patsy came up with a few options, but in general was not very effec-tive. To help her, role-playing was used (Yablonsky, 1976). The therapist and Patsy adopted different roles in the interactions she described and then exchanged roles so that each played each part. This enabled Patsy to see more appropriate mechanisms, and then she could adopt them herself. This behavioral practice paralleled some of the cognitive changes that were oc-curring as a result of the woman's consciousness raising group.

She was next given assignments to find outside situations in which she could specifically adopt more assertive behaviors. This assignment was first instituted with less threatening targets, such as a waiter at a restaurant and a clerk in a store. As she became more assertive in these situations, she was then asked to include targets that were more significant to her. At first, Patsy showed a common initial response to assertive thinking. She became ex-cessively aggressive with some of the "harmless" targets, such as waiters and clerks. She then had to learn to modulate her behavior into an appropriate though firmly assertive pattern (Lutzker & Martin, 1981).

Along with these therapy techniques and the implicit psychotherapy that accompanies most behavioral techniques, Patsy was asked to enroll in a parent training group. This was important, not only because she did not want to pass on her patterns to her child, as her mother had done to her, but also because she was going to be a single parent and wanted to optimize her chances of doing this well. The parent training group went for ten weeks, and Patsy reported she felt much more confident at the end of this period. She also noted that her daughter was showing few of the problem behaviors she had shown at the time of the divorce.

After these techniques had been integrated, Patsy was moved into a group therapy situation. This allowed her more diverse feedback regarding her new thoughts and behaviors. When she came under stress, she was inclined to regress into her passive-aggressive behaviors; the group gave her immediate feedback that helped her avoid slipping back too far. The group also provided her with more role-playing practice and served as a powerful source of reinforcers for any changes she did make. Finally, the group provided her with new contacts that she would need in her role as a single parent. Patsy's prognosis is good, in large part because she was able to make some important initial changes and also because she is highly motivated. Yet a cure won't be quick or easy, as she is trying to change some long-term facets of her personality while adapting to the stress of a new role that requires much in the way of personal resources.

Comment The concept of the passive-aggressive personality is more widely accepted among practicing clinicians than among research psychologists. Consequently, this disorder has received little empirical attention; and etiological, diagnostic, and treatment outcome variables have not been clearly delineated. The clinical conceptualizations are, however, rather consistent in the numerous case studies that have been reported. Notable among clinical observations is the extent to which passive-aggressive behavior elicits anger and frustration from other people. The tendency provocatively to test the limits of relationships presumably develops in childhood or adolescence along with other features of Oppositional Disorders. With maturation, the person learns to manipulate the environment effectively while remaining within (albeit barely) socially accepted boundaries. The person then can avoid, without cost, the overt negative consequences in the environment that would result from assertive approaches. Parents, spouses, friends, employers, and other significant others in the environments of persons with passive-aggressive personality disorders find themselves aware of manipulation but unable to express their objections in a logically consistent or socially acceptable manner—for example, Patsy's involvement in church activities to avoid her father's restrictive curfew (Barrett, 1980).

These strategies have been observed within the therapeutic relationship and frequently are prohibitive to successful treatment. Marital therapy is particularly difficult when one or, in some cases, both partners are passive-aggressive. The therapeutic response of passive-aggressive clients is primarily characterized by noncompliance and the use of "loophole" excuses. Thus, contracts and homework assignments must be carefully constructed. It is impossible to formulate a sensible behavioral contract that is completely "loophole-proof"—especially in light of their impressive acuity for finding logical inconsistencies. However, contracts that are brief and clearly specify the targeted *desired* responses generally can structure the situation such that the criteria for both compliance *and* noncompliance are immediately (and hopefully indisputably) obvious. Contracts structured in this manner increase the probability that the client's response to the contract will be overt (and possibly appropriate). More direct behavioral responses result in more accurate feedback from the social environment and, with successful treatment, the eventual acquisition of more adaptive strategies (Lutzker & Martin, 1981).

As in Patsy's case, high motivation is associated with good prognosis. Unfortunately, Patsy's insightful experiences and motivating environmental pressures are not the usual course for passive-aggressive personality disorders. Most persons with this disorder develop a chronic pattern, with the unwitting encouragement of tolerant employers, friends, and relatives. This negative prognosis should not be surprising in light of their well-learned ability to manipulate others and to avoid feedback about their problems.

REFERENCES

Barrett, C. Personality (character) disorders. In R. Woody (Ed.), *The encyclopedia of clinical assessment.* San Francisco: Jossey-Bass, 1980.

Framo, J. Family therapy and theory. *American Psychologist.* 1979, *34,* 988–992.

Gardner, E. The role of the classification system in outpatient psychiatry. In M. Katz, J. Cole, and W. Barton (Eds.), *The role and methodology in psychiatry and psychopathology.* Washington, D.C.: U.S. Public Health Service, 1965.

Hasek, J. *The good soldier Schweik.* New York: Ungar, 1930.

Lutzker, J., and Martin, J. *Behavior change.* Monterey, Ca.: Brooks/Cole, 1981.

Shneidman, E. An overview: Personality, motivation, and behavior theories. In L. Hankoff and P. Einsidler (Eds.), *Suicide.* Littleton, Ma.: PSG, 1979.

Yablonksy, L. *Psychodrama: Resolving emotional problems through role-playing.* New York: Basic Books, 1976.

11

Supplementary Conditions

This last section of the book will consider patterns that are not reflective of a clear and consistent pattern of psychopathology. Rather, they refer to situationally generated and/or transient disorders. In the DSM-III, they are for the most part referred to a V Codes (conditions not generated by mental disorder, but that still require attention or treatment).

The first selection in this section details several marital and family cases collected by Dr. Robert Liberman. Family and marital problems have been increasingly viewed as reflecting a disordered system rather than simply as being the results of disruption by a pathological member of the couple or family (Framo, 1979), a perspective seen in Liberman's approach. Effective intervention in family disorder is particularly critical, as disorder here is likely to have negative effects on any children involved, a phenomenon analogous to that seen in the child abuse cases discussed in the first section of this book.

The last case in this section, and in this book, describes General Grigorenko, a citizen of the Soviet Union, who was considered paranoid within that system, apparently for political purposes. The case as presented here is the evaluation of General Grigorenko by Western mental health experts. It shows how normality in one system may be worked into a label of psychopathology in another system. This approach could work the other way. For example, an individual who had a high ranking position in the Soviet bureaucracy, who worked very long hours with little show of affect toward coworkers, and who had no "success" in his or her personal life might be lauded as a hero; whereas such a person in western society might be considerd as showing psychopathology, such as a compulsive personality disorder. In any case, General Grigorenko's case demonstrates that normality must also be studied in order to understand abnormality. We feel that it is a fitting end to the book to focus on a basically normal individual.

REFERENCE

Framo, J. Family theory and therapy. *American Psychologist*, 1979, *34*, 988–992.

Family and Couple Therapy

Family and couple therapies have been demonstrated as effective treatments for a variety of mental disorders and situational maladjustments. The focus of the family and couple therapist is generally toward restructuring the social environment by altering contingencies in an effort to encourage more appropriate responses from all persons involved in the situation. Both psychodynamic and behavioral therapists conceive of the family as a dynamic system in which behaviors are exchanged in accordance with the laws of psychological reciprocity.

The cases reported by Liberman (a behaviorist) illustrate the impressive flexibility of family and couple therapy. In the first case, a woman who probably had a somatoform disorder received considerable relief from severe headaches as result of altered contingencies in her marital relationship. Mr. and Mrs. S., in the second case, changed the ways in which they elicited attention and communicated concern for one another. The results were an improved marital relationship and the cessation of Mrs. S.'s depressive episodes. In the third case, Liberman reports family therapy strategies for increasing the competence and productivity of a twenty-three-year-old young man who had been diagnosed as schizophrenic in childhood. As is evident, the basic therapeutic strategy for specifying contingencies and altering reinforcers was effective in each case. Yet, each family received the benefit of a treatment program designed for its unique needs.

Behavioral Approaches To Family and Couple Therapy

Robert Liberman

Case #1

Mrs. D. is a 35-year-old housewife and mother of three children who had a 15-year history of severe, migranous headaches. She had had frequent medical hospitalizations for her headaches (without any organic problems being found), and also a 1–½ year period of intensive, psychodynamically oriented, individual psychotherapy. She found relief from her headaches only after retreating to her bed for periods of days to a week with the use of narcotics.

After a brief period of evaluation by me, she again developed intractable headaches and was hospitalized. A full neurological workup revealed no neuropathology. At this time I recommended that I continue with the patient and her husband in couple therapy. It had previously become clear to me that the patient's headaches were serving an important purpose in the economy of her marital relationship; headaches and the resultant debilitation were the sure way the patient could elicit and maintain her husband's concern and interest in her. On his part, her husband was an active, action-oriented man who found it difficult to sit down and engage in conversation. He came home from work, read the newspaper, tinkered with his car, made repairs on the house, or watched TV. Mrs. D got her husband's clear-cut attention only when she developed headaches, stopped functioning as mother and wife, and took to her bed. At these times Mr. D. was very solicitous and caring. He gave her medication, stayed home to take care of the children, and called the doctor.

My analysis of the situation led me to the strategy of redirecting Mr. D's attention to the adaptive strivings and the maternal and wifely behavior of his wife. During ten 45-minute sessions, I shared my analysis of the problem with Mr. and Mrs. D. and encouraged them to reciprocally restructure their marital relationship. Once involved in a trusting and confident relationship with me, Mr. D worked hard to give his wife attention and approval for her day-to-day efforts as a mother and housewife. When he came home from work, instead of burying himself in the newspaper he inquired about the day at home and discussed with his wife problems concerning the children. He occasionally rewarded his wife's homemaking efforts by taking her out to a movie or dinner (something they had not done for years). While watching TV he had his wife sit close to him or on his lap. In return, Mrs. D was taught to reward her husband's new efforts at intimacy with affection and appreciation. She let him know how much she liked to talk with him about the day's events. She prepared special dishes for him and kissed him warmly when he took initiative in expressing affection toward her. On the other hand, Mr. D was instructed to pay minimal attention to his wife's headaches. He was reassured that in so doing, he would be helping her decrease their frequency and severity. He was no longer to give her medication, cater to her when she was ill, or call the doctor for her. If she got a headache, she was to help herself and he was to

271

carry on with his regular routine insofar as possible. I emphasized that he should not, overall, decrease his attentiveness to his wife, but rather change the timing and direction of his attentiveness. Thus the behavioral contingencies of Mr. D's attention changed from headaches to housework, from invalidism to active coping and functioning as mother and wife.

Within ten sessions, both were seriously immersed in this new approach toward each other. Their marriage was different and more satisfying to both. Their sex life improved. Their children were better behaved, as they quickly learned to apply the same reinforcement principles in reacting to the children and to reach a consensus in responding to their children's limit-testing. Mrs. D got a job as a department store clerk (a job she enjoyed and which provided her with further reinforcement—money and attention from people for "healthy" behavior). She was given recognition by her husband for her efforts to collaborate in improving the family's financial condition. She still had headaches, but they were mild and short-lived and she took care of them herself. Everyone was happier including Mrs. D's internist who no longer was receiving emergency calls from her husband.

A follow-up call to Mr. and Mrs. D one year later found them maintaining their progress. She has occasional headaches but has not had to retreat to bed or enter a hospital.

Case #2

Mrs. S is a 34-year-old mother of five who herself came from a family of ten siblings. She wanted very badly to equal her mother's output of children and also wanted to prove to her husband that he was potent and fertile. He had a congenital hypospadias and had been told by a physician prior to their marriage that he probably could not have children. Unfortunately, Mrs. S was Rh negative and her husband Rh positive. After their fifth child she had a series of spontaneous abortions because of the Rh incompatibility. Each was followed by a severe depression. Soon the depressions ran into each other and she was given a course of 150 EST's. The EST's had to function at home while not significantly lifting the depressions. She had some successful short-term supportive psychotherapy but again plunged into a depression after a hysterectomy.

Her husband, like Mr. D in the previous case, found it hard to tolerate his wife's conversation, especially since it was taken up mostly by complaints and tearfulness. He escaped from the unhappy home situation by plunging himself into his work, holding two jobs simultaneously. When he was home, he was too tired for any conversation and meaningful interaction was nil. Although Mrs. S. tried hard to maintain her household and raise her children and even hold a part-time job, she received little acknowledgment for her efforts from her husband who became more distant and peripheral as the years went by.

My behavioral analysis pointed to a lack of reinforcement from Mrs. S's husband for her adaptive strivings. Consequently her depressions, with their large hypochondriacal components, represented her desperate attempt to elicit her husband's attention and concern. Although her somatic complaints and self-depreciating [sic] accusations were aversive for her husband, the only way he knew how to "turn them off" was to offer sympathy, reassure her of his devotion to her, and occasionally stay home from work. Naturally, his nurturing her in this manner had the effect of reinforcing the very behavior he was trying to terminate.

During five half-hour couple sessions I focused primarily on Mr. S, who was the mediating agent of reinforcement for his wife and hence the person who could potentially modify her behavior. I actively redirected his attention from his wife "the unhappy, depressed woman" to his wife "the coping woman." I forthrightly recommended to him that he drop his extra job, at least for the time being, in order to be at home in the evening to converse with his wife about the day's events, especially her approximations at successful homemaking. I showed by my own example (modeling) how to support his wife in her efforts to assert herself reasonably with her intrusive mother-in-law and an obnoxious neighbor.

A turning point came after the second session, when I received a desperate phone call from Mr. S one evening. He told me that his wife had called from her job and tearfully complained that she could not go on and that he must come and bring her home. He asked me what he should do. I indicated that this was a crucial moment, that he should call her back and briefly acknowledge her distress but at the same time emphasize the importance of her finishing the evening's work. I further suggested that he meet her as usual after work and take her out for an ice cream soda. This would get across to her his abiding interest and recognition for her positive efforts in a genuine and spontaneous way. With this support from me, he followed my suggestions and within two weeks Mrs. S's depression had completely lifted.

She was shortly thereafter given a job promotion, which served as an extrinsic reinforcement for her improved work performance and was the occasion for additional reinforcement from me and her husband during the next therapy session. We terminated after the fifth session, a time limit we had initially agreed on.

Eight months later at a followup they reported being "happier together than ever before."

273

Case #3

Edward is a 23-year-old young man who had received much psycho-therapy, special schooling, and occupational counseling and training during the past 17 years. He was diagnosed at different times as a childhood schizophrenic and as mentally subnormal. At age 6 he was evaluated by a child psychiatry clinic and given three years of psychodynamic therapy by a psychoanalyst. He had started many remedial programs and finished almost none of them. He, in fact, was a chronic failure—in schools as well as in jobs. His parents viewed him as slightly retarded despite his low normal intelligence on IQ tests. He was infantilized by his mother and largely ignored or criticized by his father. He was used by his mother, who was domineering and aggressive, as an ally against the weak and passive father. When I began seeing them in a family evaluation, Edward was in the process of failing the most recent rehabilitation effort—an evening, adult high school.

The initial goals of the family treatment, then, were (1) to disengage Edward from the clasp of his protective mother, (2) to get his father to offer himself as a model and as a source of encourage-ment (reinforcement) for Edward's desires and efforts towards in-dependence, (3) to structure Edward's life with occupational and social opportunities that he could not initiate on his own. Fortun-ately the Jewish Vocational Service in Boston offers an excellent re-habilitation program based on the same basic principles of learning that have been elucidated in this article. I referred Edward to it and at the same time introduced him to a social club for ex-mental patients which has a constant whirl of activities daily and on weekends.

During our weekly family sessions, I used modeling and role-playing to help Edward's partners positively reinforce his beginning efforts at the J.V.S. and the social club. After three months at J.V.S., Edward secured a job and now after another seven months has a job tenure and membership in the union. He has been an ac-tive member of the social club and has gone on weekend trips with groups there—something he had never done before. He is now "graduating" to another social club, a singles' group in a church, and has started action on getting his driver's license.

The family sessions were not easy or without occasional storms, usually generated by Edward's mother as she from time to time felt "left out." She needed my support and interest (reinforce-ment) in her problems as a hard-working and unappreciated mother at these times. Because of the positive therapeutic relationship cemented over a period of nine months, Edward's parents slowly began to be able to substitute positive reinforcement for his gradu-ally improving efforts at work and play instead of the previous

*blanket criticism (also, paradoxically, a kind of social reinforcement)
he had received from them for his failures. I encouraged the father
to share openly with Edward his own experiences as a young man
reaching for independence, thereby serving as a model for his son.*

*The parents needed constant reinforcement (approval) from
me for trying out new ways of responding to Edward's behavior; for
example, to eliminate the usual nagging of him to do his chores
around the house (which only served to increase the lethargic sloth-
ful behavior which accrues from the attention) and to indicate instead pleasure when he mows the lawn even if he forgets to rake the
grass and trim the hedge. They learned to give Edward approval
when he takes the garbage out even if he doesn't do it "their" way
And they learned how to spend time listening to Edward pour out
his enthusiasm for his job even if they feel he is a bit too exuberant*
[End of Liberman excerpt]

Comment
An original impetus for family and marital therapies came from studies of
psychopathology and communication patterns in families with schizophrenic members. The results were improved functioning for all members of
the family, and the approach was extended to families in which the "identified patient" is so enmeshed in pathological family processes that individual therapy is less likely to be successful (Mishler & Waxler, 1976;
Hartley & Strupp, 1980). The success of family therapy for a variety of
specific mental disorders has led some theorists to consider the existence of a
familial pathology over and above pathological behavior on the part of individuals (Framo, 1979; Minuchin, 1974; Satir, 1967). Minuchin (1974) has
proposed a classificatory system in which the characteristic communication
styles and affective interactions among family members may be distinguished from individual adjustment problems and modified within a systems
approach to treatment.

Family therapy has been particularly effective where there are
children with behavior problems and anxiety disorders; it is often considered
the treatment of choice for adolescent adjustment problems (Korchin, 1976;
Jacobson, 1979; Hartley & Strupp, 1980). The three cases presented by
Liberman illustrate the range of situations for which the following therapeutic goals are appropriate:

1. Discover how presenting problems are maintained by familial interac-
    tion patterns.
2. Improve communication skills among family members.
3. Facilitate skill development among family members towards the ends of
    developing empathy and consideration among family members.
4. Shape and contract for more equitable and effective problem-solving
    strategies among family members.

These goals are attempted through a program uniquely designed for each family. Specific programs must consider the family's value system, lifestyle, financial resources, and the developmental levels of family members. In each of the cases described by Liberman, the targeted behavior and therapeutic strategies were implemented within the existing family structure and in collaboration with the family's stated goals; fortunately, successful outcomes were obtained.

REFERENCES

Framo, J. Family theory and therapy. *American Psychologist*, 1979, *34*, 988–992.

Hartley, D., and Strupp. H. Verbal psychotherapies. In A. Kazdin, A. Bellack, and M. Hersen (Eds.), *New perspectives in abnormal psychology*. New York: Oxford University Press, 1980.

Jacobson, N. Increasing positive behavior in severely distressed marital relationships: The effects of problem-solving training. *Behavior Therapy*, 1979, *10*, 311–326.

Korchin, S. *Modern clinical psychology*. New York: Basic Books, 1976.

Minuchin, S. *Families and family therapy*. Cambridge, Ma.: Harvard University Press, 1974.

Mishler, E., and Waxler, N. *Interactions in families*. New York: Wiley, 1976.

Satir, V. *Conjoint family therapy* (2nd ed.). Palo Alto, Ca.: Science and Behavior Books, 1967.

A Normal Person Viewed As Pathological

The Case of General Grigorenko

This book closes with a case of an apparently normal individual who has been viewed as psychopathological, specifically paranoid, within the political system in which he was raised. This case points out the contextual aspects of such judgments that undoubtedly reside in all labeling systems. We will provide some context data on General Grigorenko and then present the actual interviews with him, as well as some of the conclusions gathered by the author of the article.

General Grigorenko

Pyotr Grigorievich Grigorenko rose from meager circumstances to obtain the rank of Major General in the Red Army of the U.S.S.R. He was considered highly important as a military theoretician and received many honors and accolades. However, in the midst of these honors, during the early 1960s, he turned dissident. He was given a psychiatric examination at the time and was declared mentally ill,

*with specific reference made to paranoid thinking thought to be
generated by atherosclerotic brain disease. He was placed in a hospital
for the criminally insane. Two years later, in 1978, he was able to
reach the West, whereupon he requested a psychiatric examination.
He had hoped to use the results of that examination on his return to
the Soviet Union. However, the Supreme Soviet published a special
decree, signed by Leonid Brezhnev, which took away Grigorenko's
citizenship and in effect made him unable to return to his homeland.
He had not yet taken the examination, yet still decided to go through
with it. It was initiated in December, 1978.*

*The following selection is the part of Reich's (1980) article
that provides the interview material with Grigorenko. After the interview, Reich concludes that Grigorenko shows no signs of mental
disorder or of any impairment of thought processes. Even though
there is some evidence of atherosclerotic disease, the conclusion of all
concerned is that this does not detract in any significant way from
his ability to process information adequately and to perceive events
accurately. Psychological examination found Grigorenko to be of
superior intellectual ability, particularly in the areas of verbal learning and retention. This exam also found him able to shift his point
of view easily, which would be contrary to a paranoid diagnosis,
and then described him as having "a highly developed sense of truth,
one who characteristically seeks to understand and validate his
experiences" (p. 321).*

*To be objective, it should be noted that this examination took
place several years after the time when he was found to be paranoid
by Soviet psychiatrists, and his thought processes and emotional patterns may have changed in that duration. In any case, here is the
dialogue with General Grigorenko, which should help readers to
make their own judgments in regard to his normality.*

The Case of General Grigorenko:
A Psychiatric Reexamination of a Soviet Dissident

Walter Reich

Grigorenko acknowledged that his speech at the Party congress in 1961 was his
first public act of dissent. But upon further questioning it became clear that
the moral convictions represented by that act were evident before. He recalled
that the first time he had any difficulty was in 1941, on the day of the Nazi in-
vasion of his country, when in a private conversation that was later revealed to
his superiors he criticized Stalin's lack of planning for the war.

From: Reich, W. The case of General Grigorenko: A psychiatric reexamination of a
Soviet dissident. PSYCHIATRY, 1980, 43, 303–323. Copyright © 1980 by The William Alanson
White Psychiatric Foundation, Inc. Reprinted by special permission of The William Alanson
White Psychiatric Foundation, Inc.

Grigorenko: I was saved from death by a firing squad because Stalin fled and chaos overcame the leadership. What also helped me was that I had a very good relationship with, and was respected by, the military commander of that front, and they did their best to hush it up. If not for the confusion at the top, no one in that area would have dared defend me. But there was no reaction from above, so that the commanders (at the front) took the initiative in defending me. But of course I had to recant publicly. I had to denounce what I had done and swear I was faithful to Stalin.

Reich: Did you know what you did was dangerous?

Grigorenko: Of course I know; I didn't expect to be caught, since what I said was part of a private conversation between two people.

Grigorenko's second difficulty with authorities occurred in 1949, during his defense of his Master's dissertation. In its first chapter, the dissertation contained implied criticisms of the military theories of unnamed, high-ranking officers. Grigorenko was advised to excise that chapter from the dissertation.

Grigorenko: (*Smiles*) Finally they convinced me to change it. . . . The man who helped me (to the decision to compromise) asked me, "Do you want to make a scientific discovery or do you want a degree?" I told him that I thought that was the same thing. And he said, "No, it's not the same thing; first you get your degree and then you should make scientific discoveries." Once he explained that in that way, I followed his advice. You have to carry out a task in a stepwise fashion.

Reich: Aren't you interested in truth? Are you willing to compromise truth?

Grigorenko: (*Calmly*) Well, I think that when something concerns a matter of principle, no compromise is possible. A dissertation on such a subject, though, doesn't involve matters of principle. Truth did not vanish, it wasn't betrayed. After all, everyone read that dissertation (in the process of its consideration), and what had to be said was said. And when it was finally voted upon (at the ceremony of the defense of the dissertation), it was approved unanimously (for the first time in the history of the academy), and (the vote) was greeted with applause.

Reich: So you distinguish between important things and unimportant things—between things that are worth fighting about and things that are not worth fighting about?

Grigorenko: Of course.

Reich: So why did the Soviet psychiatrists consider you unwilling to change your views, unwilling to change?

Grigorenko: I'm prepared to change if I can be convinced, by discussion, that I'm wrong. That man, my thesis advisor, convinced me, so I changed.

I engaged Grigorenko in a further discussion of specific political views. In fact, my first challenge to him in the interview had to do with the content of his views during the mid-sixties, and that challenge provoked him to some spirited reflection on his former ideas regarding Leninism and on the revisions of those ideas that he developed during his confinement in a psychiatric hospital in 1965. It appeared that the depth of his feelings in response to this subject had to do, at least in part, with the past insistence by Soviet psychiatrists that his political ideas were somehow inadequate or that he was characterologically unable to change or moderate them. When I reminded him of his Leninist position and of his change in that position in 1965, a change he had recorded in a memoir, he acknowledged that he had decided then that it was a fundamental error to rely on the dogma of Leninism. He said that in thinking about the matter during his hospitalization, he had decided that he had been naive. He saw that it was necessary to take the present into account and that it would be impossible to go back 50 years. That revision, he said, represented a drastic change in his views. At that time, he explained, "I started to consider Leninism as a delusion. . . . I left the hospital with the idea that one had to fight in the open and appeal to the laws. I gave up on the conspiratorial, underground way to achieve change." As Grigorenko spoke about that change in his views, he grew increasingly animated. Although I attempted to ask him about other matters, he continued to return to the topic. Clearly, it had affected him and he felt the need for continued elaboration and clarification. However, there was no evidence of an inability to leave the subject of the discussion, or of an obsessional, perseverative quality to his answer.

Much of the interview was taken up with an exploration of the motivations for Grigorenko's dissent and risk-taking acts, the clarity of his purpose, and the sense he has and has had of himself—the sense, that is, of his personal power and capacities.

Reich: Why (did you persist in your struggle)?

Grigorenko: The Soviet psychiatrists asked me the same question. It's not a personal cause. It's a social, communal cause. Someone always has to start. I always liked to repeat the verse by Yevtushenko written when he was still a real poet. He wrote, "When lack of talent summons itself to fight for truth, then talent, I am ashamed of you." . . . This (Soviet) system of government should not be tolerated by people, but it never happens that everyone rises against it. There always have to be people who start—then others will follow. And those who start regardless of whether or not they are talented, or have special abilities—they become a slogan, a banner, for those who follow. This places a particular responsibility on them and they should not abandon the cause. You are responsible not just for yourself, but also for the cause in the eyes of those who follow. During my life, in my faithful service to communism, I caused a lot of damage to my people, and I wanted, at least in my remaining days, to repair it. . . . What's the sense of living one extra year if you continue in the fraud of not facing things? It's better to live the rest of your life creatively so that you will not be ashamed in the eyes of your grandchildren. (At this point Grigorenko appeared sad, but continued to speak carefully and deliberately.) I have always considered the inner impulses to serve as a vocation inspired—instilled in my soul—by God.

Reich: Why in your soul? After all, only a few people did what you did.

Grigorenko: No, this is not true. It's just that I became known. It was just luck that I became known, mostly as a result of the campaign in my defense (organized by my wife). There are many who did more than I did, but no one knows about them.

Reich: Did God put it in their souls, too?

Grigorenko: I think so. I think that Providence plays a greater role in the lives of people than we think.

Reich: Do you think that you have some kind of special relationship with God?

Grigorenko: No. Even though I firmly believe that God exists in the world, and that there is some Supreme Reason, I unfortunately cannot absorb myself fully in prayer. . . . Some people can detach themselves and allow themselves to be fully absorbed in prayer, but I can't. For example, I feel that I can't proselytize using the name of God—I can mention it in a private conversation, but I think that there are people chosen by God for that. We have such a man in the Soviet Union. This is Father Dudko, who one can say, really contains God within him.

I further questioned Grigorenko in order to see if I could find any grandiose trends—any sense of himself as somehow superhuman, divine, possessed of extraordinary powers or knowledge, or of being centerstage, or being more important than he could possibly be. I was alerted to one possible area of grandiosity by his mention of a conversation about him that he attributed to members of the Politburo. He said that one dissident leaflet he had written, "Why We Don't Have Bread," had been discussed by them. When I explored the matter further to see whether he thought he was somehow constantly and centrally on the minds of the Soviet leadership, he explained, matter-of-factly, that a month after he had distributed that leaflet, Brezhnev had made a speech listing some of the same circumstances that were cited in his leaflet, and that he was then told about a conversation that had taken place at a high level shortly after that speech in which someone made the comment, "Well that almost sounded as if it had been written by Grigorenko."

Reich: Who said that?

Grigorenko: It was a member of the Central Committee—it was a small group that discussed it.

Reich: The Central Committee was aware of General Grigorenko?

Grigorenko: *(laughs)* Of course, I was sent to the hospital by the Central Committee—not by the psychiatrists. And it was said, "Don't allow him to get to trial."

Reich: You mean you were talked about (in high places)—Brezhnev had a discussion about you back then in 1965 or perhaps in 1969?

Grigorenko: Well, Brezhnev knows me very well . . . Khrushchev talked about me (too).

In this interchange, as well as in other parts of the interview, Grigorenko's theories of how others, including those in high places, related to and thought of him were based on reasonable evidence or conservative inference. There was no suggestion of an inflated belief in his own importance to the world as a whole or to the Soviet leadership in particular; rather, he related what he believed to have been small but significant decisions made by persons at high levels regarding his acts and his fate, as fitting responses, under Soviet political conditions, to the dissenting behavior of a Soviet Major General. Earlier, he had pointed out to me that he had personally known Brezhnev during World War II; and he later explained that it should not be inconceivable that Brezhnev would now be aware of and talk about him in his private conversations, or that he could be the focus of the conversations of other high-ranking Soviet leaders. The series of answers, in addition to previous answers regarding his relationship with God and his personal mission, suggested that his sense of himself was a modest one, that he viewed himself as relatively unimportant in the cosmic scheme of things, and that he felt that irony and chance rather than some special destiny had fashioned his prominence and his fate.

Finally, I attempted to gauge Grigorenko's capacity to assess reality, both now and in the past—his capacity to assess the nature of the historical moment and to respond to it, as well as his capacity to appreciate danger from without and to moderate his behavior in response to that danger. I brought up, again, the event that had precipitated his political troubles in 1961, the speech he made as a Party delegate criticizing certain official Party policies.

Reich: In 1961, when you made that speech, it was, after all, after the era of Stalin. The period of repression had eased; and while, obviously, it was dangerous to speak out, it was not a capital offense. Would you have said the same thing ten years earlier, during Stalin's terror—during the late forties or early fifties? Or, to put it another way, what stopped you (from speaking out then)?

Grigorenko: At that time I couldn't have made such a statement because I didn't measure up to it. I was a faithful communist. The difference between 1951 and 1961 is not just a difference of ten years, but in the fact that the Twentieth Party Congress took place in 1956, from which I learned that what I had considered to be local mistakes were really widespread perversions of the Party line. And after 1956, I had (time for) another five years for observation and reflection. This is the way I was able to become worthy of making the statement that I made (in 1961). And as for what you said, Dr. Reich (that I organized my underground group in 1963 knowing then it was not then a capital crime), let me tell you that I was convinced then that if I would be found out I'd be killed.

Reich: So if your understanding had been the same in 1951 as it had been in 1961, you would have done (then) what you did later: you would have done that under Stalin, too?

Grigorenko: (*Smiles*) As an old historian, a military historian, I have to object to that question. One cannot say what would have happened if the past was other than the way it was. I was no different then. I was the way I was. And whether I could have been different under different circumstances is just a matter of speculation. [End of Reich excerpt]

Comment In these excerpts from the extensive interviews with General Grigorenko, Reich explores the major areas through which paranoid ideation is usually manifest. First, General Grigorenko recounts the events that led to his hospitalization. Reich's questions are quite pointed and could be expected to elicit inflammatory and elaborate defenses from a paranoid individual. Instead, General Grigorenko appears to respond with the reasoned and measured thinking that is characteristic of his responses throughout the interviews. The impression is one of an intelligent and sensitive man who evaluates the validity of his conclusions. This cognitive strategy is contrary to the description of paranoid thinking proposed by Shapiro:

> . . . a suspicious person is a person who has something on his mind. He looks at the world with fixed and occupying expectation and he searches repetitively and only for confirmation of it. He will not be persuaded to abandon his suspicion or some plan of action based on it. On the contrary, he will pay no attention to rational arguments except to find in them some aspect or feature that actually confirms his original view. (Shapiro, 1965, p. 56.)

Further, Reich searches for indices of obsessional concerns, grandiose self-perceptions, and impairments in judgment. General Grigorenko evidenced an understandable concern and emotional involvement in the discussion of the evolution of his political ideas. However, as Reich points out, the inflexible perseverative quality of paranoid ideation was not evident. Nor did General Grigorenko present his difficulties as more important than those of others. Finally, General Grigorenko's ability to process reality and to consider consequences before his actions is apparent in his comparisons of political climates and his understanding of them in 1951 and 1961;

The extent to which behavior that deviates from the usual is labeled in accordance with social context variables and the biases of observers has received considerable attention (Rosenhan, 1973; Szasz, 1967; Scheff, 1975; May, 1961). Suffice it to say that the expectations of observers, the relative social status of the individual in question, and the anticipated consequences of the unusual behavior may result in such diverse labels as: emotionally disturbed, heroic, martyred, independent, egocentric, genius, rebel, with major implications for clinical diagnosis and treatment. As in the case of General Grigorenko, unusual behavior may result in ostracism, forced treatment, and/or incarceration. In this vein, all societies on occasion lean toward prejudicial labeling of nonpathological behaviors (Rosenhan, 1973); that is, the disorder may be in the eye of the beholder. Hence, expertise, consensual validation, as well as wisdom and compassion are needed to avoid problems such as those found in General Grigorenko's case.

REFERENCES

May, R. *Existential psychology*. New York: Random House, 1961.
Rosenhan, D. On being sane in insane places. *Science*, 1973, *179*, 250–258.
Scheff, T. (Ed.). *Labeling madness*. Englewood Cliffs, N.J.: Prentice-Hall, 1975.
Shapiro, D. *Neurotic styles*. New York: Basic Books, 1965.
Szasz, T. *The myth of mental illness*. New York: Dell, 1967.

Author Index

CALIFORNIA STATE UNIVERSITY, SAN BERNARDINO

PROGRAM CHANGE FORM

NAME

SOCIAL SECURITY #

SCHEDULE CODE NO.	COURSE	COURSE TITLE	UNITS	DROP	ADD	SPECIAL FEES	TERM
							DATE
							APPROVAL

OFFICE USE ONLY

Units Before Program Change
Units After Program Change

Add'l Fees Due ☐ Amt.
Refund Due ☐ Res.

Rec. #
Int.

Subject Index